The

DATE DUE DATE DE RETOUR	
FEB 2 4 1998	
MAR 2 0 1998	
APR - 2 1998	
NOV 3 - 1998	
June 14/01	

CARR McLEAN   38-296

1995

The Hunger Report: 1995

Edited by

Ellen Messer

and

Peter Uvin

Alan Shawn Feinstein
World Hunger Program
Brown University

Gordon and Breach Publishers

Australia • Canada • China • France • Germany • India • Japan • Luxembourg • Malaysia •
The Netherlands • Russia • Singapore • Switzerland • Thailand • United Kingdom

Emmaplein 5
1075 AW Amsterdam
The Netherlands

British Library Cataloguing in Publication Data

A catalogue record for this book is available from the British Library.

ISBN 90-5699-518-9 (softcover)

ISSN 1040-3604

Contents

Tables and Figures

Figures

Foreword

Overcoming Hunger: The 1990s and Beyond

Robert W. Kates and Akin Mabogunje

In November 1989, a major non-governmental initiative (*The Bellagio Declaration: Overcoming Hunger in the 1990s*) proposed four achievable goals: (1) to eliminate deaths from famine; (2) to end hunger in half of the poorest households; (3) to cut malnutrition in half for mothers and small children; and (4) to eradicate iodine and vitamin A deficiencies. Together, these comprised a comprehensive yet practical program to end half of the world's hunger in a decade by building on the better and best of existing programs and policies for overcoming hunger. The most promising programs, the Declaration found, are those that empower people to assess their own condition and to act in their own behalf, that provide short-term hunger relief while addressing deeply rooted causes, and that can be sustained over the long term.

Five years later, these goals became in one form or another the hunger agenda for the decade. Its key elements were found in the declarations of the 71 heads of state attending the World Summit for Children (1990) and the 159 nations participating in the International Conference on Nutrition (1992), and in the deliberations of the World Bank Conference on Overcoming Global Hunger (1993). To move from agenda to action, the Steering Committee for the Bellagio Declaration organized a working Conference in Thailand from November 6 to 12, 1994, on the fifth anniversary of the Bellagio Declaration.

The Conference, hosted by the Institute of Nutrition of Mahidol University in Salaya, Thailand was coordinated by the Alan Shawn Feinstein World Hunger Program at Brown University with funding from the AEON Environmental Foundation (Japan), Carnegie Corporation of New York (USA), the Swedish International Development Agency (SIDA), the United Nations Children's Fund (UNICEF), and the United Nations Development Programme (UNDP). The choice of a venue in Thailand was to highlight the exceptional progress made in East and South-East Asia in dramatically reducing hunger within the decade. As in the original Bellagio Conference, it was a non-governmental initiative. In all, some 31 community organizers, opinion leaders, and technical and policy experts from 18 countries and six international organizations participated in the Salaya Conference as individuals sharing their expertise and concern.

To prepare for the Conference, a set of papers taking stock of the efforts to date and setting out some prospects for the future were circulated prior to the conference, then discussed in Salaya, revised in light of the discussion, and edited by Ellen Messer and Peter Uvin. They constitute the bulk of this year's *Hunger Report*.

The major conclusions of the Conference are found in two documents. The collective conclusions are found in the enclosed "Salaya Statement On Ending Hunger." The review of the global effort to cut hunger in half during the 1990s is found in the "Mid-Course Review Of The Bellagio Declaration On Overcoming Hunger In The 1990s" prepared by the co-chairman of the conference, Akin Mabogunje. Together, they present a mixed and balanced picture of progress since 1989 towards cutting hunger in half for the more than a billion people worldwide who suffer from one or more nutritional deficiencies. That goal, the conference found, has already been realized in East and South-East Asia through a combination of sustained economic growth and government-led programs addressed to the health, education, and income needs of poor people.

Addressing each of the goals in turn, the conference found that:

• Famine deaths due to natural disasters have essentially been eliminated since 1989 through early warning systems and improved regional and international humanitarian assistance. In an important but little-known success story, southern Africa suffered the deepest drought of the century in 1991-92, but international assistance helped prevent death from famine. In contrast, famine deaths continue in areas of armed conflict. Feeding the hungry repeatedly has been held hostage to ethnic and religious conflicts and to the lack of consensus among powers great and small on how to bring order to a disorderly world.

• The second goal – halving hunger among the 800 million who live in households too poor to obtain the food they need – was the most difficult to meet. Nonetheless, the experience of China between 1982 and 1992 in which the number of poor households were halved demonstrates that it can be done with effective social mobilization, increased food production and economic growth. There is increasing sensitivity to issues of poverty and hunger alleviation in the work of the World Bank and other international development agencies.

• Progress toward the third goal of cutting in half malnutrition among the 400 million under-weight women and the 184 million wasted and stunted children is more encouraging. A review of 62 countries found that in a third of the countries where malnutrition was a significant problem a generation ago, there are now only negligible amounts. A third more have already met or would meet the Bellagio goal within the decade or could reach the goal with a significant allocation of resources.

• The "hidden hunger" of iodine and Vitamin A deficiencies can be eradicated by supplementing deficient diets, fortifying foods with missing minerals and vitamins, and encouraging people to include natural sources in their diets. Iodine deficiencies, marked by goiter, mental impairment and cretinism, can be eliminated with iodized salt. At last count, some 82 our of 118 countries where the disorders are known to be prevalent have instituted universal salt iodization programs. Dealing with vitamin A deficiency is more complex, but a number of countries have made rapid progress. India and Indonesia, for example, have demonstrated a dramatic reduction in vitamin A-deficiency eye diseases that blind so many children.

Additional hope was engendered by the growing efforts and varied activities reported by the grassroots organizations at the Conference. In South Asia, large, well-organized non-governmental groups drawing upon a local reserve of well-educated people have been active in thousands of villages, rivaling or even outdoing governments in their ability to mobilize people and deliver services. In Africa, lacking such a reserve, non-governmental organizations concentrate on training needed personnel or rely on spontaneous community leadership. In Brasil, a broad national coalition has campaigned against hunger.

For those who would overcome hunger, it is always a fine balance between hope and despair. Five years ago, the Bellagio Declaration declared the need to weigh in with promise on that fine balance. Now, this careful assessment clearly finds some promise realized and more still attainable.

Acknowledgments

The World Hunger Program gratefully thanks William Bender, Marc Cohen, Sidney Goldstein, Jeanne Kasperson, Thomas Marchione, Robert Northrup, Robert Paarlberg, Barry Popkin, and Penny VanEsterik for commenting on earlier drafts of these papers.

The Program also thanks Nancy Caldwell, Dorothy Campbell, Luz Contreras, Barbara DeMaio, and Jeanne Kasperson for their high-quality research and technical support.

The Program gratefully acknowledges funding for "Overcoming Hunger: the 1990s and Beyond" conference and publication expenses from the Aeon Environmental Foundation (Japan), the Carnegie Corporation of New York, the Swedish International Development Agency (SIDA), the United Nations Development Programme (UNDP), and the United Nations Children's Fund (UNICEF).

The views expressed in this report are those of each author and do not necessarily represent the views of Brown University or those organizations and individuals who assisted us.

Introduction

This year's Hunger Report highlights progress over the past five years on problems of food shortage, poverty-related hunger, maternal-child nutrition and health, and micronutrient malnutrition. It is constructed from the papers and discussions presented at the five-year follow-up to the Bellagio Declaration: "Overcoming Hunger in the 1990s" (1989).* The individual essays assess progress in achieving the Bellagio goals to overcome hunger by the end of the decade. These goals are: (1) to end famine deaths, especially by moving food into zones of armed conflict; (2) to end hunger in half the world's poorest households; (3) to eliminate at least half the hunger of women and children by expanding maternal child health coverage; and (4) to eliminate vitamin A and iodine deficiencies as public health problems. The Bellagio Declaration also affirms that food is a human right, and insists that progress will come only when the joint efforts and energies of grassroots and community organizations are combined with state and international agencies to work against hunger. The concluding essays look into the future and suggest what else might be done beyond the turn of the century to meet the Bellagio goals.

1989-1994: FIVE YEARS OF CHANGE

Since the inception of the World Hunger Program a decade ago, and the promulgation of the Bellagio Declaration five years ago, the world has experienced enormous changes. As indicated in the individual contributions, there have been major transformations in the political-economic landscape (Hyden), in food and nutrition policy (Mason, Jonsson, and Csete), in social institutions (Uvin [b], Messer [b]), and in both positive and negative world food and hunger outlooks (Messer [c], Kates). With the end of the Cold War, the world is undergoing a rising tide of democratization often accompanied by ethnic and religious aspirations for political autonomy, accompanied by violent conflict and hunger (Hyden, Messer [a]). Grassroots movements across the world also are organizing, expanding, and insisting on taking a greater role in development (Uvin [b]). Human rights increasingly provide a reference point for hunger-related policies and actions, but an end to hunger looms far into the future (Messer [b]).

Mixed (Positive and Negative) Evidence of Progress

Although the overall trends in food supply, economic growth, and nutrition appear to be positive, the hunger numbers are still large and forbid complacency. When viewed in the contexts of population, environmental, political-economic, and sociocultural trends, they suggest room for caution as well as optimism. Food supply currently appears to be keeping up with population growth, but depending on the questions asked, the models used, and whether the preconceived message is a warning to stop reckless expense of resources or a flash of technological faith, the outlook may be pessimistic or optimistic (Messer [c], Kates).

Famine is on the decline except in zones of armed conflict (Uvin [a], Messer [a]). Famines were prevented in southern and eastern Africa during the droughts of the early 1990s by appropriate and

---

*Overcoming Hunger in the 1990s: Assessing Progress in the Mid-Decade. Workshop convened at the Institute of Nutrition, Mahidol University, Salaya, Thailand, 6-11 November 1994.

timely response. These efforts demonstrate that early warning systems and response can work when governments are well-organized, have food supply and distribution systems in place, and the international community, including non-governmental organizations (NGOs), cooperate closely with the affected communities. Food shortages still prevail where political conditions are unstable, however. The most desperate cases are encountered in zones of armed conflict, which numbered over 30 active conflicts that used food as a weapon, and at least 10 more where hunger persisted in the aftermath of war (Messer [a]). Although the United Nations (UN), bilateral aid organizations, and NGOs have created the humanitarian mechanisms to negotiate access to populations deprived of food in conflict zones, this neutral stance is not removing the causes of hunger, and is creating more and more "complex emergencies" that need food and other life essentials.

Poverty-related hunger world-wide also appears to be declining, but more than three quarters of a billion people still suffer from insufficient access to food due to limited resources, and the hunger problem is growing in industrialized countries such as the United States (US). Although there have been enormous efforts to increase the variety and scope of poverty-alleviation programs, including employment, job training, food and other welfare subsidies, policy makers still do not know precisely what types of programs work best in particular socioeconomic settings or how to limit costs over time. Most economists agree that some combination of economic growth and social welfare strategies is needed to protect human beings and assure "investment in human capital", but they are still exploring what is the appropriate mix of institutions and initiatives (Landell-Mills, Reutlinger). Certain Asian governments – Thailand, Indonesia, and China – report great strides in poverty alleviation and reductions in associated hunger and malnutrition. South Asian countries, by contrast, appear to rely more on the social welfare activities of NGOs, a trend found also in Africa and Latin America. Community organizing (or reorganizing), improvements in government infrastructure, and women's education appear to be levers for nutritional improvements, even where economic growth falters (Salaya Statement).

Progress in maternal-child nutritional health also can be identified but leaves room for improvement. UNICEF, charting progress on meeting the goals of the 1990 World Summit for Children, cites advances in 31 out of 48 developing countries for which they present data. But the others show no consensus on causes of malnutrition problems, as a first step to integrating nutrition into development planning. The situation is particularly bleak in countries at war (Mason, Jonsson, and Csete).

Micronutrient malnutrition, although not yet measurably decreasing, is on the development agenda of most countries. With technical assistance from intergovernment organizations (IGOs) and NGOs they display progress in legislating and implementing universal iodization of salt and multi-sectoral campaigns to eliminate vitamin A deficiency through supplements, food fortification, and food-based strategies. But seemingly straightforward tactics, such as salt iodization, have proved to be much harder and longer-term to implement in practice (Ralte).

The growing acceptance over much of the world that adequate food is a basic human right, as established in the UN Universal Declaration of Human Rights, also favors progress. But governments continue to argue over which rights take precedence, civil-political or economic-social, and no government that champions subsistence rights has a spotless political rights record, which is cause for concern (Messer [b]). Among NGOs, a number of new alliances, including a follow-up to the ICN, and a World Alliance for Nutrition and Human Rights, promise to mobilize human rights, development, and nutrition interests toward better nutrition policy and action. Their success will depend, however, on the willingness and abilities of their participants to join legal, political-economic, and sociocultural approaches to solve nutrition problems. It will also depend on the linkage of the goal: "overcoming hunger" to other goals of development, especially economic growth, environmental protection, positive political change, and improvements in population control and public health and on the successful linkages for action among communities, central governments, NGOs, and IGOs. The question remains how local grassroots NGOs "scale up" their impact beyond the local level; it involves issues of strategy, political involvement and communication with policy makers, technical competency, and institutional development. Experiences in overcoming hunger demonstrate that NGO scaling-up strategies need to be holistic both conceptually and institutionally, but there is no single agenda and much remains unknown (Uvin [b]).

A critical issue in nutritional projections or visions is whether the world will know more peace than war, and whether the war-torn arenas of the current world will be able to stabilize and meet basic human needs (Messer [a]). Peace will prove to be at least as important as population stabilization, economic growth (with equity), development assistance (including food aid), or trade (Singer). Another critical variable will be the ways in which women participate in building future societies, economies, and diets. Technological and political surprises may yet produce scenarios with lower hunger numbers; the downward trend in hunger numbers even in countries where economic growth is faltering suggests more room for hope, less for despair, but also the need for better data and analyses to understand, reverse, and prevent the circumstances of hunger vulnerability, respectively past, present, and future.

SUMMARIES OF FINDINGS ON PROGRESS IN MEETING THE BELLAGIO GOALS IN THE MID-DECADE

The world might be well on its way to cutting hunger in half, and then to moving on to tackle the "harder" half of hunger. But progress is less and slower than anticipated.

The State of World Hunger

In his "The State of World Hunger", Peter Uvin presents an overview of recent trends in food shortage, food poverty and food deprivation. In 1993 and 1994, the world produced enough food for all its peoples, and contained enough cereal reserves to protect them against calamities. But the margins were slim: world food production was only sufficient to cover diets that are close to vegetarian, and world cereal carryover stocks were close to the lower limit that is considered safe.

New data on food poverty are not available, but in all likelihood past trends of slow improvement have continued: economic growth in most of the Third World was positive in 1993-5. As a result, and with the exception of sub-Saharan Africa, data from 46 countries in which at least two comparable surveys of the prevalence of underweight children allow one to estimate recent trends, are encouraging, with very rapid improvements observed in China. The two main exceptions to this positive picture are sub-Saharan Africa (although a few countries in the region did perform quite well) and the former Soviet Union and Eastern Europe. In each case, the catastrophic state of economies combined with civil war resulted in acute food shortage and low quality of care, the former trend since 1992. Over the same period, the international community's capacity and willingness to supply food aid is decreasing, while an increasing proportion of the remaining food aid goes to the former USSR and Yugoslavia and to African emergencies, instead of to the traditional, low-income food aid recipients in the Third World.

Food Wars: Food is Being Moved into Zones of Armed Conflict but Doesn't End Hunger

Ellen Messer's first chapter, "Food Wars: The Use of Food as a Weapon (1989-1994)" counts the growing numbers of wars and war-affected hungry populations, who suffer food shortage, poverty, and deprivation during and after the conflicts. Formerly war-torn societies in developing countries, that have known peace in the aftermath of the Cold War, still must rebuild, and there have been new wars, devastation, and hunger following the breakup of the Soviet Union and Yugoslavia, and intensifying competition for resources, abuses of (and demands for) human rights in certain African and Latin American countries. Food aid assistance, in response to human rights and humanitarian concerns, is moving to feed victims of these complex emergencies, but does not always reach those in need because of political and military diversions. The so-called "relief-to-development" continuum is becoming by default relief instead of development as aid diminishes, and development becomes more difficult in these situations of total need but social disintegration stemming from warfare. Donors need to learn how development assistance can be used to prevent conflict, not just rebuild afterwards. "Global human security" is a named goal that incorporates adequate food and nutrition, but IGOs and NGOs are just beginning to learn how to go beyond rhetoric and make nutrition a basic human right, and requisite cornerstone of international assistance.

Halving Hunger is Possible: Asian "Success Stories" of Food Self-Sufficiency, Poverty Alleviation, and Nutritional Improvement

The Chinese government has made nutritional adequacy one of its principal goals and an important objective and indicator of success in poverty-alleviation policies. Progress appears to be certain, but somewhat uneven. Chen Chunming's paper, "Progress in Overcoming Hunger in China: 1989-1994" charts nutritional progress over the period 1978 (the beginning of China's economic reforms) through 1992. Official government statistics demonstrate that food production since the reforms has increased for all crops. Correspondingly, food intakes have improved greatly and malnutrition rates have declined. All-China averages, however, hide regional and income differences. Recent data show that malnutrition, although declining, continues to exist among some 80 million people located in the more isolated rural provinces. Additionally, the data indicate considerable inequity in food consumption between urban and rural households, and among income groups, especially in their consumption of food energy from animal foods. The urban households consume 2.5 times more animal foods than their rural counterparts, while high-income rural households consume 4 times more animal foods than poorer ones. These discrepancies in quality food intakes appear to be linked to increasing income inequities between and within regions.

The government of China has adopted a series of policies to improve household nutrition, that aim to stimulate food production and improve food storage. Policies are also leading to better planning of food supplies for urban populations, stabilization of food prices for producers and consumers, rural industry development to increase income and access to food, and finally, nutrition education. A nutrition surveillance system has been in place since 1990, and a National Consultative Committee on Food and Nutrition was established in 1993.

China has also been using poverty alleviation policies as a principal tool in the fight against hunger. In 1986, an Office of Poverty Alleviation was established within the State Council which supports self-reliant community development through such programs as road construction, land development, improved agricultural technology, education, health care, and others. The poverty alleviation program, "80 million-seven years" is aimed at eliminating hunger by the year 2000 among those 80 million people still in absolute food poverty. It sets explicit food consumption targets, based on appropriate Desirable Dietary Pattern scores for each province. It also promotes a wide variety of activities designed to provide opportunities for communities to consume more and better food, and special programs for children less than 18 months of age.

Southeast Asia's nutritional progress is also mixed, both between and within countries. Daily energy supply in all countries except Cambodia is reported to be sufficient to meet aggregate population needs, but food is not evenly distributed. In spite of certain positive trends in poverty alleviation, diets and lifestyles are changing in ways that threaten good nutrition. Kraisid Tontisirin's and Pattanee Winichagoon's contribution, "Progress in Overcoming Hunger in Southeast Asia: 1989-1994" demonstrates that Southeast-Asian countries generally have made progress in reducing malnutrition since the 1980s. Particularly in Thailand and Indonesia, malnutrition trends among children under five are definitely downward. But prevalence of underweight remains high and stunting reaches close to 50% in the Philippines, Vietnam, and Laos. Data on adult Body Mass Index of selected countries also indicate chronic food energy deficits. Iodine deficiency disorders (IDD) are also a large and increasingly well documented public health problem; only Singapore and Brunei report prevalence under 10% in school-aged children. Changes in diet and life style, particularly in urban areas, also appear to be interfering with breastfeeding.

The paper very briefly summarizes the nutrition policies and relative successes of four of the countries: Thailand, the Philippines, Vietnam, and Indonesia. Nutrition has been an explicit component of Thailand's national development policy since 1977. By the Sixth Development Plan (1987-1991) nutrition was incorporated into an intersectoral approach that involved multiple ministries working together to improve quality of life through community-based programs. Nutrition is also a component of primary health care and rural development schemes, and of the Thai government's Poverty Alleviation Plan, which targets poor areas for development within macrolevel government planning. Programs attempt to streamline resource allocation procedures and also involve the communities in planning and implementing programs. Official statistics indicate marked nutritional improvements among children under five. Thailand is continuing holistic approaches and also expanding efforts to address specific nutritional problems, especially micronutrient malnutrition. But progress is neither quick nor easy. Even with government dedication and multisectoral approaches that directly involve communities, substantial reductions in childhood malnutrition have taken fifteen years, and IDD prevalence is still unacceptably high.

As documented also in Soekirman's chapter, "Overcoming Hunger and Malnutrition: The Indonesian Experience," the government of Indonesia also manifests a long-standing interest in nutrition as an integrated part of the development planning process. Its first "development era" began in 1969, and in the intervening 25 years, government statistics chart substantial progress in all aspects of nutrition. Self-sufficiency in rice, achieved in 1984, has been sustained, and per capita food calorie availability has increased from 2,035 in 1968 to 2,701 in 1990. Rural poverty declined rapidly in one generation as a result of improvements in agricultural technology, infrastructure, and communications as well as rural to urban migration. Public health, family planning, and education, combined with entitlement programs, also are credited with helping improve income, nutrition, and standards of living. Indonesia's government also developed a nutrition surveillance system (NSS) in response to the droughts and other natural disasters of the early 1980s. The Timely Warning Information and Intervention System (TWIIS) trained local-level community volunteers, leaders and district government officials to develop and use local indicators of impending food crisis, as a way to mobilize resources to respond in timely fashion to food shortages.

The Kraisid Tontisirin-Pattanee Winichagoon chapter supplies additional commentary and detail. In 1973, the Indonesian government initiated the UPGK community movement, a nationwide program that included activities in agriculture, health, family planning, rural development, and education. Village groups such as women's organizations assume responsibility for community nutrition education, nutrition services for maternal and child nutrition at a community center, and home and community gardening aimed at generating income and increasing consumption of vegetables. Subsequent five-year development plans stress improved food and nutrition security through nutrition education, dietary diversification, micronutrient nutrition, and other programs.

As a result of improved surveillance and response, no severe adult malnutrition has been reported since 1985, although mild to moderate malnutrition and micro-nutrient malnutrition are still recognized to be significant nutrition public health problems that are addressed in the second long-term development plan (1994-2018). Protein-energy malnutrition is found mostly in the poorest households, in unsanitary environments, where disease prevalence, especially of diarrhea, is high. Severe vitamin A deficiency (xeropthalmia) has been eliminated and serum vitamin levels are being improved through food-based and fortification strategies, assisted by education and marketing tactics. IDD has been more recalcitrant since thousands of small salt producers, who are dispersed throughout the country, are difficult to reach and monitor for salt iodization.

In summary, the Asian "success" stories have all achieved food self-sufficiency, poverty-alleviation, and targeted nutritional improvements. They have been "top-down" government programs, designed by nutritionists in high-level government planning positions, that have addressed simultaneously food shortage, poverty, and deprivation but have also involved the communities in implementing, monitoring, and sustaining the solutions. All have been undertaken in relatively stable political-economic environments characterized by high rates of economic growth, but also well-planned, multi-sectoral social welfare activities. Even with these advantages reported progress in each instance took at least 15 years and further poverty alleviation and elimination of micronutrient deficiencies (especially IDD) still lag. Thus, five years may be too short a time frame to expect measurable success, although one should expect to see progress in problem assessment, nutrition planning, and institutional developments to improve the situation.

Institutional Advances in Micronutrient Malnutrition

Institutional developments are the major indicators of progress over the past five years on both micronutrient and maternal-child health goals. Anne Ralte, in her paper "Progress in Overcoming Micronutrient Deficiencies: 1989-1994", reports mixed news on prevalence but mostly good news on institutional awareness and response: "Overcoming Hunger" calls for the virtual elimination of vitamin A and iodine deficiencies as public health problems by the year 2000; goals repeated in the World Summit for Children (1990), the UNICEF/WHO initiative, "Ending Hidden Hunger" (1991), and the International Conference on Nutrition *World Declaration and Plan of Action* (1992). On each occasion, more than 150 countries pledged commitment to meet these goals, and international agencies agreed to monitor progress. Countries are developing or strengthening internal collaboration and coordination through food and nutrition councils, task forces, or working groups and also establishing coordinating mechanisms with and among external agencies. FAO, WHO, and UNICEF are orchestrating regional workshops and trying to develop reliable indicators to monitor progress.

IDD constitutes the largest known public health nutrition problem. Over 1.5 billion are at risk, or 29% of the world's population; an estimated 655 million people are affected by goiter. Of 118 out of 183 countries known to have IDD, 82 are undertaking salt iodization programs, 24 have supplementation programs, and an additional 31 have plans to initiate activities soon. For VAD, WHO estimates that over 90 countries have clinical or subclinical deficiencies classified as public health problems; 230.6 million are at risk; 3.1 million of pre-school age are affected clinically, and another 227.5 million with less visible (non-eye) symptoms. South and Southeast Asia are now reporting a decline in the magnitude of severe deficiencies, although mild to moderate deficiencies persist. In Sub-Saharan Africa, where the magnitude of the problem is just beginning to be charted, 19 of 43 countries now report VAD as a public health problem, and 50 million children are estimated to have clinical eye signs. Across regions, VAD accounts for 65% of measles-associated childhood mortality and blindness. More generally, vitamin A, in a series of studies, also has been shown to reduce infant and child morbidity and mortality from illness by an average of 23%.

Mid-decade country goals for VAD include assessment of the extent of the problem, a plan and strategy to solve the problem, and VAD programs to reach all under 24 months of age who are at risk of VAD. For IDD, the goals are reduction of goiter to less than five percent, and at least 90% salt iodization. For both deficiencies, public health experts are trying to develop effective interventions to reach the most vulnerable groups by supplementation, fortification, and food-based strategies. Successful strategies, such as Indonesia's for elimination of VAD, usually mobilize grassroots organizations, especially mothers through women's organizations, to learn more about the problems and solutions, assist with capsule distribution or iodization, promote better nutrition through education, and encourage local control of the problem through participation in record keeping and monitoring.

For both problems, fortification is the strategy of choice where there exist acceptable vehicles such as sugar or salt, both widely consumed and with long shelf lives. Vitamin A-fortified margarine, MSG (Indonesia) and wheat flour are other vehicles being tested. Fortification is the strategy of choice especially in Latin America, with its advanced food technology and distribution systems and strong private sector. Bolivia's successful program to eliminate IDD through salt iodization is one example. Both supplementation and fortification strategies must be combined with nutrition and health education and community participation to be successful. Food-based strategies are considered over the long term to be the most cost-effective since the appropriate changes in nutritional behaviors should be self-sustaining. Social marketing of vitamin A-rich foods in Thailand, and home-gardening projects in Bangladesh and Niger, are examples of promising programs managed by communities, with technical assistance from consultants and NGOs. Successful programs have found that the household context, especially the nutrition education of the mother, is critical to prevent as well as alleviate micronutrient deficiency diseases. They also involve full participation of local community organizations and NGOs, and highly visible support by local leaders. Successful programs also entail good management skills, often contributed by NGOs or the private sector, to identify problems clearly, set achievable goals, monitor progress and where necessary, respond flexibly to make mid-course corrections.

Breaking the Links Between Poverty and Childhood Malnutrition Through Effective Maternal-Child Health

The synergism between malnutrition and infection, and its antecedent conditions and remedies, is addressed also in Mason, Jonsson & Csete's contribution, "Is Childhood Malnutrition Being Overcome?", which focuses on child malnutrition and examines the interactions between low birth weight, insufficient food intake, disease, and inadequate care. Especially under conditions of inadequate care, inadequate dietary intake leads to low nutritional reserves, lowered disease resistance, and illness episodes that are more frequent, more severe, and longer-lasting. The child is caught in a spiral of disease and growth failure, often ending in death.

The World Summit for Children (1990), building on the Convention on the Rights of the Child (1989), established a legal-political context in which country political leaders pledged to try to reach certain achievable goals by the end of the decade: including elimination of VAD and IDD, a reduction in the incidence of low birth weight to under 10%, a halving of severe and moderate malnutrition among the world's under-fives, exclusive breastfeeding for the first four- to six-months of a child's life, support for growth monitoring, and greater dissemination of knowledge that would enable all households to achieve food security. Data on trends (1990-1994) in child malnutrition for all continents and for 48 individual countries are not encouraging. They show sub-Saharan Africa's situation is deteriorating, South Asia's is stagnating, while trends in Southeast Asia and China, the Near and Middle East, North Africa, and Latin America are improving, with overall improvements close to those necessary to meet World Summit for Children and International Conference on Nutrition goals. South Asia needs more rapid and unobstructed improvement, while sub-Saharan Africa needs to reverse its deteriorating status.

Countries where malnutrition prevalence is below 10%, and where the prevalence was significantly higher a generation go, are located mainly in Latin and Central America. For an additional eight countries with malnutrition prevalence 10% or above, available trend data suggest the World Summit for Children goal will be met. In most of these countries, consensus exists on causes of malnutrition and appropriate nutritional strategies and reducing malnutrition is given some political priority. In another eight countries, appropriate strategies to reduce malnutrition are in place or are planned but a significant allocation of resources still is needed to establish an adequate trend to meet the end-of-decade goal. Malnutrition is declining, but not rapidly enough. In eight additional countries, appropriate program and policy strategies to reduce malnutrition are not in place and consensus on causes of malnutrition has not been reached. Meeting nutrition goals is unlikely, even with additional resources. A final eleven countries, mostly affected by war or internal strife, also are unlikely to reach the 1995 goal, although it is possible with effective planning to make progress in reducing malnutrition even during emergenci es. This last group, with the exception of Haiti, are all in Africa.

History shows accelerated improvement in nutrition is possible but not linear. Economic growth is important, but so are the ways in which additional wealth in generated, and the mix of social services which raise investment in human capital. Specific nutrition programs can prove important, but they need to be well-targeted and involve significant community participation, alongside government structures with clear responsibility and competence. Lessons from the past include the importance of involving all social levels and sectors – from central government to local communities – in assessment, analysis and action, and of addressing immediate, but also underlying causes.

Reducing Malnutrition: Economic Growth is Necessary But Not Enough

Malnutrition appears to be reduced through the combined effects of economic growth that involves the poor, plus investment in human capital and social services (education, especially of women, literacy, access to health services). Increased income thus has multiple and synergistic effects on access to food, health care, and a nurturing environment. Landell-Mills' essay, "Trends in Household Poverty and Hunger" discusses the poverty and economic growth data that tend to be associated with hunger. Here again, the numbers are not encouraging: East Asia and the Pacific is the only region where the absolute numbers and proportion of the population in poverty are estimated to have decreased over the late 1980s, and the poverty gap index, that reflects the depth of poverty, is increasing in Latin America and the Caribbean, the Middle East and North Africa, and Sub-Saharan Africa. In Latin America, the main surge is in urban poverty. In East Asia, poverty remains more a rural phenomenon, although impressive rural economic growth has reduced both poverty and related malnutrition substantially, to about 10% in China, 15% in Indonesia.

Reduction in malnutrition conventionally is associated with economic growth, but growth in itself is not enough: it must be sufficiently broad-based to impact on the incidence of poverty; and initial and subsequent income distributions, that indicate who benefits from additional income, are also factors. Recent data are encouraging; they indicate that economic growth tends to be associated with less, not more inequality, but the factors that link growth to poverty alleviation are not well understood. Additional factors associated with greater equality and better nutrition, even where growth lags, are women's education and other investments in human welfare, including health, sanitation, and family planning.

As Reutlinger emphasizes in his Discussion: "Is Economic Growth Really the Remedy for Overcoming Hunger and Poverty?" alleviating poverty sometimes involves trade-offs with growth. Strategies to raise the incomes of the poor while promoting growth are desirable, but mostly elusive. Reutlinger suggests more local-level action is needed to generate income and possibly redistribute resources, including land. He also suggests that more data is needed on which types of policies are most cost-effective; those which increase immediate entitlements, such as food subsidies or food stamp programs, or those which improve the poor's access to public services, such as health care and education, which improve their longer-term potential for better nutrition and standard of living. To design appropriate targeted interventions and to plan for more broad-based economic growth, reliable household-level data are needed that can identify the poorest and most hungry households, the principal sources of their vulnerability to hunger, and intervene. Participatory methodologies are contributing somewhat to the superior design of local and regional food security surveys that can determine the contributing factors, including food prices, occupational structure, household or family structure.

On the supply side of the food price spectrum, economists are also trying to predict the impact of liberalized trade on food prices and hunger vulnerability at the country level. Hans Singer, in his contribution "The Future of Food Trade and Food Aid in a Liberalizing Global Economy," discusses the implications of the latest Uruguay Round of the General Agreement on Tariffs and Trade (GATT), which commits member states to partial reductions in domestic subsidies for agriculture. This liberalization of agricultural policies and trade is expected to affect mainly the food-exporting developed countries, for which subsidies are to be reduced by 35% in value and 21% in volume over a period of six years. It is anticipated that as a result, food exporting countries, in particular the United States (US) and the European Union (EU), will produce less and hold lower food stocks, and that world food prices will rise. Higher food prices will hurt the poor net food-importing countries, particularly in Africa, that will likely suffer also from reductions in food aid and other non-food related outcomes of the Uruguay Round, such as the erosion of tariff preferences. However, additional factors could reduce the predicted rise in food prices, including greater agricultural production and exports from Russia and Eastern Europe, Argentina, Thailand, Zimbabwe, and other potential food-exporting countries. New breakthroughs in agricultural research and development, or wider applications of known plant-breeding, agronomic, and food processing technologies, could also lower predicted shortfalls and price increases.

Other factors, however, could dampen production and raise future food prices. These include plateauing of yields in the most intensively cultivated areas of Asia, the US, and EC, due to crop plant genetic erosion; co-evolution of crop pests combined with restrictions on the use of fertilizers, pesticides, and other chemicals for environmental and health reasons; general effects of environmental degradation; the impact of global warming and climatic change that adds temperature and moisture stress; a shift of food production into increasingly fragile areas and soils; increasing demand for imports of basic grains by China or other countries moving toward greater animal food content in diets; a reduction in the supply of food in favor of fodder and cash crops.

Compared with these factors, the impact of the Uruguay Round may be small, but the straw that breaks the camel's back. Food-importing developing countries need a safety net to cushion the possible impacts. Yet food aid, an important safety mechanism, even now is threatened by reduced surpluses and higher prices, which together allow less volume of food donations for given donor budgetary appropriations. The final act of the GATT Uruguay Round maintains the need for food aid, suggests "a periodic review" of the minimum food aid supply, and specifically asks donors to give more food aid to needy countries on a grant or concessional basis. It also asks that a rise in food prices be considered as a factor in determining access to existing and new funds from international financial institutions. It remains to be seen whether these good intentions will be matched by beneficial actions; the US decision to unilaterally cut its food aid commitments is a bad omen.

THE CHANGING INSTITUTIONAL AND POLITICAL CONTEXT

Although the Bellagio Declaration focused more narrowly on setting achievable nutrition goals, it also addressed the wider institutional and political context, which has undergone enormous transformation over five years. Goran Hyden, in his essay, "Global Changes Since 1989" discusses several trends related to hunger, which, as borne out by the hunger data, give mixed messages of progress and future prospects. The Cold War is over, but the world knows greater numbers of conflicts, tied to religious and ethnic aspirations for political autonomy. Economic growth is disappointing, but more hopefully, population growth appears to be slowing. More widespread education and family planning, and commitment to nutrition and health, are promising; but it is not clear that such efforts are yet self-sustaining, and foreign aid appears to be shrinking overall, with more allocated to the former Soviet Union and to emergency assistance than to peacetime development. Global trade has significantly liberalized, and GATT will produce hundreds of billions of new trade dollars and incomes, but outside of the EC, the US, and China, gains may be small and African countries, with their minimal bargaining power to obtain alternative compensation, may lose.

Political conditionalities seem to have strengthened the global trend towards democratization and the world seems to be moving towards greater accountability and political voice for civil society. These political developments create environments in which social justice and human rights are more easily defended and poor communities more involved in their own development, and should improve prospects for economic growth. But the flip side of the process has been a decline in state sovereignty in many developing countries. The end of Cold War-related support, persistent armed crises, as well as a growing interdependence in finance, production, and communications, have eroded central government powers especially in the poorest countries. A rise in ethnic and religious aspirations has brought about civil violence, civil war, and "food wars", as chronicled earlier in this volume. Such political strife is in part a reaction against the hegemony of science and technology that characterizes modern Western democracies, in part a perceived need by these societies to return to traditional sources of humanities and values, and a disenchantment overall with the benefits offered by the modern secular state. Hyden ends his essay with a plea for a new ethics of tolerance and respect for diversity, as well as for the equality and dignity of every human being.

One of the responses to the social fragmentation and ineffectiveness of central government has been the rise of NGOs and grassroots movements. Peter Uvin's chapter, "Linking the Grassroots to the Summit" indicates how such links, that can prevent or alleviate hunger, are constructed through processes of "scaling-up" community efforts or "scaling-down" government programs. NGOs have many origins: some form out of a desire for "self-help" or "development"; others are a reaction to the abuses or injustices of government or IGO actions. Both types of institutions would best coop-erate, but there are always constraints. Uvin, drawing on the experiences of 25 Third World grassroots organizations, analyzes the different ways in which they expand their impact: by expanding size, membership base, or constituencies ("quantitative scaling up"); by expanding the numbers or types of their activities, e.g., from agriculture to health and credit ("functional scaling up"); by moving from service-delivery to empowerment efforts, that change the structural causes of underdevelop-ment through active involvement and negotiation with government or IGOs ("political scaling up"); or through improved institutional structuring and management ("organizational scaling up").

Limited progress has been made in the scaling down process: governments and international organizations do provide some direct funding of grassroots organizations, but this resource alloca-tion does not entail any redistribution of decisionmaking power. Surprisingly, the World Bank, largely as a result of NGO pressure reinforced by some member states, has recently created a few mechanisms and the potential for greater change: (1) a World Bank - NGO consultative group, which meets twice a year, and is composed of NGOs from all regions of the world; (2) operational directives that obligate project directors to consult groups that will be affected, and assess and address possible damaging impacts before projects can be approved; (3) an independent inspection panel that hears cases of complaint by any organization representing the people affected, that the World Bank is violating its own procedures; (4) a Public Information Centre, established to make available to the public a range of operational documents that were previously restricted to official users; (5) since 1992, a series of workshops on hunger that are organized jointly with the NGO sector.

Such grassroots linkages with the summit have been instrumental in pressing forward the prac-tical and also the human rights agenda associated with overcoming hunger. Ellen Messer's over-view, "The Human Right to Food (1989-1994)" traces how food and nutrition rights have been advancing within legal, political, and sociocultural frameworks through the actions of UN, NGO, and community groups. Recent efforts to move food into zones of armed conflict and to protect the nutrition and health of children through the Convention on the Rights of the Child are two ex-amples showing where the global community has reached some consensus over the past five years. Academic and legal clarifications of: rights and obligations, what constitutes adequate food or nutrition, and the criteria by which individuals or social groups are included or excluded from community or governmental respect, protection, and fulfillment of rights, are also helping to build consensus that leads to actions to prevent and redress nutrition rights violations. The World Alli-ance for Nutrition and Human Rights and the Food First Information and Action Network are two examples of umbrella NGOs that have crystallized around nutrition and "the right to feed one-self"; they advise organizations and communities of recourse when their access to food or nutri-tional well-being is threatened. Although the right to food still remains more reference point than reality, advocacy for the human right to food is growing, as is the realization that achievement of human rights and an end to hunger are interdependent, and rely on supportive values and practices at all social levels.

ENVISIONING A FUTURE WITHOUT HUNGER

Will the world community be able to fulfill the human right to food? To answer this question, Ellen Messer's final essay, "Visions of the Future: Food, Hunger, and Nutrition," analyzes IGO and NGO projections based on environmental, political-economic, and sociocultural trends spanning the decades 2000 to 2060. At one extreme is World Watch Institute Lester Brown's pessimistic assessment, that the world has already reached a Malthusian crisis of imbalance between population and food resources; at the other, the World Bank Economic Department's optimistic outlook that envisions biotechnology, trade, and economic (income) growth adjusting to increased food demand. Hedging its bets, the International Food Policy Research Institute's (IFPRI's) "2020 Vision for Food, Agriculture, and the Environment" concludes the future of food depends on effective demand, and sustained investment in international agricultural research that will allow more widespread and sustainable agricultural intensification without environmental degradation; increases of on- and off-farm income; and affordable nutritious food. The "2050"project, a joint venture of the World Resources Institute, Santa Fe Institute, and Brookings Institute, by contrast, focuses on demand, and links sustainable future food supply to greater efficiencies throughout the food system, including a reversal of current trends toward greater consumption of animal products. Chen and Kates, of the World Hunger Program, draw on these and other scenarios as they discuss hunger-related trends in economy, population, trade and aid, and social safety nets.

These forecasts differ on whether the focus is principally supply or demand and on whether more food might be forthcoming from production or processing technologies, especially the elimination of waste. All agree that biotechnology and other tools of agricultural intensification offer great potential to produce additional food with greater efficiency, but also that it will be difficult to meet the increasing food demands, especially of burgeoning urban populations. The intermediary challenges include: maintaining investment in agricultural research and development to expand sustainable yields; reducing population growth; reducing poverty or promoting economic growth-with-equity; and nurturing a system of human values that protects and advances human development and human rights, including adequate food and nutrition. A general weakness shared by all is a tendency to provide the global assessment and then stop without offering prioritized recommendations for further action. They also fail to specify what institutional mix might facilitate progress, either on production, processing, or consumption changes or the social contexts that might encourage ecologically sustainable and less wasteful dietary habits. They give little attention to the ways in which global or national efforts might connect with grassroots community or NGO efforts. All are projections based on current trends, and with the exception of Chen and Kates, give no thought to "surprise" elements in their scenarios. Messer suggests world hunger outlooks might be modified significantly by four understudied elements: (1) peace, especially in war-torn sub-Saharan Africa; (2) effective grassroots participation in food, nutrition, and development planning; (3) dietary diversification, including greater emphasis on meeting micronutrient needs; and (4) a woman-centered approach to food and nutrition planning, from agricultural research and extension to efficient processing and consumption. The so-called visions also lack the sociocultural and moral perspectives found in prophecies or visions of the good society where everyone has a right to adequate food.

Robert Kates' contribution "Ending Hunger: 1999 and Beyond" also examines possible trends in food production, economic growth, population, and values that will influence hunger in a warmer, and more crowded, connected, and diverse world. According to one scenario generated by The International Institute of Applied Systems Analysis (IIASA) in Laxenburg, Austria, a world of ten billion, given current economic and technological trends, would require a quadrupling of food, sextupling of energy consumption, and an octupling of the world economy. Such increases seem both unlikely and unsustainable. A more likely scenario, also by IIASA, predicts that by the year 2060, GDP will increase by a factor of 4.4 over the level of 1980 and total cereal production by a factor of 2.25. Assuming no change in income distribution, this model estimates some 20% of the population will be malnourished. Numbers will be greater or lesser, depending on the region-specific impacts of climate change, that presage declines in food production and increases in food prices for the developing world.

Such scenarios, not forecasts but systematically created "what if" statements, are cautionary tales which leave room to imagine changes beyond "business as usual". Kates rejects the two scenarios as unrealistic and unacceptable, and discusses what additional factors are required for a future without hunger. First is universal respect for the individual right to food. As indicated also in Messer's "Right to Food" chapter, current institutional trends and activities, suggest considerable progress can be expected but major political-economic obstacles must still be overcome. A second requirement is sustainable food availability. As Uvin indicates in "The State of World Hunger," there currently is sufficient food in the world to feed everyone a balanced vegetarian diet, if food were equitably distributed. But for more varied diets, that include increasing demands for animal products, even today the world needs to produce much more food, especially given skewed distribution. Climate change and population growth here may soon challenge and threaten to surpass the limits of human technological ingenuity. Much will depend on how responsive human behavior becomes to ecological or social demands for environmental protection and more moderate, less wasteful, consumption.

A third factor required for a world without hunger is adequate household income, provided through economic growth, full and adequately compensated employment, and also wider and deeper social safety nets. Such safety nets include famine prevention, emergency assistance, entitlements for the food-poor, and special needs programs. Such social welfare efforts had been expanding, but ethnic conflict in Africa, Asia, and Eastern Europe, and 'compassion fatigue' among donors, are limiting disaster prevention and assistance; and competition for funds and lack of effective targeting and management threaten entitlement programs, such as food for work, fair price shops, and food subsidies, and related health and sanitation programs, especially under conditions of structural adjustment.

CONCLUSIONS

Five years is too short a time span to observe success or to predict failure in meeting Summit or "Overcoming Hunger" goals for nutrition and child survival. Reported progress in selected Asian countries has taken close to 15 years. But the institutional transformation underway to prevent childhood, maternal, and micronutrient malnutrition in developing countries may hold promise for more rapid progress for the future. A surge of peaceful conditions, sustained by international political commitments to human rights and an end to hunger, could reverse nutritional and economic declines in Africa and the former Soviet Union and Eastern Europe. A shift in focus from more narrowly defined nutrition and health goals to freedom from hunger as a human right and an end to hunger as a dimension of global human security is more than sloganeering; it broadens the constituencies concerned with hunger, and is advancing knowledge and actions.

New knowledge linking IDD and VAD respectively to child development and learning, and morbidity and mortality, draw together those concerned with hunger, children's rights, health, education, and economic development. Child survival interests, while not relinquishing their chief emphasis on health, or on nutrition as food, health and care, increasingly address wider questions of peace, environmental safety, decent livelihood, and social justice. Those concerned with economic growth probe recent findings to understand how small-scale lending to poor households, especially to women, and other anti-poverty, education and social welfare programs can most cost-effectively increase entitlements to food and other vital resources; how they can relieve suffering now but also increase future human capacities for higher incomes, standards of living, and economic growth. Burgeoning environmental interests are helping to shape the development and applications of new technologies for a more sustainable agricultural future, sufficient to feed billions more in the coming decades. Issues of good governance, local representation and participation, and human rights are being addressed together, as civil and political rights advocates recognize the human right to food to be a dimension and indicator of their legal, political, and cultural mandate. New institutions and actions linking world summits to NGOs and grassroots constituencies and actions are growing up everywhere.

New knowledge and evidence produced over the last five years also suggest that progress is and will remain uneven, but there will be more synergistic effects in positive directions. The hunger numbers based on access to minimally adequate food are unacceptably high–greater than three-quarters of a billion. Yet the under-five anthropometric data on child nutrition have begun to show that it is possible to de-link poverty and hunger with the right array of State and community actions. In spite of faltering economic growth and low levels of income, developing countries especially in Latin America appear to be improving child nutrition, creating capacity to eliminate micronutrient malnutrition, and addressing the overall conditions of food, health, and care that can lead to sustainable nutritional improvements. The different measures of food shortage, food poverty, and food deprivation, allow us to address this complexity; the apparent discrepancy between household "poverty" and individual (child) anthropometric indicators of malnutrition, as well as selective improvements in micronutrient malnutrition which are emerging in particular countries and regions. Each accurate in its own way, these measures are best used together to identify countries, households, and individuals at nutritional risk, but also to chart all possible indicators of progress. All suggest the need for better data, especially on household nutrition and dynamics: how households in low-growth economies manage scarce resources and avoid malnutrition of individual members; and from the State perspective, what types of growth can alleviate poverty; what types of poverty-alleviation policies are most cost-effective and interfere less with growth; and what types of nutrition and related health, sanitation, and education programs are most cost-effective in reducing malnutrition and contributing to longer-term growth.

None are simple questions, and they pale before the even more complex antecedents of warfare and violations of human rights, afflictions that are great cause for concern and pessimism about the future of hunger. Nevertheless, the steady progress in knowledge, in institutions, and in global to local politics addressing food shortage, poverty, and deprivation are causes for optimism–and action–now and for the future.

Ellen Messer and Peter Uvin
Providence, Rhode Island
December 1995

Chapter References

Chunming, Chen. *Progress in Overcoming Hunger in China: 1989-1994.*
Hyden, Goran. *Global Changes Since 1989.*
Kates, Robert. *Ending Hunger: 1999 and Beyond.*
Mason, John, Urban Jonsson, and Joanne Csete. *Is Childhood Malnutrition Being Overcome?*
Messer, Ellen (a). *Food Wars: Hunger as a Weapon of War in 1994.*
Messer, Ellen (b). *The Human Right to Food (1989-1994).*
Messer, Ellen (c). *Visions of the Future: Food, Hunger, and Nutrition.*
Ralte, Anne Lalsawmliani. *Progress in Overcoming Micronutrient Deficiencies: 1989-1994.*
Soekirman. *Overcoming Hunger and Malnutrition: The Indonesian Experience.*
Tontisirin, Kraisid and Pattanee Winichagoon. *Progress in Overcoming Hunger in Southeast Asia: 1989-1994.*
Uvin, Peter (a). *The State of World Hunger.*
Uvin, Peter (b). *Linking the Grassroots to the Summit.*

Acronyms and Abbreviations

ACC/SCN	Administrative Committee on Coordination/ Subcommittee on Nutrition
AED	Academy for Educational Development
AMS	Aggregate Measure of Support
AP	Associated Press
BAPPENAS	National Development and Planning Board (Indonesia)
BMI	Body Mass Index
BMN	Basic Minimum Needs
BMR	Basic Metabolic Rate
CAPM	Chinese Academy of Preventive Medicine
CGIAR	Consultative Group on International Agricultural Research
CIS	Commonwealth of Independent States
CRC	Convention on the Rights of the Child
CRS	Catholic Relief Services
CSD	Child Survival and Development
DAC	Development Assistance Committee
DALY	Disability-Adjusted Life-Year
DDP	Desirable Dietary Pattern
DES	Dietary Energy Supplies
DHA	United Nations Department of Humanitarian Affairs
ECOWAS	Economic Community of West African States
EPI	Expanded Program for Immunization
ESAF	Expanded Structural Adjustment Facility
EU	European Union
FAO	Food and Agriculture Organization of the United Nations
FFF	Food Financing Facility
FIAN	Food First Information and Action Network
FNIP	Family Nutrition Improvement Program
FYDP	Five-Year Development Plan
GATT	General Agreement on Tariffs and Trade
GDP	Gross Domestic Product
GIEWS	Global Information & Early Warning System on Food & Agriculture
GNP	Gross National Product
GONGO	Governmental NGO
GRINGO	Government-run and inspired NGO
GRO	Grassroot Organization
GRSO	Grassroot Support Organization
HDI	Human Development Index
HDVA	High-Dose Vitamin A
HIV	Human Immunodeficiency Virus
ICAAC	International Conference on the Assistance to African Children
ICC	Inter-Institutional Coordination
ICDS	Integrated Child Development Scheme
ICESCR	International Convenant on Economic, Social and Cultural Rights
ICN	International Conference on Nutrition
ICRC	International Committee of the Red Cross
ICRW	International Center for Research on Women
IDD	Iodine Deficiency Disorder
IFAD	International Fund for Agricultural Development
IFPRI	International Food Policy Research Institute
IGO	Inter-Governmental Organization
IMF	International Monetary Fund
IMR	Infant Mortality Rate
IO	International Organization
ITO	International Trade Organization
LIFDC	Low Income Food Deficit Country
LRD	Linking Relief to Development
LSMS	Living Standards Measurement Studies
LTD1	first Long-Term Development plan
LTD2	second Long-Term Development plan
MCH	Maternal and Child Health
MDIS	Micronutrient Deficiency Information System
MMR	Maternal Mortality Rate
MSG	Mono-Sodium Glutamate
NCHS	National Council for Human Science
NCIE	Nutrition, Communication, Information, Education
NGO	Non-Governmental Organization
NIC	Newly Industrialized Country
NIN	National Institute of Nutrition
NPA	National Program of Action
NRC	National Research Council
NSS	Nutrional Surveillance System
NYT	*New York Times*
OAS	Organization of American States
OAU	Organisation of African Unity
ODA	Overseas Development Assistance
OECD	Organisation for Economic Cooperation and Development
ORT	Oral Rehydration Therapy
PAP	Poverty Alleviation Plan
PEM	Protein-Energy Malnutrition
PHC	Primary Health Care
PKK	Family Welfare Movement – central Java
PPAN	Philippines Plan of Action for Nutrition
PQLI	Physical Quality of Life Index
PVO	Private Voluntary Organization
R&D	Research and Development

RDA	Recommended Daily Allowance
RUNS	Rural-Urban – North/South
SELF	Special Emergency Life Food
SIDA	Swedish International Development Agency
SPLA	Sudan People's Liberation Army
SSB	State Statistic Bureau
TFNC	Tanzania Food and Nutrition Centre
TRIMs	Trade-Related Investment Measures
TRIPs	Trade-Related Intellectual Property Rights
TWIIS	Timely Warning Information & Intervention System
U5MR	Under 5 Mortality Rate
UMRs	Usual Marketing Requirements
UN	United Nations
UNCED	United Nations Conference on Environment and Development
UNCTAD	United Nations Conference on Trade and Development
UNDP	United Nations Development Programme
UNHCR	United Nations High Commissioner for Refugees
UNICEF	United Nations Children's Fund
UNITA	National Union for the Total Independence of Angola
UNRISD	United Nations Research Institute for Social Development
UNU	United Nations University
URNG	Unidad Revolucionaria Nacional de Guatemala
USAID	United States Agency for International Development
USCR	U.S. Committee for Refugees
USDA	U.S. Department of Agriculture
USSR	Union of Socialist Soviet Republics
VAC	Vuon (garden) Ao (pond) Chuong (cage) – Vietnam
VAD	Vitamin A Deficiency
VITAL	Vitamin A League
VITAP	Vitamin A Technical Assistance Program
WANAHR	World Alliance for Nutrition and Human Rights
WCHR	World Conference on Human Rights
WFC	World Food Council
WFP	World Food Programme
WHO	World Health Organization
WIC	Women, Infants, and Children
WSC	World Summit for Children
WTO	World Trade Organization

I dedicate this article to three devoted teachers who have encouraged me to think critically. At different moments of my life, their support and confidence has meant a lot to me. I thank them very much.

Alfons Van den Eynden, Melle, Belgium (1978-1980)

Professor Helmut Gaus, Ghent, Belgium (1980-1985)

Professor Leon Gordenker, Geneva, Switzerland (1986-1990)

—*Peter Uvin*

CHAPTER 1

The State of World Hunger

Peter Uvin

This is the sixth in a series of reports on hunger from the Alan Shawn Feinstein World Hunger Program at Brown University. Three distinct but related concepts have been used to estimate the numbers of people affected by hunger and to analyze the global food situation: food shortage, food poverty, and food deprivation. They focus on different aspects of the phenomenon of hunger and different levels of aggregation involved in its study. The previous report (Uvin, 1994) presented a detailed and critical overview of a large set of recent indicators designed to measure the faces of hunger; it made substantial reference to the important work done by various UN agencies in preparation of the International Conference on Nutrition. This report will present a shorter, updated version, of the most relevant indicators, to the extent that new data are available.

Food shortage occurs when total food supplies within a designated area – the world as a whole or continents, countries, or regions within countries – are insufficient to meet the needs of the population living within that area. *Food poverty* refers to the situation in which households cannot obtain enough food to meet the needs of all their members. *Food deprivation* refers to inadequate individual consumption of food or of specific nutrients, the form of malnutrition known as undernutrition.

The relationships between these three concepts are complex. On the one hand, the "higher" levels automatically imply the "lower" ones. If there is food shortage in a region, some households are bound to be food-poor for there is simply not enough food available to feed everyone; as a consequence, at least one member of each food-poor household will be food deprived. On the other hand, the "lower" levels can exist even in the absence of the "higher" ones. Food poverty can and does exist within households in regions where there is no aggregate food shortage, while individual food deprivation can occur in households that are not food-poor. The key factor in these cases is distribution. By looking at 1993-1994 data on all three concepts, we should be able to grasp the current state of the complex phenomenon of hunger and food insecurity.

FOOD SHORTAGE
Global Food Supply

Global food supply data allow us to answer the question: is there enough food in the world to provide all human beings with an adequate diet? The 1993 data, reproduced in Table 1, say "yes." If we compute the global food supply in terms of calories and divide that number by the world's population (and assuming average per capita caloric requirement of 2350 kcal/day), there is currently enough food for 6.26 billion people – 12% more than the actual population. This continues a long standing trend: since the mid-1970s there has been more than enough food in the world to feed all its inhabitants.

The 1993 situation does represent a decline from 1992, when the corresponding figures were 6.26 billion and 112%. This is due to the fact that world food production decreased by 0.7% in 1993, while global population increased by 1.7%. This global contraction in food production is largely due to a significant drop in developed country production, which declined by 5.2%, mainly as a result of government policies designed to cut cereal production (Dyson, 1994: 400-2). Developing country production, on the other hand, increased by 1.7%, which is still slightly below population growth (and also below the previous three years). (FAO, 1994: 3) Hence, the year 1993 saw a deterioration in world food security.

If we "improve" the diet of the world's population, so that 15% or 25% of the calories come from animal products (and, in the latter case, adding a richer and more varied diet of vegetables, fruits and oils), we find that in 1993, 4.12 billion or 3.16 billion people respectively could be fed with available food supplies — significantly fewer than the actual world population of 5.47 billion and also a decline from the previous year.

Table 1.1. Numbers of People Supported by 1993 Global Food Supply with Different Diets

Population potentially supported by 1993 food supply with a	
basic diet	6.26 billion (112% of world population)
improved diet	4.12 billion (74% of world population)
full-but-healthy diet	3.16 billion (56% of world population)

Source: FAO, 1994 (SOFA computer disk).

Another indicator used to assess global adequacy of food supplies is whether in a single year there are adequate carryover food stocks in the world for the following year, should it prove to be calamitous. The only data available are for cereals, and they show that during the 1990s cereal carryover stocks have fluctuated around 20% of world cereal consumption, with a significant drop in 1993/94 (Table 2). This is slightly above the 17-18% which the FAO secretariat considers the minimum necessary to safeguard world food security. (*Food Outlook*, June 1993: 17). Note that the variations in world cereal stocks are solely explainable by changes in developed country stocks; developing country cereal stocks remained stable throughout this period. Note also that ownership of these stocks is highly unequal: rich country governments and companies own two times more cereal stocks than do poor country governments and companies, although poor countries have a population more than five times bigger than the former and hunger is concentrated in them. Hence, if a major shock were to hit the world food system, it is doubtful whether the rich country stocks would be of great direct benefit to the poor country consumers. The main advantage of these stocks, then, is that they exert a downward pressure on world market prices — which is precisely why rich country governments are adopting policies to cut down their stocks.

In 1981, FAO's Committee on World Food Security endorsed a set of indicators of global food security, of which the above discussed ratio of world cereal stocks to world cereal utilization is one (for another set, see USAID, 1994: 7). In Table 3, we synthesized some of them. Overall, these indicators show a decline in global food security over the last 2 years. Global cereal stocks are shrinking,

Table 1.2. Cereal Carryover Stocks, million tons

	1991/92	1992/93	1993/94 (estimate)
All cereals	334	379	324
of which			
Developed countries	173	215	164
Developing countries	161	164	160
Stocks as % of World Cereal Consumption	19	21	18

Source: *Food Outlook*, June 1993: 2.

especially in the major exporting countries. Cereal production in the low-income, food-deficit countries increased, but less than their population. Cereal prices declined, but were on the rise by the end of 1994, reflecting tight supplies that will negatively affect 1995. In the immediate future, the agricultural liberalization agreed upon at the end of the GATT Uruguay Round will have the likely effect of strengthening most of these trends: food stocks will continue to fall, especially in the major exporting countries, and world cereal prices will keep on rising.

Thus, most indicators suggest there is no global food shortage. In 1993 and 1994, the world produced enough food for all its peoples, and contained enough cereal reserves to protect them against calamities. But the margins were slim and they are becoming slimmer still: world food production was only sufficient to cover diets that are close to vegetarian, and world cereal carryover stocks are close to the lower limit that is considered safe. At the end of 1994, world cereal

Table 1.3. Changes in Food Security Indicators

	1991	1992	1993	1994 (est.)
Changes in Production of Cereals in LIFDCs (% Change from Last Year)	+0.12	+1.72	+2.17	+0.11
Changes in Cereal Production in LIFDCs Less China and India (% Change from Last Year)		-0.26	+4.11	+1.86
Changes in Production of Cereals and Roots and Tubers in LIFDCs (% Change from Last Year)	+0.70	+1.93	+3.22	-0.16
Ratio of World Cereal Stocks to World Cereal Consumption	20	19	21	18
Ratio of Five Major Exporters' Supplies to Requirements	1.17	1.22	1.16	1.15
Annual Average Export Price Movement (% Change from Last Year)		Wheat: +27.1 Rice: +3.8 Maize: +8.6	Wheat: -4.0 Rice: -11.8 Maize: -7.9	Wheat: -4.9 Rice: +8.2 Maize: -12.9

Source: IFAO/CFS, 1994: 8 and own calculations, based on *Food Outlook*, March/April 1995.

production and cereal stocks are declining, while prices are up. The agricultural liberalization agreed upon in the GATT will in all likelihood aggravate these trends.

Do the current declines in world food security harbinger a future in which the world runs out of food, having achieved its natural limits? No. The observed decline in world food production is almost entirely due to the effects of rich country protectionist policies: acreage reduction programs in the US and EC, and the production cutbacks suffered by Third World food exporters, such as Argentina, Taiwan or Vietnam, as a result of low world market prices (Dyson, 1994a, b). As the rich countries slowly move towards ending their protectionist policies, the world food system will evolve towards a different equilibrium, in which the Third World as a whole is likely to benefit. Indeed, most studies show that, as world food prices rise, food production in the Third World (with the exception of sub-Saharan Africa) should increase, as would Third World food exports. This quite positive picture looks different if one disaggregates to the level of individual countries, and specific groups within countries — especially the poor and the hungry. How will food importing nations fare? And how about net food-consuming groups? Some dissenting voices have argued that "agricultural trade liberalization and declining producer support in developed countries may actually decrease the welfare of low income population groups in developing nations — especially those groups from food importing nations" (Meyers, 1995).

Of course, it is of little use to separate the agricultural liberalization provisions from the overall GATT agreement, which includes unprecedented liberalization of industry, services and intellectual property. Together, these policy changes are likely to lead to important income gains — and losses for some (Goldin et al., 1993). How these income changes affect poor food consumers is at least as important to the future of hunger as the specific agricultural provisions of the GATT agreement (FAO, 1995; Helmar et al., 1994: 52).

Dietary Energy Supplies

Among the many limitations of the above data is the fact that they measure only food production and imports/exports, and neglect all other uses of food. Part of the food produced or imported in any country is not directly consumed by humans, but rather stored, lost to pests and other predators, used as seeds for the next harvest, transformed into animal feed, or used in the industry. Dietary energy supplies (DES) per capita is a set of data that includes all these elements. DES figures add to those on domestic food production the food imports and variations in food stocks of countries; they subtract their exports, estimated losses during storage and distribution, and the use of food as animal feed or seeds for the next season. They then convert these data into calories, and divide them by population numbers. The result is an indicator of the real average food availability for the (hypothetical "average") inhabitants of a region or country, expressed in calories.

Table 4 compares DES data with FAO/WHO/UNU standardized average caloric requirements at similar activity levels for all countries in the world, showing the number of countries in which food availability is not sufficient to guarantee the necessary minimum caloric intake for every citizen.

In the most recent period for which data are available, using the two-year period 1988-1990 to flatten out fluctuations, there were 48 Third World countries, with a total population of 802 million, in which the dietary energy supply was lower than that needed to adequately feed the populations. This does not mean that all persons within those countries suffer from undernutrition; even in calorie-deficit countries, some eat enough (even too much), and in calorie-surplus countries some go hungry. But it does mean that these countries cannot feed their entire populations with the food reported to be available within their borders.

Table 1.4. Countries with DES below requirement, 1988-90

	Number of countries	Population, millions
sub-Saharan Africa	32	459.1
Near East & North Africa	1	12.5
Asia	4	262.4
Latin America	7	67.2
North America, Australia, Western and Eastern Europe and the Community of Independent States (former USSR)	0	0.0
small islands	4	1.1
Total	48	802.3

Source: UNDP, 1994: Table 13. For OECD countries, Eastern Europe and the CIS, see UNICEF, 1992a: Table 2. Population data are from mid-1991.

Of these 44 countries, excluding the four islands, 11 had DES above requirement in 1981, meaning that their food availability turned from surplus to shortage. These 11 countries totaled 196.3 million inhabitants (115.8 million for Pakistan alone). This was counterbalanced, during the same period, by 11 other countries which moved out of food shortage, *i.e.*, their DES as a percentage of requirement moved above 100%. The total population of these countries was 1.01 billion (146.8 million without India).

Famine

The last indicator of food shortage focuses on the most visible and well-known hunger situation, that of famine. This is the harshest but least strident indicator. On the one hand, it represents the ultimate suffering and deprivation, often leading to death by starvation; on the other hand, the populations affected and the amounts of food needed to prevent famine are the smallest of the three indicators.

As can be seen from Table 5, the number of countries suffering from acute food shortages according to FAO's Global Information and Early Warning System has increased greatly from 1992 onwards. These figures include a substantial number of recently created countries, in the Commonwealth of Independent States (Armenia, Azerbaijan, Georgia, Tajikistan), in Eastern Europe (Bosnia-Herzegovina, Macedonia) or in Africa (Eritrea). The exceptional shortfalls coincide with civil war in five out of six European countries and in nine out of fifteen African ones (Eritrea and Ethiopia, although at peace now, can be said to suffer from the effects of decades of war). Food shortages in Haiti and Afghanistan were also coincident with war or civil unrest there; in Iraq, they relate to the lingering results of past war.

Note that these figures do not mean that all people in these countries suffered from famine, but only that they lived in countries affected by exceptional food shortage, where, if no special measures are taken by governments and international aid agencies, famine can and does occur. The number of people actually starving in these countries was certainly much lower. Reliable data on the actual extent of starvation do not exist. Using various methods, Steve Hansch of the Refugee Policy Group has recently attempted to quantify the number of worldwide deaths due to starvation. His conclusion is that "starvation deaths during the 1990s will range from 150,000 to 200,000 per year, with a likely value for 1995 of 250,000". This figure is still unacceptably high, but constitutes a continuation of a declining trend that began in the 1950s, according to the author (Hansch, 1995: 1).

Table 1.5. Indicators of Famine and Food Shortage

	FAO famine and food shortages		
	number of countries	number of people, million	percentage of world population
1992	15		
1993	22	279	5
1994	21	272	5

Source: *Foodcrops and Shortages*, 1993, 1994, all issues.

Refugees

An important category of food-short people, which partly overlaps with the preceding category of famines, is refugees and internally displaced people. Refugees are defined as people who have been driven across international borders as a result of war or civil strife. Their assets and sources of income disappear, often overnight. As a result, their entitlement set collapses, in the worst cases below starvation level. Data by the U.S. Committee for Refugees indicate that at the end of 1992, approx. 19 million persons were refugees. This figure decreased to 16.3 million in 1993, and remained stable in 1994. (USCR, 1994: 41; USCR, 1995: 42) In addition, in 1993 at the very least 26 million people forced out of their homes and regions remain within the borders of their own countries (USCR, 1995: 44; see too ACC/SCN, 1994: 58). These data continue a trend that began around 1975, in which the number of refugees has been doubling approximately every 6 years. (ACC/SCN, 1994: 57) One third of these refugees are in Africa and in the Middle East each, while 2.65 million are in Europe, the direct result of the disintegration of the East bloc.

FOOD POVERTY

Food poverty is the inability of households to obtain sufficient food to meet the nutritional needs of their members due to inadequate income, poor access to productive resources, inability to benefit from private or public food transfers, or lack of other entitlements to food. In this section, we will present estimates of numbers of people living in households that cannot afford to provide their members the dietary energy (calories) they require.

In 1992, in preparation for the International Conference on Nutrition, the FAO produced the latest estimates for the number of food-poor households in the world, including, for the first time, China and the other Asian communist countries. Currently, these data are accepted and reproduced by all international organizations. For a more in-depth discussion of the methodology behind these data, see last year's Hunger Report (Uvin, 1994: 11; also FAO, 1992).

According to these data (Table 6), the absolute number of the food poor in the world has begun to decline since 1975, from 976 to 786 million persons in 1990. The picture that emerges, then, is more positive than generally assumed: the incidence of hunger in the world has declined significantly, and fewer people are undernourished now than fifteen years ago, notwithstanding the addition of approximately 1.1 billion persons to the Third World's population.

However, this globally positive scenario masks very different regional realities. Indeed, the same data, disaggregated by geographical region, show that the 1980s have been a period of stagnation and even loss in sub-Saharan Africa and South America, both of which have seen the proportion, and the number, of food-poor households increase. South America and to a lesser extent sub-Saharan Africa have populations and hunger numbers that are small compared to Asia: both India and China have more inhabitants than these two continents combined. Thus, on a global basis, the positive trend in Asia, and especially in China, more than

Table 1.6. The Proportion and Number of Chronically Underfed

PROPORTION in percentages	sub-Saharan Africa	Near East & North Africa	Middle America	South America	South Asia	East Asia	China	All
1970	35	23	24	17	34	35	46	36
1975	37	17	20	15	34	32	40	33
1980	36	10	15	12	30	22	22	26
1990	37	5	14	13	24	17	16	20
ABSOLUTE NUMBERS in millions								
1970	94	32	21	32	255	101	406	942
1975	112	26	21	32	289	101	395	976
1980	128	15	18	29	285	78	290	846
1990	175	12	20	38	277	74	189	786

Source: ACC/SCN, 1992: 105.

compensates for the deterioration in Latin America and sub-Saharan Africa.

Trends are also worrisome for much of Eastern Europe. Economic changes, as well as warfare in some countries, have provoked a "deterioration of unparalleled proportions in human welfare throughout most of the region." (Crossette, 1994) UNICEF has documented that poverty, ill health and malnutrition are on the rise.

National Food Poverty

We have looked at the food poverty of households, defined as their capacity to gain access to sufficient quantities of food. We can also speak about the food poverty of nations, defined as their capacity to grow and import sufficient food to feed their populations. In *Hunger Report: 1993* (Uvin, 1994) we presented two indicators to measure this phenomenon of national food insecurity: quantities of available food versus food needs in a country, and a country's net food import needs versus its total import capacity (Uvin, 1994: 13-4, drawing on FAO/WHO, 1992: 3). Here we will discuss a third indicator, *i.e.* the food import dependency ratio: the percentage of domestic food availability that is imported. Table 7 shows that for the Third World as a whole, this ratio increased since the beginning of the 1970s, going from 6.7% in 1969/71 to 10.3% in 1988/90. Of course, this general picture hides divergent trends.

Table 1.7. Food Import Dependency Ratio, 1969/71 to 1988/90, in percent

	increased dependency	decreased dependency	no change
Asia	13	6	1
of which			
1st generation NICs	2		
2nd generation NICs	4		
Middle East	6	1	2
North Africa	5	0	0
sub-Saharan Africa	33	5	4
Latin America	13	7	3
small islands	10	5	5
Developing countries	80	24	15

Source: UNDP, 1994: Table 13. First generation NICs include Hong Kong and North Korea (data for Singapore and Taiwan were not available); second generation NICs include Thailand, Malaysia, Indonesia and China. Small islands have populations of less than 1 million inhabitants. "No change" is defined as a less than 10% fluctuation. Note that food exports have been deducted from this; hence, Argentina has a food import dependency ratio of 1%, although it is a large cereal exporter. It is important to note also that food aid (valued at world market prices) is included in this table. If these countries had to import on a commercial basis all the food that flows into their country, it would cost them much more, and they might import less.

However, it is unclear how to interpret this table: for some countries, increases in food import dependency might signal food security trouble, while for others, it might indicate progress. The NICs, for example, seem to be importing more food because export-led economic growth has provided enough income to their populations to import food; the same might also hold, to some extent, for some Middle Eastern and North African countries. For these countries, then, increased import dependency reveals improved food security. For many others, particularly in Africa, the same process of increased import dependency denotes real problems in food security, as local production lags behind needs. Similarly, for some African countries that have decreased their food import dependency (Zaire, for example) this might denote not so much improved local production as their incapacity to pay for needed imports.

FOOD DEPRIVATION

Food deprivation results from the inability of individuals to obtain sufficient food to meet their nutritional needs. This can be due either to overall food shortage, to household food poverty, or to the existence of a special need that is not satisfied. The latter is most often the case for pregnant and lactating women, sick persons, children, and the elderly. Here, we will briefly present some of the available data for women, children under five years old, and adolescents.

Women

The most recent global data (already reproduced in the last Hunger Report) show that 400 million women of childbearing age — or approximately 45% of the total — have a weight below 45 kg (ACC/SCN, 1992: 2). This does not mean that they are all malnourished (or that every woman weighing more than 45 kg is well nourished), but a weight this low is a readily available indicator that is more or less linked with undernutrition, and often indicates obstetric risk. This proportion varies from 62% in South Asia and 44% in South East Asia, to 21% for sub-Saharan Africa and 10% for South America (ACC/SCN, 1993: 116). Other similar indicators computed by ACC/SCN, such as the proportion of women whose height is below 145 cm., whose arm circumference is below 22.5 cm, or whose Body Mass Index (BMI) is below 18.5, basically present the same picture, including the same regional variations, with South Asia and South East Asia always having a far higher proportion than the other regions, Africa in the mid-range, and South America presenting the best picture (ACC/SCN, 1992: chapter 4).

Children

Table 8 shows that, in 1990, 184 million children age 0 to 5 years were underweight; this includes 34% of all the Third World's children. Globally, while the proportion of underweight children has continuously, albeit unevenly, declined during recent decades, their absolute number has continued to increase, from 168 to 184 million children.

Note that these data hide important national and subnational differences: in Latin America, notwithstanding impressive improvements, child malnutrition is at least 40% higher in rural than in urban areas; sometimes the difference is as much as 100 or 200% (*e.g.* Paraguay and Peru). Often, this disproportionate burden falls on the indigenous populations (Psacharopoulos, 1993).

Table 1.8. Proportion of Underweight Pre-School Children (0-60 months), in percent

	1975	1985	1990	2000 low estimate	2000 high estimate
sub-Saharan Africa	31.4	29.9	29.9	27.0	32.0
Near East & North Africa	19.8	15.1	13.4	8.0	11.0
South Asia	67.7	61.1	58.5	49.0	54.0
East Asia	43.6	34.7	31.3	22.0	24.0
China	26.1	21.3	21.8	16.0	22.0
Middle America	19.3	15.2	15.4	10.0	16.0
South America	15.7	8.2	7.7	2.5	6.0
World	41.6	35.1	34.3	27.5	32.0
Absolute number of children	168	178	184	108	206

Source: ACC/SCN, 1992: 67.

In its 1994 Update on the Nutrition Situation, ACC/SCN presents data from 46 countries in which at least two comparable surveys of the prevalence of underweight children allow one to estimate recent trends. Table 9 summarizes these trends by geographical region. Except for sub-Saharan Africa, the data are encouraging. The three non-African countries where childhood malnutrition increased are India, Nicaragua and Chile; in all three cases, the increases are very small. Observe the rapid decline in the prevalence of underweight children in China from 21.7% in 1987 to 17.5% in 1990. This is a major improvement, and very different from the increase predicted in the previous ACC/SCN calculations. It should reduce the total number of undernourished children estimated in Table 8.

Table 1.9. Number of Countries in which the Prevalence of Underweight Children Increased, Decreased or Remained Stable, according to the Most Recent Estimates

	Increased	Declined	Remained Stable
sub-Saharan Africa	5	3	3
Near East & North Africa		3	
South Asia	1	3	
East Asia		5	1
China		1	
Middle America	1	5	
South America	1	5	

Source: ACC/SCN, 1994: 3. "Stability" is defined here as a change of less than 10%.

Adolescents

The International Center for Research on Women, with funding from USAID, has produced a major study of nutrition in adolescents in 9 countries on all continents. In Table 10, we reproduce its data on the prevalence of adolescent undernutrition,

Table 1.10. Prevalence of Undernutrition, in %

	All	Males	Females
India	55	69	37
Nepal	36	49	25
Benin	23	32	14
Philippines (Cebu)	13	19	7
Ecuador	9	13	6
Philippines (Mindanao)	6	9	1
Cameroon	4	7	2
Mexico	3	n.s.	n.s.
Guatemala (metabolic)	6		
Guatemala (longitudinal)	4		
Jamaica	3		

Source: ICRW, 1994a: 10.

defined as low weight for height (body mass index) (ICRW, 1994a: 10). This indicator has recently been recommended as the indicator of choice for measuring undernutrition among adolescents and adults; for females, low values result in poor pregnancy outcomes. Generally, the data confirm expectations about undernutrition, with India and Nepal being by far the highest, and sub-Saharan Africa and Latin America showing lower scores. What is surprising, however is the fact that in all cases except Mexico undernutrition for boys was at least two times higher than for girls. The authors speculate that this is due to differential maturation in boys and girls. Note that "adolescents" were defined as comprising all people between 10 and 24 years old (approximately 30% of the world's population). This is a very large, and odd, age grouping, which lumps together ten year old premenstrual children with 24 year old housewives, who might already be in their second pregnancy. That makes interpretation of these data very difficult.

The same study proposes six principles for promoting the nutritional status of adolescent girls in developing countries. They are: improve food intake, keep girls in school, improve self-esteem, promote health and treat infections, postpone adolescent pregnancy, and reduce heavy physical workloads (ICRW, 1994b).

Effects of food deprivation

Important recent work by David Pelletier attempts to quantify the "potentiating effects of malnutrition on child mortality", starting from the well-known premise that malnutrition acts in a vicious circle with infectious disease, often with devastating consequences (Pelletier, 1994: passim; see also Mason, Jonsson and Csete in this volume). Because of this intimate connection, Pelletier argues that "it is both meaningless and misleading to ascribe a certain number of deaths to either malnutrition or infectious disease alone, as is a common practice. In developing countries with high rates of malnutrition, the excessive number of deaths attributed to diarrhea, acute respiratory infection, measles, and other common infections places primacy on the proximate and clinically obvious cause, while ignoring the potentiating effects that severe and (less obvious) mild-to-moderate malnutrition have on these diseases" (Pelletier, 1994: 412). Quantifying this interaction, he concludes that "malnutrition contributes to 56% of all child deaths due to its potentiating effects on infectious diseases. This is roughly 8-10 times higher than conventional estimates that ignore potentiating effects of malnutrition on disease and the effects of mild-to-moderate malnutrition. Of the malnutrition-related deaths, 83% are due to mild-to-moderate malnutrition, as opposed to severe malnutrition, which is significantly more than commonly recognized" (Pelletier, 1994: 414). These findings indeed modify our understanding of the magnitude of the impact of food deprivation, for recent World Bank or WHO publications had put forward much smaller figures, in the order of 2-4% (World Bank, 1993; World Bank, 1994b; WHO, 1994).

MICRONUTRIENTS

Less visible than protein-energy undernutrition are deficiencies in the micro-nutrients, mainly iodine, vitamin A, and iron. "Hidden hunger" is extremely important both because of the number of people who suffer from it, and because of its health consequences.

In a moving way, the latest *State of the World's Children* report by UNICEF describes the devastating impact of iodine deficiency on children and households:

> *In 1990, some 18 million women became pregnant while suffering from a little-known dietary disorder.... In approximately 60,000 cases, the damage caused was so severe that the fetus died or the infant survived only a few hours. For approximately 120,000 of those women, pregnancy and delivery proceeded normally, and an apparently healthy baby was born. But in the first few months of life it became clear that all was not well. The infant was slow to respond to voices, and did not seem to recognize familiar faces. ... As these children reached the age of two, most had still not learned to walk. ... Today, ... their parents know only that their sons or daughters were born as cretins, and will remain so for the rest of their lives....In approximately 1 million more of those pregnancies, early childhood appeared to proceed quite normally. But today, as those 1 million children reach school age, many are being found to have poor eye-hand coordination; others have become partially deaf, or have developed a faint squint, or a speech impediment, or other neuromuscular disorders. In another 5 million or so cases, the parents may never know that there is anything specifically wrong. But if measurements could be taken ... all of them, even the brightest, would be found to have significantly lowered IQs. And in the years to come, they will merge into the estimated total of 750 million young people in the world today whose mental and physical development, and capacity for education, are impaired by the same problem — arising either from their own diets in childhood or from the diets of their mothers before and during pregnancy. Eventually they will be added to the estimated total of 150 million adults whose diminished mental alertness and reduced physical aptitude mean that they are less able to meet their own and their families' needs (UNICEF, 1995: 13-15).*

Iodine deficiency can be avoided by salt iodization, at the low cost of 5 US cents per person per year. Since the 1990 World Summit for Children, where all countries pledged to iodize at least 95% of all salt supplies by the end of the year 1995, 58 countries with IDD, home to almost 60% of the developing world's children, are on track to achieve that goal. Another 32 countries could achieve the 1995 goal with an accelerated effort (UNICEF, 1995: 16; see also UNICEF, 1994: 8-9). Trends in iodine deficiency are negative in the former USSR and Eastern Europe, however (Crossette, 1994).

The same UNICEF report describes the impact of vitamin A deficiency on children and communities, ranging from blindness to increased morbidity and mortality as a result of measles and other infectious diseases. A recent study in Malawi even suggests that "maternal vitamin A deficiency contributes to mother-to-child transmission of HIV" (Semba et al., 1994: 1593). But also here, important progress has been made since the beginning of the 1990s: vitamin A supplementation in health care centers, or fortification of sugar, are some of the means governments are using to solve the problem. According to UNICEF, "of the 67 nations concerned, 35 are likely to come close to eliminating the problem by the end of 1995. Approximately two-thirds of the children at risk live in these countries" (UNICEF, 1995: 19; UNICEF, 1994: 10).

Iron deficiency, finally, touches most people, especially women, and can lead to "exhaustion and general poor health, ... increased risk of death in childbirth" for women, as well as "higher risk of lower birthweight and impaired development" for their babies (UNICEF, 1995: 19). It too is inexpensive to address, through supplementation tablets, for example. Yet little progress is being made on this deficiency. (UNICEF, 1995: 19-20)

No new major data on micronutrient deficiency have been produced since the previous 1991 WHO data; they continue to be used by all until today (World Bank, 1994a: 7). We reproduce them in Table 11. The only exception to this is the 1993 *Global Prevalence of IDD* report by the Micronutrient Deficiency Information System of the WHO (1993: 5), which presents much higher data for IDD — 1572 million people at risk and 655 million of them suffering from actual goiter. This is largely due to an (upwards) redefinition of the IDD threshold by the International Council for the Control of Iodine Deficiency Disorders.

Table 1.11. Number of People in Millions Affected by Micronutrient Malnutrition

	Iodine		Vitamin A (pre-school children)		Iron
	at risk	goiter	at risk	xeroph-thalmia	anemia
Africa	150	39	18	1.3	206
Asia & Oceania	685	130	157	11.4	1674
Americas	55	30	2	0.1	94
Europe	82	14	0	0	27
Eastern Mediterranean	33	12	13	1	149
World	1005	225	190	13.8	2150

Source: WHO, 1991: 5.

The above mentioned UNICEF report presents a more complex picture of the impact of vitamin A and iodine deficiencies (see Table 12).

In short, the importance of micronutrient deficiencies can hardly be overstated; ending hidden hunger is a priority for all those concerned with hunger, public health and economic growth. In the words of the World Bank (1994a: 1, 8 [italics in original]):

> To grasp the enormous implications at the country level, consider a country of 50 million people with the level of micronutrient deficiencies that exists today in South Asia. Such a country would suffer the following losses each year *because of these deficiencies*:
> - 20,000 deaths
> - 11,000 children born cretins or blinded as preschoolers
> - 1.3 million persons-years of work lost due to lethargy or more severe disability
> - 360,000 student-years wasted (3% of total student body)

Prospects for overcoming micronutrient deficiencies are hopeful, however. According to figures presented by the World Bank, vitamin A availability per person is up in all developing regions except for Africa (World Bank, 1994a: 11; see too ACC/SCN, 1993: 105; supply data for iodine do not exist). Moreover, states have committed themselves to taking serious action to eradicate vitamin A and iodine deficiency, and indeed important progress has been made in supplementation and fortification over the last five years (see Ralte, Chapter 9, this

Table 1.12. Estimated Impact of Iodine and Vitamin A Deficiency, million persons

Iodine		Vitamin A	
total population at risk	1,600	inadequate vitamin A intake	231
goiter	655	night blindness	13.5
brain damage	26	xerophthalmia	3.1
cretinism	5.7	severe eye damage/blindness	0.5

Source: UNICEF, 1995: 14, 18.

volume). The main worry remains iron: the same data show that, except for the Near East, iron availability per person is down in all developing regions, while state commitment is much weaker.

FOOD AID

Food aid is one of the primary and also one of the most visible ways in which rich countries and their citizens provide relief and support to alleviate hunger in other parts of the world. As can be seen in Table 13, global food aid reached a record high in 1992/3 and declined to a more "normal" but still high level in 1993/4.

As column 3 shows, the proportion of global food aid going to Low-Income Food-Deficit Countries (LIFDCs) has begun to decline since 1993, down to 65%, its lowest level in more than 20 years (Uvin, 1994b: 146). During most of the 1980s, this proportion fluctuated around 90%. On the other hand, the amount of structural food aid to Eastern Europe and the Commonwealth of Independent States is greatly on the increase. Donors have always maintained that food aid to the former East bloc would not be at the expense of aid to "traditional" recipients. This was more or less the case until 1991/2, but the situation seems to have changed since: our data seem to document that increased food aid for Eastern Europe and the former Soviet Union has been at the expense of the poorest, most needy, food-deficit countries. Precise trends on this matter are difficult to gauge, for since Jan 1, 1995, nine CIS republics and 3 Eastern European countries (Albania,

Table 1.13. Cereal Food Aid Shipments by Region, 1989-1994

	(1) world, 1000 tons	(2) LIFDCs, 1000 tons	(3) LIFDCs as percentage of world	(4) Economies in transition, 1000 tons	(5) Economies in transition as percentage of world
1989/90	11315	7979	71	1582	14
1990/91	12356	9799	79	1342	11
1991/92	13086	11000	84	1927	15
1992/93	15184	11073	73	4390	29
1993/94	12633	8226	65	4709	37

Source: *Food Outlook*, March/April 1995: 2, 42.. LIFDCs are Low Income Food Deficit Countries.

Macedonia and Romania) have been reclassified as LIFDCs themselves. Together, they accounted for approximately 2 million tons of food aid in 1993/4 (Foodcrops and Shortages, 1995: 60).

Hence, total food aid quantities are declining, and the first estimates for 1994/5 suggest that the decline is accelerating. Of that food aid, an increasing proportion goes to the former USSR and Yugoslavia, instead of to the traditional, low-income food aid recipients in the Third World. As we know too, the share of emergency food aid in total food aid is high and, for Africa at least, still on the rise (for the case of the US, see USAID, 1994: 11). This means that food aid, for most LIFDCs, is becoming less of a development resource, and more of an emergency feeding mechanism: fluctuating, unsure, short-term, but sometimes with the capacity to save lives.

CONCLUSION

In 1993, world food security was slightly lower than the previous years, although still sufficient to feed every one of the world's inhabitants on a basic diet if food were distributed according to need. The same seems to be true for 1994. This global trend, however, is due to the production limiting policies of a few rich countries; as far as the Third World as a whole goes, little change has occurred in 1993-4.

Over the long run, most countries are increasingly partaking in international food trade. For most of them, this makes sense: it reflects their increased ability to pay for the food imports their citizens want. For quite a few of them, however, this reflects their incapacity to produce sufficient food to feed their growing populations. For the latter category of countries, the fact that food aid is on the decline (except to the former Soviet Union and Eastern Europe) is a worrisome trend, which is likely to be aggravated by the impacts of the GATT trade liberalization agreement. The failure of these countries to produce sufficient food is largely policy-induced, and not the result of absolute environmental constraints. As such, the decline in food aid and the increase in food prices may result in medium term improvements in their domestic food production, if — and only if — government policies change, providing farmers with higher producer prices, quality extension services and a guaranteed supply of agricultural inputs (including land rights). These policies take time to be put in place, however, and their impacts are not felt immediately. In the meantime — and also in the case such policies are *not* implemented — poor net food consumers will be hurt.

New data on food poverty are not available, but in all likelihood past trends of slow improvement have continued: economic growth in most of the Third World was positive in 1993-4, and major social upheavals were absent. As a result, food deprivation in children decreased in most of these countries, with continued dramatic improvements in China. The two main exceptions to this positive picture are sub-Saharan Africa (although a few countries in the region did perform quite well) and the former Soviet Union. In both cases, the catastrophic state of economies combined with civil war to produce high food insecurity and low quality of care.

The international awareness of the importance of micronutrients continues to grow. Since the beginning of the 1990s, many governments have adopted policies of fortification and supplementation, especially for iodine and vitamin A. As a result, trends are positive for these two deficiencies. The picture is more gloomy in the case of iron deficiency: few governments have adopted policies, and the availability of iron is on the decline in almost all regions of the world.

References

ACC/SCN (1992). *Second Report on the World Nutrition Situation; Volume 1 Global and Regional Results*. Geneva: ACC/SCN.

ACC/SCN (1993). *Second Report on the World Nutrition Situation; Volume II Country Trends Methods and Statistics*. Geneva: ACC/SCN.

ACC/SCN (1994). *Update on the World Nutrition Situation, 1994*. Geneva: ACC/SCN.

Crossette, B. (1994). U.N. Study Finds a Free Eastern Europe Poorer and Less Healthy. *New York Times*, Oct. 7: A13.

Dyson, T. (1994). Population Growth and Food Production: Recent Global and Regional Trends. *Population and Development Review*, 20, 2 (June): 397-411

FAO (1992). *World Food Supplies and the Prevalence of Hunger*. Rome: FAO.

FAO (1994). *The State of Food and Agriculture 1994*. Rome: FAO (incl. computer disk)

FAO (1995). *Impact of the Uruguay Round on Agriculture*. Rome: Committee on Commodity Problems, Sixtieth Session, 3-7 April 1995, Item 5 of the Provisional Agenda.

FAO/WHO (1992). *Improving Household Food Quality*. Rome: ICN Theme Paper 1.

Foodcrops and Shortages (1993-1994). Rome: FAO Global Information and Early Warning System on Food and Agriculture.

Food Outlook (1993-5). Rome: FAO Global Information and Early Warning System on Food and Agriculture.

Goldin, I., Knudsen, O., van der Mensbrugghe, D. (1993). *Trade Liberalization: Global Economic Implications*. Paris, Washington: OECD and World Bank.

Hansch, S. (1995). *How Many People Die of Starvation in Humanitarian Emergencies?* Washington D.C., Refugee Policy Group Working Paper.

Helmar, M.D., et al. (1994). *Impacts of the Uruguay Round on Agricultural Commodity Markets*. Ames, Iowa: Center for Agricultural and Rural Development, Iowa State University, GATT Research Paper 94-21.

ICRW (1994a). *The Nutrition and Lives of Adolescents in Developing Countries. Findings from the Nutrition of Adolescent Girls Research Program*. Washington DC: International Center for Research on Women.

ICRW (1994b). *Investing in the Future: Six Principles for Promoting the Nutritional Status of Adolescent Girls in Developing Countries*. Washington DC: International Center for Research on Women.

MDIS (1993). *Global Prevalence of Iodine Deficiency Disorders*. Geneva: Micronutrient Deficiency Information System, WHO, MDIS Working Paper No. 1.

Meyers, W. (1995). *Presentation Abstract*, panel on "Global Food Security Trends, Trade Liberalization: The Changing Diet of the Poor" at the 8th Annual Hunger Research Briefing and Exchange, World Hunger Program, Brown University, Providence, RI. (electronically available at: http://netspace.org/hungerweb/HW/WHP/briefing/3b.html#RTFToC7)

Pelletier, D.L. (1994). The Potentiating Effects of Malnutrition on Child Mortality: Epidemiologic Evidence and Policy Implications. *Nutrition Reviews*, 52, 12: 409-415.

Psacharopoulos, G. *et al.* (1993). *Poverty and Income Distribution in Latin America. The Story of the 1980s*. Washington D.C.: World Bank, Latin America Regional Study Report No. 27.

Semba, Richard D., Paolo G Miotti, John D Chiphangwi, Alfred J Saah, et al. (1994). Maternal vitamin A deficiency and mother-to-child transmission of HIV-1. *The Lancet*, 343 (June 25): 1593-1596

UNDP (1994). *Human Development Report 1994.* New York: Oxford University Press.

UNHCR (1993). *The State of the World's Refugees — the Challenge of Protection*. Geneva: United Nations High Commissioner for Refugees.

UNICEF (1994) .*The Progress of Nations*. London: Burgess of Abingdon.

UNICEF (1995). *The State of the World's Children 1995* . Oxford: Oxford University Press.

USAID (1994). *World Food Day Report. The President's Report to the U.S. Congress.* Washington D.C.: USAID, Bureau for Humanitarian Response, Oct.

U.S. Committee for Refugees (1994). *World Refugee Survey 1994*. Washington D.C.: U.S. Committee for Refugees.

U.S. Committee for Refugees (1995). *World Refugee Survey 1995*. Washington D.C.: U.S. Committee for Refugees.

Uvin, P. (1994a) .The State of World Hunger. In Uvin, P. (ed.) *Hunger Report 1993*. New York: Gordon & Breach

Uvin, P. (1994b). *The International Organization of Hunger*. London: Kegan Paul.

World Bank (1993). *World development Report 1993.* New York: Oxford University Press.

World Bank (1994a). *Enriching Lives. Overcoming Vitamin and Mineral Malnutrition in Developing Countries*. Washington DC: World Bank.

World Bank (1994b). *A New Agenda for Women's Health and Nutrition*. Washington DC: World Bank, Development in Practice Series, 1994.

WHO (1994). *Global Comparative Assessments in the Health Sector. Disease Burden, Expenditures and Intervention Packages*. (edited by C.J.L. Murray and A.D. Lopez) Geneva: World Health Organization.

CHAPTER 2

Food Wars: Hunger as a Weapon of War in 1994

Ellen Messer

In 1989, "Overcoming Hunger in the 1990s" set ending famine deaths as one of four achievable goals for halving hunger by the year 2000. Affirming food and nutrition as basic human rights, the document recognized that expanding early warning systems to monitor and respond to conditions that cause famine could eliminate most famine deaths. The remaining challenge was to deliver aid to areas created by armed conflict where denial of food was being used as a weapon.

Policy principles and logistics developed in the late 1980s included cross-border operations, massive airlifts of emergency food, and creation of "safe havens" in existing or new civilian zones where non-combatants received protection and emergency subsistence – such efforts had succeeded in delivering food and saving lives in the prolonged civil wars in Ethiopia and the Sudan. "Overcoming Hunger" proposed that such efforts be expanded by intergovernment organizations (IGOs), non-governmental organizations (NGOs), or governments and insurgents working together to eliminate hunger, even if they could not eliminate warfare.

For persistent "complex emergency" zones with their combined elements of political and environmental disaster, the international relief community over the last five years has been increasing the amount of assistance allocated to emergency feeding, including refugees and those internally displaced by conflicts, whose numbers have grown to 40 or 50 million over this period (ACC-SCN, 1994; Payne, 1994; WFP, 1995a). It has also expanded the declarations of principles and policies that prohibit use of food as a political weapon or tool (e.g., ICN, 1992). In 1994-95, the demand for "complex emergency" assistance has increased while financial and institutional resources for international development aid have decreased. Increasingly, critics of food aid have argued that it strengthens the political and material (subsistence) conditions of military combatants who usually control its distribution, thus prolonging rather than resolving conflicts. Relief experts and organizations in 1994-95 are searching for ways to prevent food aid from prolonging conflicts and to use it for conflict prevention or resolution – and for development (Duffield, 1994a; DeWaal, 1994).

Food Wars In 1994

In 1989, the world was struggling with 19 conflicts (excluding the Eastern bloc) in which hunger was being used as a weapon or existed as a consequence of war (Messer, 1990). Today, largely as a result of the winding down of the Cold War and its accompanying arms race, peace and progress toward free elections have been formally pursued in Angola, Ethiopia, Eritrea, Mozambique, and South Africa; in

Cambodia; and in El Salvador and Nicaragua. But in all these countries, hunger remains an enduring legacy that contributes to lingering conflicts.

Additionally, regions and countries that were relatively peaceful during the Cold War are exploding into ethnic and religious conflicts. These conflicts superimpose the politics of cultural identity on that of perceived scarcity, as leaders of fragile pluralist societies mobilize supporters around struggles for control of land and other resources. In the republics of the former Soviet Union and Yugoslavia, and in the Greater Horn of Africa, a variety of economic issues, including control over development of water and oil interests, deepen tribal, religious, or other cultural-political strife. All these conflicts use food as a weapon and heighten food insecurity.

The year 1994 was marked by sudden eruptions of new violence and related hunger in Rwanda, Mexico, and Chechnya. The complex emergencies in Rwanda and the former Yugoslavia and the protracted crises in Liberia and Afghanistan absorbed 50% of WFP relief (WFP 1995a). Peoples in at least 32 countries (Afghanistan, Algeria, Angola, Armenia-Azerbaijan, Bosnia-Herzegovina, Burma, Burundi, Cambodia, Chechnya-Russia, Colombia, Croatia, Georgia, Ghana, Guatemala, India-Kashmir, Indonesia-East Timor/West Irian, Iraq, Kenya, Liberia, Mexico, Moldova, Niger, Nigeria, Rwanda, Serbia, Sierra Leone, Somalia, Sri Lanka, Sudan, Togo, Turkey, Zaire) suffered malnutrition, poverty-related limitations in their access to food, and acute food shortages as a result of armed conflict. In at least 10 more countries (El Salvador, Eritrea, Ethiopia, Haiti, Mozambique, Nicaragua, Peru, the Philippines, Tajikistan, Uganda) there was continued hunger in the aftermath of war, civil disorder, or as a result of conflict-related sanctions. Up to 50 million refugees and internally displaced persons needed food and other essential assistance (WFP, 1995a). Countries bordering conflicts received refugees while their own people suffered loss of entitlements and access to food or trade and commerce because of sanctions levied at their warring neighbors.

Food wars are defined here as the deliberate use of hunger as a weapon, or hunger suffered as a consequence of armed conflict. Each of these cases of armed conflict involved destruction or diversion of food supplies or of the potential to produce food.[1] Included in the count are cases in which repressive measures and government policy meld to deny or restrict access to productive resources and income, as in the case of forced relocation in several African civil conflicts (see Kates et al., 1988: note 8). Classifications and commentaries draw on academic, journalistic, and policy findings to catalogue food wars; describe the range of ways in which armed conflict contributes to hunger; discuss political and humanitarian efforts to limit food wars and where and why they succeed or fail; and analyze the ways in which hunger vulnerability can be reduced after the wars end (Messer, 1990; 1991; 1994a; Bohle et al., 1993; Macrae and Zwi, 1994).[2] Figure 1 identifies these countries by region. Box 1 summarizes the continuing legacy of food wars. Below, commentaries on "zones of concern" describe briefly the new or continuing hunger situations in these nations and document the multiple ways in which food wars contribute to hunger vulnerability.

Food Shortage

The most obvious way in which armed conflict causes hunger is deliberate use of food as a weapon. Adversaries can starve opponents into submission by seizing or destroying food stocks, cattle, or other assets in rural areas; cutting off sources of

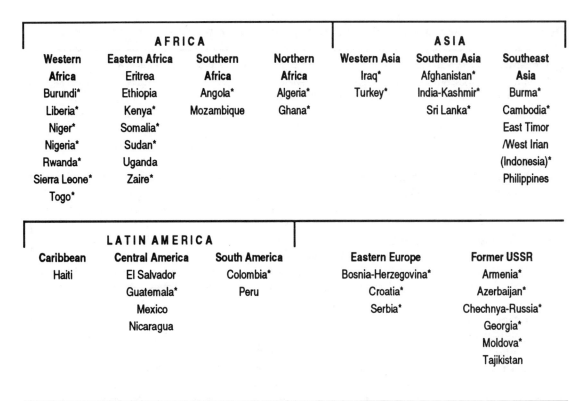

Figure 2.1. Countries Affected by Food Wars (by region).
*denotes cases of active conflict where hunger has been used as a weapon.

food or livelihood, including destruction of markets in urban and rural areas; and diverting relief food from intended beneficiaries. Land and water resources are contaminated to force people to leave and not return; the human population is reduced by direct attacks, terror, enslavement, or forced labor recruitment; health facilities are destroyed. Food shortages also occur as people flee or fear to farm agricultural lands and so set the stage for multiple years of food emergencies.

In sub-Saharan Africa, food shortage (famine) remained prominent in Angola (Sogge, 1992), the southern Sudan (Keen, 1994) and, to a lesser extent, Somalia (DeWaal, 1994). In all three instances, hunger had been created as a political tool. The international community intervened with food relief, which was manipulated as a weapon by warring parties. Millions in Rwanda and Burundi, driven from their homes, faced severe food shortages. Farmers were unable to return to plant their fields. In a newly severe regional conflict in Kenya, herders and farmers faced off in a political-economic struggle for land, that drove tens of thousands of would-be cultivators into exile.

In Asia, Cambodians experienced extreme food shortages requiring international relief, a situation exacerbated by the Khmer Rouge which chased some 100,000 western Cambodians from their homes and fields. Siege warfare and struggle for control of relief food characterized nascent and continuing conflicts in the former Soviet Union, former Yugoslavia, southwest Asia, where the Kabul area of Afghanistan remained on the brink of starvation, and southeast Asia, where the Burmese military continued to harry borderland tribes. Siege and starvation remain a tool of the persistent conflict between Tamils and Singhalese in Sri Lanka.

Box 2.1. The Legacy of Foodwars in Africa, Asia, and Latin America in the 1990s

Afghanistan (1991-94). Post-civil war fighting among Islamic factions uses siege as a tactic.

Angola (1992-94). Civil war continues (UNITA rebels vs. new govt.) despite efforts at disarmament, democratization, reconciliation, and free elections.

Burma (Myanmar) (1985-1994). (govt. vs. tribal peoples and other dissidents) disrupts access to land and livelihood, and creates refugees and hunger.

Burundi (1993-1994). Ethnic conflict (Tutsi vs. Hutu) kills and displaces thousands, disrupting food system

Cambodia (1991-1994) Civil conflict and disruption to agriculture continue despite end of civil war (Khmer Rouge vs. govt., 1975-1990).

El Salvador (1991-94). Resettlement, reconciliation and reconstruction after civil war (govt. vs. guerrillas) delayed by lack of access to land, employment.

Ethiopia and **Eritrea** (1991-94). Reconstruction and reconciliation after civil war (Eritrean and Tigrean insurgents vs. the govt. of Ethiopia, 1979-1990) slowed by lack of resources.

Guatemala (1966-1994). Civil war (military vs. indigenous population and other dissidents) continues dislocation and destruction, despite the return of some refugees.

Indonesia vs. East Timor (1975-1994). The Indonesian military continues to use hunger as a weapon against East Timorese, who want autonomy.

Iraq (1991-1994) UN sanctions, and govt. repression (against Kurds in the North and Shi'ites in the South) increase food poverty, malnutrition, and child mortality.

Liberia (1990-94). Civil war (intertribal fighting vs. govt. vs. West African coalition) causes widespread food shortage and population displacement.

Mozambique (1993-1994). Population, especially returning refugees, remain dependent on food aid, after destruction of agriculture and markets in civil war (Government vs. RENAMO rebels, 1981-1992), but no reported famine deaths

Nicaragua (1989-94). Post-war poverty and related brigandage persist, despite end of civil war (Sandinista govt. vs. U.S.-backed Contra rebels).

Peru (1983-1994) Widespread poverty and destruction continue to disrupt food systems despite capture of Shining Path rebel leaders and hopes for peace.

Rwanda (1993-94). Aftermath of civil war (Hutu govt. vs. Tutsi and other opponents) continues widespread displacement., disruption of livelihood and food production.

Sierra Leone (1991-1994) Civil war (Revolutionary United Front vs. govt.) disrupts food trade, aid, and production and displaces thousands.

Somalia (1981-1994). Intertribal fighting continues, perpetuating civil disorder and hunger.

South Africa (1990-1994) The legacy of apartheid government's policy toward Black minorities, including restricted access to productive resources and income and forced resettlement, contributes to widespread food poverty and malnutrition.

Sri Lanka (1984-1994) Civil war (government vs. Tamil and Sinhalese guerrillas) threatens famine and food poverty due to interference with food production, storage, and marketing.

Sudan (1984-1994) Civil war (Islamic government vs. Southern insurgents and intertribal fighting contribute to famine and disruption of food production and marketing and the provision of food aid.

Local indigenous populations of Chiapas, Mexico and Guatemala were also food short, denied access to land or livelihood and depending on the military for relief. Wide-spread use of field mines in southern Africa, Afghanistan, and Cambodia ensures that underproduction and food shortages will exist for some time. In Africa, and reportedly in Mexico, poisoning of water sources continues to be another destructive tactic with longer-term consequences for food production; land is rendered untillable and uninhabitable.

More positively, as a result of famine early warning and international response, the only places where famines were reported in 1994 were African and

Asian zones of armed conflict. In the aftermath of war and severe drought, Ethiopia and Eritrea averted famine through timely appeal for and delivery of food relief; external food sourcing is likely to be necessary here for years to come: lands, seeds, farm animals, and water systems have been destroyed along with the human communities (Cliffe, 1994). Similarly, the international community met food needs in Mozambique, which was struggling toward peace and construction of a new economy after a generation of conflict (Green, 1994).[3]

Food Poverty

Food shortages are also entitlement failures, as individuals, whole communities, or regions suffer from direct and indirect impacts of armed conflict. In post-war Eritrea, for example, to rebuild communities, the people, including demobilized soldiers, must first gain title to land, reconstruct waterworks, replant trees for fuel, food, and fodder, and acquire seeds and animals, or other sources of livelihood – all difficult tasks (Cliffe, 1994). Underemployment, lack of skills, and poverty present a great challenge to social reconstruction in all the former war zones where banditry often replaces political death squads.

As countries and communities lumber toward social reconstruction, self-reliance, and food security, food aid provides some immediate relief but other strategies are needed. Some have pointed out that obviously much relief food might be better utilized as "food for work" that creates employment and constructs infrastructure. But "linking relief to development" (LRD) strategies are expensive and involve tradeoffs. Those who are most hungry may not be able to work. In addition, in countries with weak central governments, such as Ethiopia, LRD strategies cannot draw on the capacity to plan and implement infrastructure-building programs (Maxwell and Lirensu, 1994). The most successful approach to reconstructing sustainable livelihoods should be work with and through local communities or indigenous NGOs, but in many instances, particularly where large populations have been in exile a generation or more, such communities and leaders are hard to identify and to link up with still-weak central governments (Davies, 1994).

Poverty and reduced access to food bring with them brigandage and disorder, and contribute to nostalgia for the Old Order that provided food for some, even if that was a part of military repression and forced dependence for others. Longing for the former regimes has been noted by journalists covering citizen reactions to the social-political disorders in the former Soviet Union, former Yugoslavia, and Nicaragua.

Food Deprivation

Even where food resources are available, certain members of the population – because of gender, age, or cultural identity – have less access. Women and children remain the most notable victims in food wars, left behind as men migrate in search of food, away from violence, or are conscripted into the armies. They suffer disproportionately from illness, as a combination of malnutrition and destruction of health services renders them more vulnerable. Even where food is present, refugee populations are vulnerable to the respiratory and gastrointestinal disorders that, as well as cholera, threaten lives in war-related situations due to lack of sanitation, water, and health services (Winter, 1995).

Reporting the needs of nutritionally vulnerable children, UNICEF estimates that over 1.5 million have been killed, over 4 million physically disabled, and over

12 million rendered homeless in conflicts this past decade (Grant, 1993, 1994; see also UNICEF's series, *Children on the Front Line*). Children are especially vulnerable to the micronutrient deficiencies that generally characterize emergency food rations, which supply predominantly calories through cereals, legumes, and edible oils – although providing adequate micronutrients in emergency feeding situations is an increasing concern of both donors and service providers.[4]

Women also are special victims of violence and hunger, especially in refugee situations where male thugs may control distribution of emergency rations (Amnesty International, 1992). Critics of indiscriminate methods of food distribution (e.g., African Rights, 1994) urge that food be distributed directly to women to protect them and their children. Targeting reproductive-age women to receive adequate micronutrients, especially iodine, is also a concern (see Ralte, this volume).

In emergency situations, the cultural identity of selected groups may mean denial of food even where rations or other foods are available, as illustrated especially by the Bosnian Serbs' treatment of Bosnian Moslems, in particular males of military age, who were seized and starved.

The human costs of sanctions combine elements of all three hunger types. International sanctions have been the strategy of choice where military intervention is counter-indicated and the international community desires and tries to mandate political change. International sanctions have been implemented by the UN in Iraq, Bosnia, and Haiti; in each case, the objective is to remove the ruler from power and bring about positive (democratic) change. With the possible exception of the return to power of Haiti's President Aristide in 1995, sanctions have been considered to be politically ineffective and a humanitarian disaster. Although essential foods and medicines are explicitly excluded from embargo, the poor have less access to nutrition and medicine because of cutbacks in petroleum and other items essential for moving food, and higher prices for foods and medicines are magnified by reduced earning power in a failing economy. NGOs still have not discovered good ways to reach those most disadvantaged by sanctions, and continue to disagree over their logistical value.[5] In sanction situations, as in those characterized by military or other humanitarian assistance, NGOs also face the dilemma of identifying responsible community leaders, organizations, or structures that can help move people away from hunger and relief, to food security, to human security. All are part of the longer-term equation for political stability, economic development, and human rights (Messer, 1995).

Underlying Conditions

Food wars themselves have been fueled by political-economic policies and sociocultural attitudes that contribute to social and economic inequities, to the "silent" or "quiet" violence of hunger, and to political unrest (Messer, 1994:47, see also Hartmann and Boyce, 1983; Reyna, 1991; Macrae and Zwi, 1994). Since colonial times in Asia, Africa, and Latin America, land-use policies have favored commercial over local subsistence production and created highly specialized economies that are extremely vulnerable to world market fluctuations. The collapse of the coffee economy in Rwanda, a case in point, left local cultivators vulnerable to hunger and hopelessness and ripe for political manipulation into violence (Uvin, 1995).

Government allocations to military rather than social expenditures (Sivard, 1994; Stewart, 1993) have led to national societies characterized by limited basic skills, food insecurity, and malnutrition, as well as discontent and despair.[6] Military preparedness in this manner creates conflict potential, and constitutes one of the underlying conditions of food insecurity that leads to war.

International donors, especially multilateral banks, may exacerbate such underinvestments by demanding more fiscal responsibility from governments. Policy makers often translate this fiat into lower levels of expenditures for health, food subsidies, and other human services programs (see e.g., Serageldin and Landell-Mills, 1994) and consequent reductions in health, nutrition, education, and quality of life. In view of the debts, destitution, and conflicts characterizing many developing economies, some analysts are questioning the wisdom of such policies. Stewart (1993) criticizes economic adjustment policies that force governments to cut services for the poor even as social tensions are running high. Smith (1994), analyzing for UNDP the development levels of countries at war, insists that debt repayment not take precedence over human well-being. Both writers trace conflict potential to indicators of underdevelopment. Other studies have suggested that donors devote more resources to zones of low economic potential, thus identifying and defusing with well-targeted development assistance potentially volatile areas, since conflict prevention is far less costly than conflict resolution or relief after tensions have boiled over into violence (Messer, 1995; WFP, 1995a,b).

How effective are such efforts if the underlying conditions are more cultural and psychological than political and economic? National, ethnic, religious, occupational and gender perspectives which classify non-members as less than human rationalize violence, including using hunger as a weapon (Messer, 1990; 1991). Alleging cultural superiority and dehumanizing or demonizing "the others," elites in Latin America, and to a lesser extent in Asia and Africa, characteristically have deprived local indigenous (tribal, minority, ethnic) populations of access to land, livelihood, and full economic and political participation, including basic civil rights. Such peoples as the Maya of Chiapas, Mexico, rebel and demand their rights as they gain education and exposure to non-indigenous ideas and agencies.[7]

Alternatively, as in Rwanda or Sri Lanka, violence may feed on its own history or quasi- (mythic) past, without appeal to external legal or moral frameworks. Combatants in these latter settings rationalize their actions by an enduring enmity between "us" (the "real" human beings, deserving of rights, especially to land) and "them" (the barbarians or illegitate "others"). New or renewed conflicts based on such enmities in 1994 included those between Hutu and Tutsi in Rwanda and Burundi and the violent uprooting of ethnic Kikuyu-Luo-Luhya farmers by Maasai-Samburu-Turkana-Kalenjin pastoralists claiming to be the legitimate owners of disputed Kenyan lands (Human Rights Watch/Africa 1994b). Even without historic or mythical enmity, a psychology of dehumanization helps justify inhuman hunger and violence perpetrated against others. Anti-Serbian and anti-Muslim rhetoric in the former Yugoslavia, especially in Bosnia, and the bloody, dismembering Hutu-Tutsi violence in Rwanda provide the most recent examples of how the psychology of dehumanization allows one group to violate another through starvation in addition to arms (see Messer, 1994:48). All are examples of the ways in which ethnic/political/religious leaders or groups, referring to non-inclusive cultural classifications of human beings, exclude entire ethnic, socioeconomic, gender, or age groups from basic human rights and protections.

Limiting Hunger and Destructiveness in War

Countering such cultural restrictiveness, every age has also witnessed some "law of nations," an internationally respected set of cultural rules that limits permissible violence and destructiveness, in war and in peace.

Religious and Cultural Codes

Jewish, Islamic, Christian, and Eastern religious traditions contain codes of behavior that limit violence toward non-combatants, the environment, and future sources of livelihood. Biblical Deuteronomy XX severely restricts the circumstances under which siege warfare is permissible and insists that combatants save fruit-bearing trees. Islamic sources command combatants to spare old people, children, or women who do not take part in the war (*Sura II*:190,192,194, see El Dakkak, 1990; Mansour, 1965) and also single out trees and especially date palms for protection (*Ibid.*) Chinese military sources, sometimes cited to document how destruction of grain supplies has been intrinsic to military strategies across the globe, nevertheless suggest that siege, with its total destructiveness, is a tactic of last resort since it leaves little of worth for either side (Griffith, 1963). Although some interpret these religious or cultural codes as the forerunners of contemporary humanitarian or human rights laws, the weakness of these earlier or sectarian codes is their insularity: rules usually apply only to co-religionists or members of one's own cultural group with everyone outside the protected group "beyond the pale" of protection (Messer, 1991:5-7).

Similar restrictions have been alleged and criticized in cases where religious groups deliver food and other essential aid to war and famine victims. Non-fundamentalists and non-Moslems accused fundamentalist Islamic NGOs in the Sudan and Somalia of using food as a lure to attract adherents (Noble, 1993); the Islamic government of Sudan and Somali Muslims in return leveled the same charges against Christian charities providing essential food to dissident Southern Sudan and predominantly Muslim Somalia (AP, 1993).

International Humanitarian and Human Rights Codes

By contrast, international humanitarian covenants, which include provisions for emergency feeding of civilian populations, are meant to be universal. Humanitarian laws and the first Geneva Convention that guarantee humane treatment for the wounded and sick date to the 19th century. The second, third, and fourth Geneva Conventions (1949) and Additional Protocols (1977) which provide guidelines to combatant parties for meeting essential humanitarian needs and ensuring basic subsistence rights of civilian populations experiencing armed conflict, were promulgated after World War II (1949). Their precedent is the Hague Convention of 1899, which states that "the right of belligerents to adopt means of injuring the enemy is not unlimited."

Relief organizations such as the International Committees of the Red Cross/Crescent (ICRC) and NGOs, when intervening to move food into zones of armed conflict, refer to this legal framework and also to more recent non-political humanitarian principles contained in their charters or mission statements (e.g., US Committee on Refugees, 1995; WFP, 1995a) or multilateral statements of humanitarian principles, such as the Providence Principles (1992). These humanitarian conventions and protocols enrich the Human Rights principles of the UN, expressed in the Charter and Universal Declaration of Human Rights (1948) which declare that food is a basic human right and a principal component of the right to life. The proposition that food must never be used as a political tool, derived from this principle, is contained in the ICN World Declaration and Plan of Action for Nutrition (1992) and the Vienna Declaration on Human Rights (1993). These UN human rights documents, signed by member states, provide a common reference point and standard for action for the UN community of nations, member states, and agencies. Increasingly, they are also recognized as guiding principles for other human communities, including NGOs which increasingly contribute to development and emergency-assistance activities orchestrated and funded by bilateral and UN organizations.

A third set of principles, promulgated in UN documents and humanitarian law, protects the rights of those who have crossed borders or are otherwise stateless and therefore beyond protection of any UN member. The UNHCR reported some 19 million refugees in 1994, but expressed hope that the second half of the decade might be a time for repatriation. It scheduled $382 million to help 3 million victims of civil war, persecution, and famine return home in the calendar year 1994 (Lewis, 1994). Planning, funding, and administration of refugee-assistance activities are orchestrated with respect to refugee law, but the number of those displaced within their country's borders now swamps those displaced across borders.

Preventing International Assistance from Prolonging Conflicts

IGOs and NGOs trying to implement these combined legal principles over the last five years have offered a variety of options for meeting emergency needs – and raised troubling questions about the way aid is being handled and the consequences. Some have suggested that all assistance meant to limit the hunger and destructiveness of war instead prolongs conflict, allowing combatants to focus on military matters rather than subsistence needs (Anderson, 1994). Even multi-lateral efforts such as food relief through Operation Lifeline Sudan, and cease-fires negotiated by UNICEF to immunize children, have been criticized for giving military (especially insurgent) leaders greater recognition, and possibly a respite that encourages them to fight on. Such war-prolonging outcomes, critics argue, may outweigh the immediate benefits in saved lives. These arguments form part of the critique of NGOs' self-proclaimed right of negotiated humanitarian access versus the rights of their alleged beneficiaries to choose the manner of their relief, and of military humanitarianism, the other major mechanism used to move food into zones of armed conflict since 1989. All contribute to the search for new models of global security that might limit scarcity, hunger, and conflict – and food wars – in the near to medium-term future.

"Negotiated Access": Politics Beyond Neutrality

In the 1990s NGOs have increasingly arranged with local, insurgent, state, or other military authorities to deliver humanitarian aid on a case-by-case basis. Maintaining a stance of neutrality, they have assumed responsibility for negotiating the quantities and terms of food delivery. Their ability to function depends on their willingness to deliver more aid when conditions make it possible and cut back when conditions are dangerous.

The advantage of this process is that NGOs can maintain a variety of options for reaching vulnerable populations with food aid. Donors select one or more organizations from the UN multilateral institutions, bilateral institutions, or NGOs operating in a given zone. One disadvantage of such flexibility is that it discourages multilateral cooperation when solidarity and coordination are needed if shrinking resources are to be used to best advantage. Another disadvantage, from international legal and political perspectives, is that NGOs, while assuming a political role usually reserved for governmental agencies, are responsible only to their donors and may be distorting or preventing local action, expression of interests, and negotiations (e.g., African Rights, 1994). As they move bilateral food aid on contract, NGOs' very neutrality makes them the political tools of donors and recipients. They often find themselves in the position of buying intelligence and security, dealing with the very thugs the world community is seeking to control (Anderson, 1994).

As the ICRC, the WFP, other UN agencies and NGOs are asked to respond to multiplying protracted, complex emergencies, they are forced to assume higher levels of financial and administrative planning that may make them political actors, even though their effectiveness as humanitarians demands they remain non-partisan. They are caught in a no-exit option of international welfare (Duffield, 1994a) for which they are ill-equipped (see Walker, 1994).

The WFP has tried to clarify its "non-political status...through a policy and *practice of impartiality*, as opposed to the more passive concept of neutrality. Impartiality implies being fully aware of the political implications of food interventions, and seeking to keep food aid out of the political and military equation" (WFP, 1995b:65). The Programme plans additional Codes of Conduct, still under development, that will guide future partnerships for aid delivery.

NGOs face the same challenges. All these new efforts focus on ways to deliver assistance that hold conduit operations more responsible. They also urge that food aid be better positioned to improve capacities for self-reliant development and sustainable food security. And they call for better aid coordination among UN agencies, governments, NGOs, and communities. These suggested efforts ultimately rely on "communities" to assume more of the burden for transforming relief into development. But identifying representative institutions and individuals remains a great challenge (Davies, 1994), one of the reasons proponents of military humanitarianism would like to see more, not less, emergency assistance delivered through military channels.

Military Humanitarianism

Since 1989, military support of humanitarian action has been used to allow victims of disaster rapid access to food in Iraqi Kurdistan (1991-92), Somalia (1992), Bosnia (1993-94), and most recently, Rwanda (1994). In each case, the logistic and security requirements of emergency relief were judged beyond the capacity of civilian mechanisms. Military assistance has also been favored in circumstances where UN peacekeeping (or observing) operations and aid delivery have coincided on the ground, as in Cambodia and Angola. Regional West African military forces and US troops have been employed to protect relief in Liberia and Haiti, respectively. In 1994, certain smaller-scale military operations in active or immediate post-conflict situations also were labelled or publicized as "humanitarian." For example, in Chiapas, Mexican army personnel were reported to be delivering food to villages ransacked by Zapatistas and in the Guatemalan highlands, local or US military forces were reported to have helped dig latrines or install potable water systems.

None of these operations, can be judged a success from humanitarian or military perspectives. Supporters insist the problem is not enough resources.

Opponents counter that military humanitarianism inevitably intensifies armed aspects of conflicts by providing food, employment, and income for local armed units: the sizable quantities of dry foods and arms moved by the military are fungible and invite pilferage (see e.g., Duffield, 1994b, Keen and Wilson, 1994). Military operations also assume the continued militarization of conflict zones by organizing relief as a military campaign dominated by military interests. Large scale and expensive, they tend to marginalize smaller-scale relief operations, even though community-based wet-feeding programs, as in Somalia, are less likely to be vandalized and more likely to involve communities and local leadership (African Rights, 1994). And where military discipline dominates relief, it allows less scope for civilian development programs. Although these criticisms have been leveled particularly against military-dominated relief in Somalia, where international forces have been involved, they also apply in Guatemala, which has been relying on a combination of national army and US military "humanitarian" assistance to rebuild communities. Such operations do deliver essential foods and medicines, and contribute to the construction of infrastructure, such as water works and sanitation channels, but they also increase community dependence on external agencies (in this case, the military) and discourage communities from increasing their own capacities to rebuild.

Human rights advocates note that "military humanitarianism" and negotiated access also may distort the human rights picture. Whereas the emphasis should be on the community's right to survive, and within that the right of individuals not to starve, aid donors have focused on *their* rights of access, evaluating success in terms of tons of food moved rather than benefits to recipients (Danish Red Cross, 1995).

US military officers caution that relief missions, such as those in Rwanda and Haiti, are too costly, unsustainable, and detract from essential combat readiness.[8] Development policy makers and field practitioners also bemoan the expense of military operations as overall development assistance is shrinking (e.g., Cohen, 1995).

From Military to (Global) Human Security

Global human security, an umbrella concept that subsumes the three concepts – meeting basic needs, maintaining armed readiness (security), and achieving human rights, has been gaining ground (see Messer, 1994a). It recognizes that programs to fight poverty, disease, malnutrition, and environmental damage can contribute to political stability, avoid costly conflicts, and avert humanitarian disasters and expensive emergency interventions. UN agencies, such as UNICEF and UNDP, have advocated replacing circa 3% of military spending or 20% of developing-country government budgets with social expenditures for basic human needs (Grant, 1995:42). They have called for a political commitment to action. Significantly, by the end of 1995, at least 181 countries had ratified the Convention on the Rights of the Child. UNICEF also has been careful to set goals and chart progress in meeting needs, such as access to safe drinking water, that serves as an indicator of progress in development (and in overcoming hunger).

Studies by UNDP (Smith, 1994) and UNICEF (Grant, 1994) show how progress in overcoming hunger has been hampered by political-economic disorganization and social disintegration. Countries that demonstrate the least progress toward meeting the goals of the World Summit for Children are those at war (see Mason et al., this volume). Indebtedness, violent conflict, and lack of progress in development coexist in most war-torn countries, where armed struggles tend to be aggravated by international demands for fiscal austerity (Smith, 1994).

Emergency assistance to victims of armed conflict has been reducing the levels of international expenditures for peaceful development that might prevent future conflict (Messer, 1995). The relative scale of international spending on complex emergencies versus longer-term peacetime aid has been demonstrated by WFP, an organization founded to provide development assistance as well as to meet immediate food relief needs. In 1994, in a complete reversal of earlier allocation patterns, two of every three tons of food WFP distributed went to emergency relief. This change reflects relative demand, and also the disruptive effects of conflict on infrastructure and government capacity to absorb and administer development assistance in several priority countries (WFP, 1995a). In addition, increasing aid to the former Yugoslavia, former Soviet Union, and other Eastern bloc nations, depleted the resources available to other poor areas of the world. The former Yugoslavia alone received 13% of total WFP emergency food distributions; huge catastrophes such as Rwanda took another 22%.

More evidence on the relative balance of relief spending and economic aid comes from the Organization for Economic Cooperation and Development (OECD): development assistance declined by 6% in real dollar terms to $566 billion in 1993; and further in 1994 (Cohen, 1995). Although the UN target for donor aid as a percentage of GNP is only 0.7%, the average donor country allocated a mere 0.3% in 1993, down 0.03% from 1992. After administrative costs are subtracted, total bilateral funds available for longer-term development in poor countries declined more than 0.8% (to $33.2 billion) in 1993. General fiscal austerity and an end to military aid linked to the Cold War account in part for observed declines. Another likely factor is "donor fatigue," a growing sense of hopelessness, futility, or waste in areas like Afghanistan, where recipients of would-be development assistance remain mired in self-destruction. Multilateral and bilateral donors face a two-fold challenge: to maintain development resources and to find ways to use emergency aid more effectively for development.

Relief to Development in Complex Emergencies

Multiple efforts are underway on the "relief-to-development" continuum, but operational challenges are enormous. Case studies presented at Institute for Development Studies (University of Sussex) workshop, *Linking Relief to Development* (Maxwell and Buchanan-Smith, 1994), revealed why it is so difficult to use food aid less as a dole and more in ways that create employment, build infrastructure, and increase the capacity of local communities to feed themselves (e.g., Maxwell and Lirenso, 1994). In Ethiopia, Eritrea, Mozambique, and other countries that are moving toward peace, weak central governments, non-existent infrastructure and communications, and newly emergent but still leaderless communities make "experts'" prescriptions for more effective use of food aid and "bottom-up" development and "grassroots" development partnerships more sloganeering than operational planning (Davies, 1994). NGOs tend to be championed as the critical link to communities, able to reach those outside governmental jurisdiction or interest. However, Mozambique's recent experience with a proliferation of NGOs and NGO activities suggests a cautious, critical approach that distinguishes between indigenous and outside organizations, all of which are "non-governmental," but which have varying capacities to mobilize local, sustainable food-security activities. Some relief and advocacy organizations, to prevent fragmentation of relief efforts, have been emphasizing activities that might strengthen new governments, or the ties between communities and governments (Messer, 1994b; Winter, 1995).

Another concern is how development assistance can help prevent further conflict by addressing zones of high conflict potential. To help donors focus on such zones, conflict (ethnic and political) early warning systems and pre-emptive response mechanisms identify areas of actual or potential food insecurity and a high potential for political ethnic violence. One promising possibility is to link program practitioners carrying out food security risk assessment – CRS-UK has a pilot project underway – with those monitoring conflict potential either on the ground (e.g., as proposed by the Human Rights Watch Committees, Neier, 1991) or from data bases (e.g., the University of Maryland Minorities at Risk project, Gurr and Haxton, 1995). But some agencies also must be prepared to act on the findings and try to pre-empt conflict through wiser and more humane economic policies and educational programs that might reduce insecurities and discrimination which exacerbate attitudes that lead to violence.

None of these is a simple issue, particularly in the absence of strong, effective international UN agency coordination or action (Slim and Penrose, 1994) and in the context of increasing competition for scarcer resources. Academics, policy-makers, and practitioners studying the underlying etiological relationships of hunger, scarcity, and conflict are identifying, at least at this stage, more constraints than opportunities. To implement more comprehensive "global human security" will entail broadening the contexts or perspectives for moving relief to development. Existing or new institutions or organizations must find new ways to unite multiple constituencies. In 1994-1995, new or renewed NGO and IGO coalitions have taken a few new steps in such confederating directions.

Nutrition, Human Rights, Development, and Human Security

In the arena of human rights, the World Alliance for Nutrition and Human Rights (WANAHR, 1994) has taken a positive step to assemble together human rights, development, and nutrition advocates under a single NGO umbrella to pursue a common agenda. This framework provides an important point of reference for charting principles, partnerships, and plans of action to limit war-associated hunger and to monitor rights and obligations of all parties involved. At least three transformations have been suggested to make the framework more effective. The first is to move human rights from the domain of international lawyers, debating words and principles, to the field practitioners in conflict prevention and resolution, who ultimately respect, protect, and fulfill human rights by their deeds.

The second is to enhance coordination of humanitarian efforts along the lines of human rights. The rationale for human rights food aid interventions continues to be to protect and fulfill the individual human right to food. All sides participating in food aid negotiations, especially outside donor agencies, must work to implement the principle, "food aid must not be denied because of political affiliation, geographic location, gender, age, ethnic, tribal, or religious identity" (ICN, 1992). One simple gesture might be to insist that representatives of the most vulnerable social categories (e.g., women) be part of the negotiating team for all sides. The third is to abandon agencies' idea that human rights are exclusively an interstate concern between central governments and the UN and recognize that where states are weak, most obligations for protection and fulfillment of food rights fall on other agencies or levels of social organization (see also Tomasevski, 1994; Eide, 1989)

Ultimately, the right to food and the elimination of hunger as a weapon of war will only be achieved when individuals, communities, and nations have overcome tendencies to dehumanize and brutalize each other. But setting relief and conflict-prevention (development) activities firmly in a human rights framework that affirms the worth and dignity of every human being and adequate food as a moral minimum for action can work against such destructive, conflict-fomenting, dehumanizing psychological processes that historically have characterized human society.

Food Security, Livelihood Security, and Environmental and Health Protection

The International Food Policy Research Institute, in its project, "2020: A Vision for Food, Agriculture, and the Environment" provides a second possible focus for comprehensive human security. As indicated in this volume, the project seeks to unite several competing technical, trade, environmental, and social agendas as it charts paths toward safe, adequate, and environmentally sustainable food systems for the next 25 years. Conflict prevention and institutional approaches to restoring post-war food security are two additional considerations for this agenda, which promises to set priorities in international agriculture for the near future (Messer, 1995). Like the five-year assessment of progress on the four "Overcoming Hunger" goals, the 2020 Vision has diversified beyond agriculture. It addresses, in addition to the International Agricultural Research Centers' conventional agenda, issues of investment in women's capacitation, clean water, micronutrient nutrition, and intra-household distribution of resources. The Salaya Statement (this volume), which reported progress on the four Bellagio goals, similarly recognizes that such investments are likely to yield greater nutritional benefits than conventional nutrition programs. All are aspects of a 1990s vision looking toward the next century and a global community that affirms human rights, economic development, an end to hunger, and crisis prevention. Only through such visions and supporting actions will the global community reach sustainable human security, a security that begins with an end to food wars.

Zones Of Concern

AFRICA

The food outlook for many African nations in 1994 was grim, as drought, war, and cutbacks in international assistance threatened food shortages and hunger for millions.

In *Angola*, fighting (government versus National Union for the Total Independence of Angola [UNITA]) and the use of siege and food deprivation as weapons continued despite the alleged peace agreement of 1992 and UN efforts to feed the hungry. Reportedly, more than a million people were at risk as a result of the war and the continuing drought (Darnton, 1994b). In February, the government halted aid flights to UNITA-controlled areas of the country in retaliation for an offensive that halted aid to the besieged town of Cuito, where some 30,000 were estimated to have died due to lack of food, water, or medicine (Brittain, 1994; *NYT*

(1993). Starvation threatened thousands in the central highlands as a result of drought and civil disorder (Maier, 1994). In June, Angolan rebels were still barring relief flights to areas they controlled, threatening millions with cutoffs of critical supplies of foreign food (*NYT*, 1994h). Perversely, the war continued partly as a result of foreign food aid, which the UN divided evenly between government and UNITA rebel forces. In addition, "The government has access to oil to purchase guns and the rebels smuggle out diamonds through Zaire" (Darnton, 1994a). In October, the UN brokered another agreement under which UN troops would keep the peace and the two sides share political power (*NYT*, 1994g).

In *Burundi*, fighting between Tutsi and Hutu in the capital, Bujumbura, followed a coup attempt in March causing up to 1000 deaths and disruption, and thousands to flee into neighboring Zaire (*NYT*, 1994c). After the violent death of their president (April 6), violence continued; numerically minor but politically dominant Tutsis who control the army, fear disruptions by Hutu militants. Burundians also fear the civil war in Rwanda will spill over into their territory and violence by Rwandan refugees fuels the potential crisis. Periodic strikes and market violence disrupt the economy (*NYT*, 1994e). Despite much international rhetoric and concern about "conflict prevention" on the part of the international community, little has been done to avert the crisis.

Eritrea, sometimes portrayed in the media as an "oasis of civility" with free markets and democracy, declared itself a nation in May, 1993, after a 30-year war for independence from Ethiopia, but remains highly reliant on external sources of food aid and economic assistance (Brooks, 1994). Water and fuel (firewood) are extremely scarce and rebuilding local economies and communities a major challenge. The population of 3.5 million is divided among nine ethnic lines and further split between Christianity and Islam. The impending return of half a million refugees from neighboring Sudan portends a resettlement and employment challenge of major proportions. The aggregate food shortage for 1994 was threatened further by weather-related crop failures estimated as high as 80%.

Ethiopia, facing severe drought in the aftermath of thirty years of war, averted starvation through timely delivery of external food aid. But politically the country remains fragmented and potentially volatile, with no real basis for national cohesion among competing ethnic and religious interests; communities and local leadership are still coalescing (Messer, 1995). After Mozambique, Ethiopia is the poorest country in the world; more than half its 50 million people live below poverty level and some 20 million are unemployed (Lorch, 1994d). Regional and local fighting persist and renewed fighting at larger scale is threatened by political divisions along ethnic lines and food insecurity. People were reported to be dying of hunger by the thousands in a few areas scourged by drought and cattle disease (Sly, 1994). In the context of severe drought and crop losses, international relief officials feared food shortages of calamitous proportions if threatened cuts in food aid reduced external sources of food (Parmelee, 1994).

In *Ghana*, ethnic fighting in the north between Nanumba and Kokomba, in February 1994 killed thousands, destroyed dozens of villages, and forced thousands more to flee into neighboring Togo, which declared itself under attack from Ghana. (Wall Street Journal, 1994; *NYT*, 1994a).

More than 10,000 *Kenyans* have been displaced in clashes that pit Maasai/Turkana, Samburu, and Kalenjin pastoralists against Kikuyu, Luo, and Luhya farmers in a struggle for increasingly scarce land. Their conflict replicates a larger national rift between President Moi, who stems from indigenous pastoral peoples who claim the land versus the opposition, who represent the other farming groups (Press, 1995). Farmers leave the land in search of safety or otherwise restrict production. Resettlement schemes funded by external donors go largely unimplemented because of the continuing risks of attack and government harrassment of the displaced. Church relief and press report political harrassment of their attempts to deliver relief and give voice to those locally involved in the clashes (Human Rights Watch/Africa, 1994b).

Across *Liberia* continued fighting forced foreign aid agencies out of the country (McGreal, 1994). Nearly half of Liberia's former 2.6 million people have fled the country, immiserating them and many in the neighboring lands that host them (French, 1994). The fighting spills over into the bordering countries, highlighting the failure of those nations to forge a peace despite their armed intervention. Of special concern is the fate of children as young as 9 or 10 who are conscripted as soldiers and lose traditional community socialization and sources of support.

In *Mozambique*, children also continue to suffer the aftermath of war. Two years after the accord of 1992 the country appears largely at peace. But armed violence continues in the form of banditry as demobilized guerrillas and other former soldiers take hostages, block roads, loot and riot, and raise serious questions about the possibility of stable governance and security. The country has little formal work. The demobilized armies have no education and few skills and many have no socialization or social reference points to speak of. They continue pillage as a way of life begun in the military (*NYT*, 1994f; Drogin, 1995). More than three-quarters of national income comes from international aid, but the informal economy provides hope for some 1.7 million refugees, resettled at a cost of $1.2 billion by the UNHCR, who must find ways to support themselves in agricultural areas still riddled with mines or towns still littered with destruction (*Economist*, 1995).

Nigeria's military dictatorship continued to violate human rights. In active conflict (government of Nigeria vs. Ogoni), government forces burned and looted villages, destroying food production and other means of livelihood (Human Rights Watch/Africa, 1994a).

In *Rwanda* violence erupted on April 6, 1994 with the killing of their President. Over two million refugees struggled for life in neighboring Zaire and Tanzania. Crops and fields remained untended and 1994 harvests were estimated at 40% below 1993 levels. Donors estimated that 2.5 million people would need five months of direct food aid (Dahlburg, 1994). Some 250,000-300,000 refugees were dependent on humanitarian relief for food, water, and shelter in the Benaco refugee camp and Ngara in Tanzania (Lorch, 1994b). To feed those in the Goma Zaire camps, relief workers had to overcome logistical difficulties of moving and distributing massive amounts of food, the predation of Zairian soldiers, and the continuing violence within the refugee populations themselves. Hutus, responsible for the earlier massacre of tens of thousands of Rwandans, terrorized refugee camps in Zaire, seizing and distributing relief food, usually denying access by the neediest (Bonner, 1994b). Return of the refugees demanded a secure supply of relief food, water, and medicines to stave off potential cholera and other epidemic diseases, as well as protection.

Within Rwanda, UN convoys attempting to deliver food to 9000 refugees living in squalor near Kigali were delayed by the continued fighting between government and rebel forces. French soldiers and relief workers mid-year located thousands of starving refugees in inaccessible parts of the country and as many as 600,000 Rwandan refugees sought food and shelter in a French-controlled security zone as Rwandan rebels tried to halt their progress (*NYT*, 1994d). Although millions of dollars in assistance is pouring into Rwanda, the government languishes unfunded, without resources to reorganize operations after the latest civil war (Lorch, 1994c).

In *Sierra Leone*, the rebel Revolutionary United Front, led by Foday Kankoh, who in 1991 launched a civil war against the government with the help of Liberia's former rebel leader, Charles Taylor, stepped up attacks against civilians, military, and the mining industry. The civil war forced 50,000 residents to flee the city of Kenema, displaced up to 100,000 from nearby villages, and cut off food supplies, trade, and aid (French, 1995).

In *Somalia*, the struggle for land and other resources, which some interpret to be the main source of the clan-based civil war, continues to ravage the country (Omaar and De Waal, 1994). The UN finally pulled out its multi-lateral forces which had been protecting food convoys.

In the *Sudan*, hunger persisted with more than two million in the south at severe risk of food shortage as a result of drought and renewed fighting (Government of Sudan vs. Sudan People's Liberation Army (SPLA)), in what were judged to be the worst conditions since the famine of 1988 (Lorch, 1994a). Irregular rains and insecurity caused up to 90% of the lands in the Habila plain to be uncultivated and up to 10,000 people from this region were reported on the move in search of food. In addition to formal attacks by government and opposition troops, banditry was rampant. The government and southern insurgents agreed in March 1994 to let aid reach the millions facing famine due to drought and strife in the southern region and designated safe routes for relief workers (*NYT*, 1994b).

There appeared to be little effort from external sources to resolve the lengthy conflict between the northern, Muslim government forces of the politically-economically dominant North and the southern, Christian or African religious economically marginal South. An estimated 4.5 million, 16% of the population, have been displaced by the war, and virtually all are hungry (Hundley, 1993). The Sudanese government continues impoverished but defiant, blaming outsiders for Sudan's problems (Richburg, 1994).

Togo received thousands of refugees fleeing fighting in neighboring northern Ghana; refugees from Togo's 1993 civil war continued to need food aid from international sources.

While *Uganda* rebuilt its economy, finding roles for former soldiers in the civilian sphere, border areas received up to 100,000 refugees fleeing armed conflict in southern Sudan, and the Rwandan Patriotic Front used other border lands as a launching area for attacks (Carrington, 1994; Tebere, 1994).

In *Yemen*, two months of civil war subjected the city of Aden to food and water shortages and a cholera epidemic, as Yemen's President Ali Abdullah Saleh took over the besieged southern city of Aden in July, and consolidated government control by delivering food and water (Whitaker, 1994).

In *Zaire*, people fleeing destitution and violence in Shaba province penetrated neighboring Zambia in search of work and food to eat and smuggle back. This followed events of 1993, in which indigenous Luba drove out Kasai settlers, destroying agriculture, mining, and other sources of income and leaving many children and women without male providers (Peters, 1994). General violence escalated as a result of the economic crisis characterized by rampant inflation (up to 80%) and collapse of the copper mining industry, which together engendered widespread hunger and disease. Localized shortages of food and medicine were exacerbated by army looting (Human Rights Watch/Africa (1994c:33). Although events led to bloodshed, it was not widespread; some commentators suggested that greater violence might be prevented by timely embargo of arms and increased food aid (N'Galamulume, 1994).

ASIA

In *Afghanistan*, two years after Islamic guerrillas toppled the Soviet-backed government in Kabul, no end to the fighting is in sight. In the first seven months of 1994, more than 11,000 people were killed and 500,000 fled as fighting among the various factions of the mujahedeen continued (Darnton, 1994c). International donors worried that reconstruction efforts had been futile, and also that the war might spill over into other parts of Central and South Asia (Bokhari, 1993). By early October an estimated 17,000 had been killed in three weeks of heavy fighting by Shi'ite factions in and around Kabul, and the border with Tajikistan was also open to conflict as 25,000 Russian-led troops attempted to control order in the former Soviet republic (Bourke, 1994).

In Thai border areas of *Burma (Myanmar)*, ethnic populations were subjected to hunger and human rights abuses, including outright attacks, intimidation, mistreatment, forced relocations, and forced labor (Human Rights Watch/Asia, 1995). The Thai military was accused of razing refugee camps and other human rights violations (Human Rights Watch/Asia, 1994b) including refusing to let refugees receive humanitarian assistance, thereby forcing them back into Burma. Burmese Muslims residing in reported squalid conditions in Bangladeshi refugee camps were still reluctant to return, despite UN repatriation efforts (Coughlin, 1994).[9]

In *Cambodia*, the Khmer Rouge continues to savage the peasantry, production, and peace. The 1991 peace agreement, supposed to lead to free elections in 1993, has not ended the reign of terror. In the first year of its democratically elected government, civil war has displaced tens of thousands, with severe human rights abuses reported on both sides. An estimated 50,000 have fled the government onslaught, only to return to homes and lands that had been looted and mined in their absence (Human Rights Watch/Asia, 1994a: 10). In early 1995, the Khmer Rouge were still reported to be attacking communities in western Cambodia; burning crops, slaughtering livestock, and forcing survivors to flee. More than 10,000 refugees need food aid, that must be stretched to feed others suffering from a year of severe drought and underproduction. The Khmer Rouge operations are sustained by widespread dissatisfaction with the corruption of the Cambodian government and also by financial infusions from sales of timber and gems, especially to Thai merchants (Shenon, 1995).

In Kashmir, *India*, a five-year war for independence (Muslim militants versus Indian government) has destroyed towns, agriculture, and commerce and killed 20,000.

In *Indonesia*, hunger and other human rights abuses oppress Timorese (with spillover effects in West Irian) as new migrants flock to the contested areas (Crossette, 1994). Asian trade meetings in Indonesia focused attention on the annexation of and human rights abuses in the former Portuguese colony as well as violations of workers' rights linked to impressive economic growth in the region (Human Rights Watch/Asia, 1994a).

Iraq continues to sink into poverty and hunger five years after the Persian Gulf War. Pillage is increasing because of income and market failures but the government shows no sign of falling (Ibrahim Youssef, 1994). Proponents and opponents of the US-led, four-year old international economic embargo continued to debate its merits as household food security and public health deteriorated, while Iraq showed persistent defiance of international demands to cease provocation and of international efforts to monitor missiles and arms. In northern Iraq, Kurdish rebels, with Western assistance, have established an autonomous state, but continued fighting jeopardizes well-being there (Hedges, 1994).

The *Philippines* government, January 30, 1994, signed a cease-fire pact with Muslim separatists as a critical step to end the 20-year conflict that has killed more than 50,000 people. National peace efforts sought to shift emphasis from Cold War to trade war concerns, as President Fidel Ramos and US President Clinton pledged economic coooperation. The Philippines also ceased to host more than 3000 Vietnamese refugees on the western island of Palawan.

In *Sri Lanka*, more than 50,000 people have been killed in the continuing civil war, where tactics have included siege and starvation.

In *Turkey*, more than 1000 villages have been razed as part of the government's crackdown against the Kurdish Workers Party, a separatist movement (Hundley, 1994).

Some North Koreans, in the absence of armed conflict but the presence of severe shortages, have indicated they would face the hardships of war to reunite with South Korea and improve their life chances (Branigin, 1994). Sanctions against N. Korea temporarily raised the spectre of war.

FORMER UNION OF SOVIET SOCIALIST REPUBLICS

Internal civil wars and wars for independence from Russia threaten the food supply and access to food within and among the former Soviet socialist republics. Russia juggles conflicts throughout the former USSR territories: the most active remaining in Chechnya and Abhkhazia (Boudreaux, 1994).

In *Armenia-Azerbaijan*, the six year conflict continued over Nagorno-Karabakh, home to most Christian Armenians but within Muslim Azerbaijan. More than a million Azerbaijanis have been uprooted; blockade has been used as a weapon against Armenia; and both countries suffer the economic devastations of war. Armenian troops wrested control of the breakaway province; razing Azeri villages in their path and driving their inhabitants into refugee status (Specter, 1994). Adding to the competition for land and ethnic-national identity is the struggle for potential oil revenues: Azerbaijan engineered an oil investment deal designed to provide $7 billion in Western investment (Sloane, 1994b).

The northern Caucasus republic of *Chechnya* continued its fight for independence, begun in 1991. Escalating hostilities in 1994 and the first half of 1995 brought the food supply situation of war-affected populations to "critical" levels (GIEWS, 1995:1).

In *Georgia*, disruption of rail traffic and streams of refugees have caused energy and other shortages. In February, 1994, fighting resumed in the disputed territory of Abkhazia (Bohlen, 1994); with tacit UN approval, Russian troops took up peace-keeping in June and were supposed to provide security for 250,000 returning refugees (Bird, 1994). South Ossetia, separated from Georgia in June, 1992, sought independence from Georgia and North Ossetia, which is under Russian protection (Bonner, 1994a).

In *Moldova*, suffering a simmering crisis exacerbated by drought, energy shortages, and economic difficulties, a referendum reported 90% in favor of independence as a member of the Commonwealth of Independent States. Russia signed an accord in October, 1994, to withdraw troops from the would-be breakaway region of Trans-Dniester, although some predicted this risked reigniting the conflict (Kamm, 1994).

In *Tajikistan*, two years after the 1992 civil war, some 30,000 refugees who fled to Afghanistan and perhaps 90% of the total half-million displaced persons were reported to have returned; the Tajikistan Popular Front continues to visit half-destroyed villages looking for recruits and weapons (Sneider, 1994). Fighting continued between the rebels and government forces backed by Russia and the Commonwealth of Independent States even after an agreement to stop all fighting by 5 November,1994 (Sloane, 1994a). Russian bombing of border villages was rationalized as protecting the Tajikistan government from attacks launched by rebels based in Afghanistan.

LATIN AMERICA

War-related population displacement and economic upheavals continued in Central America.

In *El Salvador*, economic and political instability are a legacy of the protracted political-economic inequality and civil war. Underemployment is estimated at 48%, 57% live in poverty, and buying power has decreased; the "family food basket" of essentials for survival rose 22% in 1994 (Wirpsa, 1995c). Struggle for land is increasingly accompanied by struggle for water, following a prolonged drought (*Caribbean and Central America Report*, 1995b). Cuts in foreign aid complicate the situation. Hoping for peace and democratic transition, the US cut aid from $230 million to $94 million (Robbins, 1994), but such decreases threaten the peace process. The program of reconstruction and reconciliation was short $137 million and armed violence was imminent among up to 41,000 former rebels, their supporters, government soldiers, and others displaced by the war who still were not resettled (Crossette, 1995). Those who obtained small plots of land still had difficulty getting credit and technical assistance (Vilas, 1995). Runaway crime, a legacy of poverty and decades of political violence, was characterized as the new government's biggest political challenge (Alder, 1994). Demobilized former combatants reportedly were organizing for armed banditry with no effective police interference (Farah, 1995). Critics noted that probably $4 billion was spent by the US on overt and covert aid during the war, but it was unwilling to pay to complete land reforms and prevent further conflict (Ryan, 1995).

Peace negotiations in *Guatemala* between the government/army and the URNG guerrilla forces were ongoing (but stalled) as human rights violations, institutionalized violence, and banditry afflicted the country. Guatemalan children are malnourished in disproportionate numbers after years of war and economic structural violence denying them access to land, justice, education, and economic opportunity (Heggenhoughen, 1995). Some 10,000 Guatemalan refugees in southeast Mexico face dismal prospects for finding land to till or communities to live in, as government military-controlled base communities and civilian patrols prevent free movement of persons for economic activity, threaten peaceful return and reintegration of returning refugees, and act as death squads in the continuing violence.

When the conflict ends, the government envisions transforming civil defense patrols into "Committees for Peace and Development," "participatory" community organizations, and assigning the government military to humanitarian and development roles. In communities where these changes have allegedly taken place, the new development associations control all funds without allowing others a voice. They use food as a weapon and control access to life necessities such as water (Sinclair, 1994). Military organization and operations, even where they assist in digging latrines and building roads and clinics to serve local rural populations, do not help impoverished Guatemalans to achieve their rights to a minimum living wage, land, and basic education for their children. Such constitutional guarantees must be fulfilled by the private sector in cooperation with government; their absence is likely to lead to persistent social explosion (Orlebar, 1994).

In *Nicaragua*, although the military war is over, 70% of the population still lives in poverty; unemployment allegedly runs 60%, with activities by women and children in the informal economy the only income that keeps urban residents from starving (Witness for Peace, *Bitter Medicine*, cited in Wirpsa, 1995b). An estimated 175,000 Nicaraguans work in neighboring Costa Rica legally; another 300,000 illegally, particularly during the harvest period for sugar, coffee, and bananas (*Caribbean and Central American Report*, 1995a; Maturana, 1994).

Former government soldiers and Contra rebels fight over land in almost daily armed clashes. Nicaragua's social-services yearly expenditure per capita has fallen to $13.37, down from a 1984 high of $42; per capita health expenditure (1991) was only $17, down from $58 in 1988. Only 54% of Nicaraguans are said to have access to safe drinking water and only 27% have sewage systems (Witness for Peace, cited in Wirpsa, 1995a). A "counter-reform" peasant economy is still in a formative stage; to survive, small producers are having to re-learn the self-sufficient ways of a diversified peasant economy (Torres Escobar, 1994).

January 1, 1994 in *Mexico* marked the beginning of the Zapatista revolution, as economically impoverished and politically powerless communities of ethnic Maya voiced demands for land, livelihood, and improved access to social services and opportunities. In response, the army allegedly brutalized civilian populations (Americas Watch, 1994). Tens of thousands fled into the forest. They became dependent on humanitarian handouts permitted by the surrounding military, who publicize widely their good deeds of food distribution, vaccination, and dental and medical care (DePalma, 1994a). There were also reports of looting by Zapatistas, who allegedly picked the coffee crop of some of the locals who had fled, thereby subjecting those displaced to penury when they returned (Darling, 1994; Asman, 1994). In mid-1995, new army attacks reportedly devastated households, contaminated streams and community water sources, and drove pro-Zapatistas and whole villages into the mountains (Moguel, 1995). Some displaced were being offered economic incentives to return (if they reported on rebel activities); over 15,000 were said to be in the hills without means of subsistence. In the aftermath of the rebellion, Mexico is struggling to control soaring inflation and economic disorder, that is likely to lead to additional conflict. By early 1995, unemployment and rising prices were reducing access to food and causing malnutrition (Fineman, 1995). In the north, the worst drought in 40 years was causing widespread malnutrition and hunger-related disease among poor indigenous populations in Chihuahua (DePalma, 1994b).

CARIBBEAN

More than 30,000 migrants from Haiti and Cuba took to the sea in the summer of 1994 in an attempt to escape political violence and poverty for sanctuary in the US. In both instances, abysmal human rights conditions were attributed to some combination of political mismanagement at home and sanctions from abroad.

Cuba, responding to the collapse of energy, trade, and food subsidies from the former Soviet Union, moved toward greater austerity and freer markets. In October, 1994, the government restored free domestic agricultural markets to help ease food shortages (Gunson, 1994). Tens of thousands of Cuban refugees sought "safe havens" at US military bases as a step toward entry into the US (Fiagome, 1994). US critics of the 35 year old embargo on trade and travel to Cuba argued that it hurts children and the elderly in particular and therefore constitutes an abuse of human rights. In 1994, the embargo was blamed for increases in hunger, illlness, death, and a neurological epidemic that afflicted tens of thousands of all ages (Lynch, 1994). The cause was never pinpointed, but symptoms responded to dietary and vitamin therapy.

With elected president Aristide back in place, *Haiti* faced the daunting task of building (or rebuilding) a viable economy (Cooper, 1994).

Conclusions and Outlook

The world in 1994-95 is plagued by conflict and hunger and the use of food as a weapon and political tool. It is characterized by multiplying "complex emergencies" that combine prolonged civil-political disorder with social-economic breakdown and suggest that food shortage, dangerously restricted access to food, poor health and nutrition, and violence will be the lot of millions in former- or active-conflict zones for years to come. Basic challenges for the second half of this final decade of the twentieth century are to integrate conflict prevention into food and nutritional security and agricultural development programs, to make conflict early warning a part of food and nutritional monitoring, and to encourage delivery of emergency aid in ways that discourage conflict.

1.   Classifications of wars draw initially on Sivard (1994), *World Military and Social Expenditures*, which defines war as an armed conflict causing 1000 or more deaths. To these are added conflicts, such as Haiti's, that, even though they do not fit the criteria exactly, involve substantial conflict-related (included international sanctions-related) hunger.

2.   More detailed descriptions are based on periodical accounts indexed in INFO TRAC and Newspaper Abstracts, plus UN agency and NGO newsletters and reports and other published sources. These more extensive periodical indices replace the old FAMINDEX, which was based on reports indexed under food, famine, hunger, and war in the *New York Times* exclusively.

3.   A possible exception is North Korea, where extreme food shortages were hinted, and in an ironic twist, one account suggested only by disintegrating into civil war would North Koreans resolve their food problem.

4.   The lack of equity in designing ration "food baskets" can be illustrated with respect to micronutrients, as orange juice (to provide vitamin C) is a staple of emergency food rations for the former Yugoslavia, but not for the populations served in Africa.

5.   A session at the 1994 Brown University Hunger Research Briefing and Exchange on the Human Costs of Sanctions (in Bosnia, Iraq, and Haiti) concluded that there was no agreement among aid-givers (UN, NGOs, policy makers) on the data documenting the negative costs of sanctions or by what they might be replaced to reduce their human costs, particularly for the poor.

6.   Certain donors, notably the IMF, Germany, and Japan seek to oblige recipients to decrease excessive military spending.

7.   see essays in *Cultural Survival Quarterly*, spring, 1994.

8.   "We're an army, not a Salvation Army" US Secretary of Defense William J. Perry told the US House Appropriations subcommittee on military spending, when he asked them for an additional $270 million in emergency aid for Rwanda (Schmitt, 1994). Their humanitarian versus invasive combat roles have been at issue also in Haiti, where the military's role has kept shifting from enforcing a largely ineffective economic embargo to a military presence supposed to protect a fragile peace and transition to return of democratically elected government. Haiti also raises the issue of the human costs of economic sanctions as an alternative to military intervention.

9.   Responding to Burma's military junta's continuing human rights abuses, some stockholders in international corporations doing business there discussed a possible embargo (*Chicago Tribune*, 1993).

References

ACC/SCN (1994). *Report on the Nutrition Situation of Refugee and Displaced Populations.* Refugee Nutrition Information Systems No.5, Geneva: ACC/SCN .

African Rights (1994). *Humanitarianism Unbound?* Current Dilemmas Facing Multi-Mandate Relief Operations in Political Emergencies. Discussion Paper No. 5.

Alder, D. (1994). Crime gangs replace death squads in El Salvador. *San Francisco Chronicle* August 23, A9.

Americas Watch (1994, March). Human rights and the Chiapas rebellion. *Current History* 93, 581: 121-3.

Amnesty International (1992). *Human Rights Violations Against the Indigenous Peoples of the Americas.* New York: Amnesty International.

Anderson, M. (1994). Promoting Peace or Promoting War? The Complex Relationship Between International Assistance and Conflict. Mimeo. 16 May.

Asman, D. (1994). Mexican rebels show their guts with Indian blood. *Wall Street Journal* February 11, A13.

Associated Press (AP) (1993). Western charities are hit in Somalia. *New York Times* December 27, A7.

Bird, C. (1994). Russian troops in new role as Abkhazia peacekeepers. *Los Angeles Times* June 28, A6.

Bohle, H.G, T.E. Downing, J.O. Field, and F.N. Ibrahim, eds. (1993) . *Coping with Vulnerability and Criticality: Case Studies on Food-Insecure People and Places.* Saarbrücken and Fort Lauderdale: Verlag breitenbach Publishers.

Bohlen, C. (1994). Russia and Georgia sign military cooperation today. *New York Times A15.*

Bokhari, F. (1993). Aid donors, too, are scared off by the fighting. *Christian Science Monitor* July 6, 11.

Bonner, R. (1994a). Separatists in Georgia look to Russia for protection. *New York Times* June 12, 18.

Bonner, R. (1994b). Rwandans who massacred now terrorize camps. *New York Times* October 31, A1.

Boudreaux, R. (1994). Moscow juggles conflicts in former Soviet territory. *Los Angeles Times* September 18, A4.

Bourke, G. (1994). Thousands injured as battling Shi'ite factions continue the relentless destruction of Kabul. *Guardian* October 4, 1,11.

Branigin, W. (1994). Defector says many N. Koreans think war could improve their lot. *Washington Post* July 7, A14.

Brittain, V. (1994). Angola stops aid to Unita areas. *Guardian* February 12, 1,14 .

Brooks, G. (1994). Postwar promise: Africa's newest nation, little Eritrea emerges as an oasis of civility. *Wall Street Journal* May 31, A1.

Caribbean and Central American Report (1995a). *Caribbean and Central America Report* , April 6, 3.

Caribbean and Central America Report (1995b). *Caribbean and Central American Report* May 18, 4.

Carrington, R. (1994). Recycling soldiers: poor lands try to cope with residue of war; their leftover armies. *Wall Street Journal* December 12, Al.

Chicago Tribune (1993). Abuses in Burma stir questions of conscience. *Chicago Tribune* October 25, 3.

Cliffe, L. (1994). The Impact of War on Food Security in Eritrea: Prospects for Recovery. In *War and Hunger*, J. Macrae and A. Zwi, eds., London: Zed Books, pp. 161-78.

Cohen, M., editor (1995). *Hunger 1995.* Washington, DC: Bread for the World.

Cooper, H. (1994). Mountain to climb: For Haiti, corruption, crime, and deprivation hobble economic plan. *Wall Street Journal* November 4, A1.

Coughlin, C. (1994). Burma's Muslims returning home. *San Francisco Chronicle* May 23, A10.

Crossette, B. (1994). New migrants flock to contested areas. *New York Times* October 30, 4.

Crossette, B. (1995). Peace program is in danger, Salvadorans tell the UN's chief. *New York Times* January 5, A7.

Dahlburg, J-T. (1994). Long-term food aid for Rwanda seen. *Los Angeles Times* September 1, A4.

Danish Red Cross (1995). Programming Relief for Development. Recommendations from the Copenhagen Workshop. Mimeo.

Darling, J. (1994). Chiapas refugees struggle back...cautiously. *Los Angeles Times* March 28, A7.

Darnton, J. (1994a). Civil war of nearly two decades exhausts resource-rich Angola. *New York Times* May 9, Al.

Darnton, J. (1994b). At war, Angola's bread basket lives, barely, on handouts. *New York Times* May 15, 4.

Darnton, J. (1994c). Forgotten by the world, Afghans plunge into misery. *New York Times* August 11, A4 .

Davies, S. (1994). Public Institutions, People, and Famine Mitigation. In *Linking Relief and Development*. IDS Bulletin 25,4: 46-54.

DePalma, A. (1994a). For Mexico's oppressed Indians, smothered hopes and promises not kept. *New York Times* June 15, A12.

DePalma, A. (1994b). Dying babies are witness to proud people's crisis. *New York Times* October 31, A4.

DeWaal, A. (1994). Dangerous Precedents? Famine Relief in Somalia 1991-93. In *War and Hunger*, J. Macrae and A. Zwi, eds., London: Zed Books, pp. 139-59.

Drogin, B (1995). Sending children off to war: From Mozambique to Bosnia. *Los Angeles Times* March 26, A1.

Duffield, M. (1994a). Complex Emergencies and the Crisis of Developmentalism. In *Linking Relief and Development*. IDS Bulletin 25,4:37-45.

Duffield, M. (1994b). The Political Economy of Internal War: Asset Transfer, Complex Emergencies and International Aid. In *War and Hunger*, J. Macrae and A. Zwi, eds., London: Zed Books, pp.50-70.

Economist (1995). *Economist* August 5, 336-7926:42-43.

Eide, A. (1989). *Food As a Human Right*. Paper No.1. Geneva: United Nations Commission on Human Rights.

El Dakkak, S. (1990). International humanitarian law lies between the Islamic concept and positive international law. *International Review of the Red Cross* .

Farah, D. (1995). Salvadorans complain postwar crime defeating rebuilt police force. *Washington Post* March 15, A24.

Fiagome, C. (1994). Cubans in the US push asylum for refugees detained at bases. *Christian Science Monitor* November 8, 3.

Fineman, M. (1995). Peso: Mexican currency's collapse puts many lives on hold. *Los Angeles Times* February 16, A3.

French, H. W. (1994). Liberia's war refugees now united in misery. *New York Times* September 17, A3.

French, H. (1995). For Sierra Leone, Elections and Starvation. *New York Times* September 26, A3

GIEWS (Global Information and Early Warning System on Food and Agriculture), FAO (1995, May/June). *Food Outlook* 5/6.

Grant, J. (1993). *The State of the World's Children 1993*. New York: Oxford University Press.

Grant, J. (1994). *The State of the World's Children 1994*. New York: Oxford University Press.

Grant, J. (1995). *The State of the World's Children 1995*. New York: Oxford University Press.

Green, R.H. (1994). The Course of the Four Horsemen: Costs of War and Its Aftermath in Sub-Saharan Africa. In *War and Hunger*, J. Macrae and A. Zwi, eds., London: Zed Books, pp.37-49.

Griffith, S., trans. (1963). *Sun Tzu: The Art of War*. Oxford: Oxford University Press.

Gunson, P. (1994). Market food feeds Cuba reform lobby. October 3, *Guardian* 10.

Gurr, T.R. and M.L. Haxton (1995). The Minorities At Risk Project: An Ongoing Effort to Understand the Nature of Ethnopolitical Conflict. *Conflict Processes Newsletter* of the American Political Science Association, T. David Mason, ed., November 1994.

Hartmann, B. and J. Boyce (1983). *A Quiet Violence: View from a Bangladesh Village*. London: Zed Books.

Hedges, C. (1994). Quarrels of Kurdish leaders sour dreams of a homeland. *New York Times* June 28, A1.

Heggenhoughen, K. (1995). The Epidemiology of Functional Apartheid and Human Rights Abuses. *Social Science and Medicine* 40,3: 281-284.

Human Rights Watch/Africa (1994a). Human Rights in Africa and US Policy. *Human Rights Watch/Africa* June, 6,6.

Human Rights Watch/Africa. (1994b). Kenya: Multipartyism betrayed in Kenya. *Human Rights Watch/Africa* July, 6,5.

Human Rights Watch/Africa (1994c). Sudan. "In the Name of God" Repression Continues in Northern Sudan. *Human Rights Watch/Africa* November, 6,9.

Human Rights Watch/Asia. (1994a). Human Rights in the APEC (Asia-Pacific Economic Cooperation) Region: 144. *Human Rights Watch/Asia* November, 6,13.

Human Rights Watch/Asia (1994b). The Mon: persecuted in Burma, forced back from Thailand. *Human Rights Watch/Asia* December, 6,14.

Human Rights Watch/Asia (1995). Abuses linked to the Fall of Manerplan. *Human Rights Watch/Asia* March, 7,5.

Hundley, T. (1993). Food a weapon in Sudan. *Chicago Tribune* September 29, 1,1.

Hundley, T. (1994). A remote and dirty little civil war. March 15,*Chicago Tribune* 1.

Ibrahim Youssef, M. (1994). Iraqi officials say military won't attack. *New York Times* 16 October, 12.

International Conference on Nutrition (ICN) (1992). *World Declaration and Plan of Action on Nutrition.* Rome: FAO/WHO.

Kamm, H. (1994). Russian Troops quitting a hot spot in Moldova. *New York Times* October 28, A12.

Kates, R.W. et al. (1988). *The Hunger Report:1988.* Providence, Rhode Island: Brown University World Hunger Program.

Keen, D. and K. Wilson (1994). Engaging with Violence: A Reassessment of Relief in Wartime. In *War and Hunger,* J. Macrae and A. Zwi, eds., London: Zed Books, pp. 209-21.

Lewis, P. (1994). Agency hopes for fall in number of refugees. *New York Times* 21.

Lorch, D. (1994a). Drought and fighting imperil 2 million in Sudan. *New York Times* February 10, A3.

Lorch, D. (1994b). Out of Rwanda's horrors into a sickening squalor. *New York Times* May 8, 1.

Lorch, D. (1994c). In Rwanda, government goes hungry. *New York Times* September 18, 1,4.

Lorch, D. (1994d). Hunger and dissent stalk a struggling Ethiopia. *New York Times* October 26, A3.

Lynch, C. (1994). US embargo is blamed for increase in Cuban deaths, illness). *Boston Globe* September 15, 12.

Macrae, J. and A. Zwi (1994). Famine, Complex Emergencies, and International Policy in Africa; An Overview. In *War and Hunger,* J. Macrae and A. Zwi, eds., London: Zed Books, pp.6-36.

Maier, K. (1994). Angola's war burns on, and thousands starve. *Washington Post* February 7, A12.

Mansour, A. (1965). *The Islamic Sharya and Public International Law.* The Council of Supereme Islamic, Book I.

Elisa Maturana (1994). Quoted in *La Tribuna* (Managua), (1994, April) Nicaragua: No way out? World *Press Review* 30.

Maxwell, S. and M. Buchanan-Smith, eds. (1994). *Linking Relief to Development.* IDS Bulletin 25,4.

Maxwell, S. and A. Lirensu (1994). Linking Relief and Development. An Ethiopian Case Study. In *Linking Relief and Development.* IDS Bulletin 25, 4:65-76.

McGreal, C. (1994). Liberians 'out of reach' of aid. *Guardian* October 6, 1,18.

46   Ellen Messer

Messer, E. (1990). Food Wars: Hunger as a Weapon of War. In *The Hunger Report: 1990*, R. Chen, ed. Providence, Rhode Island: Brown University World Hunger Program.

Messer, E. (1991). *Food Wars: Hunger as a Weapon of War in 1990*. Providence, Rhode Island: Brown University World Hunger Program Research Report.

Messer, E. (1994a). Food Wars: Hunger as a Weapon in 1993. *The Hunger Report*, P. Uvin, ed. Yverdon: Gordon & Breach, pp.43-70.

Messer, E. (1994b). The International Conference on Nutrition: An NGO Perspective. *The Hunger Report*, P.Uvin, ed. Yverdon: Gordon & Breach.

Messer, E. (1995). Food from Peace. Manuscript. World Hunger Program, Brown University.

Moguel, J. (1995). Army moves against Zapatistas. *NACLA Report on the Americas* May-June, 1: 1.

Neier, A. (1991). Ethnic conflict and human rights. An overview: Ethnic conflict critical factor in rights abuses worldwide. *Human Rights Watch 1*.

New York Times (1993). Food reaches Angolan city where 30,000 died. *New York Times* October 17, 1,16.

New York Times (1994a). Togo says it is under attack from Ghana. *New York Times* January 7, A8.

New York Times. (1994b). Sudan and rebels to let aid in to the south. *New York Times* March 24, A9.

New York Times (1994c). Thousands fleeing the ethnic violence in Burundi's capital. *New York Times* March 25, A10.

New York Times (1994d). Rwandan rebels halt drive toward French-held haven. *New York Times* July 7, A2.

New York Times (1994e). Violence paralyzes the capital of Burundi. *New York Times* August 10, A6 .

New York Times (1994f). Mozambique struggling to cope with raging crime wave. *New York Times* October 14, A5.

New York Times (1994g). UN Negotiates End to Angolan Civil War. *New York Times* October 18, A10 .

New York Times (1994h). Angolan rebels bar aid. *New York Times* June 15, A11.

N'Galamulume, O-J. (1994). Arms embargo, food aid could stay Zaire's crisis. *Christian Science Monitor* March 16, 32.

Noble, K.B. (1993). Islamic militants, pushed aside, express anger in Somali port. *New York Times* March 15, A9.

Omaar, R. and A.De Waal (1994). Sowing the seeds of famine and war. *Guardian* February 25, 2,15.

Orlebar, E. (1994). Guatemala plagued by historic inequity. August 30, *Los Angeles Times* .

Parmelee, J. (1994). New famine could loom in Ethiopia. *Washington Post* March 31, A28.

Payne, P. (1994). The Growth of Numbers of Refugees and Displaced People. *SCN News*.II.

Peters, A.(1994). Hunger forces Zaireans across the border. *International Press Service Harare.* January 10.

Press, R. (1995). Nomads and farmers feud over increasingly scarce land. *Christian Science Monitor* January 18, 6.

Reyna, S.P. (1991). What is to be Done? An Historical, Structural Approach to Warfare and Famine. In R.E. Downs, D.O.Kerner, and S.P. Reyna (editors). *The Political Economy of African Famine*, Philadelphia: Gordon & Breach, pp. 339-71.

Richburg, K.(1994). Sudanese government is impoverished, defiant. *Washington Post* April 2, A13.

Robbins, C.A. (1994). US, cutting Salvador aid, may regret loss of leverage in fragile peace process. *Wall Street Journal* A6.

Ryan, N. (1995). Deal to end El Salvador war threatened by slow reforms. *Christian Science Monitor.* January 17.

Schmitt, E. (1994). Pentagon worries about cost of aid missions. *New York Times* August 5.

Serageldin, Ismail and Pierre Landell-Mills, eds. (1994). *Overcoming Global Hunger.* Washington, DC: World Bank.

Shenon, P. (1995). Rebels still torment Cambodia 20 years after their rampage. *New York Times* 6 February, Al.

Sinclair, M. (1994). Patrols in Guatemala's highlands: A death grip on indigenous societies. *Christian Century*, 4 May 1994:466-69.

Sivard, R. (1994). *World Military and Social Expenditures.* Leesburg, VA: WSME Publishers.

Slim, H. and A. Penrose (1994). UN Reform in a Changing World: Responding to Complex Emergencies. In *War and Hunger*, J. Macrae and A. Zwi, eds., London: Zed Books, pp. 194-208.

Sly, L. (1994). New agony for Ethiopia. *Chicago Tribune* July l, 1,1.

Sloane, W. (1994a). Tajikistan government and rebels reach cease-fire agreement. *Christian Science Monitor* September 19, 5.

Sloane, W. (1994b). Azeri government thwarts a putsch linked to oil deal. *Christian Science Monitor* October 6, 5.

Smith, D. (1994). *War, Peace, and Third World Development.* Occasional Papers 16. Oslo: International Peace Research Institute, Human Development Report Office.

Sneider, D. (1994). Refugees rebuild in Tajik village. *Christian Science Monitor* May 19, 6.

Sogge, D. (1992). Sustainable Peace: Angola's Recovery, Harare, SARDC. In *War and Hunger: Rethinking International Responses to Complex Emergencies.* J. Macrae and A. Zwi, eds., London: Zed Books, pp. 92-110.

Specter, M. (1994). Azerbaijan, potentially rich, is impoverished by warfare. *New York Times* June 2, Al.

Stewart, F.(1993). *War and Underdevelopment: Can Economic Analysis Help Reduce the Costs.* Oxford: International Development Centre.

Tebere, R. (1994). Rwandan rebels staged their attack from Uganda. *Christian Science Monitor* June 8, 19.

Tomasevski, K. (1994). Human Rights and Wars of Starvation. In *War and Hunger*, J. Macrae and A. Zwi, eds., London: Zed Books, pp. 70-91.

Torres Escobar, E. (1994). Will Central America's farmers survive the export boom? *NACLA Report on the Americas* 28,3.

US Committee for Refugees (1995). *World Refugee Survey.* New York: US Committee for Refugees.

Uvin, P. (1995). Genocide in Rwanda: The Political Ecology of Conflict. Research Report RR-95-2. Providence, RI: World Hunger Program, Brown University.

Vilas, C. (1995, May/June). A painful peace: El Salvador after the accords. *NACLA Report on the Americas* 28, 6.

Walker, P. (1994). Linking Relief and Development: The Perspective of the International Federation of Red Cross and Red Crescent Societies. *Linking Relief and Development.* IDS Bulletin 25,4: 107.

Wall Street Journal (1994). Ethnic fighting in Ghana. *Wall Street Journal* February 15, A1.

Whitaker, B. (1994). Most of Aden in Northern hands. *Guardian* July 7, 1,15.

Winter, R. (1995). The Year in Review. In *World Refugee Survey*, New York: US Committee for Refugees.

Wirpsa, L. (1995a). Bitter Medicine. Structural Adjustment in Nicaragua. *National Catholic Reporter* May 26, 31:8.

Wirpsa, L. (1995b). Poor seek way out of Nicaraguan crisis. *National Catholic Reporter* 31,30: 7-8.

Wirpsa, L. (1995c). Tensions persist in postwar El Salvador. *National Catholic Reporter* 31: 26.

World Alliance for Nutrition and Human Rights (WANAHR) (1994). Report of WANAHR Inaugural Meeting 18-21 May 1994. *WANAHR Bulletin* 5.

World Food Programme (WFP) (1995a). *Annual Report of the Executive Director 1994 – Linking Relief to Development.* CFA: 39/4.

World Food Programme (WFP) (1995b). *Food Aid For Humanitarian Assistance.* Proceedings of the UN. World Food Programme Africa Regional Seminar. Addis Adaba, Ethiopia, 5-9 February 1995. Rome.

CHAPTER 3

Global Changes Since 1989

Goran Hyden

The Bellagio Declaration was launched in the spirit of 1989, when optimism about the ability of humanity to make a positive difference for itself and for future generations was on the rise. Although participants were careful to identify the structural constraints on human betterment, notably heavy debt burdens, environmental degradation, and continued rapid population growth, emphasis was still on the prospective dividends of peace and democracy. The meeting took place *before* the full implications of the ongoing political turmoil in Eastern Europe and the Soviet Union were known, but even so, the participants sensed that this was a turning point, an opportunity for concerted action. A year later there was little doubt about the fundamental nature of the changes that were occurring: the world would not be the same again.

Now the question increasingly being asked is whether we missed the opportunities presented five years ago. The British historian, G.M. Trevelyan (1922:292), said of the events of 1848, when uprisings against autocratic regimes erupted across Europe: "the year 1848 was the turning point at which modern history failed to turn. The military despotisms of Central Europe were nearly but not quite transformed by a timely and natural action of domestic forces. It was the appointed hour, but the despotisms just succeeded in surviving." Are we keeping our appointment, or are we, too, about to miss it?

Failure to seize our time would be so much more disturbing, for it is widely agreed that we possess today the knowledge and the means to improve the quality of life substantially for far larger numbers of people than was possible in the past. If we are so minded, overcoming hunger in our time is not beyond reach. In the past, the Good Society was, as Plato put it, a model set up in the sky. Today, we are not asking for the impossible when proposing to halve world hunger within ten years. But are we losing the political will to do so?

This paper addresses these questions by examining what has happened since 1989. It tries to provide an analysis of the global context in which the Bellagio initiative is being pursued. More specifically, it looks at the economic and political factors that are likely to determine the choices and courses of actions open to us. Needless to say, the account leaves out some factors that others would have included. All the same, I hope that it will provide a useful backdrop to discussions of what should and what can be done to eradicate hunger from this world.

Economic Changes

It could be argued that paying attention to what has happened in the global economy in the last five years is a waste of time. After all, five years is a very short span in the long haul. Yet, short-term trends often become the foundation on which long-term projections are made. Our sense of promise and peril for the future is very much determined by what we read into the present. This is evident from examining the reports issued by authoritative international agencies. In this section of the paper, I will look at four variables that are likely to shape analysts' and policy-makers' perception of what can be done to overcome hunger at the global level: 1) economic growth; 2) population growth; 3) foreign aid; and 4) world trade.

Economic Growth

As the 1992 *World Development Report* notes, the 1990s began badly for developing countries (World Bank 1992:32-33). In both 1990 and 1991, their per capita income as a whole fell, after rising every year since 1965. Some of that can be attributed to recession in high-income countries, but also important were extraordinary events such as the Gulf War and the economic contraction in Eastern Europe and the former Soviet Union following the demise of Communism. How much of this slowdown in economic growth can be attributed to external as opposed to internal variables is hard to know. The World Bank, for example, operates on the assumption that the effect of domestic policies on long-term growth is about twice as large as the effects attributable to changes in external conditions. This is a principal reason why the Bank insists on the dogged pursuit of domestic economic reform in developing countries. Given the heavy individual sacrifices and sufferings that are associated with strong structural adjustment policies, it is quite remarkable how far these reforms have been taken in both Latin America and Sub-Saharan Africa. To be sure, the record is mixed. Some countries have fared much better than others. Typically, reforms have been more successful wherever the political leadership has taken the lead to pursue them rather than leaving them to be driven by the international finance institutions. Chile, Ghana, and Uganda stand out as successful cases in point.

Citing the patient effort in the early 1990s by many developing countries to reform their economies, the Bank makes the assumption that economic growth rates will be higher in the 1990s than they were during the 1980s. GDP growth for the developing countries is projected at 5% for the decade, with Asia emerging as the fastest growing region. Growth will pick up in all the other regions too, but the gains per capita will be small in Sub-Saharan Africa.

The long-term projections that follow from these estimates are interesting. World GDP could rise from US $20 trillion in 1990 to US $69 trillion in 2030. For developing countries as a whole, per capita incomes could triple: from US $750 today (the level of Ivory Coast) to US $2,500 in 2030, the level in Mexico today. Although in the aggregate the gap between developing and industrialized countries would narrow, the fruits of such a tremendous economic expansion would not be shared evenly among the regions of the world. Because of rapid rates of growth in Asia, the average per capita income in East Asia would be US $3,300 in 2030, while in South Asia it would reach US $1,000. Average per capita incomes in the Middle East and Latin America could exceed US $5,000 and US $4,000 respectively, considerably above the average for developing countries in that year. The projections for Sub-Saharan Africa are particularly sobering: under present productivity trends and population projections output in total would rise fourfold, but per capita incomes would still reach only US $400. This is considerably more pessimistic than the projections provided a few years ago. For instance, when researchers at the World Hunger Program assembled data to make development projections for Sub-Saharan Africa up to year 2057, the official statistics available estimated a per capita income at that time of US $3,800, the equivalent Greece's per capita income in 1980 (Achebe et al, 1990:3036). The figure now being offered for year 2030 is lower than the 1957 per capita income for the region: US $440.

It is obvious that the increasingly pervasive "Afro-pessimism" is responsible for this drastic revision of projections. However, such trajectories are burdened with two weaknesses: they are "surprise-free," in that they do not account for unanticipated events; and they are based on normative assumptions associated with a particular point in time.

Population Growth

One of the key variables in all economic projections is population growth. For example, the somber figures for Sub-Saharan Africa are based on the premise that Africa's growth rate will still be 3% or above per annum for some years to come. Today, this looks less certain. One of the most remarkable findings in recent population research is the 20% fall in fertility rate from 6.7 in 1989 to 5.4 in 1993 (National Council for Population and Development, 1994). Another recent study, of low-income Bangladesh, suggests a fertility decline there from 7.0 per woman in 1975 to 4.2 in 1990 (Population Council, 1994).

Both reports tend to attribute the reported declines to successful population programs. There is some evidence to back it up. For example, contraceptive use in Bangladesh has risen from 3% in 1969 to 45% in 1990. Today about one-third of Kenyan women use contraception, compared to a mere 7% in 1978. The fertility decline there has been particularly sharp in the last five years. The prevalence of AIDS is likely to be one factor that explains this change in behavior, but we know too little about the variables that influence attitudes towards the use of contraceptives. There seems to be a link to education: the Kenyan research found that only 15% of women without formal education use contraception, in contrast to 45% of those with at least some secondary education. The figure for women without formal education, however, is as interesting as the other, because in previous fertility studies, the figure for such women was much lower. This suggests that even uneducated women are becoming more inclined to use contraceptives, maybe because they (and their spouses?) realize that having many children in dire economic circumstances is associated with costs that they cannot meet. In short, it is not only in the upper social and economic echelons that fertility behavior is likely to take place; the most dramatic change may well be at the very bottom among those whom we often find hardest to reach.

There is reason to look at this type of data side by side with the more pessimistic forecasts that tend to prevail in the public media. The demographic momentum towards "replacement level" also appears to be accelerating in recent years in places for which no such predictions existed just a few years ago. This is not to ignore the possibility that there will still be too many people in relation to available resources. The International Labor Organization reports that fully 30% of the world's labor force does not earn enough to rise above the poverty line. The International Food Policy Research Institute draws attention to the failure in recent years to expand investment in agricultural research, something that may show up in production shortfalls in ten to 20 years. These are real concerns that must be assessed in conjunction with any discussion of population growth, but there is no reason to view only the perils. As one analyst of our ethical predicament has noted: "whoever inspects the social record of our species on planet Earth confronts a medley of contrasts and contradictions, inextricably intertwined – of good and evil, wisdom and folly, compassion and cruelty" (Lipson 1993:11). As he implies, the discrepancy between promise and practice is a cause for social action. The qualifier I offer here is that if that discrepancy generates too much pessimism it may paralyze mind and energy. The good news is important too, particularly in the present when doomsday prophets easily get an audience.

Foreign Aid

Transfer of resources from the rich to the poor countries is an important dimension of any effort to reduce global economic inequities and, more specifically, to pave the way for a significant reduction in global hunger. On this front, the last five years have brought both good news and bad news. The bad news is that an increasing number of countries has fallen further behind the OECD goal of 0.7% of GNP as the target for foreign aid among its member countries. The average for these countries in 1992 was less than half of that – 0.34%.

There are significant, and growing, differences, however, among the industrialized countries. The gap between the more generous donors – the three Scandinavian countries – and the rest has widened in recent years. While they continue to give a full 1% of GNP or a little more, the share of the other countries has declined. The result is that in 1992 Scandinavians gave twice as much aid per person as the French, Germans, or Canadians, three times as much as the Japanese, four times as much as the Italians, five times as much as the British, and six times as much as the Americans. As suggested in Table 1, if all countries were to reach the target aid figure of 0.7% of GNP, an additional US $67 billion a year would be made available – more than enough not only to overcome half the world's hunger but also to make a serious dent in the bulging poverty problem.

A few clarifications may be necessary to ensure that too much is not read into these figures. Countries vary in terms of what they define as official development assistance. For instance, security assistance (like what the US gives to a few countries in the Middle East) may be included together with economic or development assistance. Another important clarification is that the figures above do not cover the increasing amounts of money donated by nongovernmental organizations. This type of contribution is particularly significant in the case of the US. These points notwithstanding, the general message of the above table is clear when it comes to actual aid flows: they fall far short of agreed targets, and the gap seems to be growing.

It is against this background that the right column of the table offers a glimmer of hope. Opinion polls conducted in European countries in the early 1990s – at a time of economic recession – show that a significant majority of voters are in favor of increasing aid levels. Survey results from other countries, notably Japan, Canada, Sweden, and the US are not comparable, as respondents were also asked if they supported *maintaining* or increasing aid levels. In Japan, over 80% answered "yes" to this question. In Sweden, 53% were in favor: a noticeable decline from polls conducted in the 1980s. In Canada, over 50% approved of maintaining or increasing aid.

Surveys in the US tell a different and less upbeat story. Only 43% want the US to supply aid at all. What is particularly distressing is that support is weakest among young Americans: only 34% of those under 30 years of age approve of economic assistance.

These figures indicate essentially three things of significance for the task of overcoming hunger in the 1990s. Plagued by growing budget deficits, most governments are likely to treat foreign aid as an expendable item. The figures also confirm that the political will to protect foreign aid varies from government to government, thus providing a measure of shame that can be used by concerned groups to argue their case for more foreign aid. Finally, the poll figures do suggest that large numbers of people in many industrialized countries wish to see the levels of foreign aid at least maintained, in many cases increased.

Table 3.1. The Aid Gap

Country	Aid as % of GNP 1992	Total aid ($billions) 1992		Aid per person ($) 1992			% in favor of increasing aid 1991
		Actual	Total if 0.7% of GNP	Actual	Total if 0.7% of GNP	Diff'rence	
Norway	1.11	1.2	-	288	180	+108	63
Sweden	1.05	2.5	-	270	189	+81	-
Denmark	1.04	1.4	-	250	182	+68	80
Netherlands	0.88	2.7	-	167	144	+23	75
France	0.61	7.8	8.9	132	157	-25	60
Finland	0.55	0.6	0.8	141	163	-22	-
Switzerland	0.46	1.1	1.7	160	256	-96	-
Canada	0.44	2.5	3.9	96	145	-49	-
Portugal	0.41	0.3	0.5	25	52	-27	75
Belgium	0.40	0.8	1.5	79	147	-68	53
Germany	0.38	7.0	13.0	109	161	-52	67
Italy	0.35	4.1	8.3	68	144	-76	69
Australia	0.32	1.0	2.1	58	119	-61	-
Japan	0.32	11.1	24.6	83	197	-114	-
U.K.	0.31	3.1	7.2	54	124	-70	70
Austria	0.30	0.5	1.2	64	157	-93	-
Spain	0.28	1.5	3.8	36	98	-62	78
New Zealand	0.24	0.1	0.3	30	83	-53	-
U.S.A.	0.18	10.8	41.3	45	162	-117	-
Ireland	0.16	0.1	0.3	18	86	-68	69

Sources: Aid: OECD, *Development Cooperation*; GNP: *World Bank Atlas 1994*; Public opinion polls: *Eurobarometer No 36* and Norwegian Social Science Data Service, September 1991.

Global Trade

Some analysts, who believe that foreign aid is neither cost-effective nor helpful to its potential beneficiaries because it tends to encourage a sense of dependency, argue that the best way to reduce the gap between rich and poor countries is to increase global trade by liberalizing it. In that spirit, government representatives from around the world completed the eight-year-old Uruguay Round of trade talks in 1994 by signing a joint protocol in Marrakech in Morocco. The agreement has cut tariffs and for the first time brought trade in agriculture and services under the

GATT regime. This agreement has been heralded by many as a victory for everybody, although it is clear that a freer global trade regime also has its strong opponents and has differential consequences for individual regions and countries around the world.

Looking first at the anticipated effects of the latest GATT agreement, figures available from the World Bank and OECD paint a rather disturbing picture of clear winners and losers. The following projections to year 2002 suggest that the new trade regime is likely to exacerbate rather than reduce the economic gap between rich and poor countries.

Table 3.2. GATT Winners and Losers
(Projected Net Annual Losses or Gains)

Region/country	Gain/loss
European Community	plus US$ 80.7 billion
China	plus US$ 37.0 billion
United States	plus US$ 18.8 billion
Latin America	plus US$ 8.1 billion
E. Europe + Former USSR	plus US$ 2.2 billion
Gulf/Mexico	plus US$ 1.5 billion
Africa	minus US$ 2.6 billion

Source: *Africa Recovery*, Dec. 1993/March 1994: 9.

The scenarios worked out by the World Bank and the OECD of the likely consequences of the Uruguay Round show African export revenues declining as liberalized world trade erodes existing tariff preferences for Africa. Most of Africa's countries are net food importers, and they will also be hit by anticipated higher world food prices brought on by cuts in agricultural subsidies in developed countries. The overall effect is that African countries will suffer a further deterioration of their balance of payments situation and worsening of their debt servicing problems unless measures are taken to offset the projected losses. Both the Bank and the OECD have recommended compensatory transfers, financing, or access to markets but, given current preoccupations with their own balance of payments or budget deficits, industrialized countries may be reluctant to take on such extra financial burdens. African countries are also under pressure from other sources. For example, the Latin American countries have in the past few years complained to GATT that their access to the European market is hampered by preferences contained in the Lomé Convention, meant to regulate access to the European market for commodities coming out of the African, Caribbean, and Pacific regions. The original dispute focused on access for Latin American bananas, but the complaint was subsequently broadened, and GATT has now ruled that Lomé preferences generally contravene free trade conventions.

The predicament of the poorer countries is exacerbated by their lack of power to bargain for a better deal. In the increasingly competitive global environment, developing countries now compete for access to markets and scarce foreign capital, leading to the fragmentation of their coalitions, such as the G-77 Group, which in the past gave them bargaining capabilities in international fora. The low-income countries, in particular, have no choice but to abide with the new economic and political conventions. In this respect, they have dramatically changed their attitude to the external world. As one economist observer recently noted, they no longer adhere to the dictum, associated with the dependency approach, that "integration into the world economy leads to disintegration of the national economy" (Bhagwati, 1994:21). In fact, many leaders of developing countries see more positive effects with global integration today than do leaders of the industrialized countries. In this respect, the world in the mid-1990s has moved 180 degrees from where it was a quarter-century ago. It is not clear that the present situation will necessarily facilitate the achievement of social-development objectives on a global scale.

Political Changes

The five years since the Bellagio Declaration was adopted have bristled with political changes. Existing structures at both national and international levels have experienced difficulties in adjusting to the new political realities. The most obvious change is the collapse of Communism and the end of the bipolar world order, the effect of which, among other things, has been a further decline in the bargaining capabilities of developing countries in the global arena. In the past, it was possible for poor nations to play one superpower against another as a means of gaining resources. The changes of the past five years have not made it any easier for developing countries to gain ground.

In this section I intend to discuss four aspects of the new political situation that are of relevance to the task of overcoming hunger in the 1990s: 1) democratization; 2) political conditionalities; 3) declining state sovereignty; and 4) ethnic and religious aspirations.

Democratization

The recent expansion of democracy, what Huntington (1991) has called "the third wave," began in the mid-1970s in southern Europe and continued in the 1980s in Latin America and Asia. In the 1990s the process has intensified, as countries in Eastern Europe, the former Soviet Union, and Africa have joined the ranks of those attempting to democratize. The participants at Bellagio in 1989 could only sense the beginning of this transformation. Few would have suggested that by of the end of 1993 no less than 107 out of 186 countries would have introduced competitive elections and various guarantees of political and individual rights – that is more than twice the number two decades earlier (*Freedom Review* 1993:3-4, 10). Democracy is weakest in Islamic countries and in parts of Africa, although more than 30 on that continent are now in the process of transition from an authoritarian civilian or military government to one that is more pluralistic.

The move towards democracy is not a simple one; it would be premature to draw far-reaching conclusions from the evidence available at this stage. Reversals like those in Burma and Nigeria are likely to occur elsewhere. All the same, the probability of a widespread return to authoritarianism is relatively small, at least in the time period we are considering here. Two aspects of the move to democracy are particularly relevant.

The first is the greater transparency and public accountability that governments are being pushed to adopt in a competitive political setting. While democracy will not in itself eliminate corrupt behavior in official circles, it is likely to make such behavior more costly for the individual, and to that extent create an environment in which social justice and human rights are more easily defended. The rapid growth of privately owned media in many of these countries is particularly important in fostering checks on official behavior. These media are likely to provide the early warnings of crises, much as Amartya Sen (1981) suggested with reference to famines in India.

This greater openness is also likely to promote the growth of civil society, notably voluntary associations engaged in development work. The last five years have seen a tremendous expansion of NGOs both at the global and the national level. While there may be questions about the democratic character of some of these organizations, few observers question their potential contribution to poverty alleviation. To be sure, these organizations typically operate on a small scale, but more and more is being learned on how to spread their impact. A particularly interesting case is the community bank movement in Nigeria, where savings by individuals and local community or hometown associations are being matched by federal contributions. The advantages that the NGOs provide over government departments include their ability to tailor their programs to local needs and interact more closely with the prospective beneficiaries. In the current democratic environment these organizations can more easily be sustained and developed, and hence the voice of the people more effectively guaranteed an influence on matters that affect their lives.

Political Conditionalities

The 1980s were characterized by the growing importance of the International Monetary Fund and the World Bank in the management of national economies, especially in Africa and Latin America. Governments were asked to retreat from much of their direct involvement in economic activities and through a variety of liberalization measures "get the prices right". These policy recommendations were accompanied by a series of conditionalities. For example, new credit would be made available only if these governments demonstrated progress in adjusting their economies. The bite of the international finance institutions became much more effective as bilateral donors generally supported the new policies and also threatened suspension of aid if structural adjustment was not followed.

Since 1990 bilateral donors have decided to add a set of political conditionalities. Believing that respect for human rights and practice of multi-party democracy are good for development, these donors have made it clear that grants or loans will not be issued afresh unless recipient governments change their political behavior in a democratic direction. For example, the Kenya Government was faced with a suspension of foreign aid in 1991 because President Moi rejected the idea of such political reforms. Following a meeting with the donors in Paris, he had to give in to their demands. Kenya could not afford a suspension of foreign aid. In 1993 the same donors made it clear to the President of Zambia that his country could not count on further assistance unless he got rid of three cabinet ministers who were documented drug smugglers.

This new demand to "get politics right" has bolstered the aspirations of the political opposition in countries undergoing transition from authoritarian to democratic rule. The latter have generally welcomed the tougher stand taken by the donors. In those countries where the parliament still remains weak, however, the tendency for key decisions to be made in Paris (under the auspices of OECD's "Paris Club") has also made many people in these countries rather cynical about the role of their own legislature. The Paris Club is referred to in many African countries as a "second parliament."

Controversy still surrounds the issue of whether democracy and political freedom are necessary or good for development. The statistical correlation between levels of economic growth and political democracy has been known at least since the days of Lipset's (1960) seminal work, *Political Man*. Debates, however, have raged over whether economic growth comes before democracy or vice versa. In the last five years, the question has earned increased relevance because of the alternative routes out of Communism adopted by, on the one hand, China and Vietnam, and, on the other, the former Soviet Union and its Eastern European satellites. Governments of the former two have opted for economic liberalization first, holding back on granting political freedoms to their citizens. In this respect, they have followed a pattern adopted by other non-Communist East Asian countries, notably South Korea and Taiwan. Governments of the latter group, however, allowed political freedoms to precede (or coincide with) economic reforms. Looking at the economic records of the first group, there is a tendency to conclude that political freedom and democracy are not necessary for development.

Leaving alone the question whether economic liberalization and an ensuing rapid economic growth undermine the basis for authoritarian rule – a question that most observers answer in the affirmative – the debate has recently taken a new twist with the issuing of a four-year study of the relationship between political freedom and economic growth by Surjit Bhalla (1994) using data from 90 countries for 1973-1990. He concludes from his carefully crafted research that the impact not only of economic but also of *political* freedom on economic growth is robust.[1] After controlling for three educational attainment variables, the variables pertaining to political and economic freedom are positively, and significantly, associated with improvements in economic welfare (measured in terms of three income and two social variables). This is the most extensive study to date that confirms that getting both policies and politics right facilitates economic and social development. As Bhalla (1994:51) concludes:

> *The right policies can be defined* ex ante *– economic policies which allow the maximum freedom to individuals. As a shortcut, such policies should insure that domestic tradeable prices are close to international tradeable prices, investors should be allowed freedom, and exchange rates should be allowed to move freely. The right political policies are the ones that provide the maximum freedom to individuals. The shortcut to this goal is the provision of a free press and a 'free-wheeling' democracy. In conclusion, free markets, and free societies, are the important ingredients to rapid economic development.*

This may not be the last installment in this debate, but it is a good indication of where the winds are blowing these days, not only in policy circles but also among academics around the world.

Declining State Sovereignty

The growing significance of political conditionalities in foreign aid is only one sign of the decline in state sovereignty that has become increasingly apparent in the past five years. The principle of state sovereignty dates back to the Peace Treaty of Westphalia in 1648, and has been the fundament of international law ever since. The Wilsonian principle of national self-determination that became so important in this century has helped pave the way for people under colonial tutelage to create new states, but it has not really been used in other contexts to effectively challenge the notion of states as sovereign entities with the legitimate right to handle all domestic affairs at their own discretion. The United Nations Charter clearly identifies it as an association of independent sovereign states.

Even though state sovereignty remains the dominant principle, its exclusivity can no longer be taken for granted, as in the past. One reason for this is that the end of the Cold War, and thus the disappearance of a bipolar power structure, means that the weaker states have fewer means of resisting the will of the mighty. Another reason is the growing global interdependence in a number of fields, such as technology, finance, migration, and communications, which has encouraged the influence of non-state actors. The financial stability of a nation-state is being challenged, for example, by the international money markets which move approximately one trillion US dollars every day, of which only a small fraction has anything to do with productive investments (Childers and Urquhart, 1994:16). Yet another reason is the growing inability of many states to protect their own citizens. In the more extreme cases, such as Bosnia-Herzegovina, Liberia, Rwanda, and Somalia, government authority has virtually collapsed. In other places, Haiti, for example, the concept of state sovereignty is being challenged because of violations of democratic and human rights by those who unilaterally seized power in 1992.

These circumstances have led to a debate about where rights and obligations of states start and end. While controversy still rages over the right of the international community to intervene in the affairs of an independent state, certain things are becoming clearer. The time of absolute and exclusive sovereignty has passed. Individual governments can no longer get away with breaches of universally adopted declarations about human rights, governance, and peace in the way that happened in the past. As the U.N. Secretary General argues in his *Agenda for Peace* (Boutros-Ghali, 1992:paragraph 17): "It is the task of leaders of States today to … find a balance between the needs of good internal governance and the requirements of an ever more interdependent world".

If the pattern of the early 1990s is any guide, the United Nations has increasingly come to play an active role in situations that earlier would have been left to regional organizations to deal with (Gottlieb, 1993:108). In Central America the UN acted to end the civil war in El Salvador in an area that had traditionally been the exclusive preserve of the Organization of American States (OAS). The Arab League was unable to respond to the Iraqi aggression against Kuwait, and King Hussein's appeal to allow the Arab states to deal with the crisis went unheeded. Again, it was the UN rather than the Organization of African Unity (OAU) that brought the conflict in Namibia to an end and was called upon to intervene when authority crumbled in Somalia and Rwanda.

The third thing that seems to stand out from the experience of the early 1990s is that there is a growing requirement to employ military might to help quell ethnic violence, create humanitarian space, and protect fundamental human rights (Weiss, 1995). Realization of this objective, however, has been fraught with political, financial, and logistical difficulties. UN peace-keeping efforts in recent years have been hampered by lack of timeliness, robustness, and consistency. The governments of the richer nations are reluctant to make commitments to peace-keeping efforts, and poignant media coverage usually elicits only halfway measures. In addition, the command and control system within the UN system has serious problems. The capacity to plan, support, and command peace-keeping is no greater now than it was during the Cold War, in spite of a dramatically increased demand. The inability of the UN to develop and strengthen its military professionalism leaves a serious gap at a time when the demand for peace-keeping and peace-enforcing missions is on the increase.

Ethnic and Religious Aspirations

Another significant change in the past five years has been the global resurgence of ethnic and religious aspirations. This manifests itself in many different ways. One is the "new" nationalism that is thriving in the wake of the breakup of the Soviet empire. No less than 15 new states have emerged in that region since 1990. Another manifestation is the growth of ethnicity or regionalism as catalyst for new political parties. This phenomenon is evident not only in Africa and Asia but also in Europe, notably in Italy and Spain. Even redistricting, that is, changing the boundaries of electoral constituencies, in the US to accommodate specific ethnic groups is a response in recent years to the same concern.

In the religious realm the new aspirations are no weaker. They appear as a more general resurgence of interest in religious issues even in societies that have for quite a few generations been predominantly secular. Faith in religious deities at the end of the second millennium is certainly not in decline. This is particularly obvious in those circles where religious resurgence has been turned into a fundamentalist revival. The latter is most evident in two of the major monotheistic religions, Christianity and Islam but, interestingly enough, has also occurred, albeit in a different form, in polytheistic Hinduism. Although the fundamentalist strand is by no means new to either Christianity or Islam, it has continued to grow strong in many countries. Christian evangelism in Central America is one case in point, the spread of Islamic fundamentalism to Algeria, Egypt, and the Sudan in recent years another.

These new aspirations have many explanations. More generally, however, they are associated with three phenomena of our time. The new religious ferment is often a response to the hegemony of science and technology during much of this century. Seen by many in the past as the prime driving force behind development, science and technology have often preempted other values in public policy. This has had two types of effects. In industrialized societies, the reaction has been that science and technology have been taken too far. The answers to the problems of our time do not lie in their blind use to foster economic growth. Although some people have responded to this issue by focusing their concern on the environment, they share the same "post-materialist" orientation (Inglehart, 1991) as found among the Christian right where people are agitated over the issue of abortion.

The notion that science and technology have been taken too far is shared also in other circles, notably among Muslims, as the recent population conference in Cairo has indicated. The principal reaction to the hegemony of science and technology in developing countries, however, is that not enough has been achieved. The secular, positivist, and materialist orientation that was given special impetus in those places by the modernization efforts in the past 50 years has not paid expected dividends. Although food security may have improved on an aggregate national or global scale, large numbers of rural and urban households in developing countries experience investments made by governments and private corporations as either inadequate or inappropriate. They feel let down by the promise of science. It is only understandable that many of them turn to something more proximate and intimate: their God.

A second feature of our time is the global spread of the notion that the market economy provides the answer to present developmental challenges. While no doubt many individuals around the world respond to this with confidence and seize the new opportunities it opens up for self-improvement, others – and they may be the majority – experience this situation as threatening. It increases the uncertainty surrounding their livelihood and they sense the world is becoming increasingly callous. In this situation, it is very likely that people seek comfort and strength among those who are close and familiar. This may be one's own kith and kin, members of the same ethnic group, or fellows of the same religious denomination.

The significance of the ethnic and religious aspirations, however, can only be fully understood if we also consider a third feature of our time: the move to democracy. Without wishing to suggest that authoritarian regimes are immune to ethnic or religious conflicts – see for example the cases of Iraq and Syria – it must be recognized that democratization is associated not only with promise but also with peril, particularly in culturally plural societies. The essence of democracy is the readiness of political leaders to accept electoral defeat, and that does not always come easily. They are understandably inclined to maximize their chances of being returned to office. A shortcut that they usually adopt to ensure victory is to create and manipulate social categories, such as ethnicity and religion, with which people can easily associate. This tendency has been an almost integral part of the politics of democratization. Religious and ethnic sentiments that were previously dormant are being whipped up to serve elite aspirations. In many countries this politicization of ethnic and religious identities has been possible to contain, but in many others it has caused civil violence or even civil war. Several of the so-called food wars that Ellen Messer (1994:43-70) discusses in the *1993 Hunger Report* are the consequence of manipulation of ethnic or religious identities for political ends. In the mid-1990s, the growing ethnic and religious aspirations clearly constitute a challenge to which neither the old nation-state nor the international community has yet found an adequate way of responding in a constructive fashion.

Conclusions

Do the changed conditions since 1989 make our task of overcoming hunger in the 1990s easier or more difficult? The assessment I have tried in this paper suggests a mixture of positive and negative factors, none of which can necessarily be given a particular weight. Even if we accept that, on balance, circumstances are more difficult, it would be wrong to accept the almost apocalyptic perspective of Robert Kaplan (1994), who argues that we are heading towards a global anarchy characterized by tidal flows of refugees, armed bands of stateless marauders, and wars over scarce resources. Nor is there anything inevitable in Huntington's (1993) argument that the next wars will be fought between civilizations, not nation-states. To the extent that these arguments imply that the Middle Ages are coming back to haunt us, they are wrong.

Kaplan may still have a role to play as a Jeremiah warning us about something that is not explicit in his article but which is nevertheless possible to deduce from his analysis: an ethical crisis. The failures that this paper has recorded, and many others that could be listed, are not, foremost, the consequence of lack of technical and financial means, but instead of what Lipton (1993:283) calls an "ethical meltdown." Such a crisis arises when one value is being advanced at the expense of others that are important to human beings. There are at least two dimensions of such a meltdown that should concern us as we deliberate on what to do next to realize the objectives of the Bellagio Declaration.

The first concern is the recognition that a people emerges into prominence by utilizing some talent, or developing some trait, in which it excels, but that later it declines if the same advantage is pushed to harmful excess. Individualism is a case in point. It was the emphasis on the enterprise and initiative of individuals that unleashed the energies of people in countries that are now developed; the US, with its immigrant population, is the best illustration of this scenario. But when overemphasized at the expense of countervailing values, individualism produces negative outcomes. It leads to excessive selfishness, to disregard for others, and to a lack of concern for the public good. Such one-sided individualism may have already have reached its peak but it is still contained in a chorus of well-orchestrated voices on the global scene intoning the litany that private activity is invariably superior to public, that government is the source of society's problems, not the solution, that each individual should make and take whatever the opportunities allow. Even if many people around the world display cynicism and alienation towards public authority, the answer does not lie in a crude form of individualism. Such an approach is a shortcut to a self-inflicted decline, to the kind of global anarchy that Kaplan speaks of.

The second dimension is our inclination to prioritize means over ends, facts over values. Those scientists who claim to absolve themselves from the ethical consequences of their discoveries, those economists who maintain that production for profit is independent of morality, those students of politics who restrict themselves to the phenomenon of power, the types of techniques, and the behavior of systems of government – all these condone what is socially pernicious by their vows of abstinence from the knowledge of good and evil. The peak of this orientation may already have been reached, but it still has a hold on many scientists, including those who work on issues that affect the lives of people. Even here values need to be balanced. Thought by itself moves nothing, as Aristotle, a rationalist philosopher, noted long ago.

No one wants to underestimate the complexity of the task of overcoming hunger. It does require work on many fronts. But if we are concerned with expanding the outer boundaries of our mission, the lessons that we can learn from the past five years point as much in the direction of human ethics as anywhere else. To engage people's imagination on the side of higher ethical values may well be the prime task of the next five years. To close the horrendous gap that separates the majority from the minority in terms of standard of living and quality of life requires not only capital and knowledge. It requires a normative reorientation that fosters a tolerance of diversity, both in matters of belief and in patterns of culture, that trains children to grow up to be more altruistic and less self-serving, and that treats every individual with equal consideration for his or her dignity as a human being. We do not have to miss the appointment that 1989 provided us with, but as Lord Acton once said: "All it takes for evil to triumph is that good men do nothing."

62   Goran Hyden

Notes

1. The paper by Bhalla was also the subject of a recent article in *The Economist* (August 27-September 2, 1994) titled "Democracy works best".

References

Achebe, C., G. Hyden, C. Magadza and A. Pala Okeyo (1990) *Beyond Hunger in Africa*. Nairobi: Heinemann Kenya.

Bhagwati, J. (1994) *Democracy and Globalization*. Uppsala, Sweden: Paper presented at the Nobel Symposium on "Democracy's Victory and Crisis", August 27-30.

Bhalla, S. S.(1994) *Freedom and Economic Growth: A Virtuous Circle?* Uppsala, Sweden: Paper presented at the Nobel Symposium on "Democracy's Victory and Crisis", August 27-30.

Boutros Ghali (1992) *An Agenda For Peace*. Report of the Secretary General. New York: United Nations.

Childers, E. and B. Urquhart (1994) *Renewing the United Nations System*. Uppsala: Dag Hammarskjold Foundation.

Freedom Review (1993) Freedom Around the World. *Freedom Review*, 24, 1 (Special Issue): 3-67.

Gottlieb, G. (1993) *Nation Against State: A New Approach to Ethnic Conflicts and the Decline of Sovereignty*. New York: Council on Foreign Relations.

Huntington, S. P. (1991) *The Third Wave: Democratization in the Late Twentieth Century*. Norman: University of Oklahoma

Huntington, S. P. (1993) "The Clash of Civilizations?" *Foreign Affairs*, 72, 3 (Summer): 22-49.

Inglehart, R. (1991) *Culture Shift*. Princeton: Princeton University Press.

Kaplan, R. D. (1994) The Coming Anarchy. *Atlantic Monthly*, 273, 2 (February): 44-76.

Lipset, S. M. (1960) *Political Man*. New York: Doubleday.

Lipson, L. (1993) *The Ethical Crises of Civilization: Moral Meltdown or Advance?* Newbury Park CA: Sage Publications.

Messer, E. (1994) Food Wars: Hunger as a Weapon of War in 1993. in Uvin, P. (ed.) *The Hunger Report: 1993*. Yverdon, Switzerland: Gordon and Breach Science Publishers.

National Council of Population and Development (1994) *Kenya Demographic and Health Survey 1993*. Nairobi: Government Printer.

Population Council (1994) *The Determinants of Reproductive Change in Bangladesh: Success in a Challenging Environment*. New York: The Population Council.

Sen, A. (1981) *Poverty and Famine: An Essay on Entitlement and Deprivation*. Oxford: Oxford University Press.

Trevelyan, G. M. (1922) *British History in the Ninenteenth Century*. New York: Longman's Green.

Weiss, T.G. (1995) On the Brink of a New Era? Humanitarian Interventions, 1991-94. in Daniel, D. C.F and Hayes, B.C. (eds.) *Beyond Traditional Peacekeeping*. London: Macmillan.

World Bank (1992) *World Development Report*. Washington DC: The World Bank.

CHAPTER 4

The Human Right To Food (1989-1994)

Ellen Messer

The year 1994 began with a demand from Zapatista rebels in Chiapas, Mexico for land, livelihood, adequate food and access to health care and education, expressed in terms of the basic human right to subsistence. This uprising of indigenous Maya indicates how far the concept of "human rights" now permeates grassroots consciousness and politics. In the five years since the *Bellagio Declaration: Overcoming Hunger in the 1990s* (1989) there has also been substantial advocacy at the summit for the human right to food (Table 1), and in some cases measurable goals have been set.

> *Bearing in mind the right to an adequate standard of living, including food, contained in the Universal Declaration of Human Rights, we pledge to act in solidarity to ensure that the freedom from hunger becomes a reality* (International Conference on Nutrition (ICN) World Declaration on Nutrition 1992, para.1).

> *The World Conference on Human Rights calls upon States to refrain from any unilateral measure not in accordance with international law and the Charter of the United Nations that creates obstacles to trade relations among States and impedes the full realization of the human rights set forth in the Universal Declaration of Human Rights and international human rights instruments, in particular the rights of everyone to a standard of living adequate for their health and well-being, including food and medical care, housing, and the necessary social services. The World Conference on Human Rights affirms that food should not be used as a tool for political pressure.* (World Conference on Human Rights (WCHR), Vienna, 1993, para. 31, The Vienna Declaration and Programme of Action).

Table 4.1. International Conferences, 1989-1994, Containing References to the Human Right to Food

1989	Bellagio Declaration: Overcoming Hunger in the 1990s
1989	Convention on the Rights of the Child
1990	World Summit for Children
1991	UNICEF/WHO Conference on Ending Hidden Hunger (Micronutrient Malnutrition)
1992	International Conference on Nutrition (ICN, 1992)
1992	UN Conference on Environment and Development (1992)
1993	World Conference on Human Rights (WCHR, 1993)
1994	International Conference on Population and Development

Academic researchers and advocates have been advancing:

> ...an analytical framework for food security and its expansion into "nutrition security" which can form a basis for translating food and nutrition development goals into rights and obligations as they are embedded in international legal instruments (Oshaug, Eide, and Eide 1994:491).

New nongovernmental organizations (NGOs) have been mobilizing around advocacy for human rights, nutrition, and development:

> The purpose of the World Alliance for Nutrition and Human Rights [WANAHR] is to improve nutrition, food, health, and care, using a human rights approach. Compared with current efforts this will provide stronger ethical as well as legal basis for actions to reduce malnutrition... (WANAHR, 1994:2).

The right to subsistence constitutes an essential human right in all societies[1] and "freedom from want," construed as adequate food and nutrition, provides a cornerstone of the United Nations [UN] human rights framework that defines the individual's right to life vis-a-vis state government. Progress and backsliding have been chronicled in Uvin's "State of World Hunger" and other chapters in this volume. The sections below examine what difference the international enunciation of human rights makes as a reference point for policies and actions against hunger. The analysis draws on a legal-political/economic-sociocultural framework developed for analytical and teaching purposes in an "Advanced Seminar on Special Topics in World Hunger: Human Rights to Food and Freedom From Hunger" (Messer, 1992).

Food and Nutrition Rights Within the UN Human Rights Framework

For fifty years the legal and political concept of human rights has been evolving as a set of universal norms for states and the international community. The rights established in international agreements are broad and general standards, given concrete meaning and made enforceable through clarification and implementation in their country-specific legal systems.

UN Legal Framework

Paragraph 25 of the Universal Declaration of Human Rights (1948), whose content is reflected in the opening citations of this paper, declares:

> ...everyone has the right to a standard of living adequate for the health and well-being of himself and his family, including food...

The Covenant on Economic, Social, and Cultural Rights (1966) adds:

> ...State Parties to the present Covenant [on Economic, Social, and Cultural Rights] recogniz[e] the fundamental right of everyone to be free from hunger... (art. 11)

and obligates signatories "...to take steps to the maximum of...available resources, with a view to achieving progressively the full realization of the rights recognized" in the Covenant.[2]

Approximately 200 additional UN instruments address the right to adequate food and nutrition within *civil-political, economic-social-cultural, development,* and *indigenous* rights constructions. Although food is considered predominantly an economic right, linked also to rights to land, work (just wages), health, a clean environment, and a just economic order, a decent standard of living depends also on personal security, fulfillment of civil-political rights, freedom from violence, and "freedom from fear" (see e.g., Eide, 1989). Country case studies such as Guatemala and South Africa increasingly illustrate that those denied civil liberties suffer disproportionately from social injustices, including hunger-related diseases and mortality (Heggenhoughen, 1995); and the significance of freedom of speech, free press, and freedom of assembly for the protection of economic rights, including the right not to starve, has been amply illustrated for India and certain African nations (Dreze and Sen, 1989; Howard, 1986).

The human right to food is also indispensable for human development, and itself a development right (UN Declaration on the Right to Development, 1987); access to clean water, protection of a sustainable environment, a just and peaceful world order, and freedom from extreme want are dimensions of "development" or "solidarity" rights formulated and advocated by Third World political leaders that illustrate the interdependence of economic-social-cultural and civil-political rights (e.g., Tomasevski, 1989; 1993; Okoth-Ogendo, 1993).

The human right to food also is considered within the domain of indigenous and collective rights, especially the cultural group's or community's rights to land, water, and natural or economic resources sufficient to feed group members and keep them from extreme want (Messer, 1993). The individual's right to food also is coupled with humanitarian and refugee law; all three legal frameworks provide a rationale for moving food into zones of armed conflict where individual noncombatants may be starving (Tomasevski, 1994). Programs of UN agencies, including those in food and nutrition and technical assistance, increasingly invoke this pluralistic understanding of human rights in undertaking their activities (e.g., Eide et al., 1984; ICN, 1992; Grant, 1994).

State Legal Frameworks

Despite international proclamations and actions, few state constitutions guarantee individuals the right to food;[3] and those states that champion a "right to subsistence", such as China[4] and certain African states (Howard, 1986), often exclude interdependent and complementary political rights and civil liberties that give the hungry voice and redress in states such as India or the US, which does not recognize a legal right to subsistence or the general economic-social-cultural rights category (Alston, 1990). Developing countries in general advocate subsistence rights, and when criticized by the US and other Western nations for poor human rights records in turn criticize them for not meeting the subsistence needs of all their own citizens. In either case, state legislation promoting agricultural production, environmental protection, just wages, fair food prices, and social security programs, especially universal access to health care and education, advances fulfillment of the right. State-level legal instruments also provide for both emergency and on-going nutrition measures, monitoring nutrition conditions and setting in place food security warning systems that respond to conditions of extreme food insecurity due to environment, poverty, or deprivation.

Insuring adequate micronutrient nutrition (see Ralte, this volume, for a discussion of the case of iodine deficiency) is an additional way states respond to nutritional inadequacies with legislation and regulation of the private sector (e.g., the iodization of salt or vitamin A fortification of basic foods) to ensure populations a basic right to adequate nutrition and health. Efforts move from assessment of nutritional needs, to claims, to rights, to law, and finally to practice.[5]

The effectiveness of partnerships with and regulation of the private sector for programs such as iodization of salt, vitamin-A fortification of selected commodities, and production of low-cost, nutritionally-balanced children's biscuits and beverages, depends on adherence to codes by the food-processors and marketers and on nutritionally favorable consumption patterns by the general public.

UN Monitoring Mechanisms

To measure achievement, the UN Committee on Economic, Social, and Cultural Rights, established in 1987, is charged with clarifying states' obligations, monitoring their progress, hearing complaints of violations, and trying to bring about changes to rectify abuses. Member states that have signed the Covenant document their adherence by reporting evidence of nutritional status in their countries (a general measure of realization of the right to food in the country), indicating supporting legislation (e.g., food subsidies, primary health care, and infant feeding programs), and describing the measures necessary to implement the right to food with regard to "vulnerable groups" such as children, women, or other social classes subject to discrimination. UNICEF and the member states have launched a diagnostic, planning, implementation, and evaluation process to meet the end-of-decade goals of the World Summit for Children, which provides an illustration of how "achieving progressively the full realization" of the human right to food might proceed (see chapter by Mason et al., this volume). Through changes in reporting mechanisms, and the strategic assistance of NGOs (such as FIAN, the Food First Information and Action Network), individuals and collectivities can now raise complaints of violations of economic and social rights, including the right to food, before the Committee.

Academic and NGO Advocacy

Academic and NGO advocates, mobilizing around goals for nutrition, development, and human rights (e.g., FIAN, 1994 a,b; WANAHR, 1994), have assisted the clarification and monitoring process through a series of conferences and publications (Eide et al., 1984; Alston and Tomasevski, 1984) that go "beyond misery research" and analyses of political-economic exploitation to consider hunger as a violation of human rights and ending hunger as a political obligation of states and the international community. Locating the causes of hunger in socioeconomic structures that discriminate against the poor, participants begin to build the case for human rights against economic-growth policies that fail to respect and protect the land and life-sustaining resources of poor people, structural adjustment policies that eliminate vital food subsidies, and political-economic policies that further marginalize pastoralists or smallholders. Tomasevski (1987) reviews the UN legal discourse relevant to nutrition. Additional studies further clarify the legal and political "food and nutrition security matrix" of obligations and actions necessary to respect, protect, and fulfill the right to food at international, state, community, and household levels (Eide, 1989; Oshaug et al., 1992;[6] and Oshaug et al., 1994). In "Human Rights: a Normative Basis for Food and Nutrition-Relevant Policies" (Oshaug et al., 1994) the organizing question shifts from: "why take a human rights approach [in analyzing the causes of, and possible solutions for, hunger]?" (Eide et al., 1984) to "how can the international human rights system be an instrument in helping states to secure freedom from want for their inhabitants?" (Oshaug et al., 1994:492). The authors urge states to locate the rationale for food and nutrition policy goals in obligations to guarantee the human right to food.

Drawing on such analyses, FIAN, based in Heidelberg, Germany, provides "Guidelines for Parallel Reporting to the UN Committee on Economic, Social, and Cultural Rights" and undertakes "urgent actions" where land, labor, and other economic rights violations threaten "the right to feed onself" (FIAN, 1994a,b; see also Frente por el Derecho a la Alimentacion, 1994). FIAN's and other NGOs'activities[7] clarify where food rights are infringed, draw international and national attention to specific violations, seek to obtain pronouncements of the Committee on these breaches, and use the UN attention to create awareness and promote solutions within the country (FIAN, 1994a,b). In India, FIAN helped halt a Shrimp Project in Lake Chilika that would have dispossessed local fisherfolk (FIAN, 1994c) and in Kenya, protested state failure to protect the subsistence rights of tribal and pastoralist peoples chased from their territories (FIAN, 1994b).[8]

FIAN also works with national human rights organizations, e.g., the Mexican Front for the Right to Food, which, encouraged by FIAN information, reports abuses of malnutrition, unemployment, urban chaos, and associated reductions in public social security investments and programs, and demands that the human right to food be incorporated into the Mexican constitution and legally and politically implemented.[9] In the conflict-ridden regions such as Chiapas, FIAN and the Front work with the Zapatistas: protesting violations of food rights in the war zone, organizing collection and transfer of humanitarian food aid, and pressing for human rights (Frente por el Derecho a la Alimentacion, 1994).

The progress of the UN, NGO, and state support from rhetoric to actions can best be summarized by first, considering transformations in the three components of the human right to food: (1) rights and obligations; (2) what constitutes adequate food and nutrition; and (3) who is classified as a human being, a full member of society deserving food and rights; and second, considering changes from legal, political, and sociocultural perspectives.

The Human Right to Food

Rights and Obligations

Oshaug et al. (1992) summarize state obligations:

> ...to respect *the freedom of individuals and groups to solve their own problems,* ...to protect *them in their efforts, and*...to assist *and* fulfill *their rights when the individuals or groups concerned are unable by their own to secure the enjoyment of their rights* (Oshaug, Eide, and Eide, 1992:4, emphasis added on pp. 9-10);

Translated into practice, states have duties to *respect* individual and collective actions taken on behalf of meeting the minimum nutritional needs of individuals; e.g., people's rights to land and to the use of vital resources for food production and income; to *protect* individuals and groups against violations; e.g., against land or resource seizures, enslavement or demeaning, life-threatening wage rates or working conditions. States also have the obligation to *fulfill* the substance of rights where respect and protection prove insufficient; e.g., to provide special feeding and health care for needy young children and social security programs for the needy elderly. Entire populations suffer risk of starvation and destitution in cases of natural disasters or civil conflict and states have the obligation to be prepared, informed, and to intervene. Overall, states are obligated to provide a political-economic environment where individuals can fulfill their rights to food (see Oshaug et al., 1994).

States' failures to achieve this can be interpreted as a problem of clearly stated legal obligation or of political will. The Universal Declaration of Human Rights is not a binding legal obligation, states that have not signed the Economic-Social-Cultural Rights Covenant categorically reject any legal obligation, and even those that have signed interpret the obligations to be vague and subject to interpretation (i.e., available financial, material, and social resources). Most have yet to develop national legal frameworks surrounding food, and there are no international sanctions against states that "allow" malnutrition – only public censure and embarrassment.

Against this background, the only component of the human right to food on which there is widespread consensus is the right not to starve (e.g., ICN, 1992), for state obligations to prevent starvation are clearer than those to provide a political-economic order that allows self-fulfillment of the right to adequate nutrition: the technology exists to avert starvation; starvation today entails not only a failure of economic, but also political rights; and the historic Geneva Conventions lend additional humanitarian weight to interventions. Early warning systems for food shortage are well developed; states receive multiple lines of assistance to prevent famine. As witnessed in "Overcoming Hunger," the "Providence Principles," and other statements by humanitarian agencies, the international community agrees that there is a right to food for civilians in zones of armed conflict and intervenes (see Messer, Food Wars, this volume).[10]

However, consensus is still missing on state or international obligations in cases of malnutrition – mild or extreme – in war or in peacetime. Agreement is even more problematic on the right of every human being to be free from chronic hunger, which is usually associated less with war and more with poverty, ignorance, and milder forms of deprivation. Specific ways to measure whether the outcome of "adequate food" is being violated are not sufficiently clarified in international or national law to allow claims against a state or international intervention. One exception is the child's right to survival (nutrition and health), specified in the Convention on the Rights of the Child (1989) and the World Summit for Children (1990). These agreements, establishing end-of-decade goals for child survival, obligate signatory governments to monitor child nutrition problems and work toward their alleviation. In articles 24 and 27 of the Convention on the Rights of the Child (1989), states recognize that every child has a right to enjoy "the highest possible standard of health" and states obligate themselves to "diminish infant and child mortality" by reducing severe and moderate malnutrition by half, eliminating micronutrient deficiencies, and improving access to clean water and food. States also assume responsibility for disseminating nutrition education and encouraging breast-feeding. The child survival goals are also repeated in the ICN *World Declaration on Nutrition* (1992), which pledges to reduce malnutrition and to eliminate famine deaths, but sets no other measurable, achievable goals.

Nutritionally Adequate Food

Achieving the right to food via state fulfillment of obligations is also hampered by disagreements over what constitutes fulfillment. Notions of "adequate food" range from meeting minimum nutritional standards (defined as calories, protein, micronutrients) to ensuring a culturally acceptable diet. "Adequate food" also is variously defined at different social levels; concerns over the past twenty years have shifted from global to household food security as the goal of nutrition policy (ICN, 1992). A 1992 preparatory paper to the ICN defined "food adequacy" from the *supply* side as availability of sufficient quantities of the types of foods necessary to meet nutritional needs for energy and quality, and are also culturally acceptable and safe (free from toxins). The authors added that the supply must also be sustainable environmentally and socially. Food production and processing must not degrade the environment and access in one era not preclude social support networks to provide food later (Oshaug et al., 1992; see also Oshaug et al.'s 1994 "food and nutrition security matrix").[11]

The *consumption* side of "food adequacy" also has undergone change since 1989, from an emphasis mostly on calories (minimum acceptable intake up to 1.54 BMR, from 1.4 BMR) and nutrients (a new emphasis is on adequate micronutrient nutrition, especially iodine, vitamin A, and iron) to nutrition as "food, health, and care". Food and agriculture (including food safety and food trade) are important themes in the ICN; but so are breast-feeding, micronutrient nutrition, and nutrition monitoring; control of infectious diseases; nutrition planning and development policy. Women's rights to food as individual human beings are highlighted as well as their roles as food providers and nurturers of children, and nurturance ("care") at household and community levels, where individuals, such as female children, or whole social or ethnic-religious categories, may be left out of access to adequate food and health care.

Who is Human with Rights Respected, Protected, and Fulfilled?

No one is supposed to be denied adequate nutrition because of age or gender, or ethnic, religious, geographic, political, or tribal identity (ICN, 1992, para.15). Yet sociocultural factors continue to be significant causes of undernutrition, even where food supply may otherwise be sufficient at household, community, regional, or national levels. UNICEF, WHO, and NGOs, including WANAHR, place special emphasis on the nutritionally vulnerable group, children. The ICN (1992, para.13) also singles out women as deserving of basic human rights, including nutrition. More generally, the ICN developes the theme: "Caring for the socio-economically deprived and nutritionally vulnerable." Collectivities, especially indigenous communities, receive heightened attention; in the year 1992 the UN community marked UNCED, the ICN, and also 500 years of cross-hemispheric exchange and moved closer to an indigenous rights declaration. Indigenous and other cultural communities also frame demands for land, control over resources and development, and political autonomy in terms of food and human rights.

Additional populations "left out" of state respect, protection, and nutrition- and health-security programs are refugees and displaced persons, now numbering between 40 and 50 million. Other nutritionally deprived peoples include the economically marginalized, especially pastoralists, subsistence agriculturalists, and those dependent on single cash crops over which they have no market control. Members of ethnic and religious groups outside of (or antagonistic to) prevailing political state political authorities also suffer discrimination, even where states otherwise accept nutrition and human rights obligations. All of these nutritionally vulnerable groups need and, to a greater or lesser extent, receive special international attention as a result of their being singled out and excluded from rights by communities, regions, or states. They suggest opportunities to link food and nutrition rights to other human rights, including the rights of children, women, minorities and other cultural communities, and to build broader-based advocacy and action (Messer, 1994).

Politics and Progress in Nutrition Rights

An alternative assessment of progress on rights, nutrition, and inclusion in the category "human" can be made in legal, political, and sociocultural terms.

Legal Perspectives

Since 1989 there has been a rise in the acceptance of collective as well as indigenous rights; greater understanding of the interconnectedness among four so-called "generations" of rights: civil-political, economic-social-cultural, development, and indigenous; and pressure on governments by the UN Committee on Economic, Social, and Cultural Rights, IGOs, and NGOs to meet nutrition needs as basic human rights (e.g., Berting et al., 1990; Messer, 1993; WANAHR, 1994). More countries have signed the Covenant on Economic, Social, and Cultural Rights, obligating them to work toward improved nutrition. Additional Conventions and Summits have affirmed more specific obligations. And legal experts have been improving formulations to make nutrition monitoring and identification of violations clearer. Table 2 (see appendix) summarizes the 1994 status of signatories on the major relevant covenants and conventions; the Convention of the Rights of the Child being the most widely adopted.[12] Additionally, NGO institutions that address hunger, development, and human rights within a legal framework are growing.

Political Perspectives

Good nutrition is also increasingly "good politics" and nutrition advocates and agencies, especially UNICEF, have advanced a politics of constructive embarrassment of states that do not meet minimum moral obligations to child survival and nutrition. UN agencies such as WHO, WFP, and IFAD offer project assistance that especially benefits those who in the past have been mostly left out: the poor and female, who are benefiting nutritionally from farming, health, and nutrition programs aimed at them. Elevated ACC/SCN nutrition monitoring, refugee surveys, and multi-lateral efforts meeting needs of the destitute in situations of complex emergencies are all indicators of "progress" toward meeting broad nutrition and human rights goals.

NGOs, framing activities in human rights, nutrition, and development terms, increasingly intervene to improve livelihoods, access to food, and respect for human rights where states fail; they suggest that responsibility and accountability for meeting nutrition goals also lies outside the state, while they continue to press states to enact into law and then meet nutrition and human rights obligations.

Sociocultural Perspectives

Such emphasis on legal and political measures, however, deflects attention from sociocultural concerns that either ensure or interfere with human rights to food. To prevent iodine deficiency disease, for example, governments may join an international consensus for salt iodization and implement central iodization with technical assistance from UN agencies and through national laws mandating that all salt be iodized. But at the household level, iodine-deficient individuals still must consume iodized salt to prevent deprivation, and it is at this household level of economic access and cultural dietary preference (or social exclusion from some of the "good" but expensive foods of the culture) that the right to adequate nutrition may be denied. Fulfillment of the right thus demands multiple social levels of obligation and action. From a practical perspective, in addition to summit, state, and NGO efforts, human rights achievements entail obligations for individuals, households, and communities that have their own cultural moral codes affecting access by individuals to adequate nutrition (Messer, 1993). Universal human rights and an end to hunger will only be achieved when these cease to be viewed principally as a legal matter for state-to-state negotiation, and instead penetrate and draw on local and other cultural traditions for effective conceptualization and fulfillment (Messer, 1993; see also Food Wars, this volume).

Prospects for the Future

The optimistic outlook for the end of the Cold War is a greater voice for communities and individuals in selecting governments and policies to improve their conditions; free and representative elections, accountable democratic governance, free press, the right to organize for fair working conditions, wages, and personal and social security benefits. But the picture is mixed at best as the world witnesses multiplying and escalating armed conflicts that deny entire ethnic or religious groups access to food and use hunger as a weapon, failed states – even without conflict – that are unable to create or sustain the conditions where all people can access adequate food, and sub-state cultural groups that try to fill the gaps and seek greater political power but tend to be selective, exclusive, or worse in allocating resources and respecting, protecting, and fulfilling basic rights. States and sub-groups in developing countries also confront diminishing development assistance with cuts overall, and especially in non-emergency aid. Although aid agencies continue to talk about "relief-to-development" the aid picture for the short term may be relief in lieu of development.

Yet five years is too short a time to judge the future impact of the human rights framework on hunger. The ten-year time frame of the published literature (1984-94) encouragingly suggests considerable progress in research and advocacy leading to social mobilization and action. Although the precise definition of a right to nutrition will likely remain country- and culture-specific, the individual's right not to starve is widely affirmed in international declarations and NGO principles justifying actions.[13] In parallel, more than 170 countries, with the assistance of UNICEF, other IGOS, and NGOs have signed the Convention on the Rights of the Child, and most are initiating supporting actions to allow every child food, health care, and nurturing adequate to support full human development. Major international financial institutions, such as the World Bank are devoting additional attention to hunger and protection of human rights, including indigenous rights (e.g., Cernea, 1991; Serageldin and Landell-Mills, 1994), although their adherence and accountability to the human-rights framework in decisionmaking remains problematic (Alston, 1987). A critical question for economic and food and nutrition policy planners is how to avoid damaging consequences of free market development and trade liberalization through public policy that will promote growth while improving food security of low-income groups (Sahn, 1994; Marchione, in press).

Conclusions

Human rights remains "a common standard of achievement for all peoples and nations" (UN Universal Declaration of Human Rights, 1948). Political priorities, particularly in contexts of scarce resources, currently seem to favor arms and military preparedness over food and nutritional or human security, and economic growth over "the human being as the central object of development" (see chapter by Landell-Mills, with rejoinder by Reutlinger, this volume). Social and cultural customs of inclusion or exclusion at the community and household level further condition fulfillment or denial of both nutrition and human rights. But human rights logically and practically could provide a common reference point, and rationale for economic, agricultural, and human development programs; and a standard against which to judge the appropriateness and effectiveness of planned change.

Legal, political-economic, and sociocultural perspectives suggest that human rights offers a central mobilizing theme to unite international (IGO and NGO), national (state), and local (community) actions against hunger. Although the persistance of hunger and malnutrition in a world capable of providing adequate food for all highlights current failures of achievement, human rights standards serve as a reference point for human values. Failure to achieve the substance of rights 50 years after the founding of the UN in no way diminishes their importance as a unifying goal for the world community. Effective implementation of human rights, however, awaits both positive and negative actions at multiple social levels: preventing the major sources of violations, not only at the level of the state but also at less-inclusive social levels; and joining the efforts of individuals, communities, and NGOs to those of states and the international community to guarantee subsistence and global human security.

1. Human rights as a philosophical concept refers to certain reasonable demands for basic well-being that all individuals should be able to make on the rest of humanity by virtue of their being members of the human species (Shue, 1980). Among human rights, adequate food (subsistence), along with personal security, constitutes an *essential right*:

    ...a moral minimum...the lower limits of tolerable human conduct, individual and institutional...the least that every person can demand and the least that every person, every government, and every corporation must be made to do...

    The principle of human rights also carries with it attendant duties if rights are to be fulfilled; for individuals: (1) the duty to avoid deprivations of the substance of the right (in this case, food); (2) the duty to protect against deprivation; and (3) the duty to assist someone who is nevertheless deprived.

2. Almost all countries sign the Declaration as a "rite of passage" for entry into the UN community. Apart are the binding legal obligations of signing the Convenants. The countries obligating themselves to achieve human rights to food by signing the Covenant had increased to 131 by 1994, up from 85 in 1989, but the numbers of signatories to the Covenant on Economic, Social, and Cultural Rights has been inflated since 1989 by the numbers of newly independent states signing the Covenant following the breakup of the USSR.

3. Tanzania under Nyere, Nicaragua under the Sandinistas, and Cuba under Castro are possible exceptions.

4. The *Beijing Review* and *China Daily* in 1992, remarking on the occasion of the Quincentennary, ran a series of articles with titles such as: "Subsistence: The Primary Human Right" *Beijing Review* 35,1:12 (January 6, 1992); "The Right to Subsistence Not To be Shunned" *Beijing Review* 35,2:13 (January 13, 1992); "Developing Countries Seek the Right to Subsistence" *Beijing Review* 35,8:12 (February 24, 1992).

5. This framework has been developed by WANAHR (1994).

6. *The Right to Adequate Food as a Human Right* (Eide, 1989), was a study of a particular economic right commissioned by the UN Human Rights Commission; *Food, Nutrition, and Human Rights* (Oshaug et al., 1992), was a country paper submitted by the Norwegian government contribution to the ICN.

7. See the papers cited above (f.n.6), plus FIAN (1994a) *Breaches of the Human Right to Feed Oneself. FIAN Guidelines for Parallel Reporting to the UNO Committe On Economic, Social, and Cultural Rights.*

8. FIAN (1994b) The Right to Adequate Food (Art.11) in Kenya. Parallel information to the initial report of Kenya concerning the right to adequate food as enshrined in the International Covenant on Economic, Social, and Cultural Rights (ICESCR, art.11). FIAN International Secretariat. Heidelberg, Germany.

9. The Front also recommends specific actions, such as integrated education, health, and horticultural programs for rural areas, community kitchens to elaborate affordable nutritious foods, investment in "alternative" nutritional products, such as amaranth, and nutrition and health education, especially for mothers.

10. The 1989 Bellagio Declaration on Overcoming Hunger in the 1990s states:

    The major obstacle to eliminating famine remains the destruction or interdiction of civilian food supplies in zones of armed conflict. The rudiments for international protection of civilian rights to food exist in international law, most specifically in the 1977 protocols to the Geneva Conventions of 1949 that prohibit starvation of civilians as a means of combat. More recnelty, there is renewed interest in an international or regional covenant for the sanctity of civilian food supplies and the safe passage of emergency food relief. Such a covenant could bind nations to provide safe passage and might permit convoy by UN peacekeeping forces within their national territory.

    The UN and humanitarian NGOs have since advanced principles to justify interventions.

11. The nutrition matrix of Oshaug et al. (1994) uses the "food security" categories "nutritionally adequate," "safe and of good quality," "culturally acceptable," "environmental sustainability," "social sustainability" (equitable and accessible distribution), viable procurement (vulnerable groups should be able to meet their basic human needs), and the additional nutrition categories of "adequate care" and "adequate prevention and control of disease."

12. Legal experts have also suggested that the right to food would achieve greater adherence were states to sign an additional optional protocol obligating them to adhere to nutrition rights.

13   ICN (1992); WCHR (1993), WANAHR (1994) are just three of many documents that specifically ban food (hunger) as a weapon or political tool; WANAHR has established a task force on "food as a weapon". Kates' brief reference to human rights and hunger of the future (this volume) also is restricted to this narrower dimension of the right to food.

References

Alston, P. (1987). The International Monetary Fund and the Right to Food. *Howard Law Journal* 30:473-82.

Alston, P. (1990). US Ratification of the Covenant on Economic, Social, and Cultural Rights. *American Journal of International Law* 84: 365-93.

Alston, P. and K. Tomasevski, eds. (1984). *Right To Food*. The Hague: Nijhoff.

Berting, J., et al., eds. (1990). *Human Rights in a Pluralist World. Individuals and Collectivities*. Westport, Connecticut: Meckler.

Cernea, M., ed. (1991). *Putting People First. Sociological Variables in Rural Development*. 2nd ed. New York: Oxford for the World Bank.

Dreze, J. and A. Sen (1989). *Hunger and Public Action*. Oxford: Clarendon Press.

Eide, A. (1989). *Right to Adequate Food as a Human Right. Human Rights Study Series 1. UN Publicaton No.E89 XIV.2.* Geneva: UN Centre for Human Rights.

Eide, A., W. Eide, S. Goonatilake, S. Gussow, J. Omawale, eds. (1984). *Food as a Human Right*. Tokyo: UNU Press.

FIAN (1994a). *Breaches of the Human Right to Feed Onself. FIAN Guidelines for Parallel Reporting to the UN Committee on Economic, Social, and Cultural Rights*. Heidelberg (Mimeo).

FIAN (1994b). The Right to Adequate Food (Art. 11) in Kenya. Presented at the tenth session of the Committee on Economic, Social, and Cultural Rights (2.-22. May 1994). Heidelberg, Germany.

FIAN (1994c). Actions. *Hungry for What is Right* No.2 (April, 1994).

Frente por el Derecho a la Alimentacion (1994). El Accesso a la Alimentacion es un Derecho Humano. Mimeo.

Grant, J. (1994). *The State of the World's Children 1994*. New York: Oxford University Press.

Heggenhoughen, K. (1995). The Epidemiology of Functional Apartheid and Human Rights Abuses. *Social Science and Medicine* 40,3: 281-284.

Howard, R. (1986). *Human Rights in Commonwealth Africa*. Totowa, NJ: Rowman & Littlefield, pp.60-90.

ICN (1992). *World Declaration and Plan of Action on Nutrition*. Rome.

Marchione, T. (1996). The Right to Food in the Post-Cold War Era. *Food Policy*. 21.

Messer, E. (1992). *Advanced Seminar on Special Topics in World Hunger: Human Rights to Food and Freedom From Hunger*. Providence, RI: Brown University, Mimeo.

Messer, E. (1993). Anthropology and Human Rights. *Annual Review of Anthropology* 22:221-49.

Messer, E. (1994). The Human Right to Food and Other Human Rights: Perspectives in 1994. *Abstracts of the 93rd Annual Meeting of the American Anthropological Association*, p.248.

Okoth-Ogendo, H.W.O. (1993). Human and People's Rights: What Point is Africa Trying to Make? *Human Rights and Governance in Africa*. R. Cohen, G. Hyden, and W. Nagan, eds. Gainesville, FL: University of Florida, pp. 74-85.

Oshaug, A., W.B. Eide, and A. Eide (1992). *Food, Nutrition, and Human Rights*. First Preparatory Committee for the International Conference on Nutrition. Geneva, August, 1992. Conference Paper Submitted by Norway.

Oshaug, A., W. B. Eide, and A. Eide (1994). Human rights: a normative basis for food and nutrition-relevant policies. *Food Policy* 19:491-516.

Sahn, D. (1994). Economic Crisis and Policy Reform in Africa. In *Adjusting to Policy Failure in African Economies*. D.Sahn, ed. Ithaca, New York: Cornell University Press.

Serageldin, I. and P. Landell-Mills, eds. (1994). *Overcoming Global Hunger. Proceedings of a Conference on Actions to Reduce Hunger World Wide*. World Bank Environmentally Sustainable Development Proceedings Series No.3. Washington, D.C.: The World Bank.

Shue, H. (1980). *Basic Rights: Subsistence, Affluence, and U.S. Foreign Policy*. Princeton, New Jersey: Princeton University Press.

Tomasevski, K. (1987). *The Right to Food: Guide Through the Applicable International Law*. Dordrecht: M. Nijhoff.

Tomasevski, K. (1989). *Development Aid and Human Rights. A Study for the Danish Center of Human Rights*. NY: St. Martin's.

Tomasevski, K. (1993). *Development Aid and Human Rights Revisited*. NY: Pinter.

Tomasevski, K. (1994). Human Rights and Wars of Starvation. In *War & Hunger*, J. Macrae and A. Zvi, eds., pp.70-91. London: Zed (with Save the Children).

WANAHR (World Alliance for Nutrition and Human Rights) (1994). Founding Document: The Mission of the World Alliance for Nutrition and Human Rights. *WANAHR Bulletin* No.5.

WCHR (World Conference on Human Rights) (1993). *The Vienna Declaration and Programme of Action*. Vienna, Austria.

Table 4.2. Chart of Ratifications of International Instruments

States	Cov. Econ/Social/Cultural	Covenant Civil/Political	Elim. Racial Discrimination	Crime of Genocide	Rights of the Child	Discrim. Agnst. Women	Geneva Convention III	Geneva Convention IV	Geneva Protocol I	Geneva Protocol II
	(1)	(2)	(3)	(4)	(5)	(6)	(7)	(8)	(9)	(10)
Afghanistan	X	X	X	X	X	S	X	X		
Albania	X	X	X	X	X	X	X	X	X	X
Algeria	X	Xa	Xb	X	X		X	X	X	X
Angola	X	X			X	X	X	X	X	
Antigua & Barbuda			X	X	X	X	X	X	X	X
Argentina	X	Xa	X	X	X	X	X	X	X	X
Armenia	X	X	X	X	X	X			X	X
Australia	X	Xa	Xb	X	X	X	X	X	X	X
Austria	X	Xa	X	X	X	X	X	X	X	X
Azerbaijan	X	X			X					
Bahamas			X	X	X	X	X	X	X	X
Bahrain			X	X	X		X	X	X	X
Bangladesh			X		X	X	X	X	X	X
Barbados	X	X	X	X	X	X	X	X	X	X
Belarus	X	Xa	X	X	X	X			X	X
Belgium	X	Xa	X	X	X	X	X	X	X	X
Belize					X	X	X	X	X	X
Benin	X	X	S		X	X	X	X	X	X
Bhutan			S		X	X				
Bolivia	X	X	X	S	X	S	X	X	X	X
Bosnia Herzegovina	X	Xa	X	X	X	X			X	X
Botswana			X				X	X	X	X
Brazil	X	X	X	X	X	X	X	X	X	X
Brunei Darussalam									X	X
Bulgaria	X	Xa	Xb	X	X	X	X	X	X	X
Burkina Faso			X	X	X	X	X	X	X	X
Burma see Myanmar										
Burundi	X	X	X		X	X			X	X
Cambodia	X	X	X	X	X	X	X	X		
Cameroon	X	X	X		X	X	X	X	X	X
Canada	X	Xa	X	X	X	X	X	X	X	X
Cape Verde	X	X	X		X	X	X	X		
Central Afr Rep	X	X	X		X		X	X	X	X
Chad			X		X		X	X		
Chile	X	Xa	X	X	X	X	X	X	X	X
China			X	X	X	X	X	X	X	X
Colombia	X	X	X	X	X	X	X	X		

States (continued)	(1)	(2)	(3)	(4)	(5)	(6)	(7)	(8)	(9)	(10)
Comoros					X	X	X	X	X	X
Congo	X	Xa	X		X	X	X	X	X	X
Costa Rica	X	X	Xb	X	X	X	X	X	X	X
Cote d'Ivoire	X	X	X		X	S			X̶	X̶
Croatia	X	X	X	X	X	X			X̶	X̶
Cuba			X	X	X	X	X	X	X̶	
Cyprus	X	X	Xb	X	X	X	X	X	X	
Czech Republic	X	X	X	X	X	X	X	X	X̶	X̶
Dem. People's Rep. Korea	X	X		X	X		X	X	X	
Denmark	X	Xa	Xb	X	X	X	X	X	X	X
Djibouti					X		X	X	X̶	X̶
Dominica	X	X			X	X	X	X		
Dominican Republic	X	X	X	S	X	X	X	X		
Ecuador	X	Xa	Xb	X	X	X	X	X	X	X
Egypt	X	X	X	X	X	X	X	X	X	X
El Salvador	X	X	X	X	X	X	X	X	X	X
Equatorial Guinea	X	X			X	X	X	X	X	X
Eritrea					X					
Estonia	X	X	X	X	X	X			X̶	X̶
Ethiopia	X	X	X	X	X	X	X	X		
Fed. States/Micronesia					X					
Fiji			X	X	X		X	X		
Finland	X	Xa	X	X	X	X	X	X	X	X
France	X	X	Xb	X	X	X	X	X		X
Gabon	X	X	X	X	X	X	X	X	X	X
Gambia	X	Xa	X	X	X	X	X	X	X̶	X̶
Georgia	X	X		X	X	X				
Germany	X	Xa	X	X	X	X	X	X	X̶	X̶
Ghana			X	X	X	X	X	X	X	X
Greece	X		X	X	X	X	X	X	X̶	X̶
Grenada	X	X	S		X	X	X	X		
Guatemala	X	X	X	X	X	X	X	X	X	X
Guinea	X	X	X		X	X	X	X	X	X
Guinea-Bissau	X				X	X	X	X	X	X
Guyana	X	Xa	X		X	X	X	X	X	X
Haiti		X	X	X	S	X	X	X		
Holy See			X		X		X	X	X	X
Honduras	X	S		X	X	X	X	X		
Hungary	X	Xa	Xb	X	X	X	X	X	X̶	X̶
Iceland	X	Xa	Xb	X	X	X	X	X	X	X
India	X	X	X	X	X	X	X	X		
Indonesia					X	X	X	X		
Iran (Islamic Rep.)	X	X	X	X	X		X	X		
Iraq	X	X	X	X	X	X	X	X		
Ireland	X		S		X	X	X	X		
Israel	X	X	X	X	X	X	X	X		
Italy	X	Xa	Xb	X	X	X	X	X	X	X
Ivory Coast							X	X		

States (continued)	(1)	(2)	(3)	(4)	(5)	(6)	(7)	(8)	(9)	(10)
Jamaica	X	X	X	X	X	X	X	X	X	X
Japan	X	X			X	X	X	X		
Jordan	X	X	X		X	X	X	X	X	X
Kazakhstan					X				X̲	X̲
Kenya	X	X			X	X	X	X		
Kiribati										
Kuwait			X		X	X	X	X	X	X
Kyrgyzstan	X	X			X	X			X̲	X̲
Lao Pple's Dem. Rep.			X	X	X	X	X	X	X	X
Latvia	X	X	X	X	X	X			X̲	X̲
Lebanon	X	X	X	X	X		X	X		
Lesotho	X	X	X	X	X	S	X	X		
Liberia	S	S	X	X	X	X	X	X	X	X
Libyan Arab Jamahiriya	X	X	X	X	X	X	X	X	X	X
Liechtenstein				X	S		X	X	X̲	X̲
Lithuania	X	X			X	X				
Luxembourg	X	Xa	X	X	X	X	X	X	X̲	X̲
Macedonia	X	X	X		X	X				
Madagascar	X	X	X		X	X	X	X	X̲	X̲
Malawi	X	X			X	X	X	X	X̲	X̲
Malaysia				X			X	X		
Maldives			X	X	X	X			X̲	X̲
Mali	X	X	X	X	X	X	X	X	X̲	X̲
Malta	X	Xa	X		X	X	X	X	X̲	X̲
Marshall Islands					X					
Mauritania			X		X		X	X	X	X
Mauritius	X	X	X		X	X	X	X	X	X
México	X	X	X	X	X	X	X	X	X	
Monaco				X	X		X	X		
Mongolia	X	X	X	X	X	X	X	X		
Morocco	X	X	X	X	X	X	X	X		
Mozambique		X	X	X	X		X	X	X	
Myanmar				X	X					
Namibia	X	X	X	X	X	X	X	X		
Nauru					X					
Nepal	X	X	X	X	X	X	X	X		
Netherlands	X	Xa	Xb	X	S	X	X	X	X	X
New Zealand	X	Xa	X	X	X	X	X	X	X	X
Nicaragua	X	X	X	X	X	X	X	X		
Niger	X	X	X		X		X	X	X	X
Nigeria	X	X	X		X	X	X	X	X	X
Norway	X	Xa	Xb	X	X	X	X	X	X	X
Oman							X	X	X	X
Pakistan			X	X	X		X	X		
Panama	X	X	X	X	X	X	X	X		
Papua New Guinea			X	X	X		X	X		
Paraguay	X	X		S	X	X	X	X	X̲	X̲
Peru	X	Xa	Xb	X	X	X	X	X	X̲	X̲

States (continued)	(1)	(2)	(3)	(4)	(5)	(6)	(7)	(8)	(9)	(10)
Philippines	X	Xa	X	X	X	X	X	X		X
Poland	X	Xa	X	X	X	X	X	X	X̄	X̄
Portugal	X	X	X		X	X	X	X	X̄	X̄
Qatar			X		S		X	X	X	
Republic of Korea	X	Xa	X	X	X	X	X	X	X	X
Republic of Moldova	X	X	X	X	X	X			X̄	X̄
Romania	X	X	X	X	X	X	X	X	X̄	X
Russian Federation	X	X	Xb	X	X	X			X̄	X̄
Rwanda	X	X	X	X	X	X	X	X	X	X
Saint Kitts and Nevis					X	X	X	X	X	X
Saint Lucia			X		X	X	X	X	X	X
St. Vincent & Grenadines	X	X	X	X	X	X	X	X	X	X
Samoa					X	X	X	X	X	X̄
San Marino	X	X			X		X	X		
Sao Tome and Principe					X		X	X		
Saudi Arabia				X			X	X	X	
Senegal	X	Xa	Xb	X	X	X	X	X	X	X
Seychelles	X	X	X	X	X	X	X	X	X	X
Sierra Leone			X		X	X	X	X	X	X
Singapore							X	X		
Slovakia	X	X	X	X	X	X			X̄	X̄
Slovenia	X	Xa	X	X	X	X			X̄	X̄
Solomon Islands	X		X				X	X	X	X
Somalia	X	X	X		S		X	X		
South Africa	S	S	S		S	S	X	X		
Spain	X	Xa	X	X	X	X	X	X	X̄	X̄
Sri Lanka	X	Xa	X	X	X	X	X	X		
Sudan	X	X	X		X		X	X		
Surinam	X	X	X		X	X	X	X	X	X
Swaziland			X		S		X	X		
Sweden	X	Xa	Xb	X	X	X	X	X	X	X
Switzerland	X	Xa	X		X	S	X	X	X	X
Syrian Arab Republic	X	X	X	X	X		X	X	X	
Tajikistan					X	X			X̄	X̄
Thailand					X	X	X	X		
Togo	X	X	X	X	X	X	X	X	X	X
Tonga			X	X			X	X		
Trinidad and Tobago	X	X	X		X	X	X	X		
Tunisia	X	Xa	X	X	X	X	X	X	X	X
Turkey			S	X	X	X	X	X		
Turkmenistan			X		X				X̄	X̄
Tuvalu							X	X		
Uganda	X		X		X	X	X	X	X̄	X̄
Ukraine	X	Xa	Xb	X	X	X	X	X	X̄	X̄
United Arab Emirates			X				X	X	X	X
United Kingdom	X	Xa	X	X	X	X	X	X		
United Rep. of Tanzania	X	X	X	X	X	X	X	X	X	X
United States of America	S	Xa	X	X		S	X	X		

States (continued)	(1)	(2)	(3)	(4)	(5)	(6)	(7)	(8)	(9)	(10)
Uruguay	X	X	Xb	X	X	X	X	X	X	X
Uzbekistan					X					
Vanuatu					X		X	X	X	X
Venezuela	X	X	X	X	X	X	X	X		
Viet Nam	X	X	X	X	X	X	X	X	X	
Yemen	X	X	X	X	X	X	X	X	X̲	X̲
Yugoslavia	X	X	X	X	X	X	X	X	X	X
Zaire	X	X	X	X	X	X			X	
Zambia	X	X	X		X	X	X	X		
Zimbabwe	X	Xa	X	X	X	X	X	X	X̲	X̲
Total Number of States Parties	131	128	141	115	174	135	165	165	126	117
Signatures not followed by ratification	3	3	7	3	11	8				

(1)   International Covenant on Economic, Social and Cultural Rights.
(2)   International Covenant on Civil and Political Rights.
(3)   International Convention on the Elimination of All Forms of Racial Discrimination.
(4)   Convention on the Prevention and Punishment of the Crime of Genocide.
(5)   Convention on the Rights of the Child.
(6)   Convention on the Elimination of All Forms of Discrimination against Women.
(7)   1949 Geneva Convention III Relative to the Treatment of Prisoners of War.
(8)   1949 Geneva Convention IV Relative to the Protection of Civilian Persons in Time of War.
(9)   1977 Geneva Protocol I Additional to the Geneva Conventions of 12 August 1949, and Relating to the Protection of Victims of Non-International Armed Conflicts.
(10) 1977 Geneva Protocol II Additional to the Geneva Conventions of 12 August 1949, and Relating to the Protection of Victims of Non-International Armed Conflicts.

X   Ratification, accession, approval, notification or succession, acceptance or definitive signature.
X̲   Ratification, accession, approval, notification or succession, acceptance or definitive signature given after Jan. 1989.
S   Signature not yet followed by ratification.
Xa   Declaration recognizing the competence of the Human Rights Committee under article 41 of the International Covenant on Civil and Political Rights.
Xb   Declaration recognizing the competence of the Committee on the Elimination of Racial Discrimination under article 14 of the International Convention on the Elimination of All Forms of Racial Discrimination.

• Chart of Ratifications of International Instruments (1) through (6). Source: United Nations.
   International Instruments: Chart of Ratifications as at 31 December 1994, New York and Geneva, 1995 – See foreword to Human Rights – Status of International Instruments (ST/HR/5), United Nations publication (Sales No. E.87.XIV.2); replaces text of 30 June 1994.

   Instruments (7) and (8): Information supplied in communications from the Swiss Federal Department for Foreign Affairs in July-September 1988. (Source: International and Non-International Armed Conflicts. p.459).

   Instruments (9) and (10) as at 16 July 1993. (Source: United Nations, General Assembly. A/INF/48/3. 30 August 1993).

CHAPTER 5

Linking the Grassroots to the Summit*

Peter Uvin

The war against world hunger is fought on many battlefields by troops seeking to increase agricultural production, improve basic health care, increase poor people's incomes, design safety nets against exceptional entitlement shortfalls, improve the quality of the environment, change dietary practices, curb fertility rates, assure access to land, seeds, water etc. Third World governments, and bi- and multilateral development agencies are all active in these fields, yet their capacities, willingness, and resources are limited and the size of the problems often daunting.

Increasingly, we realize that the answers to these problems must come primarily from the local communities themselves – if that is not happening already. In this respect, the veritable explosion of community-based, participatory, grassroots action in most of the Third World over the last two decades is very encouraging: everywhere one looks, people are organizing to fight erosion, increase production and incomes, create safety nets, supply credit and other inputs, improve their own and their children's health, etc.

Yet, recognizing the importance of such participatory initiatives in the fight against hunger should not imply that there is no longer a role for governments or international organizations. The summit remains crucial in the fight against hunger. The issue is not its destruction, or neglect, but rather the creation of links between the grassroots and the summit. There are various reasons for this.

One is that most grassroots initiatives are small, underfunded, poorly staffed, slow and localized in contrast to the immensity of the problems of poverty, hunger, and environmental degradation facing hundreds of millions of people. They thus remain actions at the margin, capable of providing local relief and empowerment, but not of tackling the larger challenge. Governments and international organizations, on the other hand, usually possess vastly more resources, especially financial and material, than grassroots organizations. This situation is unlikely to change soon. Moreover, governments have capacities and responsibilities most grassroots organizations will never possess. They are responsible for the wellbeing of all people within the national territory. They are endowed with the capacity to create binding laws and enforce them. They can use this power to promote the eradication of hunger and the development of grassroots initiatives, or for different (if not opposing) purposes, and, short of civil war, there is no way NGOs can take it away. In addition, in the present interdependent world, many problems felt locally have national or international origins or are of a transboundary nature. Governments and international organizations are the main actors capable of dealing with such problems.

Hence, governments and international organizations remain crucial actors in the fight against hunger and its many causes. They, along with grassroots organizations, are needed to work, if not in collaboration, then at least in parallel, to eradicate hunger and poverty. Along these lines, the first "Overcoming Hunger in the 1990s" meeting, in its final Bellagio declaration, talked about "linking the grassroots to the summit."

"Linking the grassroots to the summit" implies two processes. One is "scaling up," a term referring to the process by which grassroots organizations expand their impact and enter into relation with the summit. Less often discussed, but equally necessary, is another process, whereby the summit "scales down," adopting new modes of functioning that allow for meaningful interaction with the grassroots. This paper will deal with both these processes, focusing mainly on the former. Before doing so, however, it will present some remarks about factors that, although beyond the immediate scope of this paper, frame and condition its subject.

Some Cautionary Remarks About Grassroots-Summit Interaction

"The grassroots" have always participated in the fight against hunger, both individually and collectively. Throughout Africa and Asia, for example, thousands of traditional mutual help mechanisms, self-help institutions and collective organizations exist, linking people of all walks of life. In rural and in urban areas, providing food security to each other is one of their foremost functions. These institutions are intimately linked to social structures of allegiance, alliance, religion, power, clientelism, and exclusion. In other terms, these mechanisms are by no means necessarily or always consensual, inclusive, just or egalitarian. They exclude some, profit more to some than to others, are imposed on still others, etc. These traditional mechanisms and institutions provide if not the point of departure, then at least the frame of reference for the new grassroots organizations (Kwan Kai Hong, 1991: 25). As such, the latter are also subject to (or part of) the same social structure of values, power, clientelism, and exclusion. The dynamic of grassroots organizations and NGOs can only be understood in this light: the interaction between the "traditional" values, structures, and practices from which they emerge and in which they are embedded, and the new ones they seek to acquire or cope with.

Similarly, "the grassroots" have always interacted with the summit. Often, the summit (whether colonial or post-independence) has deliberately sought to destroy the grassroots' traditional organizations, including its mechanisms for collective action and self-help (Uphoff, 1993: 618). This was done for political reasons (get rid of competing mechanisms that are uncontrollable to politicians, especially from other ethnic groups) or for ideological ones (these values and practices are backward). In both cases, this destruction or displacement may not have been a deliberate objective, but the side effect of policies of "development," "modernization" or "administrative efficiency".

Faced with these challenges, the grassroots have adopted a variety of reactions. One is withdrawal and so-called passivity, whereby individuals and local communities minimize their contact with the summit. Another, occurring only under very rare circumstances, has been revolt: peasant uprisings against perceived injustice. A third and common reaction has been for the grassroots to formally join the programs proposed to them but attempt to modify them from within, engaging only in those aspects which interest them. Finally, in those cases where the propositions of the summit have been considered by peasants to be in their interest, they have wholeheartedly interacted with the summit's propositions. The present phenomenon of the emergence of myriad grassroots organization constitutes a new response to the summit, whereby people pool their resources so as to compensate, complement, or combat the summit's deficiencies.

In most countries, from the point of view of the hungry and the poor, the history of grassroots-summit interaction is filled with broken promises, deceptions and deceits, losses and lies, as well as occasional gifts and other forms of clientelism. Small wonder that the new grassroots organizations are reluctant to deal with the summit, usually defining themselves precisely through their capacity to bypass the summit, to go it alone – or, in some cases based on their habits of client-patron relationships, dealing with the summit as beggars, habitual clients. We cannot wish that history away. Even though very good arguments can be made that NGOs should collaborate with the state or with international organizations, there are strong historical constraints on doing so. The real question, then, is whether changes have occurred in the nature of the grassroots or the summit that would render their future interactions different from their past ones.

"The grassroots" also covers a large variety of phenomena and processes. One way to distinguish them is by asking "why do people join grassroots organizations"? On the most general level, people organize or join organizations – or do not organize and do not join organizations – because they perceive it to be in their interest. This is easy to understand.

The nature of this self-interest, however, is often misunderstood by idealistic outsiders, who project their own images and ideologies on others. Outsiders usually believe that all cases of farmers joining organizations are cases of self-help, based on an assessment (often the result of "conscientization") by these same farmers that mutual organization for autonomous development is to their interest. Outsiders do not realize that self-interest can be defined in many ways, and that the benefits of mutual organization are only one of them. Schematically, we can distinguish at least three types of self-interest that can motivate people to join organizations or programs.

Joining an organization or a program can be based upon peoples' realization that they can do more with their own resources, that by joining hands they can achieve more, etc. These are cases of self-help. The self-interest the joiners are satisfying here is based on the realization that they can create their own solutions to the problems they face. This is an internal process (which does not mean that there may be no external involvement), linked to peoples' capacities and desires. It is also without doubt the most difficult to bring about and to maintain. Organizations resulting from this motivator will have a tendency to be small, for to very poor people, only small-scale projects offer the potential for benefits accruing directly to them; larger-scale ones risk being taken over by intermediaries or local elites (Chowdhury, 1989: 211). Hence, the potential for sustainability of such organizations is high, but so are the difficulties in creating them and increasing their size.

Joining an organization or a program can also be motivated by the possibility of grants, credit, jobs, training opportunities, and other benefits offered by the aid system. This can occur even when there are no actual handouts or immediate benefits to be obtained: the mere belief that they exist suffices. In much of the Third World, there is a long history of handouts and free aid; as a result, people have a tendency to equate the presence of almost all foreigners (including people from the capital) with free gifts, even if the foreigners work with a different vision (Mayfield, 1985: 80). The sustainability of organizations resulting from this motivator will depend either on the continued presence of the carrot, or on the transformation of the original dependency/gift dynamic into the self-help type. Both are highly unlikely: the first for it is very costly, especially on a large scale, and the second because it is organizationally and psychologically very difficult to change dynamics once they have been set in motion.

Finally, people may join organizations or programs because they consider they have no choice. Perhaps if they do not join, they will have no access to a given resource anymore (the current movement toward privatization of water supply and health care into community-managed and community-financed systems is a good example); maybe they risk sanctions (certain cooperatives, official youth or women's movements in repressive states); or perhaps they feel pressured by local authorities (traditional authorities or local elites who adopt a strategy of coopting modern aid programs, for example). This motivator is also very unsustainable. Whenever the original constraint disappears, or whenever people feel strong enough to fight it, the motivation for joining is likely to disappear with it, and the process to fall apart. Only to the extent that the situation has been modified into one of self-help, or that new constraints arise, is participation likely to continue.

Hence, the constitution or growth of grassroots organization can be due to a variety of perceived self-interests. In all three cases, people and communities can create organizations, elect leaders and adopt statutes, receive money and invest some of their own resources, or build primary schools and health centers. Yet, beneath their common appearances, these three types of motivators create different organizational dynamics. The biggest difference lies in their degree of sustainability, *i.e.*, their capacity to continue over time, especially after withdrawal of the external intervention.

This discussion is important for our subject, for the summit, whenever it enters into relations with grassroots organization, has a tendency to promote the second and the third motivators. International organizations lack the time and the closeness to promote people's understanding and capacity for "real" self-help. They want to achieve fast results, disburse large sums of money, touch many people, etc. With their large resources, there is an almost irresistible tendency to use free gifts to encourage grassroots organization. Governments and government personnel similarly lack closeness to and understanding of poor people's needs and aspirations; moreover, they want to tightly control the outcome of any process of grassroots organization they set in motion. As a result, they are inclined to use pressure or sanction to promote grassroots organization.

In conclusion, we made three points that, together, provide caution against overly optimistic assessments of the likelihood or the benefits of grassroots-summit interaction. First, grassroots organization exists since time immemorial, and is embedded in societies' structure of hierarchy, clientalism, and exclusion. There is no reason to assume that the "new" grassroots organizations are independent of these complex social factors. Second, grassroots organizations, whether old or new, have always interacted with the summit, usually with preciously little benefit to themselves. This has made the grassroots very distrustful of the summit. Third, there are real dangers associated with getting the summit involved in grassroots organization, for the summit displays strong and inherent tendencies to provide motivators based either on carrots or on sanctions. Both are likely to be unsustainable.

One can also look at the above in a different manner and conclude that grassroots-summit interaction is likely to be sustainable and beneficial for local communities only when grassroots organizations result from internal processes of self-help, and have gone through a period of successful activity and autonomous growth. Their interaction with the summit will be from a position of strength, as part of a process of scaling up on their own terms. This is what we will deal with in the next section of this article

SCALING UP

A Definition and Taxonomy of Scaling Up

Different definitions of scaling up have been used in the literature. In a recent USAID evaluation of two innovative Freedom From Hunger credit projects in Africa (Ashe et al., 1992), the term scaling up – the focus of the study and explicitly mentioned in its title – is equated with 'expansion', or, more precisely, the need to "reach several times the actual number of members" in the countries concerned. This definition of scaling up as expansion of membership or target group is probably the one most commonly used.

Social scientists propose more complicated definitions. Robert Berg (1986), for example, talks about scaling up organizationally, managerially and financially, while Goran Hyden (1992) differentiates between scaling up organizationally and functionally. "Organizationally" is defined by both authors as "serving larger constituencies," *i.e.*, the same organization, keeping the same goals, grows in size. This, then, is the same meaning of the term as "expansion." "Functionally" means that the same organization increases or diversifies its range of activities, regardless of size. Howes and Sattar (1992) talk about "intensification," referring to the addition of new activities to existing programs.

Clark (1991) makes a different distinction among three types of scaling up: project replication, building grassroots movements, and influencing policy reform. The first two are linked to expansion, but the latter is new. Fisher (1993) also defines scaling up as the process of influencing policy; she uses the term "scaling out" to describe expansion. Although he does not use the term scaling up in this context, Korten (1990) clearly discusses a similar type of scaling up where he advocates so-called "third generation" NGOs. The latter are distinct from first and second generation ones by their concerns for "bridging the gap between micro and macro" (*i.e.*, quitting the local level) and their desire to deal with the (political) root causes of underdevelopment, and not its manifestations. This involves the creation of relationships with governments as well as international partnerships. Therefore, Korten, Clark, Fisher and many others consider influencing politics to be an important form of scaling up.

Finally, coming from a different tradition, Bernard Lecomte (1991), a French grassroots specialist with decades of field experience in Africa (and co-founder of the "Six-S" movement) writes about different phases in the maturing of self-help organizations – phases mainly characterized by increased capacity to innovate, generate local resources, and improve organizational capacity. His scaling up is a matter of autonomy, self-reliance, independence.

This variety of definitions is important. It allows us to look at the phenomenon in several different ways, giving some insight into the complexity of the associative sector. It also suggests that there are different types of scaling up, which often go together but are not identical. Below, we look at structures, programs, strategies and resource base to develop a typology of scaling up.

Structure

The first type is where a program or an organization expands its size, through increasing its membership base (for grassroots organizations – GROs) or its constituency (for grassroots support organizations – GRSOs) and, linked to that, their geographic working area or their budgets. This quantitative scaling up is the most evident type, equaling 'growth' or 'expansion' in their basic meanings. It happens when participatory organizations draw increasing numbers of people into their realm.

Programs

A second type occurs where a community-based program or a grassroots organization expands the number and the type of its activities. Starting in agricultural production, for example, it moves into health, nutrition, credit, training, literacy, etc. This functional scaling up. takes place when participatory organizations add new activities to their operational range.

Strategies

The third type refers to the movement of participatory organizations beyond service delivery towards empowerment and change in the structural causes of underdevelopment – its contextual factors and its socio-political-economic environment. This political scaling up will usually mean active involvement with the state. This process is similar to a graduation to higher generations in Korten's parlance.

Resource Base

Finally, community-based programs or grassroots organizations can increase their organizational strength to improve the effectiveness, efficiency, and sustainability of their activities. It can be done financially, by diversifying their sources of subvention, increasing the degree of self-financing, creating activities that generate income, or by assuring the enactment of public legislation earmarking entitlements within the annual budgets for the program. It can also be done institutionally, by creating external links with other public and private actors, and by improving the management and learning capacities of the staff allowing the organization and its programs to grow, to improve, to change. This type we call organizational scaling up.

We will now briefly present the relevant results of a case study of the processes of scaling up followed by 25 Alan Shawn Feinstein Hunger Award winners and nominees (for the full results of the case studies, see Uvin, 1995a). This case study will illustrate, through the experience of some organizations that are perceived to be highly successful in the fight against hunger, the extent to which grassroots-summit interaction takes place, and the nature of this interaction. This will allow us to continue with a discussion of the factors that favor grassroots-summit interaction, as seen from both sides of the relationship.

Methodology And Presentation of the Sample

Since 1986, Brown University yearly grants three ASF Hunger Awards, one of $25,000 and two of $10,000 each. According to the statutes of the Awards, the winners are organizations or people who have made "extraordinary efforts or contributions to the reduction of hunger in the world or its prevention in the future." Yearly, between 30 and 50 nominators – academicians and practitioners from around the globe – submit on their own initiative detailed descriptions and justifications for candidates for the Awards. Brown University's Board of Trustees, assisted by a special Selection Committee, chooses the three winners.

While the criteria are flexible, the nominees for the Hunger Awards can be considered as judged by their peers or by independent scholars to be especially meritorious in combating world hunger. The nominators would most likely not have gone through the trouble of sending in fully confidential and quite detailed nominations had they not thought highly of these organizations. As such, the universe of candidates for the Hunger Awards can be taken to represent a selection of people and organizations that are considered to have significantly impacted upon hunger. Realizing that the process is subjective and that high-quality data on the real impact of the nominees' programs on hunger do not exist, we believe that the universe of nominees – a total of 120 – constitutes interesting material for a closer analysis.

For this article, we selected those nominees that are Third World organizations, i.e. we excluded all individuals as well as all First World or international organizations.[1] For the remainder, we used the materials sent to us by the nominators: this usually included a quite large selection of annual reports, mission statements, newsletters, evaluations, videos, and letters of recommendation. For some organizations, such as BRAC, Plan Puebla and Sarvodaya Shramadana, we added other readily available sources of information. We dropped those nominees for which we did not find sufficient information. The total number of organizations retained was 23. Of these, eight are award winners, and 15 are nominees that have not won awards. For reasons of confidentiality, we will not identify the latter. The 23 organizations are spread quite evenly across the three continents, with a slight preponderance of Asia.

The Organizations

The first 8 organizations (hereafter called the "core" group) are the following:

- Bangladesh Rural Advancement Committee (BRAC)
- Committee for the Fight to End Hunger, Senegal (COLUFIFA)
- Foundation for the Cooperation between Displaced Persons, El Salvador (CORDES)
- National Farmers' Association of Zimbabwe (NFAZ)
- Papaye Peasants' Movement, Haiti (MPP)
- Plan Puebla, Mexico
- Sarvodaya Shramadana, Sri Lanka
- Women's Organization of Independecia, Peru (WARMI)

Of these, three – COLUFIFA, MPP, NFAZ – are member-based GROs, while the other five are grassroots support organizations, working directly in the community, soliciting popular participation. Of the other 15 organizations (hereafter the "nominee" group), 12 are GRSOs – including two international NGO coalitions – and three are GROs. Of the latter, two are government-initiated.

Of the ten core organizations, BRAC is probably the best known to people interested in grassroots mobilization in the Third World. Indeed, it is probably the single largest community based development program in the whole of the Third World. It is active in all fields of rural development: agriculture, credit, health, nutrition, education, handicraft, etc.

Sarvodaya Shramadana, founded by A.T. Ariyaratne, is also a very large and well-known organization, touching several million villagers in Sri Lanka. It draws on Buddhist values to promote moral and social improvement and to encourage non-violent change in all fields of development: protection of the environment, health, agriculture, etc.

The "Mouveman Peyizan Papaye" of Haiti is generally considered by those who know Haiti as the largest and most successful peasant self-help group in Haiti. It has worked under very adverse conditions to promote small-scale rural development. It has been a major force behind the "Operation Lavalas" that brought Rev. Aristide to power.

The National Farmers Association of Zimbabwe is a countrywide organization representing more than 800,000 communal and resettlement farmers. It acts as a spokesman for these small, black farmers towards government and international organizations. It is also active itself in rural development programs, and supplies cheap agricultural inputs to its members.

COLUFIFA was created in 1984, after a severe famine hit the Casamance region in Senegal for the first time in man's memory. It was the outgrowth of a farmers' organization that has more than 25,000 members, and some of the same leaders. It is a peasant organization, in which all decision-making positions are occupied by farmers from the region. It seeks to improve food security in the region through income diversification, cereals storage, and improved health.

Plan Puebla was started by a motivated team of agricultural technicians from CIMMYT (Centro Internacional de Mejoramiento de Maiz y Trigo) and the Postgraduate College at Chapingo working with small Mexican farmers in a participatory manner. As a result, the agricultural yields of hundreds of thousands of small farmers have trebled; its innovations have spread from one region through all of Mexico, and now even to Africa and Asia.

CORDES and WARMI, finally, are both organizations typical of different but very real Latin American problematiques and the answers local people have developed towards them: one works with displaced persons and their resettlement under conditions of war and violence; the other deals with the massively increased urban poverty in a country plagued by hyper-inflation and guerrillas. WARMI consists of hundreds of volunteer women managing soup kitchens in a poor Lima neighborhood. CORDES is a self-reliance promoting NGO assisting returning refugees in 12 of the 14 provinces of El Salvador.

Table 5.1. Main Features of the "Core Organizations"

	Country	Type Of Organization	Year of Creation	Population Involved
BRAC	Bangladesh	GRSO	1972	550,000 (plus 11 million in ORT program for UNICEF)
COLUFIFA	Senegal	GRO	1984 (1974)	20,000
CORDES	El Salvador	GRSO	1987	100,000
MPP	Haiti	GRO	1973	30,000
NFAZ	Zimbabwe	GRO	1980	800,000
Plan Puebla	Mexico	GRSO	1967	50,000 in original region
Sarvodaya	Sri Lanka	GRSO	1958	more than 3 million
WARMI	Peru	GRSO	1985 (1971)	80 soup kitchens (1991)

As can be seen, these eight organizations range from the small to the very large, involving vastly different budgets and people, with very different aims. All of them have a history of more than one decade behind them, either in their present structure, or in "embryonic" form (dates between brackets).

The other 15 nominated organizations range in size from a small grassroots organization in Guinea-Bissau to Asian GRSOs touching millions of persons in thousands of villages. Their activities range from participation in international policy debates in the case of the Asian NGO networks, over integrated rural development programs (Swaziland, Nigeria, Bangladesh, India, the Philippines, West Africa) to self-help for slum dwellers and women in India, and rural credit on all continents.

Grassroots-Summit Relations: Results From the Case Studies

Quantitative Scaling Up

All 25 organizations scaled up quantitatively, and often dramatically so. Yet, this only rarely involved building links to the summit. Most of the time, it took place solely within the NGO sector, through "spread," the process in which increasing numbers of people spontaneously adhere to the organization and its programs; or through "replication," whereby a successful program (methodology and mode of organization) was repeated elsewhere, usually by the same NGO.

In only three cases did strong links build with the summit as part of a process of quantitative scaling up. All three did so through "integration," where an NGO program is taken over by government structures after it has demonstrated its potential. Integration can come about as a result of demand by the NGO, which persuades a government agency to take over a successful program it launched (the case of Plan Puebla, where Jimenez Sanchez convinced the Ministry of Agriculture to take over his program methodology on a large scale, as well as one of the two nominees), or as a result of independent state action (case of one nominee in the Philippines). Such integration is often argued to be an important mechanism to increase impact and assure sustainability of NGO-initiated participatory programs (Lovell, 1992: 187; Howes & Sattar, 1992: 109; Morgan, 1990; Tendler, 1982: 9 & 91). As can be seen, it rarely occurs, however, for it goes against the ideological and organizational dynamics of most NGOs and governments.

Political Scaling Up

Most organizations in our sample of 25 scrupulously attempted to avoid the political arena. Only eight were politically active. Of these, four were born as third-generation organizations: the National Farmers' Organization of Zimbabwe, which set out to act as a lobbying group for farmers' interests at the governmental level, and three of the nominees, which were also deliberately created for the purpose of influencing politics (two Asian organizations working at the national and international levels, one African NGO at the national level). The three latter organizations are all examples of an oft taken path for political scaling up: "aggregation," whereby NGOs create federative structures designed to influence policy making. The number of member-NGOs that make up these federation ranges from four for the African case, to more than 20, many of which are federations by themselves for one of the Asian cases.

The four other organizations – two award winners (MPP and CORDES), and two nominees – began as first or second generation ones, and scaled up politically.

Both CORDES and MPP did so mainly through the path of networking, *i.e.* the more-or-less informal pooling of their numbers and resources with like-minded organizations. In 1991, MPP took the initiative in creating a National Peasants Movement, with the direct aim of confronting the government. MPP also offered training courses for the leaders of other emerging peasant organizations in Haiti in the hope of building a large movement of actors representing the interests of the rural sector. In 1990, CORDES, together with seven other NGOs, created an Inter-Institutional Coordination, aimed at promoting community development "on a large scale." This IIC subsequently went on to organize a conference in San Salvador, attended by representatives of over one hundred Salvadorian and foreign NGOs, at which a "New Initiative for Popular Self-Development in El Salvador" was adopted. It is explicitly seen as an attempt to "create models that can be expanded nationwide as the political space opens."

None of the 25 organizations of our sample followed the path of direct entry into politics (although A.T. Ariyaratne of Sri Lanka or Chavannes Jean-Baptistes of MPP certainly have taken on high political profiles – and have been the subject of harassment by government). On the other hand, the leaders of the three national NGO coalitions described above all have held high political office in the past – they are former politicians who provide their knowledge of the system and their connections as a tool for the representation of grassroots causes.

Finally, note that the generational hierarchy a la Korten is not as fixed as often thought. Both the NFAZ and CORDES provide examples of parcours that do not follow a mechanistic generational scaling up. The National Farmers Association of Zimbabwe started as a third-generation type of organization, representing its members' interests at the level of government and foreign donors. Afterwards, taking on rural development activities and the delivery of cheap inputs, it moved into second generation types of activities. CORDES started as a first generation organization, providing emergency type aid to returning refugees who lacked everything. Yet, at the same time, it was also firmly a third generation organization, having developed a forceful and coherent vision of self-reliance, and building up national and international alliances to create the environment conducive to such development. Since the end of the civil war in El Salvador, it increasingly acts on the second generation level, promoting rural development in one region (San Vincente), working in the fields of irrigation, credit, and marketing.

Organizational Scaling Up

Organizational scaling up is about assuring sustainability. It involves some very important processes organizations must go through so as to ensure their survival: improve management, adopt monitoring and evaluation routines, create various institutional structures, diversify funding sources, and increase the degree of self-financing. It is in this field, and especially the latter two objectives, that we find most NGO-summit interaction.

Most organizations in our sample receive funding from more than one source – in four cases more than ten sources. Our group of "nominee" organizations presents the same picture. All except three of the organizations receive funds from more than ten foreign donors; in one case, there are more than 50 of them! These donors are almost exclusively foreign, consisting (in order of decreasing frequency) of international PVOs, international organizations, rich country governments (the US, Switzerland), and their own governments.

This successful donor diversification implies four points. First, this sample shows that successful grassroots organizations (or, more precisely, grassroots organizations *perceived* to be successful) can count on large amounts of foreign aid: donors are, in a way, scrambling over each other to finance the "good" NGOs. Second, this situation certainly decreases NGO dependency upon one single donor, increasing their survival chances. Third, grassroots organizations are forced to adapt their mode of functioning to the divergent if not conflicting requirements of their donors, and to spend many human resources in satisfying various administrative requirements. This is costly, and can decrease their accountability to the communities they serve. Fourth, none of the organizations in our sample finances its activities by its own resources, or even by national resources. Hard data on this matter are unavailable, but it seems clear that self-financing is far away for all but a few of the organizations studied.

Various attempts have been made by NGOs to increase their financial autonomy as part of a strategy of organizational scaling up. A few of the nominees supplied consultancies to governments and foreign aid organizations; some others organized training for fees to other organizations and even government employees; three organizations created banks and cooperatives as autonomous profit centers. But the main mechanism has been subcontracting for government, whereby the state pays the NGO to deliver certain services it feels the NGO can better provide. In our sample, BRAC, as well as five of the nominees, undertake a significant part of their activities under subcontracting arrangements.

Much is written about the dangers of such subcontracting. It is thought that NGO subcontracting to the state, as well as to international organizations, risks obliging or tempting them to "sell out" their principles for the sake of income. Yet, in the cases of our sample, their subcontracting rather seems to entail a recognition from the state that their mode of functioning (more participatory, flexible, and effective) is superior to the mode of functioning of the public sector in certain sectors (savings and credit, primary health, and education). Hence, for the NGOs, this is a way to scale up their impact and increase their degree of auto-financing, while for the state this is a more cost-effective delivery mechanism.

Conclusion: Why the Grassroots Links Up to the Summit

Most Third World NGOs came into being to work with and in civil society. They work in a participatory manner, dealing with local issues considered by their members or constituencies to be of primary importance to their lives. Most often, their history with the state is one of mutual antagonism or at best mutual neglect (indeed, many NGOs came into being precisely because state actions were not considered by local communities to address their problems – if they were not the cause of these problems). Yet, increasingly (although by no means generally) we see NGOs seeking to link up to the state, and to international organizations, as part of a process of scaling up. Why do NGOs seek to move beyond their local implantation and perceived history to interact with the summit?

Our case study, as well as the available literature, suggests there are basically three reasons: the possibility of expanding and securing "good" programs, the necessity to influence government policies that have local impacts, and the availability of funds. The same factors more or less explain why NGOs seek to link with international organizations. In this case, however, a fourth factor can be added: the possibility to influence state behavior through these organizations.

A first reason for NGOs to seek collaboration with the state is the need to secure the future of their programs. As most NGO programs with the poor are not self-financing and not likely to become so, NGOs have a permanent need to secure external financing. Originally, this usually comes from foreign NGOs, foundations, international organizations, and a few bilateral aid agencies. Such funding is always limited in time, often to a very short time. The only source of money and entitlement that has the potential to be permanent is the state. As a result, it makes sense for NGOs to integrate their programs, if proven successful, with those of the public sector, so as to guarantee their survival. A related argument is the one of expanding good programs to the national level, which, again, can basically only be done by the state. In short, the state is the only institution with a national mandate and a guaranteed existence, and it makes sense to transfer successful programs to it in order to scale up their impact.

A second reason for seeking collaboration with governments is that many of the constraints on development emanate at the national policy level. Hence, even though NGOs might have purely local objectives, they need to "go national" to address the profound causes of their local problems. This could be because of the negative impacts of certain state policies, or because the state neglects to fulfill certain functions, or because the type of solutions proposed by the state is harmful to local interests. In all cases, it is crucial for NGOs to influence government policy: it is a prime form of political scaling up required to change local conditions.

Third, grassroots initiatives that are solely funded by internally mobilized resources and external development aid have a limited capacity to expand activities, or touch more people, by themselves. They need external money for quantitative and functional scaling up. BRAC could not provide ORT to 11 million children without millions of dollars of UNICEF money, nor could the Grameen Bank extend its program without government as well as IFAD and World Bank grants. Governments (and IOs) have financial resources that dwarf the grassroots' own resources, or anything they could ever hope to mobilize from local private sources. Access to these resources is one of the main reasons why Third World NGOs seek to build relations with the governments.

Fourth, and applying only to the case of NGOs building links with international organizations, NGOs can seek to change government policies through international organizations (Bebbington & Farrington, 1993: 211). NGOs can also gain greater local recognition and freedom through these links. Indeed, the World Bank sometimes puts pressure on national governments to establish more favorable public policies towards NGOs or to allow their participation in Bank-funded projects (Cernea, 1989: 134-5). NGOs lobby IFAD or the UNDP so that the latter "advocate links with NGOs at the start of [their] dialogue with governments" (*Monday Developments*, 1990: 8). In these cases, too, NGO interaction with IOs is motivated by considerations of political scaling up, the target being the national government.

The View From the Summit

In this section, we ask the inverse question from the previous section: why do governments, and international organizations, want to increase the level of NGO participation? In the past, they have usually neglected the grassroots if not often actively undermined their independent actions, believing them to be misguided, unimportant, or threatening. Yet, nowadays we see many instances of governments and IOs seeking collaboration. We distinguish five related reasons for this process. increased funding, ideological preferences, program effectiveness and sustainability, external pressure, and the creation of constituencies.

First, since the mid-1980s, many Third World governments have faced severe budgetary crises; most of them have undergone, and are still undergoing, structural and sectoral adjustment, causing severe cutbacks in their real spending capacities. Other funding sources have to be found, among others in the poor communities themselves. NGOs are seen as good at mobilizing local resources, financial, material, or human. Hence, collaborating with NGOs may lower the cost of programs or provide community-based maintenance (Bhatnagar, 1992: 29) – an important argument in times of budget distress. The same argument holds more or less for international organizations, whose budgets are generally far smaller than their mandates, and who are similarly interested in tapping new local resources.

Second, it is increasingly recognized that including NGOs in project management and design can entail major benefits in terms of project effectiveness and sustainability. Evaluation after evaluation has shown that the projects financed and managed in a top-down manner tend to lack sustainability, and the prime cause for this is failure to involve local communities and to ensure participation (for the World Bank, see Cernea, 1988: 28; Cernea, 1989: 12). NGOs are seen as having comparative advantages in precisely these fields: flexibility; community trust; capacity to work with the poorest of the poor and in remote areas; independence from governments. (Clark, 1994: 5-6; Refugees, 1989) NGOs are also considered useful mediums for adapting national or international programs to local realities, and for informing central ministries or headquarters about local conditions.

Third, increasingly, governments and international organizations are ideologically in favor of the associative sector. Economically liberal regimes, such as in Brazil or Bangladesh, or more social-democratic ones, such as Burkina Faso under Sankara, now promote the creation of NGOs, albeit usually under as strict as possible government control. In the case of international organizations, their dominant development ideology since the 1980s is predisposed in favor of the private sector: enterprise to produce wealth, and NGOs to redistribute it (Clark, 1994: 4-5; Bebbington & Thiele, 1994: 200).

A fourth, related, factor is that many governments and IOs are under external pressure to work with NGOs. Part of this pressure emanates from the NGOs themselves, with thousands of them pushing for collaboration, proposing models, fighting projects they consider against their interests, and generally imposing themselves as unavoidable partners. Another source of pressure can be found in some rich-country governments that are ideologically attached to grassroots participation, and are increasingly channeling bilateral and multilateral development assistance to projects involving NGOs.

Finally, NGOs can fulfill one more important function for governments and IOs alike: they can help build local constituencies for their policies and programs. In countries with multiparty elections, political parties from all sides like to be seen to be associated with NGOs and their works. It is this process (combined with the desire to capture some of the available international aid money) that has led to the creation of so-called GONGOs (governmental NGOs) or GRINGOs (government-run and inspired NGOs). A similar consideration exists for the international organizations. As a matter of fact, NGOs are obliged by UN resolution 1296 to "undertake to support the work of the UN and to promote knowledge of its principles and activities." UNHCR, for example, recognizes that support for refugees depends on the attitude of ordinary people, and NGOs can better and more freely campaign to change these attitudes than can the UNHCR, which has to avoid controversies with member governments (*Refugees*, 1989: 29; *Monday Developments*, 1991: 1).

Some Problems with Linking Up to the Summit

Notwithstanding the potential, there are also important problems and risks associated with processes of scaling up. On a most practical level, NGO participation in international policy making is a very costly business (time, human resources). This cost has to be weighed against direct help to the poor and the hungry. This is extremely hard to do, but the issue needs constant consideration.

Moreover, the professionalization of staff and procedures and the increased travel that follow from participation in national and international policy making may pull the grassroots organizations' ideology and style of functioning in new directions which the grassroots does not control. There are two aspects to this. The first is that NGOs, as they engage more of their time, energy, and personnel in policy influence, lose their contact with the grassroots, and can actually end up promoting grassroots apathy. This seems to be very much the case of the US, where NGO advocacy is by far the strongest in the world. As Fowler (1992: 2) puts it:

> *Public interest advocacy in the U.S. has apparently failed to strengthen broad citizen participation, and allowed NGOs to rely on governmental or elite patronage in lieu of grassroots support. If NGOs take on professional policy roles without building popular participation in the process, they may unintentionally become part of a system that ignores grassroots input in spite of their initial values and commitments*

The second is that, as NGOs learn how to be effective players in national and international debates, they may lose sight of their goals of empowerment and structural change, and "soften" their positions to be more acceptable to the summit. As Elliott puts it: NGOs may come to emphasize "modernization goals" over "empowerment." (Elliott, 1987; Shaw, 1990: 13; Fowler, 1991: 59. 70; Nerfin, 1992: 90) This can be deliberately sought for by governments: witness the oft-discussed problem of cooptation.

Moreover, to the extent that states and international organizations remain top-down, or repressive or disempowering, working with them risks supporting or legitimating these processes. Fowler states it quite well: "increasingly, NGOs are required to fit into non-participatory systems of development administration." (Fowler, 1991: 67; Brodhead, 1992: 101) A related risk is that, by collaborating with them, organizations become dependent on governments and international organizations, and their vagaries. As governments change, their attitude to collaboration with specific NGOs may shift dramatically, hurting the organizations that have become exposed to them. This risk of course exists also with the donor community: what happens to the hundreds of farmers organizations that worked with USAID projects and funds in the tens of countries where these projects now stop almost overnight?

Finally, increased funding, and the requirements attached to it, as well as the necessity to sustain it over time (so as not to have to cut staff, cars and perks) create a dynamic in favor of staying in business at all cost. It also leads to actions being undertaken because funding is available, and not necessarily because people want or need them (Nerfin, 1992: 84; Kiriwandeniya, 1992; Constantino-David, 1992).

As Peterson (1992: 388) says: "connection to a state may weaken societal actors by reducing their credibility as autonomous actors or by encouraging them to rely on state resources rather than their own efforts. Yet the money and other resources a state transfers to the societal actors it selects as partners can be used by them to build up their own capacities to accomplish goals." The issue boils down to this: to what extent can NGOs become effective actors at the national and international level without losing their strengths as NGOs: their links to their communities, their participatory methodology, their position in favor of structural change? Or, in other terms, how to scale up without becoming like the summit?

SCALING DOWN

Theoretical Rationale for Scaling Down

It is generally held that for the interaction between scaled up NGOs and the summit to be meaningful, the latter should also scale down, *i.e.*, adopt structures and modes of operation that allow local communities and NGOs to build their conceptual, operational, and institutional capacity. This implies the need for what Fowler calls "management for withdrawal," *i.e.*, the development of structures and practices that are geared not to perpetuate or enhance the hold of the summit over the grassroots, but rather towards beneficiary scaling up and autonomy.

On a technical level, scaling down is about the creation of structures and procedures of accountability to and participation of local communities in the development programs that concern them, about hiring and training personnel who are respectful and responsive to the needs of poor people, about the provision of facilities for self-help such as credit, advice, and legal recognition of grassroots organizations, about development programs that are smaller, more participatory, more flexible and based on local learning, about the protection of the livelihoods and the culture of the weak, etc. (Uvin, 1995b). Fundamentally, scaling down is a political affair, entailing an abandonment of power by the summit, as well as a profound attitude change. As such, it is not surprising that it does not happen without significant resistance from the summit, nor that it has not advanced far yet.

Scaling down is an important element of the pressure the NGO community brings to bear on the summit: indeed, thousands of NGOs, in various ways, are putting pressure on their governments, as well as on the World Bank and UN institutions, to adopt a more participative, accountable and decentralized mode of functioning.

Experiences to Date with Scaling Down

During the last decade, an undeniable ideological change has taken place within the summit towards a greater acceptance of the need for grassroots participation and community involvement. This change seems to be caused to a large extent by two simultaneous trends that most of the Third World has been confronted with since the 1980s. The first is the financial crisis facing most Third World governments, and the resulting need to tap new resources for development. This has led to the dominance of a liberal ideological position, emanating from the international financial institutions and the donors and now officially accepted in most Third World countries, that favors self-help and community participation, seen as instruments of economic growth and budgetary savings. The second trend is the widespread erosion of the legitimacy of the state and the pressure for political change many governments face. The end of the Cold War, as well as the decline in politically motivated development aid and the increase in political conditionality, are causal parts of this trend, but its main sources are internal. In many Third World countries, especially in Africa, urban and rural populations as well as elites have been voicing demands for political change, often violently. Powerholders have been forced to provide at least a semblance of change, recognizing organizations of civil society and allowing a greater space for their voice.

Together, both these processes have led to decentralization of government decision-making, increased recognition of and freedom for NGOs, increased funding of NGOs, and opportunities for participation in the implementation if not the decision-making of sectors that were previously under the exclusive control of governments and donors (health, water, education). As a result, grassroots organizations have found a new margin for maneuver, which they have not hesitated to fill. This process of scaling down, then, is not so much the result of a sudden conversion by governments to the virtues of community self-help, as a process grudgingly allowed to take place under the influence of strong financial, economic and political pressures at the international and domestic level.

Important changes have also taken place at the level of international organizations. To a certain extent, financial pressure has played a role here too, but ideological change is more important. Many donors have adopted mechanisms to allow NGOs to scale up on their own terms – a new phenomenon in international aid. The USAID Special Facility allows its mission heads to fund small grassroots actions. UNDP's Partners in Development Program since 1990 offers small grants ($25,000 per country) to NGOs to implement community-based initiatives in more than 60 countries (Livernash, 1992: 16; Nerfin, 1992: 85). All these mechanisms are cheap and small – cynically spoken, crumbs that fell off the table. They do *not* modify the mode of functioning of the summit, or change the spending patterns of most of their activities – which is what scaling down is really about.

Other processes, however, hold the promise of scaling down. Here, we will provide some examples from the World Bank and UNDP. In 1984 the Bank created a mechanism which meets every six months for regular consultation with NGOs. NGOs also currently participate in 40% of Bank projects, albeit largely at the "junior implementation partner" level. More recent changes, however, move the Bank further in the direction of scaling down.

First, the Bank has expressly written consultation with affected groups and NGOs into its operational directives. This was done under pressure from the US, and against the will of most Third World member states, who considered this a violation of their sovereignty. Note that the language of this directive states that consultation shall be done by the borrowing government ("the Bank expects the borrower to consult with affected groups and local NGOs"), which is logical in Bank language, for theoretically the Bank always acts through the government.

Second, as a result of NGO pressure, and "following a new policy of disclosure of operational information approved by the Executive Directors in August 1993," the World Bank has created a Public Information System, designed to "make available to the public a range of operational documents that were previously restricted to official users." Ordinary citizens now have access to more project information than before – albeit by no means all.

Third, the Bank created an independent inspection panel, composed of three persons, that can deal with complaints that the World Bank is violating its own procedures. Cases can be brought before the panel by any organization representing the people affected. This is very difficult, for it necessitates excellent knowledge both of the project itself and of the Bank's procedural guidelines. In practice, that means Southern NGOs can only lodge complaints with strong Northern NGO backing. Recently, the first case regarding the Arun dam project in Nepal has been presented to that panel (*Monday Developments*, 1994: 4; Bradlow, 1994: 8).

As for the UNDP, it created its own body for regular consultation with NGOs in 1984, and developed innovative funding mechanisms for them. Among the latter are the Grassroots Initiatives Support Fund, which provides small grants to self-help initiatives in Africa, and the Africa 2000 Network (followed by similar initiatives in Asia and Latin America) which supplies grants and technical assistance to Southern GROs and GRSOs that are active in ecologically sustainable development (Nerfin, 1992: 86; Brodhead, 1992: 104-6). In November 1993, UNDP endorsed a strategy paper that stresses the need to include NGOs in its policy dialogue with governments and to develop new operational frameworks and procedures that allow for effective capacity building of NGOs. The latter category implies potentially important processes of UNDP scaling down: modification of operational procedures regarding contracting and procurement; reformulation of UNDP staff recruitment, training, and performance criteria; increased freedom for national country representatives to conduct dialogues and collaborate with NGOs; funding for dissemination of NGO publications, etc. These innovations are still young, but they have the potential to create a new learning process whereby the UNDP and its staff, traditionally highly government-centered, learn to work in a meaningful manner with NGOs (UNDP, 1993, 1994; personal communication with Sarah Timpson, UNDP Deputy Assistant Administrator, Bureau for Programmes and Policy)

Conclusion

NGOs are scaling up and acting on higher levels than they used to. They now lobby governments and international organizations, implement development programs with million dollar budgets, participate in international conferences, and propose workable innovative development models to their governments. This does not apply to all NGOs: many of them lack both the desire and the capacity to do so. But there is a worldwide trend for grassroots organizations to scale up in the ways described above.

The summit – both governments and international organizations – has its own reasons to allow this to happen, if not to encourage it. Some of these reasons are ideological, having to do with a sincere commitment to participation and self-help. Other reasons are opportunistic, the result of budgetary distress and the need to push the cost of services down. Still others are the result of external pressure, from international organizations and foreign donors, but also from the NGOs themselves. Whatever the reasons, opportunities have emerged for the grassroots to link up to the summit as serious, unavoidable actors.

In building links with NGOs, the summit is under pressure to scale down, to adopt more flexible, respectful, and accountable procedures and structures, so as to turn interaction into partnership – and, again, there is significant NGO pressure to do so. This does not take place without resistance, but, for a variety of reasons outlined in this article, change is taking place.

This is not necessarily all for the greater good of everyone. The past teaches us that scaled up NGOs risk losing their initial strengths, that the grassroots-summit interactions often turn to the detriment of the grassroots, that it is dangerous to carve up countries into a multitude of NGO-dominated small territories, that the summit's commitment to self-help and participation is fickle and can be reversed whenever vested interests feel threatened, and that NGOs can be fickle, opportunistic, inefficient too. But the promise exists that some of these new relations will in fact fulfill their potential, and provide innovative coalitions to combat hunger and poverty throughout the world.

Notes

*   I thank Marc Cohen, Ellen Messer, David Miller, Robert Northrup, and Paul Wapner for their comments.

1.   Hence, we excluded Amartya Sen, Representative Tony Hall, James Ingram, Prof. Carlos Ochoa, Prof. Yuan Long Ping, the International Committe of the Red Cross, Bread for the World, and others.

References

Ashe, J. *et. al.* (1992).*Access to Credit for Poor Women: A Scale-Up Study of Projects Carried Out by Freedom From Hunger in Mali and Ghana.* Bethesda: GEMINI, Technical Report No. 33.

Bebbington, A. and J. Farrington. (1993). "Governments, NGOs and Agricultural Development: Perspectives on Changing Inter-Organisational Relationships." *The Journal of Developmental Studies* 29, 2 (January).

Bebbington, A. and G. Thiele (eds) (1994). *Non-Governmental Organizations and the State in Latin America. Rethinking Roles in Sustainable Agricultural Development.* London: Routledge.

Berg, R (1987). *Non-Governmental Organizations: New Force in Third World Development and Politics.* East Lansing: Center for Advanced Study of International Development.

Bhatnagar, B. (1992). "Participatory Development and the World Bank: Opportunities and Concerns." Washington D.C.: World Bank Discussion Papers No. 183.

Bradlow, D.B. (1994). "You Can Help Hold the World Bank Accountable," *Monday Developments,* May 9.

Brodhead, T. (1992). "Cooperation and Discord Towards Collaboration among NGOs, Aid Donors and Third World Governments." *Development, International Cooperation and the NGOs. First International Meeting of NGOs and the United Nations System Agencies.,* 97-107. Rio de Janeiro: IBASE/UNDP.

Cernea, M. (1988)*Nongovernmental Organization and Local Development,* Washington D.C.: World Bank Discussion Paper 40.

Cernea, M. (1989). "Nongovernmental Organizations and Local Development." *Regional Development Dialogue ,* 10, 2.

Chowdhury, A. N. (1989). *Let Grassroots Speak. People's participation, self-help groups and NGOs in Bangladesh.* Dhaka: University Press.

Clark J. (1991)*Democratizing Development: The Role of Voluntary Organizations.* West Hartford: Kumarian Press.

Clark, J. (1994)*The Relationship between the State and the Voluntary Sector.* Electronic message: International Development and Global Education List, intdev-l&uriacc.bitnet, June 13.

Constantino-David, K. (1992). The Philippine experience in scaling up, in Edwards, M. and D. Hulme (eds.). *Making a difference: NGOs and Development in a Changing World.* London: Earthscan.

Elliott, C. (1987). "Some Aspects of Relations between the North and the South in the NGO Sector." *World Development* 15, Supplement.

Fisher, J. (1993.). *The Road from Rio: Sustainable Development and the Nongovernmental Movement in the Third World.* Westport, Connecticut: Praeger.

Fowler, A. (1991). The Role of NGOs in Changing State-Society Relations: Perspectives from Eastern and Southern Africa, *Development Policy Review*, 9, 1.

Fowler, A. (1992). "Building Partnerships between Northern and Southern Development NGOs: Issues for the Nineties." *Development, Journal of SID* , no. 1.

Howes, M. and M.G. Sattar (1992). Bigger and better? Scaling up strategies pursued by BRAC 1972-1991, in Edwards, M. and D. Hulme (eds.) *Making a Difference: NGOS and Development in a Changing World*. London: Earthscan.

Hyden, G. (1992). *Some Notes on Scaling Up*. Gainesville, FL: unpublished paper.

Kiriwandeniya, P. A. (1992). The growth of the SANASA movement in Sri Lanka, in Edwards, M. and D. Hulme (eds.). *Making a difference: NGOs and development in a changing world*. London: Earthscan.

Korten, D. (1990)*Getting to the 21st Century. Voluntary Action and the Global Agenda*. West Hartford: Kumarian Press.

Kwan Kai Hong (1991). Concilier la cooperation avec le developpement: les perspectives offertes par l'auto-promotion. In Kwan Kai Hong (ed.) *Jeux et enjeux de l'auto-promotion. Vers d'autres formes de coopération au developpement*, Geneva, Paris: Institut Universitaire d'Etudes du Développement, Presses Universitaires de France.

Lecomte, B. (1991). "Processus d'autopromotion et formes d'appui adaptées." In Kwan Kai Hong (ed.) *Jeux et enjeux de l'auto-promotion. Vers d'autres formes de coopération au developpement*, Geneva, Paris: Institut Universitaire d'Etudes du Développement, Presses Universitaires de France.

Livernash, R. (1992). The Growing Influence of NGOs in the Developing World. *Environment*, 34, 5 (June).

Lovell, C. (1992). *Breaking the Cycle of Poverty. The BRAC Strategy*. West Hartford: Kumarian Press.

Mayfield, J. B. (1985). *Go to the People. Releasing the Rural Poor though the People's School System*. West Hartford: Kumarian Press.

Monday Developments (1990). "IFAD, NGOs Agree on Measures to Strengthen Collaboration" July 9: 8.

Monday Developments (1991). "High Commissioner Calls for Partnership with NGOs" Sept. 30: 1.

Monday Developments (1994). "World Bank Panel Will Soon Begin Hearing Complaints" May 9: 4.

Morgan, M. (1990). Stretching the Development Dollar: The Potential for Scaling up. *Grassroots Development*, 14, 1.

Nerfin, M. (1992). The Relationship NGOs/UN Agencies/Governments: Challenges, Possibilities, Prospects. In *Development, International Cooperation and the NGOs. First International Meeting of NGOs and the United Nations System Agencies.*, 79-96. Rio de Janeiro: IBASE-UNDP.

Peterson, M.J. (1992). Transnational Activity, International Society and World Politics. *Millenium*, 21, 3: 371-388.

Refugees (1989). Facts and Feelings: the UNHCR/NGO Relationship" Sept. 1989: 29.

Shaw, T. (1990). "Popular Participation in Non-Governmental Structures in Africa: Implications for Democratic Development." *Africa Today*, 3rd Quarter.

Tendler, J. (1982). *Turning Private Voluntary Organizations into Development Agencies: Questions for Evaluation.* Washington D.C.: USAID Program Evaluation Discussion Paper 12.

Uphoff, N. (1993). Grassroots Organizations and NGOs in Rural Development: Opportunities with Diminishing States and Expanding Markets. *World Development*, 21, 4.

UNDP (1993). *UNDP and Organizations of Civil Society: Building Sustainable Partnerships.* A Strategy Paper presented to, and endorsed by, the Strategy and Management Committee on 23 Nov. 1993.

UNDP (1994). *Note to the Administrator on Progress in UNDP Cooperation with Institutions of the Civil Society,* New York.

Uvin, P. (1995a). Fighting Hunger at the Grassroots: Paths to Scaling Up, *World Development*, 23, 6 (June).

Uvin, P. (1995b). Scaling Up the Grassroots and Scaling Down the Summit: the Relations between Third World Nongovernmental Organizations and the United Nations. *Third World Quarterly*, (Sept.).

CHAPTER 6

Progress in Overcoming Hunger in China: 1989-1994

Chen Chunming

Since implementation of the economic reform and "open to the world" policy in 1978, China's agriculture production system has fundamentally changed from a system of collective responsibility to one of family responsibility. This has greatly enhanced farmers' initiatives, and agricultural production has grown tremendously: grains production rose from 304.77 million tons in 1978 to 442.66 million tons in 1992. As the increase in population during 1978-1992 was approximately 200 million (from 970 million to 1.17 billion), the national average of per caput grain production increased from 314kg to 378kg. Simultaneously, urban and rural income have been growing. Urban household income in 1978 was 316 Yuan RMB per caput, and 1,826 in 1992 – a deflated increase of 228%. Rural household income was 133 Yuan RMB in 1978 and 784 Yuan RMB in 1992 – a 328% increase.

Table 6.1 National Average Food Consumption (kg/year)

	1*	2	3	4	5	6	7	8	9
1978	195.5	1.60	7.67	0.75	0.44	1.97	3.50	3.42	2.57
1979	207.0	1.96	9.66	0.82	0.57	2.08	3.22	3.56	2.98
1980	213.8	2.30	11.16	0.83	0.80	2.27	3.41	3.83	3.41
1981	219.2	2.94	11.08	0.85	0.84	2.44	3.57	4.10	4.42
1982	225.4	3.53	11.75	1.03	1.02	2.52	3.85	4.41	5.24
1983	231.5	4.01	12.31	1.10	1.18	2.95	4.00	4.46	5.79
1984	249.7	4.66	12.93	1.23	1.35	3.88	4.32	4.85	6.55
1985	251.7	5.08	13.84	1.31	1.56	4.93	4.84	5.57	7.61
1986	252.7	5.17	14.22	1.31	1.72	5.20	5.33	6.04	8.97
1987	248.9	5.60	14.39	1.43	1.71	5.50	5.49	6.59	10.39
1988	246.1	5.87	14.73	1.58	1.75	5.74	5.66	6.17	11.42
1989	239.1	5.35	15.36	1.58	1.79	5.88	6.17	4.92	11.33
1990	238.8	5.67	16.64	1.73	1.73	6.27	6.53	4.98	11.63
1991	234.5	5.89	17.44	1.79	1.98	7.10	6.79	4.98	11.93
1992	235.9	6.29	18.22	2.05	2.31	7.75	7.29	5.42	12.94

Source: 1993 Yearbook of Statistics of China, China Statistical Publishing House, Beijing, 1993.
* 1=cereals 2=vegetable oil 3=pork 4=mutton and beef 5=poultry 6=eggs 7=fish and shellfish 8=sugar 9=wine

The national average of food consumption shown in Table 1 indicates that the food security problem has been solved nationally since 1984: from 1984 to 1982, grain consumption has been maintained at about 250 kg per capita per year, and consumption of meat has increased 5 kg, poultry and eggs 5 kg, and fish 3 kg per year. Table 2 shows that the dietary pattern has been substantially improved.

Table 6.2. Consumption of Energy, Protein, and Fat (National average)

	Energy (kcal)	Protein (g/day)		Fat	
		g	% total energy	g	% total energy
1978	1833	46.5	10.1	28.2	13.8
1979	2010	49.4	9.8	32.5	14.6
1980	2105	51.5	9.8	36.2	15.5
1981	2175	52.3	9.6	38.1	15.8
1982	2271	54.7	9.6	41.4	16.4
1983	2341	56.3	9.6	44.0	16.9
1984	2532	61.0	9.6	48.1	17.1
1985	2590	62.3	9.6	51.1	17.8
1986	2621	62.9	9.6	52.3	18.0
1987	2617	62.3	9.5	53.3	18.2
1988	2625	62.8	9.6	51.9	17.8
1989	2535	60.9	9.6	53.8	19.1
1990	2524	61.3	9.7	56.7	20.2
1991	2550	61.0	9.6	58.7	20.7
1992	2597	62.2	9.6	61.4	21.3

Source: Calculated from data in 1993 Yearbook of Statistics of China, China Statistical Publishing House, Beijing, 1993.

Household Food Security

Since national-average figures always conceal geographical or income group differences, Tables 3 through 8 present household food consumption/intake data collected by 1) the State Statistic Bureau through the national household survey; 2) the Nutrition Surveillance System 1990 pilot study carried out jointly by the Chinese Academy of Preventive Medicine (CAPM) and the State Statistic Bureau (SSB) with a subsample of the national household survey; and 3) the Third Nationwide Nutritional Survey carried out by the Institute of Nutrition and Food Hygiene, CAPM. This discussion of household food security will focus on rural households, since in 1993 the income of urban residents reached 2337 RMB, 2.5 times the income of rural residents: 921 RMB (State Statistic Bureau, 1993), and complete household food consumption data for urban residents are difficult to obtain because of the increasing frequency of meals outside the home.

Table 3 shows the food consumption of rural households. Cereal consumption has remained around 250 kg per capita per year since 1978, but meat consumption has increased from 5.76 to 11.03 kg, poultry from 0.15 to 1.49 kg, eggs from 0.80 to 2.85 kg, and vegetable oil from 1.96 to 5.85 kg. Nutrient intake data also indicate

Table 6.3. Food Consumption in Rural Households (kg/caput/year)

	1	2	3 & 4	5	6	7	8	9	10*
1978	248.0	1.96	5.76	0.25	0.80	0.84	0.73	1.22	142.0
1980	257.0	2.49	7.75	0.66	1.20	1.10	1.06	1.89	127.0
1985	257.0	4.04	10.97	1.03	2.05	1.64	1.46	4.37	131.0
1988	260.0	4.76	10.71	1.25	2.28	1.91	1.41	5.93	130.0
1989	262.0	4.81	11.00	1.28	2.41	2.10	1.54	5.95	133.0
1990	262.1	5.17	11.34	1.26	2.41	2.13	1.50	6.14	135.0
1991	255.6	5.65	12.15	1.34	2.73	2.21	1.40	6.38	127.0
1992	250.5	5.85	11.83	1.49	2.85	2.25	1.54	6.56	129.1

Source: 1993 Yearbook of Statistics of China, National Statistic Publishing House, Beijing, 1993.
* 10=vegetables

the quality improvement of the diet in rural households (Table 4). The energy intake of rural households has reached 2597 kcal per person per day and intake of protein is at 63.5 g per day. Animal protein, which was 3.5% of total protein intake in 1978, increased to 7% in 1985 and to 8% in 1992. Energy from fat, 10.4% in 1978, increased to 15% in 1985, and to 17% in 1992.

Table 6.4. Consumption of Energy, Protein, and Fat (in rural households, China)

	Energy (kcal)	Protein g	Protein % total energy	Fat g	Fat % total energy
1978	2310	60.3	10.4	26.7	10.4
1980	2432	63.0	10.4	33.2	12.3
1985	2531	64.3	10.2	42.1	15.0
1988	2581	64.9	10.1	44.1	15.4
1989	2636	65.5	9.9	44.9	15.3
1990	2631	66.0	10.0	45.8	15.7
1991	2594	64.6	10.0	48.3	16.8
1992	2559	63.5	9.9	48.4	17.0

Source: Calculated from data in 1993 Yearbook of statistics of China

Tables 5 and 6 data collected through the 1990 pilot study of the National Nutritional Surveillance System show food consumption and nutrient intake of rural households by income groups (Chen & Shao, 1994). Even the lowest-income groups in the seven provinces had energy intakes ranging from 87% to 106% of the RDA.

Table 6.5. Food Consumption of Rural Households (Pilot survey of Food and Nutrition Surveillance System) in 1990 (kg/caput/year)

Province*	BJ	HB	HL	NX	ZJ	GD	SC
Cereals	207	239	314	274	289	279	258
Veg. oil	4.7	3.5	8.4	5.8	2.6	3.8	1.8
Meat	12	7	11	10	13	17	18
Poultry	0.7	0.3	1.7	0.4	1.7	4.8	0.9
Eggs	4.8	2.9	3.7	1.3	2.4	2.3	2.2
Beans	1.3	3.0	1.9	4.1	2.2	1.1	1.2
Bean prod.	3.6	4.2	9.6	1.6	1.0	5.6	3.6
Vegetables/fruits	131	104	95	87	105	110	154
Sugar	2.0	1.3	1.9	2.0	3.2	4.7	1.9
Wine	9.6	3.5	9.1	1.1	16.1	4.8	4.4

Source: Food, Nutrition and Health Status of Chinese in Seven Provinces 1990, China Statistical Publishing House 1994.

*Provinces:
BJ = Beijing Municipality   NX = Ninxia Hui Autonomous Region   SC = Sichuan Province
HB = Hebei Province   ZJ = Zejiang Province
HL = Helongjiang Province   GD = Guangdong Province

Data from the Third Nationwide Nutritional Survey in 1992 are shown in Tables 7 and 8. The national average energy intake was 2328 kcal (92% of RDA). For the urban population, it was 2395 kcal (99.8% RDA), for the rural population, it was 2294 kcal (95.7% RDA). The national average protein intake was 68 g; for urban and rural populations it was 75.1 g and 64.3 g, respectively. When low-, medium-, and high-income households are compared, there is no significant difference in energy intake, but protein and fat intakes are strongly correlated with income (Ge & Zhai, in press).

These data show that food security at the household level has been largely achieved in the past 15 years. However, because of the unevenness of economic development among areas of the country, food insecurity problems still exist. The 1990 nutrition surveillance data indicate that about 8% of rural households had an energy intake lower than 1500 kcal per Reference Man [male adult under conditions of light labor] (Chen & Shao, 1994); 42% of them belonged to the 10% lowest income households. The inequity in food consumption among income groups and between urban and rural residents is worth noting: the energy contribution of animal foods to the high-income group is 4 times that for the low-income group; urban households got 2.5 times more energy from animal foods than rural households (Ge & Zhai, in press). In 1990, the energy contribution of fat to 75% of the rural households was below 15%. Animal protein intake is lower in the north; here the highest-income households eat about 9% animal protein, compared to the 11% eaten by income group 3 (medium income) in the southern provinces (Chen & Shao, 1994). Child nutrition surveillance in 101 poor counties revealed that the total energy intake of infants 6-11 months old, including breast milk and supplementary food, only met 64% of the RDA and protein intake met only 48%; for children aged 12-23 months the situation was a bit better: 75% of the energy RDA and 56% of the protein RDA (Li & Zhai, in press).

Table 6.6. Energy, Protein and Fat Intake of Income Groups of Rural Households in 1990

Income Group*	BJ	HB	NX	ZJ	GD	SC
Energy Intake, kcal						
1	1960	1970	1819	1917	2129	1889
2	1855	2093	2142	2217	2174	2068
3	2091	2201	2319	2314	2191	2271
4	2371	2256	2480	2559	2583	2485
5	2605	2284	2642	2711	2532	2606
6	2972	2559	3074	2983	2797	2852
Energy Intake, %RDA						
1	88	92	89	95	106	87
2	88	96	92	100	106	88
3	99	99	98	101	106	93
4	97	99	105	110	112	99
5	121	98	109	114	106	107
6	110	103	120	117	112	112
Fat, % total Energy intake						
1	17.4	12.5	10.6	9.2	12.2	12.1
2	17.4	12.5	10.8	10.7	13.5	12.1
3	17.3	13.0	12.3	11.5	14.1	12.9
4	17.3	13.9	12.9	12.3	14.8	13.8
5	17.7	14.9	14.1	13.2	14.9	15.0
6	18.8	16.1	14.3	14.3	16.3	18.1

Protein Intake, g (Animal Protein in % of total protein intake)

Income Group*	BJ	HB	NX	ZJ	GD	SC
1	58.9	59.4	54.9	51.0	51.9	48.1
	(9.3)	(3.9)	(3.1)	(8.8)	(13.9)	(9.4)
2	54.4	64.7	64.6	57.0	53.0	52.5
	(7.9)	(4.2)	(4.0)	(10.0)	(13.6)	(9.6)
3	60.8	67.9	65.4	59.6	58.4	55.4
	(9.3)	(4.6)	(5.0)	(11.9)	(15.9)	(10.5)
4	68.1	70.2	68.7	65.6	64.5	61.0
	(11.3)	(5.4)	(6.8)	(10.6)	(16.9)	(11.5)
5	77.2	71.4	72.5	70.7	64.7	66.6
	(10.9)	(6.4)	(9.1)	(14.0)	(20.6)	(13.2)
6	86.5	80.8	84.5	79.2	71.8	73.6
	(14.2)	(8.9)	(9.6)	(16.3)	(24.3)	(16.3)

Source: Food, Nutrition and Health Status of Chinese in Seven Provinces, 1990, China Statistical Publishing House, Beijing, 1994.

*Group 1 to 6 ranks the households into lowest to highest income groups: Group 1: the lowest 10 percentile, Group 2: 11 to 25 percentile, Group 3: 26-50 percentile, Group 4: 51-75 percentile, Group 5: 76-90 percentile, Group 6: 91-100 percentile.

110   Chen Chunming

Table 6.7. Intake of Energy, Protein, and Fat of The Chinese People
(1992 Nationwide nutritional survey)

	Urban		Rural		National average	
	Mean	%RDA	Mean	%RDA	Mean	%RDA
Energy (kcal)	2395	99.8	2294	95.7	2328	97.1
Protein (g)	75.1	98.7	64.3	85.9	68.0	90.3
Fat (g)	77.7		48.3		58.3	
Source of energy (%)						
Cereals	54.7		71.7		66.8	
Legumes	2.1		1.7		1.8	
Animal foods	15.2		6.2		9.3	
Energy distribution (%)						
Protein	12.7		11.3		11.8	
Fat	28.4		18.6		22.0	
Source of protein (%)						
Cereals	48.8		68.3		61.6	
Legumes	5.8		4.8		5.1	
Animal foods	31.5		12.4		18.9	
Source of fat (%)						
Animal	38.7		36.4		37.2	
Vegetable	61.3		63.6		62.8	

Source: 1992 Third Nationwide Nutritional Survey, in press.

Table 6.8. National Average of Macronutrient Intake by Income Groups
(Per reference man per day)

			Income groups		
			Low	Medium	High
	Urban	2395	2299	2384	2500
Energy (kcal)	Rural	2294	2292	2274	2315
	U&R	2328	2294	2285	2410
	Urban	75	65	76	84
Protein (g)	Rural	64	62	63	68
	U&R	68	62	65	77
	Urban	78	60	81	92
Fat (g)	Rural	48	38	46	61
	U&R	58	40	55	80

Source: 1992 Third Nationwide Nutritional Survey, in press.

Table 6.9. BMI Distribution of Adults Aged 20–45 in China

| | % of adults aged 20–45 | |
	BMI<18.5	BMI>25
Urban		
1982	11.5	7.2
1989	10.1	12.0
1992	9.0	14.9
Rural		
1982	9.0	5.5
1989	7.7	7.5
1992	8.0	8.4

Source: (i) 1989 Nutritional Survey of Elderly
(ii) 1982 Second Nationwide Nutritional survey
(iii) 1992 Third Nationwide Nutritional Survey

Nutrition Status

The nutrition status of Chinese adults, as measured by Body Mass Index (BMI), is basically good: data from the 1992 nutritional survey showed the proportion of adults aged 20–45 with a BMI <18.5 was 9.0% in urban and 8% in rural populations. For a BMI >25, the proportions were 14.9% in urban and 8.4% in rural areas. Thus, 76.1% of the urban and 83.6% of the rural populations have a normal BMI. Table 9 compares data on the BMI in 1982 and 1989 (Chen, 1993; Ge, in press). The trend to overweight among adults is evident, and the percentage of underweight is decreasing in both urban and rural populations (Ge & Zhai, in press). This may illustrate the nutritional improvement of Chinese adults in general.

Table 6.10. Prevalence of Underweight (% wt/age < standard mean-2 SD)

| | Urban | | | Rural | | |
Province@	1987*	1990*	1992#	1987*	1990*	1992#
HL	9.0	5.3	3.2	15.2	17.6	10.3
NX	16.6	5.3	4.6	17.4	14.5	13.0
SC	25.1	10.4	8.5	31.4	27.1	23.9
GD	24.0	11.1	11.3	40.7	32.6	31.1
ZJ	6.5	10.1	4.8	13.4	16.0	9.5
NM	8.6	-	4.3	14.2	-	10.9
YN	15.5	-	15.0	40.1	-	27.4
HUB	10.0	-	7.7	18.5	-	15.7
SD	5.1	-	1.6	9.4	-	9.6
HB	-	4.2	4.0	-	13.8	11.8

@ NM = Neimung Mongolian Autonomous Region   YN = Yunnan Province
HUB = Hubei Province   SD = Shandong
HL, NX, SC, GD, ZJ and HB are the same as in Table 5
* Age below 6
# Age below 5

Table 6.11. Prevalence of Stunting (% ht/age < standard mean -2 SD)

Province	Urban			Rural		
	1987*	1990*	1992#	1987*	1990*	1992#
HL	11.8	12.7	9.9	28.3	32.9	28.0
NX	21.6	6.1	7.6	33.1	24.6	29.3
SC	29.8	10.1	14.7	51.5	54.8	51.3
GD	18.9	14.3	14.0	48.7	49.2	46.7
ZJ	7.0	4.8	5.1	21.4	25.0	22.9
NM	12.2	-	9.9	24.1	-	34.7
YN	8.9	-	24.9	50.9	-	50.8
HUB	10.0	-	18.5	28.7	-	42.4
SD	8.8	-	5.1	15.6	-	25.8
HB	-	5.7	8.8	-	27.0	32.0

* Age below 6
# Age below 5

Recent surveys also show an improvement in children's nutrition status. Tables 10 and 11 compare the prevalence of underweight (percent of children whose weight for age is below the standard median – 2 SD) and stunting (percent of children whose height for age is below the standard median – 2 SD) among children below 6 years of age from 1987 to 1992. The prevalence of underweight decreased at least 50% in all urban areas except Yunnan Province. In rural areas, the prevalence decreased by only 15-32% in this period, except for Shandong Province, where the prevalence was quite low even in 1987. The prevalence of stunting decreased much more slowly urban areas, while there was very little change among rural children. There were clear increases in the prevalence of stunting in rural Inner Mongolia, Hubei and Shandong and Hebei, and in urban Yunnan, Hubei and Hebei. This needs further analysis.

Table 6.12. Comparison of Growth Distribution (ht/age Z score)

	1987		1990	
	mean	SD*	mean	SD
Rural				
HL	-1.50	1.19	-1.66	1.34
NX	-1.68	1.15	-1.34	1.10
ZJ	-1.40	0.95	-1.28	1.34
GD	-2.15	1.14	-2.10	1.38
SC	-2.27	1.03	-2.23	1.35
Urban				
HL	-0.88	1.03	-0.60	1.42
NX	-1.36	1.13	-0.45	1.17
ZJ	-0.66	0.96	-0.37	1.03
GD	-1.15	1.07	-0.86	1.10
SC	-1.49	1.14	-0.79	1.10

Source: Food, Nutrition and Health Status of Chinese in Seven Provinces 1990, China Statistical Publishing House, Beijing 1994, p 75.

Table 12 shows the standard deviation of the height-for-age Z score in 1987 and 1990. Although the overall mean growth of rural children did not change much after 1987, growth composition did change, becoming more heterogeneous in terms of distribution: the standard deviation of the Z score in most provinces increased over time. In contrast, the distribution of growth in urban children has been constant except for one province, Helongjiang (HL), where it seemed more homogeneous over the whole distribution. Increasingly uneven income distribution during 1987 to 1990, as well as the possibly increasing inequity in dietary quality, is also a factor causing the gap in nutrition status between the urban and rural population.

Actions for Overcoming Hunger

Promote Agricultural Production

In order to achieve food adequacy at the household level, the Chinese government has put agricultural production at the top of the list of economic development programs. Grain production is always the first priority. The "Household Production Responsibility System" made dramatic and continuous growth in agricultural production in the last 15 years: total grain production was 304.8 million tons in 1978, 456.7 million in 1993. During the transition from a planned to a market economy, agriculture faces the challenge of a decline in interest in grain production due to farmers' interests in the higher profit of cash crops. To address the issue at the national level the government has been establishing policies to encourage grain production:

First is a "National Program on Food Structure Reform and Development in the 1990s," which was promulgated in 1993. The program has a nutritional emphasis and aims at future food production that is economically sustainable and nutritionally adequate and healthy. The 1990s will be the critical time for coordinating food production with food consumption and nutritional requirements.

The recommended dietary pattern for year 2000 is:

(a) daily energy intake 2400 kcal/reference man;
(b) energy from cereals/tubers 65% of total energy intake;
(c) daily 70 g intake of protein for 14% of total energy intake; 40% of protein from beans and animal foods;
(d) fat intake 25-30% of total energy intake;
(e) salt intake less than 10 g.

Second is a corresponding food production strategy, with set objectives for urban/rural, developed/poor areas to meet to achieve the consumption goal of basic foods (kg/caput/year) by the year 2000. The goals for urban and rural areas will be, respectively: cereals 150 and 230, meat 34 and 23, eggs 12 and 9, aquatic 12 and 8, vegetables 140 and 115, fruits 33 and 14. For the poor areas, goals will be: cereals 250, meat 16, eggs 4, aquatic 4, vegetables 140, fruits 9.

Third is the Program's emphasis on coordinated policies: related governmental sectors have been requested to set up matched economic policies, policies for technology development and for management, and policies for pre- and post harvest. Measures specifically mentioned in the document are: 1) adjustment of the food production structure emphasizing a shift from grain-cash crops to grain-feed-cash crops and soybean production; 2) development of animal foods, including reducing the proportion of pork to 70% of meat production and raising chicken meat to 18%; 3) development of the international food trade; 4) facilitating food processing, storage, and transportation; 5) orientation of food consumption behavior toward a healthy dietary pattern; 6) increasing investment in fundamental facilities for food development, such as improved varieties and fine breed, immunization, warehouses, transportation, etc.; 7) upgrading scientific and technological development and promoting intensive production of foods; 8) education and human resource development; 9) strengthening food safety controls; 10) perfection of nutrition management and the food and nutrition surveillance system. According to the Program document, a National Consultative Committee on Food and Nutrition was established in 1993 as an advisory body to the State Council on food and nutrition policy. The Committee consists of 26 members from various sectors. The Program is now implemented at the provincial level; training courses for the provincial officers supported by FAO were finished in May of this year. 1994.

Fourth is Central Government investments in agricultural production, which have been increasing for 15 years: an increase of 35.6% was planned for 1994. Investment at the local level has been encouraged, as has been the accumulation of production resources by individual farmers.

Since 1982, measures have been taken to develop commodity grain production: 274 counties were selected in main grain-producing areas as commodity grain bases. After eight years, the system for popularizing agricultural and breeding techniques has become established in these counties. The arable land of these counties accounted for only one-fifth of the country total, but grain output accounted for more than one-fourth, and for 40% of total commodity-grain production. The number of grain bases was increased to 362 in 1993 and another 100 were planned in 1994.

It appears that the high grain-producing counties have become "poor counties" in recent years due to increased production costs and the limited price adjustment. Actions and policies to support overall capacity development in these counties aim at income generation, technology upgrading, and community development, such as investing in township/small city establishment; a pilot project is underway in 100 counties. The plan aims at utilizing foreign resources for projects such as agricultural construction; importing seeds of good varieties of grains; providing credit for township food-processing industries; and building warehouse for grain storage. In addition, two billion Yuan RMB/year from 1993-1996 are allocated to "Work for Food" programs for the poor populations within the counties, and the incentives for grain exportation will be granted to provinces supplying grain to other provinces.

Various other incentives are also in the Plan, including a three-year tax exemption for agricultural projects using presently uncultivated land/water and area/shoal.

Protect Grain Producers and Grain Consumers

After the grain production boost in 1978, the grain supply in the market greatly increased and the agroproducts/grains subject to State imposition and monopoly for purchase and marketing were gradually reduced. By 1993 all agroproducts were managed through the market mechanism. Since 1993, food rationing at low fixed prices for urban residents has been ended, and subsidies are now given to the residents for compensation. Grain pricing, both the government purchase price and the market price, is critical to producers and consumers. The government must play an important role in protecting producers from losses during bumper harvests, and in keeping food affordable for consumers during times of scarcity, when market forces work against them. The Chinese government has been making great efforts in this regard:

It has established a "protection price," on the basis of production cost plus moderate profit, for State grain purchase by contracts and for buffer stocks to maintain a stable price even in a falling market. The "protection price" is subject to gradual increase.

It has also established a National/Provincial Risk Fund for Grain Production to be used to level the market price. When it is lower than the protection price the Government will purchase grains from farmers at the protection price; when the market price is too high the Government will sell grains to the market at a reasonable price. The Risk Fund is used to balance the deficit caused by such adjustments.

It has strengthened the Grain Buffer Stock System by setting up a Grain Stock Fund to facilitate the capability of grain price modulation. A Bureau of Grain Stock affiliated with the State Council, launched to work on market price leveling and food for disaster relief, has proven very effective in addressing the food supply for the flooded areas in 1991 and in leveling off rising grain prices at the end of 1992.

These price adjustment policies have encouraged farmers to grow cereals and have played an important role in increasing total grain production and in slowing down the land loss for grain in the past decade.

Reduce the Cost of Agricultural Production

In shifting to a market economy, the price incentives for fertilizers and diesel oil have been eliminated, resulting in increased production costs for farmers. The Government has compensated with an extra price subsidy added to the regular purchase price when buying grain from affected farmers. In addition, limits have been mandated for production costs at State-run factories to control the ex-factory price.

Ensure The Food Supply for The Urban Population

In addition to providing for a government-ensured supply of affordable grain for the urban population, the State Council requested all city mayors to plan and implement a "Food Basket Program" to ensure an adequate supply of non-staple foods. Since 1987 this approach has played an important role in promoting food availability in the cities and controlling the market price of non-staples. Production of meat, milk, and poultry organized by the Programs has increased 19-28%, fish production has reached 15.6 million tons. Food diversity has been achieved in the marketplace and a better dietary pattern is within reach of the urban population.

A Risk Fund for Vegetable Production has been set up to compensate producers for losses caused by accidents or climate. For example, Harbin City received 100,000 Yuan RMB from the Fund after the county's vegetable crop was decimated by hailstones.

It is also proposed to establish a Price Adjustment Fund for both grains and non-staple foods, to organize a market monitoring system and an information system, and to build production bases and cold storage houses. A part of this fund should be used for price adjustment.

Finally, a system for the storage, transportation, and distribution of food stocks, including basic facilities and market management, would be developed.

As the result of these plans, the income of the rural population participating in the Programs is going up dramatically and it has become possible to modulate price fluctuations in urban areas.

Poverty Alleviation

China has worked to alleviate poverty since 1978 with a great degree of success. In 1986, an Office of Poverty Alleviation was established within the State Council and the main strategy shifted from food/cash aid to assisting investment in economic development with the purpose of enhancing the capability for self-reliance. Funds allocation was made on a project rather than a per capita basis; input in kind was emphasized over input in cash; an administrative framework and an economic development organization were required rather than a purely administrative framework. These changes are producing results. From 1986 to 1992 the number of absolute poor decreased from 125 million to 80 million – an average annual reduction of 6.4 million.

At this time, China has 80 million poor (8.87% of the rural population), living in around 600 of its 2680 counties. By initiating economic development to support self-reliance while emphasizing agricultural infrastructure such as roads construction, land development, improving food production technology, etc., the Poverty Alleviation Program intends to achieve sustainable development while maintaining food security – always a major priority.

Recently, the central government formulated a National "80 million-seven year" Poverty Alleviation Program aimed at elimination of absolute poverty in the country by year 2000. The goal includes adequate food consumption; increased income; the availability of arable land; orchard or cash cropping; more widespread education and health care; market development; road construction and better water supplies; electrification, etc. The State Council has put investment figures to the components and asked the Ministries/Commissions and the developed provinces to help in the development of the poor counties.

Information on food consumption and nutrition status in low-income

Table 6.13. Comparison of Dietary Patterns (Rural households)

Income group	HB GP 5	NX GP 6	ZJ GP 2	GD GP 1	SC GP 2
Income/capita/year, Yuan	948	1395	508	433	347
Energy intake (%RDA)	98	120	100	106	87
Source of Energy (% total energy intake)					
Cereals	80.7	80.7	82.8	81.2	82.3
Animal food	4.1	4.8	5.3	6.4	6.4
Legume & products	3.2	1.1	2.4	1.9	1.3
Vegetables & fruits	2.9	3.1	3.0	2.8	3.6
Added fat & oil	5.5	7.0	3.1	4.4	3.3
Sugar	1.2	1.8	1.5	1.9	1.0
Nuts & seeds	0.5	0.3	0.2	0.3	0.3
Wine	1.1	0.5	1.1	0.6	1.3
DDP-China Score	70.5	70.3	69.3	71.9	70.5

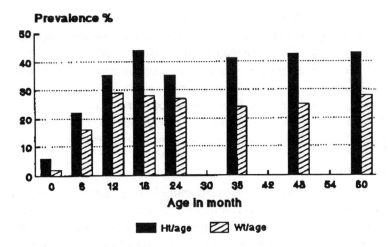

Figure 6.1. Prevalence of Stunting and Underweight, % in Age Groups.

households has been provided, an estimate of food consumption at an income level of 500 Yuan RMB – the income criterion for poverty alleviation – has been made, and a specific goal for food consumption based on the Desirable Dietary Pattern score (DDP), the quality score of a diet, has been recommended in the various provinces (Table 13) (Chen & Shao, 1994). With these data, food production can be planned with good nutrition in mind and money for foods can be spent in an efficient manner.

Nutrition improvement at the household level can be achieved through community nutrition education and mobilization of community organizations and women's groups to implement measures, such as home gardening, animal raising, and breastfeeding promotion, that are recommended by nutritionists based on current science and experiences in the rural communities.

Since the Nutrition Surveillance survey in 101 poor counties demonstrated that the prevalence of underweight and stunting peaked at 18 months of age and the prevalence of wasting peaked at 12 months (Figures 1 and 2), the recommendation is made to focus on the ages below 18 months for improving child nutrition in the poor areas.

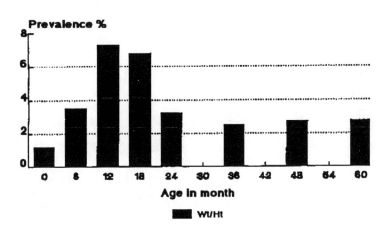

Figure 6.2. Prevalence of Wasting, % in Age Groups.

Development of Rural Industry

Since the early 1980s, rural industry has become the main support of the rural economy and one of the major pillars of the national economy. In 1992, the rural industry accounted for 51.6% of the net increase of GNP and 68.2% of the net increase of revenue; 67% of the per capita income of the rural population is attributed to rural industrial development. Rural industry has become the foundation for the development of townships and small cities adjacent to or within rural areas and the essential means of income generation.

Conclusion

China's present success in overcoming hunger is the fruit of historical efforts and of policies that have been followed in conjunction with economic development. Data on household food consumption of different income groups indicate that food security has improved as a result of general economic development as well as progress in agricultural production. Even the 10% poorest households are now at the margin of security. Recent policies for food production and distribution have focused on adjusting subsidies and price protection for both producers and consumers. The creation by government of funds for the modulation of supply and demand have been effective.

Poverty alleviation actions have performed quite well since 1986 and will play an extremely important role by the year 2000, if food and nutrition goals can be integrated into poverty alleviation activities. Yet, the nutritional status of many adults and children, especially in the rural areas, although improved, still lags behind, constituting a real challenge. In the process of transition from a planned economy to a socialist/market economy, problems such as economic inequity, lack of efficient health care and disease prevention, environmental deterioration, and the like put at risk the nutritional status of vulnerable populations. Continuous surveillance of food and nutrition status coupled with socioeconomic development and policies for nutrition improvement will be absolutely necessary. A National Plan of Action for Nutrition has been formulated to make nutritional adequacy a major goal of national economic development.

References

Chen C.M. and Shao Z.M. (1994) *Food, Nutrition and Health Status of Chinese in Seven Provinces 1990.* Beijing: China Statistical Publishing House.

Chen X.S. et al (1993) Blood pressure and nutrition survey of middle age and elderly in Chinese population with various dietary habits. *Gerontology,* 13 suppl. 170.

Ge K.Y. (in press) *Report of the Third Nationwide Nutritional Survey.*

Ge K.Y. and Zhai F.Y. (in press) *Report of the 1992 Third Nationwide Nutritional Survey.*

Li W.J. and Zhai F.Y. (in press) *The Report of Baseline Survey for Child Nutrition Surveillance for 101 Poor Counties 1990.* Proceedings of the 14th International Congress of Nutrition, Adelaide, Australia, 1993.

State Statistic Bureau (1993) *1993 Yearbook of Statistics of China.* Beijing: National Statistic Publishing House.

CHAPTER 7

Progress in Overcoming Hunger in Southeast Asia: 1989-1994

Kraisid Tontisirin and Pattanee Winichagoon

Hunger, poor health, and malnutrition are manifestations of social and economic inequity. Since the 1970s, most countries in the Asian region have made marked progress, both in their food production and in overall economic growth. Yet, despite these positive trends, high morbidity, mortality, and malnutrition persist. Overt starvation from lack of food may be heard of occasionally in pockets of populations, but is much less prevalent in the Southeast-Asia region than in some other parts of the world. Thus, the focus of attention in these countries will begin to shift to the more subtle or chronic hunger manifested as malnutrition and the poor health related to it.

In this paper, we will discuss human development, nutrition and related trends for ten Southeast Asian countries: Brunei, Cambodia, Indonesia, Laos, Malaysia, Myanmar, the Philippines, Singapore, Thailand, and Vietnam. However, little attention will be given to Singapore and Brunei, both of which, judged by the Human Development Index (HDI) (UNDP, 1994), are more advanced in their development. This paper examines the progress made by the other eight countries during the period from the late 1980s to the present. It will present three sets of data: macro-economic data on trends in economic production, poverty, and food production; figures on household food security, child malnutrition and micronutrient deficiency; and a few related and relevant indicators such as population growth, breastfeeding, literacy, and access to health. This article will also briefly present the nutrition policies and relative successes of four of these countries: Thailand, the Philippines, Vietnam and Indonesia. Much progress has been made in the region, and much can be learned from this success, yet there is still a long way to go before hunger will be fully eradicated for all.

General Macroeconomic Trends

Poverty

Singapore obviously surpassed other countries in economic status, followed by oil-rich Brunei. Cambodia, Vietnam, Laos and Myanmar still lag far behind in terms of per capita GNP.

The Human Development Index is a composite index of life expectancy at birth, educational attainment, and real adjusted GDP per capita (UNDP, 1994). It classifies the ten Southeast Asian countries as high-, medium-, and low-HDI (Table 1). Both Singapore and Brunei have a high HDI, 0.8 and above; the five in the medium group (Thailand, Malaysia, the Philippines, Indonesia, and Vietnam) have HDIs ranging from 0.5 to under 0.8; and the three in the low group (Myanmar, Laos, and Cambodia) have HDIs under 0.5.

Table 7.1. Indicators of Economic Development

Countries by HDI rank	Human Development Index	GNP per capita	Percentage of population in absolute poverty	Ratio of income share of highest 20% to lowest 20%
	1990	1992	1980-90	1980-91
High				
Singapore	0.836	15750		9.6
Brunei	0.829			
Medium				
Thailand	0.798	1840	30	8.3
Malaysia	0.794	2790	16	11.7
Philippines	0.621	770	54	7.4
Indonesia	0.586	670	25	4.9
Vietnam	0.514		54	
Low				
Myanmar	0.406		35	
Laos	0.385	250		
Cambodia	0.307	200		

Source: UNDP, 1994: Tables 1, 2, 18.

It is alarming that over half of the Philippine and Vietnamese populations live in absolute poverty. The figure is lowest for Malaysia (16%). Table 1 also shows that for the five countries for which data were available, the income disparity between rich and poor (ratio of the income share of the highest 20% and to the lowest 20%) was smallest in Indonesia and highest in Malaysia.

Food production

Except for Singapore and Brunei, the other Southeast Asian countries remain major food producers. Table 2 shows that the food production index has increased in all of them since the beginning of the 1980s, except for the Philippines.

Food imports dependency – i.e. the ratio of food imports to the food available for internal distribution, with the latter being the sum of food production plus food imports, minus food exports – was extremely high in Singapore (417%) (UNDP, 1993), and high in Brunei (93.5%) and Malaysia (51.3%). Among the other countries, this rate was very low, i.e., below 10% except for the Philippines (11.4%). In these countries much of the labor force is engaged in agriculture; this was particularly true of the three low-HDI countries (70% or more), and of Vietnam, Thailand, and Indonesia in the medium-HDI group (more than 55%).

Hence, including food imports, daily calorie supply for all countries in Southeast Asia except Cambodia is enough to meet the aggregate requirements of their population. However, these are average values, and do not account for disparities in food availability among socioeconomic or geographic groups. Neither are variations in intrafamilial distribution reflected by this indicator. It is striking, moreover, that the supply of micronutrients (particularly iron and vitamin A) may be inadequate (Table 2). The estimated daily iron supply was lower than the usual recommended dietary allowances. Much more attention to micronutrient adequacy is needed.

Malnutrition

Malnutrition persists to a much greater extent than would be expected from figures showing food self-sufficiency at the national level. In Southeast Asian countries the prevalence of malnutrition among children under five continues to be high. In addition, data on adult Body Mass Index (BMI) in selected countries also reflect the existence of a chronic energy deficit. This is the case because macro-level data do not reflect consumption at lower-aggregate levels. The actual consumption by households and individuals is determined by food accessibility and affordability, food habits, and cultural beliefs and practices, to name a few important factors. In this section, we will discuss available data on child malnutrition, low birthweight and maternal mortality, infant mortality rates, and micronutrient deficiency.

Child Malnutrition

As expected, the two high-HDI countries have quite low mortality rates for infants (IMR), children under five (U5MR), and mothers (MMR) (Table 3). In the medium-HDI group, Malaysia performed the best in these indicators; the mortality rates for infants and children under five have declined substantially. Thailand follows quite closely, although its IMR and U5MR are nearly double those of Malaysia. Mortality rates for infants and children under five remain quite high in all three countries in the low-HDI group, and in Indonesia in the medium-HDI group. Vietnam (medium HDI) performed quite impressively in bringing the 1992 IMR and U5MR down by almost 50% from the 1989 rates (Table 3).

Table 7.2. Food Production and Nutrient Availability

Countries by 1992 HDI rank	Food production per capita index (1979-81 = 100)		Per capita daily energy availability (1988-1990)		Daily dietary supply of micronutrients (1987-89)	
	1989	1991	Kcal	% Req	Iron, mg.	Vit A ug RE
High						
Singapore	93					
Brunei						
Medium						
Thailand	108	106	2052	103	9.2	650
Malaysia	153	159	2404	121	11.2	1609
Philippines	88	88	2109	109	8.6	357
Indonesia	124	135	2345	121	11.9	34.8
Vietnam	113	124	1994	103		
Low						
Myanmar	120	100	2208	114	10.3	396
Laos	120	141	2219	109		
Cambodia	145	111	1910	92		

Sources:UNDP,1994; RAPA/FAO, 1991.

Table 7.3. Mortality, Low Birthweight and Total Fertility Rates of Southeast-Asian Countries

Countries by HDI 1994 rank	Infant mortality rate/1000 LB		U5 mortality rate		Maternal mortality rate		% Low birth-weight		Total fertility rate	
	1989	1992	1989	1992	1980-1988	1992	1980-1988	1990	1989	1992
High										
Singapore	8	5	12	7	.05	0.1	7	7	1.8	1.7
Brunei		9								
Medium										
Thailand	27	26	35	34	0.5	0.5	12	13	2.3	2.3
Malaysia	22	14	30	19	0.59	0.6	10	10	3.9	3.7
Philippines	44	40	72	60	0.93	1	18	15	4.2	4.0
Indonesia	73	68	100	111	4.5	4.5	14	14	3.3	3.1
Vietnam	61	36	84	49	1.4	1.2	18	17	3.9	3.9
Low										
Myanmar	67	98	91	113	1.4	4	16	16	3.8	4.2
Laos	106	107	156	145		3	39	18	6.7	6.7
Cambodia	127	112	200						4.6	4.5

Sources:UNDP, 1994; UNICEF, 1991 & 1994.

Southeast Asia is one of the world's regions where considerable progress has been made in alleviating malnutrition; this is particularly true of Thailand and Indonesia. Due to intensive efforts during the 1980s, malnutrition among childen under five showed a clear trend of improvement, which has continued into the 1990s in both countries. Nevertheless, the prevalence of underweight remains rather high in the region as a whole. Moreover, stunting is still prevalent in almost every country, being reported as almost 50% in the Philippines, Vietnam, and Laos. There are limited national data in this respect in most countries (Table 4).

As for maternal mortality, most countries have sustained their low rates of the 1980s. Indonesia, Myanmar, and Laos, however, still report a relatively high MMR compared to the other countries. There were no data from Cambodia.

The trends in low birthweights have not changed significantly except in Laos, which has reduced its rate by one-half. The prevalence of low-birthweight infants in all countries in this region is much lower than in South Asia, where rates are still 30-40%.

Hidden Hunger

"Hidden hunger" has been the catch-phrase for micronutrient deficiencies, particularly deficiencies in iodine, iron, and vitamin A. Among the best documented is the global problem of Iodine Deficiency Disorder (IDD) (Table 5).

Many Southeast Asian countries have recently reported either a recurrence of iodine deficiency or an occurrence where it had not been previously observed - the central region of Thailand, for example. The iodine content of sea salt has been reported to be much lower than expected. It is believed that the washing away of topsoil results in decreased environmental iodine, thus diminishing the iodine content of foods. Singapore is virtually free from the problem of IDD, and a small magnitude was reported in Brunei. The prevalence in other countries in this region has been more than 10%, much higher than the level defined as a public health concern (below 5% in school-age children). The problem is particularly high in Indonesia, both in terms of the total goiter rate (i.e., clinical symptoms detected), which is 27.7%, and the number of people affected and at risk - 53 and 95 million, respectively. Malaysia, Vietnam, Laos, and Myanmar are also widely affected relative to the size of their populations (in Vietnam, with 13.9 million affected, the problem seems quite serious).

As can be expected, iron-deficiency anemia exists in all the countries, with the exception of Brunei, where none was reported. Anemia has been overlooked because its symptoms are less severe and its health consequences less obvious. In Singapore, the prevalence of anemia during pregnancy was about 18% - much lower than the 30% or above in most developing countries. In countries where data were available, anemia was also widespread among lactating and nonpregnant women, as seen in the statistics of the Philippines, Indonesia, and Thailand. Iron deficiency has been speculated to be the major cause of anemia in these populations. In these women, iron status due to a diet low in iron may have been poor prior to pregnancy, and anemia may be easily precipitated by the significant increase in iron requirements as pregnancy progresses. It is now known that not only the amount, but also the form of iron in diets, the presence of absorption inhibitors (*e.g.*, phytate in cereals, tannin in tea) and absorption enhancers (*e.g.*, vitamin C, meat protein) determine the amount of iron available to the body. Folic acid is also found to be deficient in some countries in Asia.

Xerophthalmia as the end result of vitamin A deficiency has been well-documented in Southeast Asia. Vitamin A-deficiency deaths associated with measles or other infections have been less well reported than in other regions of the world; however, the problem, ranging from subclinical deficiency to clinical manifestations of various stages of xerophthalmia, has been widespread (Table 4).

Table 7.4. Nutritional Status of the Underfives*

Countries by HDI rank	Nutritional status (1980-1992)		
	underweight	wasting	stunting
High			
Singapore	14		
Medium			
Thailand	26	10	28
Philippines	34	14	45
Indonesia	43/33		43/41
Vietnam	42	12	49
Low			
Myanmar	32		
Laos	37	20	44

Source: UNICEF 1994. Data for Indonesia, from National Survey on Xerophthalmia (1992), Harvard std. cutoff below -2, for Boy/Girl.

*Prevalence was based on NCHS reference and cutoff below -2. Data may be from national sample or small scale survey as available.

Table 7.5. Micronutrient Nutritional Status of Countries in Southeast-Asia

Countries by HDI rank	Iodine deficiency disorder			Iron deficiency (IDA)			Vitamiun A deficiency (VAD)
	TGR children	population affected, million	population at risk, million	pregnant women, %	lactating women, %	non pregnant women, %	
High							
Singapore	0	0	0	18			
Brunei	2	.005	.01				
Medium							
Thailand	12.2	6.8	20	30-40 (1991-93)		22*	20% preschool and school-aged children, subclinical deficiency (1990)
Malaysia	20	3.7	4.8	34 (1982)		59 (1986)	
Philippines	14.7	9.6	15.3	45 (1987)	51 (1987)	26-27 (1987*)	.8-4.4 %NB, .2-2.9% Bitot's spot (1987-91, selected areas)
Indonesia	27.7	53	95	74 (1986)	36/65	29-88	.64/1000 corneal lesion (1977-79, national survey)
Vietnam	20	13.9	17				.07% Corneal lesion, 12% scar (1985-87)
Low							
Myanmar	18	7.9	42-72 (1968-82)	42 (1968-72)	.7-3.3% Bitot's spot		.7-3.3% Bitot's spot (1976-90)
Laos	25	1.1					
Cambodia	15	1.8					

Sources:WHO/UNICEF/ICCIDD,1993;WHO,1992; Udomkesmalee,1992.

Vitamin A, iodine, and iron are needed in only minute amounts, yet changing environments and living patterns may have resulted in increasingly lower intakes from habitual diets. Vitamin A, for example, can be widely obtained from animal and vegetable sources. The deficiency may be a result of poor eating habits, such as low consumption of beta-carotene from dark green, leafy, and yellow vegetables or low intake of fat or other micronutrients needed for metabolism of the vitamin. Iron and iodine differ from vitamin A in terms of their availability. We have already mentioned the problem of iodine in the food supply. Habitual diets high in plant foods may have a low iron and iodine content and some plants contain inhibitors to iron absorption and iodine utilization.

Hunger-Related Indicators

Population growth rates

Four countries in the medium-HDI group (Thailand, the Philippines, Indonesia, and Vietnam) are relatively large, with populations above 50 million; the fifth, Malaysia, has only 20 million people. Population growth rates have been lowered impressively in Thailand and Indonesia, as a result of active implementation of their population policies since the 1970s (Kachondham et al., 1992; Soekirman et al., 1992). The other countries, including Malaysia, still have a population growth rate above 2%. All in this group were among the most active in development during the 1980s. Their performance, however, depended on each country's political and economic situation. This resulted in a wide variation in several health and nutrition indicators.

In the low-HDI group, Myanmar is the only large country, with a population of 45 million. In Cambodia, although it has a small population, the ratio of females to males is unusually high as a result of a large number of male deaths in the internal conflicts of the last two decades.

Singapore (high HDI) and Thailand (medium HDI) are moving toward the replacement level in terms of population growth (Table 6). Their total fertility rates (TFR) are much lower than those of other countries in this region. Laos (low HDI) ranked the highest in this regard. This may have been a result of the country's population policy (personal communication, Dr. Saysawan, School of Public Health, Laos).

Life expectancy at birth in all countries in the medium-HDI group is above 60 except for Indonesia, at just 60 years. On the other hand, in all low-HDI countries life expectancy is below 60 years; in 1992 it remained relatively unchanged or had worsened compared to that reported in 1989.

Literacy and the Economic Situation

The adult literacy rate is quite high in eight out of the 10 countries (Table 7). Only in Laos and Cambodia was the literacy rate reported at 55 and 37.8%, respectively. Nevertheless, the mean duration of schooling was only half a year in Brunei, despite the reported adult literacy rate of 86%. The Philippines reports the most years of schooling (more than seven), followed by Malaysia (5.6) and Vietnam (4.9). The percentage of school entrants who complete primary education was highest in Singapore and the Philippines (100% and 96%, respectively); in Vietnam it was only 58%; for the three low-HDI countries, no data are available. However, educational attainment in these countries is much lower than for the rest in this subregion.

Table 7.6. Basic Demographic Information in Ten Southeast-Asian Countries

Countries by HDI rank 1994	Total population (million)		Population annual growth rate, %		Life expectancy at birth	
	1989	1992	1987	1992	1989	1992
High						
Singapore		2.9	1.1	1.2	74	74
Brunei		0.3				71
Medium						
Thailand	54.9	59.4	1.8	1.4	66	69
Malaysia	17.4	19.5	2.3	2.3	70	71
Philippines	60.9	68.7	2.6	2.4	64	64
Indonesia	180.1	199.7	1.8	1.6	61	60
Vietnam	65.3	73.1	2.2	2.3	62	65
Low						
Myanmar	41.0	45.4	2.1	1.9	61	59
Laos	4.0	4.7	2.1	2.9	49	51
Cambodia	8.1	10.3	2.6	2.9	50	49

Source: Human Development Index, 1994.

Table 7.7. Education and Economic Situation

Countries by HDI rank	Adult literacy rate % 1992	Mean year of school 1992	Complete primary education 1990, %	Per capita GNP, US $		
				1989	1991	1992
High						
Singapore	92	4	100	10450	14210	15750
Brunei	86	.5				
Medium						
Thailand	94	3.9	87	1220	1570	1840
Malaysia	80	5.6	96	2160	2520	2790
Philippines	90	7.6	70	710	730	770
Indonesia	84	4.1	77	500	610	670
Vietnam	89	4.9	58	240	240	
Low						
Myanmar	82	2.5		220	220	
Laos	SS	2.9		180		250
Cambodia	38	2.0			200	200

Sources:UNDP, 1994; UNICEF,1992 & 1994.

Table 5 shows the data on literacy and economic status of countries in the region. Literacy rates in almost all the countries are quite high (>80%), except, as noted above, for Laos and Cambodia. The Philippines ranked the highest in mean duration of schooling, but Malaysia had the highest percentage of people completing primary education. There is a clear need to improve literacy, especially among the three low-HDI countries.

Access to Basic Health Services

Access to various basic health services is quite good in the high-HDI group, i.e., Singapore and Brunei. In the medium-HDI group, although accessibility to general health services is apparently good, the access and (possibly) compliance to more preventive and promotive health services, namely, clean water and sanitation, antenatal care, and childbirth care are variable. Immunization is the only clear success in almost all countries, except for Laos, where only one-fifth of the infants had been immunized, and Cambodia, where the comaparable rate is one-third, with a small improvement in 1990-92 (Table 8). Access to clean water and sanitation is still rather low in Vietnam, and moderately low in Indonesia. Antenatal services are less utilized in Thailand and Indonesia, and childbirth attended by health personnel remains infrequent in Indonesia, despite good progress in other community-based primary health care activities. The use of contraception was quite good in Thailand (66%), followed by Indonesia (53%), but in Singapore it was the best accepted (74%). Family planning has been considered quite successful in both Thailand and Indonesia.

Breastfeeding and Weaning

Breastfeeding is still almost universal in rural areas in all these countries. In urban areas, its prevalence is generally lower, but still considerably higher than in developed countries. The mean duration of breastfeeding in Thailand, the Philippines, and Indonesia is satisfactory (longer than one year). However, much more attention must be given to the timing of weaning and to feeding during the process. In Thailand, for example, exclusive breastfeeding for four months has been virtually non-existent due to early introduction of semisolid food during the first week of life. The practice may have changed somewhat, in that it may be delayed for a month or two, but it continues to be substantial, particularly in rural areas. In urban areas there is an increased trend to bottle feeding due to changing lifestyles and the increasing need for women to work outside the home.

Policies and Programs Addressing Hunger and Malnutrition

Southeast Asia was very active in nutrition and development during the 1980s, and the momentum has continued into the 1990s. Thailand and Indonesia have made considerable progress in nutrition improvement through their community-based organizations. Similar efforts were made in the Philippines, but were less successful because of economic recession and frequent natural calamities. Vietnam has had a good start in improving family nutrition, particularly through its family VAC system, which is being expanded. The rest of the countries are preparing their nutrition policies and programs, as well as developmental approachs to tackle the root causes of poor health and nutrition: poverty and ignorance. This section will review the experiences, current policies and programs, and future plans in selected countries.

Indonesia has a longstanding interest, dating back to the 1930s, in addressing nutritional problems through sectoral programs such as salt iodization. In the

Table 7.8. Immunization Coverage

Countries by HDI rank	1988-1989					1990-1992				
	BCG	DPT	Polio	Measles	TT	BCG	DPT	Polio	Measles	TT
High										
Singapore	99	90	90	87		99	85	85	90	
Brunei	98									
Medium										
Thailand	99	84	84	66	70	99	85	84	74	72
Malaysia	99	72	72	50	54	99	90	90	79	83
Philippines	89	79	78	83	43	94	92	92	90	52
Indonesia	85	75	77	68	41	95	91	91	89	44
Vietnam	80	68	68	71		91	88	89	90	42
Low										
Myanmar	66	45	45	50	42	80	73	73	71	72
Laos	29	21	22	20	4	39	25	25	55	19
Cambodia	42	22	22	20	22	50	32	32	33	22

Source: UNICEF, 1994.

1980s, the Family Nutrition Improvement Program (FNIP) community movement was implemented as a nationwide program. The FNIP started in 1973 in eight provinces covering 1600 villages, and by 1989 had expanded in all 27 provinces to include about 65,000 villages. FNIP activities consist of agriculture, health, family planning, rural development, and education. The approach is a community-based effort involving village organizations like Village Women as well as religious organizations. The three main activities are: community nutrition education; nutrition services for maternal and child nutrition at the Posyandu (community centers); and home and community gardening aiming at income generation and home consumption.

In the country's next five-year development plan nutrition will continue to be an important consideration. The goal has been set to increase community self-sufficiency in nutrition; improve the physical wellbeing, intelligence, and productivity of the people; and to increase food security through food and dietary diversification. The Family Nutrition Improvement Program will still be the main thrust, with more attention to using effective nutrition information/education/communication strategies. Improvement of human resources will also include Nutritional Institution Programs. The major problems will be protein-energy malnutrition and the three micronutrient deficiencies, as well as ensuring food security.

The Philippines has been one of the leading countries in pioneering the community-based approach. Its Operation Timbang was one such attempt to improve the nutrition of young children. However, its progress was interrupted in the mid-1980s because of political instability. The country has recovered and development policies and programs have been revitalized. The Philippines Plan of Action for Nutrition (PPAN) for 1993-1998 aims to improve the nutrition situation using two main strategies: ensuring household food security, and the prevention, control, and elimination of micronutrient malnutrition.

Excellent progress has been made in *Thailand* in improving infant and child nutrition through the broad rural development and nutrition programs that form part of the national development plan. By the mid-1980s, regular growth monitoring took place routinely in 90% of the villages, and serious malnutrition had been almost eliminated. Still specific nutritional deficiencies remain prevalent in pockets, particularly in the north and northeast.

Since 1977, which was the beginning of the fourth five-year development plan, nutrition has been an explicit component of national development policy. The policy and strategies have evolved, and by the sixth plan (1987-1991), were aimed at improvements in the quality of life, incorporated in an intersectoral approach of various ministries via the community-based programs. Nutrition has been made a component of the primary health care (PHC) and rural development schemes, and of the Poverty Alleviation Plan (PAP). While PHC provides a main thrust for community-based implementation, the evolving concept of Basic Minimum Needs (BMN) has made its community effort a holistic development for achieving a good quality of life. The PAP, on the other hand, made a great contribution to macro-level planning by using an areas-targeted approach. Communities were defined as being under the poverty line, and received priority in community development. Resource allocation was streamlined to focus on those communities most in need of help. Further, planning at the community level has become more decentralized through the communities' efforts. This has resulted in marked improvement in the nutrition status of children under five, as well as heightened awareness of the importance of nutrition in human resources development. Both the holistic approach, as described, and followup by individual programs addressed specific nutrition and health problems, such as the national iodine disorder program, the iron deficiency program, and the expanded program for immunization.

Like other countries in the region, *Vietnam* has very good natural resources for agriculture and the potential of being self-sufficient in foods. Despite this, malnutrition remains a major public health problem. Up to the present, there have been several projects with developmental objectives that are potentially expandable. Some examples are: the VAC system for improving household food security with particular attention to supplementary foods for young infants; the national vitamin A program; and the nutrition component of the program in family planning and primary health care. Currently, a draft of the National Plan of Action on Nutrition is being formulated.

Other countries in the region are catching up with those that already have developmental policies and planning in place. International agencies, like FAO, WHO, and UNICEF, are attempting to assist them in formulating policies and programs to improve health and nutrition.

Conclusion

Countries in Southeast Asia have made significant progress in economic and social development. At present, these countries vary considerably in their progress, both in terms of having policies and plans in place, and in the actual implementation and impacts. The socio-demographic situation, economic development, internal conflicts, and natural calamities are among important factors that have contributed to these variations. Nevertheless, there are lessons to be learned from those countries that have already made some progress.

References

Kachondham, Y., Winichagoon, P., and Tontisirin, K. (1992). *Nutrition and Health in Thailand: Trends and Actions.* An ACC/SCN case study presented at the XV International Congress of Nutrition, September 26–October 1, 1993, Adelaide, Australia.

RAPA/FAO (1991). *Expert Consultation on Food and Nutrition.* FAO: RAPA/FAO, Bangkok, Thailand.

Soekirman, Tarwotjo, I., Justat, I., Sumodimingrat, G., and Jalal, F. (1992). *Economic Growth, Equity and Nutrition Improvement in Indonesia.* An ACC/SCN case study presented at the XV International Congress of Nutrition, September 26–October 1, 1993, Adelaide, Australia.

Udomkesmalee, E. (1992). Vitamin A Deficiency in Asia. *Vital News,* 3 (3): 1-5.

UNDP (1993, 1994). *Human Development Report.* New York, Oxford: Oxford University Press.

UNICEF (1991, 1992, 1994). *State of the World's Children.* New York and Oxford: Oxford University Press.

WHO (1992). *The Prevalence of Anemia in Women: A Tabulation of Available Information.* Geneva: World Health Organization, Maternal Health and Safe Motherhood Program.

WHO/UNICEF/ICCIDD (1993). *Global Prevalence of Iodine Deficiency Disorders.* Geneva: Micronutrient Deficiency Information System, MDIS Working Paper #1.

CHAPTER 8

Overcoming Hunger and Malnutrition: The Indonesian Experience

Soekirman

Indonesia entered the development era 25 years ago with a very low economic and social base. One of the poorest countries in the world, it had a per capita income of US $50, roughly half that of India, Bangladesh, and Nigeria. Over 60% of the population (about 70 million people) lived in poverty. Hunger and malnutrition were widespread; illiteracy was high; life expectancy was about 50 years.

In April 1994, Indonesia started its second long-term development plan (LTD 2) for the years 1994-2018. The first long-term development plan (LTD 1), initiated in 1969, had stimulated an annual economic growth rate of 7%, reduced poverty, and eliminated severe hunger and malnutrition, one of the most fundamental problems in developing nations. Self-sufficiency in rice was achieved in 1984, and has been sustained. Food and calorie availability per capita, 95.9 kg and 2,035 kcal, respectively, in 1968, increased by the 1990s to 154 kg (1992 data) and 2,701 kcal (1990 data). This success in food production and availability was followed by improved food distribution and consumption at the household level. Since 1985 no case of overt hunger (severe protein-energy malnutrition, or PEM) has been reported either in adults or in children, not even in Central Java or Lombok provinces, areas that had known chronic hunger. However, the "hidden hunger" of malnutrition, especially mild and moderate PEM among children under five, is still a problem to be addressed in LTD 2.

In this paper I will describe the development policies that have had a significant impact and examine the four distinct but related issues of self-sufficiency, food availability, food entitlement, and nutritional capability as enumerated by Dreze and Sen in their book on *Hunger and Public Action* (Dreze and Sen, 1989). I will also take a more in-depth look at Indonesia's successful program to eradicate xerophthalmia, and describe the nutritional surveillance system for coping with food crises arising from natural disasters.

Food Self-Sufficiency and Availability

Indonesia achieved rice self-sufficiency with the aid of high-yield technology developed at the International Rice Research Institute, combined with newly developed agricultural infrastructure: irrigation, rural roads, and new marketing institutions supported by rural credits for agricultural inputs.

Until the 1970s, Indonesia had been known as the world's biggest rice importer - an annual drain of about 25% of the country's foreign exchange. Rice imports began to decline in 1974, falling from about 1.2 million tons to almost nothing by 1988. It has been argued that achieving food sufficiency improves food security at both national and household levels. A recent analysis indicates that Indonesia has already achieved better food security according to two sensible measures: trade balance and available calories per capita (Peter Timmer, personal communication). Between 1985 and 1992, food exports rose by $236 million per year; each year the surplus of exports over imports increased by $120 million. According to the food balance sheet (as computed by Timmer, 1994), in 1976-1978 an averaage of 2,321 calories was available per capita per day; of these, 2,217 calories were from domestic products. By contrast, in 1990-1992, the average calorie supply per capita per day was 2,855, less than the average of 2,868 calories produced domestically. Thus, there was a surplus of calories available in this period, a finding consistent with the food self-sufficiency indicated by the trade balance (Timmer, 1994).

Food Entitlement and Nutrition Capability

However, an approach to hunger and starvation dominated by the examination of food trade or calorie supply ignores the complex problem of the relationship between food and people. The food entitlement approach, as described by Amartya Sen, provides a more comprehensive account of an individual's ability to command commodities in general and food in particular: famines and hunger should be viewed more as economic disasters than as simple food crises (Sen, 1982). People lack food because they lack income and the ability to acquire it for various reasons. Nutrition capacity is the outcome indicator of the entitlement system.

Poverty in Indonesia

Poverty in Indonesia had its origins in 350 years of Dutch colonial oppression and three years of Japanese occupation. The devastating social, economic, and political conditions during the colonial era were, not surprisingly, one of the major factors in the birth and growth of the nationalism that resulted in Indonesia gaining independence in 1945, at the end of World War II. Poverty alleviation has been one of the Indonesian government's main concerns ever since, and was the reason for initiating LTD 1 in 1969.

In the *World Development Report* on poverty of 1991 (World Bank, 1991) Indonesia was cited as a country where economic growth has had a major impact on poverty reduction. The poverty line adopted by the Indonesian Central Bureau of Statistics shows that the incidence of 40.1% of the population (54.2 million) living at or below that line in 1976 had declined to 14% (25 million people) by 1993. In less than one generation, over 29 million people (more than 50% of the total number of the poor) were raised out of poverty. Data gathered in 1990 show this reduction occurring relatively faster in rural than in urban areas. In 1976, 18% of the 54 million poor were located in the cities, 82% in the countryside. By 1990 this had changed to 35% urban and 65% rural, a shift due in part to the success of agricultural development, in part to rural-to-urban migration.

This large reduction is also the result of sustained broad-based economic growth, particularly in the agricultural sector (Nitisastro, 1994). The policy of according priority to agriculture, which is labor-intensive and employs most of the population, was primarily responsible for the improvement in food entitlement and nutrition. The policy was reinforced by nationwide improvements in primary health care, basic education, and the family planning programs that have succeeded in reducing population growth from 2.32% in 1971 to 1.66% in 1993 (Government of Indonesia, 1994).

Nutritional Improvements and Challenges

Overt hunger in adults, the form of severe PEM known as hunger edema, has not been reported since the late 1980s, either formally (through health centers) or informally (by the press), despite several long droughts in the 1990s (the most recent in 1994) that resulted in significant harvest failures. This would indicate that food self-sufficiency does assure food security at the household level. In addition, due to increased income and better rural infrastructure, many villages no longer depend on local production: more people can afford to buy food at markets.

"Hidden hunger," however, remains a national problem. Recent data on the prevalence of mild and severe malnutrition (weight for age below 70% NCHS standard) show a 37.7% decrease over the last two decades; but with a 1993 income level of $700 per capita Indonesia would be expected to have a malnutrition rate of about 20%, not 40%. Instead, it continues to have one of the worst rates in Asia (compared, for example, to the Philippines at 34% or Thailand at 13%).

A 1990 analysis of data on moderate and severely underweight children according to household expenditure reveals that most of these children come from poor households. In 1993 about 14% of the population was still living below the poverty line, although this number is shrinking. The prevalence of underweight children is thought to be closely related to the relatively large number of families in poverty. The high incidence of diarrhea and the limited availability of clean water and sanitation facilities in Indonesia, as compared with other Asian countries, have also contributed to this situation.

In addition, problems continue with the provision of specific micronutrients. Indonesia still faces technological and managerial problems in tackling major deficiencies. For instance, the salt iodization program to combat Iodine Deficiency Disorder (IDD), in operation for almost two decades, has not yielded satisfactory results. Universal iodization entails the complex problem of dealing with thousands of small salt producers across the country, which leads to further problems of distribution, pricing, and quality control. The IDD control program will continue in LTD 2, and will receive more attention, especially on the managerial front.

Indonesia has also been unsuccessful in solving the problem of iron deficiency. The distribution of iron supplements to pregnant women through community health centers and "Posyandu" (Village Integrated Service Posts) organized by village women's organizations also seems to be faced with various managerial problems. In the meantime, iron fortification of foods is still in the experimental stage.

In short, despite long-term efforts to eradicate micronutrient deficiencies, most results remain unsatisfactory. Stronger managerial capabilities are still needed (Soekirman, 1994). The one encouraging victory has been eradication of xerophthalmia through a nationwide high-dose vitamin A intervention. Efforts are being made to sustain this achievement by encouraging consumption of fruit and vegetables to improve the vitamin A serum level (Soekirman, 1994). If this program is successful, it may offer useful lessons in the policy, planning, and operational aspects of nutrition programs.

Eradicating Xerophthalmia: A Case Study

Indonesia has long been considered a "traditional home" of xerophthalmia (Sommer, 1982). The prevalence of vitamin A deficiency (VAD), with or without xerophthalmia, was detected and documented in no fewer than 10 surveys conducted between 1930 and 1950 (Soekirman, 1974). However, an early (and initially successful) effort to find a solution, a pilot trial of red palm oil processed for children's consumption, had been abandoned in the 1950s because of problems of procurement, distribution, and (probably) unacceptable taste and color. A 1962-1963 WHO survey of xerophthalmia in nearly 50 countries indicated that Indonesia was still one of those most affected (Oomen, 1974). In 1978, 13 out of every 1,000 Indonesian children under five suffered from blindness caused by VAD. By 1992, using a new technology for producing high-dose vitamin A (HDVA) developed in the early 1970s (World Bank, 1994), the rate had been reduced to 3 per thousand.

Technology Field Trial

Indonesia's field trial for HDVA, a milestone for the national nutrition program, was based on a longitudinal epidemiological study initiated in 1975 in cooperation with Helen Keller International (HKI). The study was terminated in 1979, and in the 1980s followup studies were conducted in various provinces to evaluate the impact of HDVA intervention. The technology for producing vitamin A-fortified MSG, which has been successful in the Philippines and other countries, has now been developed in Indonesia.

Policy and Program Development

It is important to note that nutritional improvement is explicitly described in the state Policy Guidelines for National Development, and has therefore become a political commitment. In his Martin Forman Memorial Lecture on malnutrition and "nutritional engineering," Alan Berg reminds us that in dealing with malnutrition we "need always be cognizant of its political and economic context" (Berg, 1992). One of the requirements for successful nutrition advocacy in the national development agenda is an understanding of both the political and the bureaucratic process.

My experience in Indonesia indicates that there are at least four prerequisites for nutrition to be adopted as one of the priority goals and programs in national development. Each has played a role in Indonesia's program to eliminate VAD.

First, we have to promote nutrition awareness in the general public and among policy makers through effective nutrition, communication, information, and education programs (NCIE). In particular, effective NCIE, or nutrition education as it is traditionally known, is the key to making nutrition a priority. The findings of research and development (R & D) on nutrition should be used as the main inputs for NCIE, and should also be utilized to update the messages and technology for effective NCIE. For VAD, we are developing NCIE social-marketing approaches for the HDVA capsule and vegetable consumption.

Second, we have to be supported by a wide range of professional organizations, the scientific community, and the press, both nationally and internationally. International agencies, bilateral and multilateral NGOs, etc., are essential to the promotion of nutrition. In the case of VAD control in Indonesia, the assistance of UNICEF, FAO, the World Bank, WHO, USAID, and HKI has been instrumental in terms of funding, but more important in terms of advocacy.

An established method for obtaining wide support in Indonesia is a periodic National Workshop on Food and Nutrition, organized every five years prior to the preparation of a new five-year development plan (FYDP). This high-level workshop is the most prestigious gathering of the nutrition community, inaugurated by the President and followed by keynote addresses by prominent ministers related to food and nutrition. International scholars are invited to attend. The first workshop in 1969 was organized in cooperation with the US National Academy of Sciences. Its salient recommendations, including those for controlling VAD, were adopted as priorities in the State Policy Guidelines and in the FYDP. Five more workshops have since been organized by the Indonesian Institute of Sciences in cooperation with the Indonesian Society and Professional Organizations.

Third, we have to be able to present and propose a good and sound program that meets several criteria set up by the Planning Agency and Ministry of Finance. Programs must be consistent with the goals defined in the FYDP, and it must be clear how the activities of the programs are related to or complement programs of other sectors, such as health, education, family planning, agriculture, industry, and transmigration. No nutritional problem, including VAD, can be effectively solved by one single strategy, such as the HDVA capsule. In addition, of course, the program must be implementable, cost effective, sustainable, gender sensitive, environmentally friendly, and promote people's empowerment.

Fourth, a sustainable nutrition program requires community participation in the form of a strong social infrastructure at the grass-roots level. Indonesia is fortunate in having a strong family-welfare movement known as PKK, begun in Central Java in the 1950s as a volunteer village women's organization helping poor village families. It has now developed into a nationwide organization under the coordination and supervision of the Ministry of Home Affairs. PKK, with its Posyandu, is the key to success in delivering services to mothers and children in the villages, and in reaching the unreached. Most nutrition activities at the village level, including distribution of vitamin A capsules, monthly weighing, nutrition and health education, diarrhea control using oralite, and home gardening, are carried out by PKK members already trained by local health and nutrition workers.

With a token subsidy from the central as well as the local government, PKK has been very effective at empowering women to support the national development program at the village level, especially in the realms of nutrition, family planning, MCH, and immunization through Posyandu. PKK also supports informal education programs for the eradication of illiteracy, development of home industry, entrepreneurship, etc. The effective distribution of the HVDA capsule to millions of children annually is a success that can be credited to Posyandu.

Reasons for Successful VAD Prevention

Indonesia's success in preventing VAD and blindness, in my opinion, is primarily due to:

1. A macroeconomic policy conducive to improving nutrition;

2. a strong commitment to equity and poverty alleviation in the national development plan;

3. strong economic, social, and political stability, which creates a favorable environment for continuous and sustainable implementation of existing programs;

4. relatively strong institutional systems for nutrition: R & D, professional manpower development, programming, and policy institutions.

The Role of Nutritional Surveillance (NSS)

The Nutritional Surveillance System was developed in the early 1980s as a timely warning information and intervention system (TWIIS), focused primarily on areas prone to food shortage (at village, sub-district, and district levels). The system provided indicators suitable for early detection of food crises and the quick action needed to cope with declining food security at the household level. It was designed for community leaders and government officials with the authority to mobilize resources to cope with food supplies and entitlement by authorizing food-market operation to ensure adequate food at affordable prices, and by providing employment, subsidies for agricultural inputs, rural credits, health and nutrition services, etc. The data were collected in the field at community and household levels by local trained volunteers.

Since food self-sufficiency was achieved in 1984, interest in TWIIS as a remedy against hunger resulting from natural disasters has dwindled. Districts once known as food deficient or hunger prone have now become food-surplus or even food-exporting districts. In addition, there are indications that local people are more able to cope with the effects of cyclical drought. It is one of the goals of Indonesia's overall national development plan to improve food security by encouraging this empowerment and participation.

Lessons Learned

1. Indonesia's success in overcoming hunger has been due to the priority given to food and nutrition. Since the initial stages of development in the 1970s, policies have been highly committed to these basic needs. This has made agricultural development a top priority, with the special objective of providing adequate food, employment, and income in rural areas, where the majority of the population resides.

2. This success has contributed to the ability to sustain an annual economic growth rate of 7% over two and a half decades of development, which, in turn, has ensured the sustained provision of basic needs for all (food, nutrition, health, education, and employment) and reduced poverty. In addition, the development plan has pursued a dynamic national stability (political, economic, and social) in order to provide an environment conducive to sustainable development that guarantees the people's welfare and security.

3. National development gives high priority to nutritional programs as an integral part of overall economic and social development. There is an awareness that overcoming hunger does not necessarily ensure eradication of "hidden hunger." Macro- and micronutrient deficiencies are recognized as a serious problem, not only for community health but also for the quality of the nation's human resources. In the Second Long-Term Development Plan, spanning the next 25 years, the eradication of malnutrition (and also the prevention of overnutrition) will be an important goal.

4. Overt hunger is generally given a great deal of attention in the community and among government authorities: people are concerned and aware of policies and actions that pertain to the issue. In contrast, the problems of hidden hunger are usually ignored. To overcome hunger of this type will require strong and active nutrition programs, which should be vigorously promoted to the people and to policy makers and managed professionally as part of all other development programs. This requires strong linkage among four main development institutions: professional training for nutrition manpower; research and development; program design and implementation agencies; and policy and national planning organizations.

References

Berg, A. (1992). Sliding to World Nutrition Malpractice: Time to Reconsider and Redeploy. *American Journal of Clinical Nutrition*, 1992: 57.

Dreze, J. and Sen, A. (1989). *Hunger and Public Action*. Oxford: Claredon Press.

Government of Indonesia (1994). *The Sixth Five Year Development Plan (Repelito VI)*. Jakarta: Government of Indonesia.

Nitisastro, W. (1994). *Reduction of Poverty: the Indonesian Experience*. Madrid: paper presented at the conference on Fifty Years after Bretton Woods: the Future of the IMF and the World Bank.

Oomen, H.A.D.C (1974). Vitamin A deficiencies, Xerophthalmia and Blindness, *Nutrition Reviews*, 32: 161.

Sen, A. (1982). *Poverty and Famine: An Essay on Entitlement and Deprivation*. Worcester: Billing and Sons.

Soekirman (1974). *Priorities in Dealing with Nutrition Problems in Indonesia*. Ithaca: Cornell University Monograph Series no. 1.

Soekirman (1994). *Eradicating Xerophthalmia: the Indonesian Experience*. Chiang Rai, Thailand: paper presented at the Vth International IVAGC Conference.

Sommer, A. (1982). *Nutritional Blindness*. Oxford: Oxford University Press.

Timmer, P. (1994). Unpublished paper on Food Self-Sufficiency and Food Security (personal communication).

World Bank (1991, 1994). *World Development Report*. New York: Oxford University Press.

CHAPTER 9

Progress in Overcoming Micronutrient Deficiencies: 1989-1994

Anne Lalsawmliani Ralte[1]

The Bellagio Declaration, adopted in 1989, called for global action to end half the world's hunger before the year 2000 through four achievable goals, one of which was the elimination of vitamin A and iodine deficiencies. This goal was incorporated in the Declaration on the Rights of the Child developed at the World Summit For Children in 1990. National leaders and international agencies reaffirmed their commitment to these goals in Montreal in 1991 at the "Ending Hidden Hunger" conference. In 1992, at the International Conference on Nutrition, the most important global forum to debate nutrition since the 1974 World Food Conference, 159 countries pledged commitment to a set of goals and objectives, including a reaffirmation to eliminate vitamin A and iodine deficiencies by the year 2000.

This paper examines the programs undertaken to control and prevent these deficiencies, the extent to which known technologies have worked in addressing the problem, and the progress made to date. It also suggests areas that require further attention and overall steps for achieving the year 2000 goals.

Micronutrient Deficiencies – An Overview

Micronutrients are vitamins and minerals essential for normal growth and development, for maintenance of the immune system, protection against infectious disease and some degenerative diseases. Although dietary requirements are minute, the consequences of deficiencies are critical. Among them are impaired work capacity, illness, and, in severe deficiency, death. These often-"hidden" deficiencies attest to the fact that hunger problems go beyond the availability of and access to the micronutrients. In developing countries, deficiencies of vitamin A, iodine, and iron are the major contributors to the world's "hidden hunger" problem.

Vitamin A Deficiency

Vitamin A deficiency (VAD) is well recognized throughout much of South and Southeast Asia: India, Bangladesh, Indonesia, the Philippines, Thailand, and Vietnam. The trend in these countries has been a decline in its severity and magnitude, with countries like India and Indonesia demonstrating a reduction in xerophthalmia (India: from 2.0 in 1975-79 to 0.07% in the 1988-90 survey; Indonesia from 1.33% in 1977-78 to 0.34% in 1992), although subclinical deficiency is still very much a problem (ACC/SCN, 1993; Muhilal et al, 1994).

Recently, more information has become available on the magnitude of the problem in many areas of Africa, Central and South America, and the Caribbean. In 11 countries in Latin America, vitamin A deficiency can be classified as a significant public health problem, either in the country as a whole or in some regions (VITAL, 1993).

In Sub-Saharan Africa, vitamin A deficiency is a public health problem in 19 of the 43 countries; 50 million children are estimated to show clinical eye signs. Vitamin A deficiency with measles is responsible for over 65% of childhood blindness and associated mortality and morbidity (Chirambo, IVACG, 1994).

At the global level, the latest WHO estimate is that over 90 countries have either clinical or subclinical vitamin A deficiency or both, with 230.6 million at risk. Based on serum retinol levels, 3.1 million are affected clinically and another 227.5 million have subclinical deficiency at a severe or moderate level. The earlier classification of 37 countries as having vitamin A deficiency to the degree of public health significance was based on clinical eye signs (WHO, 1987). WHO now defines vitamin A deficiency as the situation that exists when tissue levels are depleted to a level at which health consequences occur even in the absence of xerophthalmia (Underwood, IVACG, 1994).

Iodine Deficiency

Iodine deficiency (IDD) is the world's single most significant cause of preventable brain damage and mental retardation: at least 110 countries are known to have the problem (WHO/UNICEF/ICCIDD - MDIS, 1993). The revised estimate of goiter is now at 655 million people affected, based on country-by-country assessment. The estimated number at risk has risen to over 1570 million, or 29% of the world's population, due to the lowered cutoff criteria used to define at-risk populations. The worst problems are largely confined to Southeast Asia (including India, Bangladesh, Indonesia) and the Western Pacific, including China (MDIS, 1993).

Although iron deficiency was not addressed in the Bellagio Declaration, it affects nearly 1.5 billion people and produces anemia in 1.2 billion. Nearly 90% of all anemia in the world is due to iron deficiency. Consequences include reduced work capacity, diminished learning ability, increased susceptibility to infection, and greater risk of death associated with pregnancy and childbirth. Of 500,000 maternal deaths ascribed to childbirth each year (essentially all of which occur in the less developed countries) anemia is the sole or major contributory cause in 20-40% (Viteri 1992).

Interventions - From Research to Applied Technologies

The initial findings of a study from Indonesia (Sommer et al, 1983) reported an increased risk of child death associated with mild vitamin A deficiency. Since then, 10 additional studies have been undertaken in Brazil, Ghana, India, Indonesia, Nepal, and Sudan to test the impact of vitamin A supplementation on mortality and morbidity. In several studies, supplementation was effective in reducing infant mortality well above 40%. A meta-analysis of the studies resulted in an average reduction of 23% in mortality rates of infants and children between six months and five years (ACC/SCN 1993).

In addition, vitamin A supplementation was linked to decreased severity of illness episodes, such as measles and diarrheal diseases, and lower rates of hospital admissions. A very important finding was that the effect on mortality was not dependent upon very-high-potency dosing, with one trial based on the weekly administration of 8,133 IU of liquid vitamin A, the equivalent of the recommended dietary allowance for vitamin A (Rahmathullah et al, 1990). Another trial was based on fortification of monosodium glutamate (MSG) with vitamin A.

Research findings indicate that, of different health and child-survival interventions, strategies to control and prevent micronutrient deficiencies are the most cost effective. A recent World Bank review (Jamison, 1993) of the significance to public health of individual diseases or related clusters of diseases and what is known about the cost and effectiveness of various interventions ranks six micronutrient interventions among those with the lowest marginal cost: $25 per DALY (disability-adjusted life-year) gained. The micronutrient interventions in this range include salt iodization; fortification of sugar with vitamin A; a semiannual mass dose of vitamin A; medical treatment of measles with vitamin A; iodine injections and daily oral iron supplements for pregnant women.

The selection of any one or a combination of the above interventions and other strategies depends on a variety of factors, including the severity and cause of the problem, its distribution within the country, the existing infrastructure, and the availability of micronutrient-rich foods. One or a package of interventions may not work in all countries; however, what emerges from the global pool of experience may be helpful in shaping future directions.

Supplementation

Depending on the selection of the delivery mechanism and design of the program, supplementation is generally low in cost, acceptable, and clinically effective within the short term. It has been the most popular strategy to date, with over 55 operational programs in vitamin A and iodine (Levin et al, 1993). Supplements can be taken orally or by injection, and the interval between dosages depends on the body's ability to store the micronutrient (four-six months for vitamin A, one year for iodized oil given by mouth or two to three years when given by injection). Most vitamin A supplementation programs have adopted a periodic high dose rather than a weekly lower dose, although the efficacy of both methods has been demonstrated. The provision of 200,000 IU vitamin A capsules was found to have at least 90% prophylactic efficacy for four to six months among children against developing mild xerophthalmia and corneal disease (Sommer et al, 1983).

Maintaining adequate and sustained coverage is a major problem with supplementation programs. In the case of vitamin A, reasonable coverage (that is, at least 65% universal distribution for a favorable impact on mild xerophthalmia) has been difficult due to a combination of factors, including access to health delivery systems, inadequate supply, and lack of personnel.

Distribution of supplements has been pilot-tested using various delivery mechanisms. In countries where vitamin A supplementation was undertaken on national immunization days coverage rose significantly, with little or no additional burden on the EPI infrastructure (IVACG, 1994). Although some countries have had positive experiences, questions remain on the effects of the logistical add-on of vitamin A to EPI and the efficacy of vaccines, particularly the sero-conversion of live measles vaccine. Three additional studies now underway will help to illuminate the scientific basis for further policy development. With the immunization program providing an opportunity to reach 500 million infants and their mothers each year, WHO and UNICEF have suggested that provision of 100,000 IU with the measles vaccine at 9 months is one important way of delivering supplements (WHO/UNICEF Joint Statement to XVI IVACG Meeting Participants, October 26, 1994).

To accelerate progress toward achieving the World Summit/ICN goals, countries are undertaking various measures. For example, the Philippines has embarked on a successful three-year campaign to universally distribute vitamin A capsules to children aged 1-4 to prevent blindness, iodized oil capsules for pregnant women to prevent mental retardation of their babies, and "mulunggay" (horseradish) cuttings and packets of vegetable and fruit seeds for all families to ensure food sources rich in iron. The campaign uses multi-media strategies: the government, private sectors, and the community participate in the once-a-year nationwide "Araw ng Sangkap Pinoy" or ASAP (translation: "a day of local ingredients" – "ingredients" is more understandable than "micronutrients"). Over 90% (vitamin A) and 86% (iodine) of the targeted groups were reached during the 1993 campaign. The cost per beneficiary is estimated at $3.06; this figure does not take into account the added economic benefits or the impact of improved micronutrient status on overall health and survival (Sangkap Pinoy, 1994).

Disease targeting gives priority to those in whom supplementation will effect mortality reduction or prevention of serious and permanent complications. Targeting vitamin A supplementation, through the routine health delivery system, to high-risk groups with xerophthalmia, severe protein-energy malnutrition (PEM), measles, and diarrhea has been pilot-tested in the Philippines, where coverage of 12-83 month old children rose from 3% to 30% after 18 months, and xerophthalmia prevalence dropped from 3.7% to 1.0%. The project also complemented supplementation with nutrition education, using mass-media and interpersonal communications targeted to mothers of 6-72 month old children. This resulted in an increase of knowledge and awareness, and intake of foods rich in vitamin A increased 65% among children and by 29% at the household level (Tan et al, HKI, 1992).

However, while disease targeting may be economically desirable, one needs to bear in mind that the children most at risk in most developing countries are usually those who do not have access to the health delivery system. That problem cluster groups are the most difficult to reach through regular health services was recognized in Indonesia as early as 1979; suggestions were made then for outreach programs to reach xerophthalmia "clusters" (Pettiss, 1984). Targeting high-risk areas, particularly where NGOs or indigenous grassroots organizations have ongoing activities, is a practical approach.

In Indonesia, the capsule coverage tripled nationwide from a reported 21% in August 1991 to nearly 60% in August 1993. Success with the biannual vitamin A capsule distribution may be attributed to the expansion of village health posts (posyandu) throughout the country, and the national and provincial promotion of capsules using the social-marketing approach as part of the Somavita program (Social Marketing of Vitamin A). Most important, locally-specific alternate distribution channels to the posyandu were organized with the involvement of grassroots groups. Religious leaders as well as traditional medicine sellers were asked to reinforce messages to mothers about capsules. The boy scouts (South Sumatra) and the military (West Sumatra) distributed capsules outside health posts. Religious women's NGOs were mobilized (Central Java) to distribute capsules at kindergartens and to produce traditional shadow puppet shows with capsule messages. Maternal knowledge and awareness were also considered key to improving coverage. The active mobilization of communities correlated with mothers' attendance at the posyandu.

In addition to effective mobilization of grassroots organizations, more attention was given to improving management and monitoring of the program, beginning with the establishment of an improved record system emanating from village health posts and ending with data compilation at the national level.

Fortification

Fortification is considered to be the most cost effective of micronutrient interventions, and is generally preferable to supplementation as a long-term strategy. Developed countries have eradicated some major micronutrient deficiencies through food fortification (for example, iodized salt, vitamin-D fortified milk); such fortification, and the restoration of nutrients to some commonly consumed foods (for example, cornmeal, white rice, and white flour) has been an effective and sustainable means of improving nutrition. Experience suggests it can be equally effective in developing countries. The advantage is the opportunity provided by the existing food distribution system to distribute the fortified agent. The primary limitation is that the poorest countries, which need fortification the most, generally lack an appropriate carrier: a dietary item widely consumed that is produced and packaged at sites where micronutrients can be conveniently added under careful regulation and quality-assurance guidelines.

Additionally, the food vehicle and the nutrient must be stable under the extreme conditions likely to be encountered in storage and distribution in these countries; substances in the food must not interfere with the use of the nutrient; and the nutrient must not interfere with the food (it must not be detrimental to flavor, shelf life, color, texture, or cooking properties) (Levin et al, 1993).

Typical food vehicles for vitamin A, iodine, and iron are salt or sugar because they tend to meet the above criteria. Other vehicles that have been pilot-tested and are at various stages of implementation and success are margarine, monosodium glutamate (MSG), and wheat flour. Some of the constraints encountered are technical, requiring adaptation of known technologies to meet the special needs of developing countries. For example, in the case of MSG, when commercially available vitamin A beadlets did not withstand the hot, humid conditions of Indonesia, efforts had to be redirected to produce a new beadlet that met the special requirements (both climatic and Muslim religious food regulations) of the country.

The recent experience of the Philippines with "Star" margarine illustrates what might be achieved in a relatively short period and at minimum cost to the health and nutrition sector, when the private sector is engaged in a dialogue in resolving health and nutritional problems. Advocacy followed by technical consultations convinced the manufacturer to improve the vitamin A content of the margarine. The manufacturer supported the costs of fortification, the efficacy field trial, and repackaging into smaller containers for the very poor who tend to purchase in small quantities. A margarine approved by the Ministry of Health is now available (Solon, IVACG, 1994). While the private sector has been involved to some degree in other fortification efforts, this is an excellent resource still very much untapped.

In Latin America, food technology and distribution systems are more advanced than in other developing regions, so these strategies have good potential. However, the lack of adequate human resources at the local level has been an obstacle and further training is needed. The private sector may have enough technical capacity to produce fortified foods and might be able to contribute to the educational component of training programs for food fortification (VITAL, 1993).

Iodization of salt is the most feasible approach to combatting IDD. In Bolivia, efforts to control IDD resulted in a reduction of the prevalence of goiter among school children from 65.3% (1983) to approximately 20% in preliminary 1989 results, and the incidence of new cases of cretinism has been nearly zero. The national program emphasized early formation of cooperatives, teaming up small producers to achieve units of salt production large enough to support iodization plants. This increased commercialization made iodized salt both accessible and economically viable at prices nearly equal to those of common salt, and covering 80% of estimated human consumption (Mannar, 1994).

It should be noted that the reduction of IDD was not achieved through fortification of salt alone. Complementary actions included: effective education about iodine deficiency; assurance of financial independence of the program through the formation of an independent salt-marketing company; and a massive campaign with iodized oil providing immediate iodine supplementation while awaiting adequate distribution of the iodized salt.

Other factors contributing to the success of the program that might be applied to any program intervention include clear identification of goals and constraints; flexible and strategic programming; strong program management; commitment; collaboration; local involvement; and appropriate international support used strategically (Mannar, 1994).

Dietary Diversification

The most appealing long-term solution for micronutrient deficiencies (particularly of vitamin A) is to increase intake of natural dietary sources. The first priority is to identify those factors responsible for inadequate intake, such as lack of access or awareness. More than any other approach, the success of this type of intervention depends on a thorough understanding of local practices and constraints, and intense work with the community is necessary to understand and alter local dietary practices. The advantage of this approach is that, once the community develops an appropriate response, it will generally be sustained at little cost and is self-sufficient within the community.

Thailand's recent experience in social marketing of vitamin A-rich foods is one of the best documented examples of how nutrition communication programs can significantly change food and nutrition practices and improve nutritional status. The project promoted home and school gardening of a locally available food, the ivy gourd plant, as well as other vegetables and foods rich in vitamin A. Its success can be attributed to the comprehensive approach, based on sound technical knowledge of the framework for behavior change, an understanding of the target population, the use of talent and creativity to produce innovative and useful messages, and the ability to work with the community as partners. Also crucial were linking nutritional messages with concrete actions and an emphasis on careful, effective management (Smitasiri et al, 1993).

More recently, preliminary results from Niger have indicated that promotion of vitamin A-rich foods could improve consumption to levels judged adequate by biological criteria, and that this occurred during significant improvements in coverage with vitamin A capsules. This finding is especially important. Niger is considered one of the more difficult countries in which to combat this deficiency, given its location in the drought-prone Sahel where, vitamin A-rich foods are scarce. The success appears to be the result of a variety of synergistic donor (USAID, FAO, UNDP) inputs (Burger, 1995). Contributions were made by the

USAID mission to support Helen Keller International's (HKI) efforts in capsule distribution; the Academy for Educational Development's (AED) Nutrition Communication Project for the promotion of increased consumption of vitamin A-rich foods shared a Ministry of Public Health vitamin A coordinator and the administrative and logistical support provided by HKI's field office. USAID's Office of Health and Nutrition (through VITAL), FAO, and UNDP supported the promotion of home gardens. Efforts were directed to strengthening local capacity to develop effective communication skills and use participatory learning activities. Creativity in the use of communication channels, such as a puppet theater, generated community enthusiasm. The National Vitamin A Committee (comprised of various government sectors) has been responsible for the high political commitment to sustain activities.

Experience with home-gardening support suggests that this can increase consumption of beta-carotene-rich vegetables and fruits and improve vitamin A status. The Bangladesh nationwide project, implemented through a network of national NGOs, complements production with social marketing and nutrition. Results have shown increased production and consumption of vegetables, and a concomitant decrease in the prevalence of night blindness. Other positive outcomes include a growing trend in funds generated from the gardening activities being spent on food, and the empowerment of women, with the adult female (70% of gardens are maintained by women) responsible for this new income. Several NGOs, under the overall supervision of HKI, have undertaken implementation of the project, including bimonthly data collection from about 4,000 households (Islam et al, IVACG, 1994).

Experience from the pilot home-gardening project in Niger described above indicates that nutrition education (the promotion of existing, naturally growing sources of vitamin A to cultivated status as well as the promotion of liver consumption) and addressing the seasonal shortage problem through food preservation and solar drying both contributed to the success of the effort (Mohamed, IVACG, 1994).

Program Elements Deserving Further Attention

There is now a body of information from programs undertaken over the last 20 years in supplementation, fortification, and in nutrition communications. Some has been published, other information still remains with program implementers. There are also certain program elements that require our further attention and exploration.

Women's Health Before and During Pregnancy

For the child, the mother is the key to survival and health, the infant's first line of defense against infectious diseases through the colostrum in breast milk, which is also the infant's best source of vitamin A. The association of breastfeeding with a substantial reduction in the risk of vitamin A and iron deficiency in infants supports the recommendation that mothers in developing countries be advised to breastfeed as long as possible. However, if the mother herself is deficient in various nutrients, the child may be born deficient and the mother's milk will be both less bountiful and less rich in vitamin A and iron. Data from Bangladesh show that children (12-59 months) of nightblind mothers are at 5-10 times higher risk of being nightblind than other children. This suggests the need for more attention to the vitamin A status of women during the reproductive years to protect both their own health and that of their children (Bloem et al, IVACG, 1994).

Maternal literacy plus access to nutrition and health information has been shown to be instrumental in substantially reducing the risk of xerophthalmia and malnutrition in young children. It appears to be an important predictor of the prevalence in a village of xerophthalmia or excessive levels of wasting (VITAL News 1992). Whether the intervention is supplementation (compliance) or nutrition education, the mother's knowledge and awareness are key to the success of improving her and thus the infant's micronutrient status.

It seems clear that increasing women's literacy should also be addressed. While micronutrient programs have prioritized the special needs of pregnant and lactating women, more attention needs to be directed to future mothers, and at least as early as adolescence. Education on the importance of micronutrients in the context of overall good nutrition and health should be introduced as early as possible through schools and other channels such as literacy programs, and the information reinforced over the years, so that the woman has the tools and knowledge necessary for motherhood. In all cases, and in all program interventions, the key motivating factor for the mother is the wellbeing of her child. She is a natural partner in the prevention of micronutrient deficiencies.

Linkages With Overall Development

The provision of information without a supportive or enabling environment is self-defeating. Access to community-based health, social, and educational services, plus adequate and balanced diets, will enable the mother to sustain the child and herself. An inadequate intake of essential vitamins and minerals is usually due to the influence of cultural beliefs and practices or food unavailability (for whatever reason), or to both. While current programs address behavior change, any lasting solution needs to explore all the causes of micronutrient deficiencies, including the lack of adequate food due to poverty.

Countries such as Indonesia and Thailand, which have addressed overall economic and national development along with nutrition and health issues, are the ones on their way to achieving the year 2000 goals in micronutrient deficiencies. The 1992 data from Indonesia show that active xerophthalmia has been dramatically reduced: the overall prevalence among preschool children declined 75%, from 1.33% in 1977-78 to 0.34% in 1992. Active corneal disease declined by 95% (1/1000 in 1977-78 to 0.05/1000 in 1992). Whether the decline is due to intervention programs (universal capsule distribution, nutrition education, social marketing) undertaken in response to the findings of the original survey is impossible to ascertain, as significant achievements were also made in national development (Muhilal et al, 1994).

The achievements in Indonesia (including economic growth, food self-sufficiency, a sharp decline in infant mortality, a reduction in population growth, a significant reduction in the number of people in poverty, and betterment of nutritional status, especially in vitamin A deficiency) were feasible within a relatively short time (10-15 years) because of consistent implementation of the Indonesian Trilogy of Development strategy. This strategy has been in place since 1969, and has made significant progress despite economic crises and structural adjustment in the 1980's (Soekirman, Kodyat, 1992).

While further progress in development efforts is desirable, this does not imply that we should wait for countries to achieve reductions in poverty or make strides in other social and health agendas to alleviate micronutrient deficiencies. It does support the conceptual framework developed by UNICEF, which defines malnutrition as the outcome of three levels of causes (Mason, Jonsson, Csete, this volume), to widen the perspective of program planners and implementers and accelerate consensus-building on the causes of malnutrition and appropriate responses. The UNICEF framework calls for a more holistic and collaborative approach in dealing with micronutrient and other nutritional goals that are inherently linked with other goals – control of diarrhea and measles, improved water and sanitation, promotion of exclusive breastfeeding, and education. The challenge is no longer *what* to do (there are effective technologies that can be vertically implemented) but *how* to effectively apply this knowledge in a broader framework and with sustained outcomes.

The Role of NGOs and Other Community-Based Groups

Non-governmental organizations (NGOs) and private voluntary organizations (PVOs), particularly those with ongoing child survival and nutrition programs, provide a cost-effective delivery channel for micronutrients. Experience has demonstrated that limited, short-term technical assistance directed to US PVOs has had a multiplier effect on local NGOs and their grassroots beneficiaries. In some cases the effect has extended to collaborating government decision-makers and national programs (HKI, 1993). NGOs/PVOs have the flexibility that governments and international agencies do not: to move rapidly forward on initiatives, to apply new strategies, or to work out operational issues. NGOs/PVOs, if equipped with appropriate knowledge and skills, have demonstrated their ability to effect sustained change at the country and community level in treating micronutrient deficiencies. In Niger, for example, contributions of PVOs supported by various USAID offices had a synergistic impact.

At the global policy level, the NGO community claimed an "historic breakthrough" (TerraViva - IPS news, 1992) in their participatory role in the formulation of the World Declaration and ICN Plan of Action for Nutrition. In particular, the NGO Working Group on Micronutrient Deficiencies took the lead in having their draft adopted by 159 countries as the official ICN Plan of Action for micronutrient deficiencies. NGOs continue to put pressure on governments to implement the ICN Declaration and Plan of Action and in some countries, Nigeria, for example, NGOs have taken the lead in followup activities (Sanusi, IVACG, 1994).

Successful national supplementation programs involved some participation of grassroots organizations. However, the potential of a fully-mobilized NGO community in this and other areas of program implementation, and particularly in assessment and analysis from which appropriate actions could emerge, is yet to be explored.

Brazil's movement to demand an end to hunger as a basic human right and utilizing "partnership" as a central concept is a lesson in mobilization and the awakening of conscience (Carvalho, 1994). It demonstrates the potential role of a catalyst or change agent, in this case, an NGO – The Citizens' Action for Life Against Hunger and Misery, and for Life (CA) – to give rise to the largest mass movement in Brazil's recent history.

Mobilization of Human Resources

Most successful programs have noted the role of management, that is, individuals, in reaching project objectives. From the clear identification of problem, solution, and goals to monitoring activities, being responsive and flexible to changing situations, dealing with communications and a magnitude of competing priorities, and steering programs towards articulated goals and objectives takes extraordinary commitment and perseverance in the face of scarce human and financial resources. Flexibility, a pragmatic approach to constraints, and a clear understanding of the scientific basis of programs all are important.

Most successful programs have had national implementers who have faced challenges with strong determination. It is this small but growing critical mass of dedicated program planners and implementers who have shown what can be achieved. If year 2000 goals are to be met, it will be necessary to institutionalize the in-country knowledge and experience of this small group through human resource development. Capacity-building of communities and leaders is crucial: they must be empowered with appropriate tools to identify and solve their own problems.

The Role of Private Industry

Private (profit-making) industry is a valuable resource not yet fully engaged. Experiences in collaborating with them, as for example, in the Philippines and Indonesia, have been positive and successful, requiring limited advocacy and technical coordination. If developing countries are to follow in the footsteps of western countries with fortification as the key strategy in overcoming some micronutrient deficiencies, private-sector companies need to be active partners, particularly those already involved in food processing, marketing, and distribution. Such programs, already in place in some countries, could provide the link with government representatives and assist in the development and/or enforcement of fortification regulations. There is also a largely untapped potential for small-scale food processing industries, for example, to work on domestic weaning-food production (Mannar, 1994). NGOs (see above) could foster linkages and coordinate incorporation of micronutrients into the products, perhaps through food cooperatives. Policy makers in governments and private sector groups need to make a more concentrated and coordinated effort in advocacy and awareness-raising.

Monitoring Progress

Micronutrient goals are being monitored by WHO and FAO as part of the overall ICN national plans of action. A report from WHO (Verster, IVACG, 1994) indicates that 121 countries have provided information on the status of their national plans of action. One-third of these countries are now finalizing their plans; half are at the preparation stage, and the rest have not yet started developing plans.

The major constraints to progress are the lack of human resources and political instability. However, 87 countries reported that ICN had led to increased financial and human resources for nutrition, with 50% of the countries making available additional government resources, while the other half received assistance from international agencies. In 25% of these countries, there was increased support from bilateral donors. Additional financial and human resources were mobilized in 24 countries by collaboration with NGOs.

The majority of countries are enhancing in-country collaboration by developing or strengthening intersectoral bodies – for example, food and nutrition councils, task forces, and working groups. Seventy-five percent of the countries have also established coordinating mechanisms with and among international agencies to achieve ICN goals.

With WHO's efforts to establish a global database on micronutrient deficiency prevalence, the Micronutrient Deficiency Information System (MDIS), global monitoring is becoming more systematic. Information from individual countries or from case studies provides some indication of overall progress and, more important, in identifying viable interventions and initiatives.

UNICEF and WHO have developed mid-decade goals for vitamin A and iodine deficiencies and established indicators appropriate for use in monitoring decade goals. The mid-decade goal for vitamin A targets 80% of all children under 24 months of age in areas with inadequate vitamin A intake. It recommends a combination of breastfeeding, dietary improvement, fortification, and supplementation to ensure an adequate intake ("adequate" being defined as the equivalent of at least 350 micrograms retinol equivalent (or 1200 IU) daily, or 2450 micrograms retinol equivalent (8400 IU) weekly. (UNICEF/WHO, 1993).

The UNICEF/WHO goal is that by 1995, all countries have determined whether they have a VAD problem and (if so) established approaches to ensure its elimination by 2000. Steps will have been taken to ensure adequate intakes in the group of children at highest risk - those under 24 months of age and those in areas where clinical VAD is recognized. Focusing on children under two years of age should result in the greatest number of lives saved and cases of childhood blindness prevented, and will set in motion progress toward sustainable strategies to achieve the decade goal (UNICEF/WHO, 1992).

Published data on the status of interventions include descriptions of fortification and supplementation programs. Supplementation programs are underway in 31 countries, compared with eight countries undertaking national prevention and control programs a decade ago (West, Sommer, ACC/SCN, 1987). Fortification activities are either underway or planned in 10 countries , with four of these countries also undertaking supplementation programs (Jamison, 1993, with personal updates). It is encouraging to note that over 69% of the countries categorized in 1984/5 as having undertaken (or partially undertaken) assessments but no programs are now doing so. And 61% of countries that in 1984/5 had yet to assess the problem, have now accomplished that and are implementing supplementation programs.

In IDD, a notable acceleration of activities has occurred at the global, regional, and country levels since the 1990 World Summit for Children. To reach the year 2000 goal requires demonstrably effective control programs in all countries with a significant IDD problem. The WHO/UNICEF/ICCIDD consultative group has developed monitoring indicators that include both IDD status and IDD control program indicators (WHO/UNICEF/ICCIDD Consultation, 1992).

Current information on 183 countries indicates that IDD exists in 118; 51 do not have the problem; no data are available from 14 (Pandav, IVACG, 1994). Of these 183 countries, 82 are undertaking iodization programs. Twenty-four countries are already undertaking iodine supplementation programs, and an additional 31 countries plan to initiate activities (Jamison, 1993).

Steps for Achieving the Year 2000 Goal

Determined political will and government action can make an enormous difference – Indonesia is a good example. To control vitamin A and iodine deficiencies by the year 2000, the following steps need to be taken:

- Establish an active, central intersectoral coordinating group to organize and oversee all phases of the program. The group must initiate the work (as in the Philippines and Niger), not simply suggest and review what implementers are doing. This requires a chairperson carrying sufficient political authority to facilitate policy decision making and implementation. Decisive political action that includes an allocation of necessary funds from government sources is needed.

- If adequate data are not available, assess the population at risk and the severity, magnitude, and distribution of the problem. For IDD, these measurements might require suitable laboratories, and the salt industry must be assessed for potential iodization. For VAD, if the problem is localized in one region, a local intervention may be adequate.

- Establish a program plan to identify why the target population is deficient, begin appropriate educational and related activities to instill community understanding, develop locally appropriate solutions to the problem, and increase intake of natural dietary sources of vitamin A. Include the education system, public health professionals, consumers, the media, the private sector, and industry – particularly, for IDD, the salt industry. Mobilize various groups to action.

- For VAD, while awaiting the effects of changes in dietary habits or of fortification efforts, establish periodic dosing as an emergency measure, beginning with existing health-care facilities and ensuring that all children with measles, chronic diarrhea, and significant protein-energy malnutrition are included in the policy. Identify high risk areas for priority interventions for more efficient use of resources. Where feasible, consider expanding to community-based mass distribution through the primary health care network, EPI, NGO network, and related systems. For IDD, iodized oil can be used as an emergency measure.

- Implement the plan, using whatever combination of specific interventions is appropriate, and include education of the population and appropriate training of program implementers, communities, and leaders. This will include organization of the supply of iodized salt, iodized oil, and vitamin A capsules, as well as the establishment of appropriate standards and regulations (for iodized salt and other fortified foods) and measures to enforce them.

- Monitor and evaluate the program. This requires outcome (or status) and process indicators developed by ICCIDD/UNICEF/WHO (1993). Determination of salt iodine levels provides a good indication of the social process of a national program. Outcome measurements include evidence of reduction of goiter size and one biochemical indicator. Core indicators for vitamin A include serum vitamin A or breast-milk retinol levels and the prevalence of nightblindness. Several process indicators have been outlined, including percent coverage of the at-risk population, increases in consumption of vitamin A-rich or fortified foods, and the percent of homes with gardens with provitamin A-containing foods.

Achievable, worldwide goals include:

- By 1995: coordinating bodies have been established; countries have determined whether they have VAD and IDD problems, and initiated appropriate intervention strategies. Steps have been taken to ensure adequate vitamin A intakes in the children at highest risk, including those with measles, chronic diarrhea, and significant PEM, as well as in high-risk areas where clinical VAD is recognized.

- By 2000, VAD and IDD deficiencies as a public health problem will be controlled, if not eliminated, in high-risk regions. This should be demonstrated by a reduction in the prevalence and severity of clinical manifestations, as well as in the improvement of overall status. If this goal is not reached in a few countries due to political instability and other realistic constraints, they will at least be on their way to achieving the year 2000 goal.

> *The time for* **bold action** *is now – what will be required to win our war against 'hidden hunger' is a global commitment of the type and magnitude that has made the immunization program such a success story.* (Grant, 1991).

1.   The views expressed in this paper do not necessarily represent the agencies with which the author is affiliated.

References

ACC/SCN (1993). *Second Report on the World Nutrition Situation, Vol. II. Country Trends, Methods and Statistics.* Geneva: ACC/SCN and Washington DC: IFPRI.

Bloem, M.W., H. Matzer, N. Huq (1994). Vitamin A Deficiency among Women in the Reproductive Years: An Ignored Problem. IVACG presentation.

Burger, S.E (1995). Draft paper – Preliminary results of a Helen Keller International/Ministry of Public Health Survey – Indirect Evidence that USAID Contributions to Promote Consumption of Vitamin A-Rich Foods in Niger had a Biological Impact. Helen Keller International.

Carvalho, F.(1994). *Citizens in Action for Life, Against Hunger and Deprivation.* Preparatory paper for "Overcoming Hunger: The 1990s and Beyond" conference, Institute of Nutrition, Mahidol University, Thailand.

Chirambo, M. (1994). Vitamin A Deficiency in Africa: Update. IVACG presentation.

Grant, J.P. (1991). The End of "Hidden Hunger" is in Sight. Address at International Policy Conference on Micronutrient Malnutrition, Montreal. New York: UNICEF.

Helen Keller International report (1993). *Assessment of the Vitamin A Technical Assistance Program (VITAP).* New York: Helen Keller International.

ICCIDD, UNICEF, WHO (1993). *Global Prevalence of Iodine Deficiency Disorders.* MDIS Working Paper #1. Geneva: WHO.

ICCIDD, UNICEF, WHO (1993). *Indicators for Assessing Iodine Deficiency Disorders and their Control Programmes.* Report of a Joint WHO/UNICEF/ICCIDD Consultation, 3-5 November 1992, WHO/NUT/93.1. Geneva: WHO.

Islam, T.A., et al (1994). Results and Lessons Learned from HKI's Home Gardening Activities in Bangladesh. IVACG presentation.

IVACG (1994). *Two Decades of Progress: Linking Knowledge to Action.* Washington DC: Office of Health and Nutrition, USAID, and ILSI.

Jamison, D. T. (1993). Disease Control Priorities in Developing Countries: An Overview. In D.T. Jamison, W. H. Mosley, A. R. Measham, and J. L. Bobadilla, eds., *Disease Control Priorities in Developing Countries.* New York: Oxford University Press for the World Bank.

Levin, H., E. Pollitt, R. Galloway, J. McGuire (1993). Micronutrient Deficiency Disorders. In D.T. Jamison, W.H. Mosley, A.R. Measham, J.L. Bobadilla, eds., *Disease Control Priorities in Developing Countries.* New York: Oxford University Press for the World Bank.

Mannar, V. (1994). Draft paper - IDD Control in Bolivia: An Evolving Success Story.

Mason, J., U. Jonsson, J. Csete (this volume). *Is Childhood Malnutrition Being Overcome?* Preparatory paper for "Overcoming Hunger: The 1990s and Beyond" conference, Institute of Nutrition, Mahidol University, Thailand.

Mohamed, M. (1994). Piloting Diet Diversification through Home Gardens: the Niger Experience. IVACG presentation.

Muhilal et al, (1994). Changing Prevalence of Xerophthalmia in Indonesia, 1977-1992. *European Journal of Clinical Nutrition* 48.

Nandi, B. (1994). FAO/RAPA's Progress in Support of ICN and Vitamin A Programming in the Region. IVACG presentation.

Pandav (1994). Progress with Universal Salt Iodisation and Lessons Learnt from the ICCIDD. IVACG presentation.

Pettiss, S. (1984). *Indonesian Nutritional Blindness Prevention Program, Historical Perspective: HKI-USAID Collaboration, 1972-1980*. New York: Helen Keller International.

Rahmathullah, L., B.A. Underwood, R.D. Thulasiraj, R.C. Milton, K. Ramaswamy, R. Rahmathullah, G. Babu (1990). Reduced Mortality Among Children in Southern India Receiving a Small Weekly Dose of Vitamin A. *New England Journal of Medicine*, 323:929-35.

Sangkap Pinoy: The Philippines Experience in Massive Micronutrient Intervention (1994). Department of Health/UNICEF/National Nutrition Council/Helen Keller International.

Sanusi, R. (1994). Food Basket Foundation International and ICN Follow-Up in Nigeria. IVACG presentation.

Smitasiri, S., G. Attig, A. Valyasevi, S. Dhanamitta, K. Tontisirin (1993). *Social Marketing Vitamin A-Rich Foods in Thailand*. Office of Nutrition, USAID and Institute of Nutrition, Mahidol University.

Soekirman (1994). Eradicating Xerophthalmia: Indonesian Experience. IVACG presentation.

Soekirman, B. Kodyat (1992). *Indonesia: Preventing Specific Micronutrient Deficiencies*. Case Study. Preparatory paper for the Break-Out Workshop on Preventing Specific Micronutrient Deficiencies, International Conference on Nutrition. New York: Helen Keller International.

Solon, F.S. et al (1994). Effect of Vitamin A Fortified Margarine in Rural Preschool Children in the Philippines. IVACG presentation.

Somavita II: The Social Marketing of Vitamin A Program in Indonesia (1991-1994). Helen Keller International documents.

Sommer, A., I. Tarwotjo, G. Hussaini, D. Susanto (1983). Increased Mortality in Children with Mild Vitamin A Deficiency. *Lancet*, 2:585-88.

Tan, J., G. Bayugo, R. Klemm (1992). *Philippines: Preventing Specific Micronutrient Deficiencies*. Case Study. Preparatory paper for the Break-Out Workshop on Preventing Specific Micronutrient Deficiencies, International Conference on Nutrition. New York: Helen Keller International.

TerraViva - Inter Press Service Publication (1992). No. 1. Rome, Italy.

Tontisirin, K., P. Winichagoon (1994). *Progress in Overcoming Hunger in Southeast Asia, 1989-1994*. Preparatory paper for "Overcoming Hunger: The 1990s and Beyond" conference, Institute of Nutrition, Mahidol University, Thailand.

Underwood, B.A. (1994). Global Prevalence of Vitamin A Deficiency and its Control. IVACG presentation.

UNICEF (1993). *The Progress of Nations*. New York: UNICEF.

UNICEF, WHO (1992). *Indicators for Assessing Vitamin A Deficiency and their Application in Monitoring and Evaluating Intervention Programmes*. Report of a Joint WHO/UNICEF Consultation, 9-11 November, 1992, WHO/NUT/94.1. Geneva: WHO.

UNICEF, WHO (1993). *World Summit for Children – Mid-Decade Goal: Vitamin A Deficiency (VAD)*. Geneva: WHO.

Verster, A (1994). ICN Follow-Up Progress in Countries (WHO). IVACG presentation.

Vital News (1992). Can Maternal Literacy Prevent Xerophthalmia? Vol 3, no. 2.

Vital report (1993). Third Regional Workshop on Vitamin A and Other Micronutrient Deficiencies in Latin America and the Caribbean, Recife, Brazil, August 23-27, 1993.

Viteri, F. (1992). *Iron Deficiency*. Preparatory paper for the Break-Out Workshop on Preventing Specific Micronutrient Deficiencies, International Conference on Nutrition. New York: Helen Keller International.

West, K. P., A. Sommer (1987). *Delivery of Oral Doses of Vitamin A to Prevent Vitamin A Deficiency and Nutritional Blindness: A State-of-the-Art Review*. ACC/SCN State-of-the-Art Series, Nutrition Policy Discussion Paper 2. Geneva: United Nations ACC/SCN.

CHAPTER 10

Is Childhood Malnutrition Being Overcome?[1]

J. Mason,[2] U. Jonsson,[3] and J. Csete[4]

What is Malnutrition? Why Do We Worry About It and How Do We Measure It?

Malnutrition in children, which results from complex societal processes, has proven a durable scourge in the modern era. It is an important determinant of mortality and morbidity, and thus of the quality of life, and an impediment to the development of individuals, communities, and nations. Its persistent presence and grievous consequences led the heads of state at the 1990 World Summit on Children to commit to halving 1990 levels by the year 2000 (UN, 1990). This goal was endorsed at the International Conference on Nutrition in 1992 (FAO/WHO, 1992), where the etiological complexity of child malnutrition was again recognized. A subsidiary goal of a 20% reduction by 1995 was later established (UNICEF, 1993a).

This paper draws on recent progress in understanding and reducing child malnutrition and suggests some factors related to that progress and to future successes. First we will consider problems of malnutrition as they affect children and the commonest indicator currently used: the prevalence of underweight children. This discussion is not meant to be a comprehensive exposition, but rather to focus on the causes and consequences of the problem in relation to rapid solutions. Second, we will introduce a broad framework for the causality of malnutrition, drawing attention to potential policy and program interventions. Third, we will examine current trends, with examples from several countries, classified by whether or not national strategies exist for nutritional improvement. Fourth and finally, we will discuss what could be done to accelerate this improvement in nutrition.

Growth Failure

Typical growth patterns for children in poor countries look something like those illustrated in Figure 1. Although such charts have been familiar for many years, our understanding has evolved, and it may be useful to revisit them before going on to the (by now) even more familiar conceptual framework discussed in the next section. Growth patterns provide an entry to considering the problem of malnutrition, why it matters, and how we measure it.

Newborn infants in poor countries are more likely to be of low birth weight (e.g., 32% in South Asia, 17% in Sub-Saharan Africa, compared with less than 5% in industrialized countries), resulting often from the equivalent of intrauterine malnutrition (see Kramer, 1987), which, in turn, is more common in stunted and currently malnourished mothers. Birth weight substantially determines the

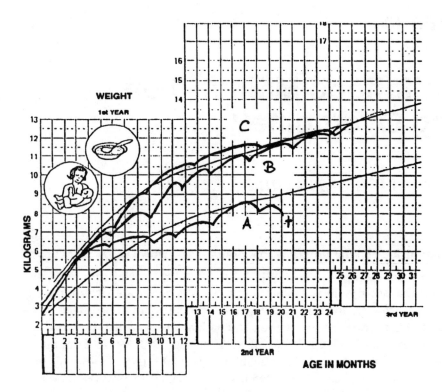

Figure 10.1: Illustration of Growth Patterns. Child A is malnourished, child B better nourished and cared-for, but with same disease incidence as child A. Child C is in less-poor environment
Source: WHO, 1986: 12.

subsequent growth pattern and risk of mortality, and it is through birth weight, to a considerable extent, that failure to grow to potential size is passed from generation to generation.

In the illustrations in Figure 1, child A has a birth weight of 2.5 kg, fairly typical in many poor countries. Both children A and B are breastfed, and grow at a good rate for the first six months or so. Child B has a birth weight of 3.0 kg, and after six months is actually slightly ahead of the usual (WHO, 1986) standard curve. Child C, from a less-poor background, is shown growing parallel to the standard curve. All three children survive the dangerous first few months, but although mortality risk declines from birth on, the nature of the risks changes too.

From around four to six months, all three are exposed increasingly to infectious diseases, especially diarrhea and acute respiratory infections. They are caught in a cycle of malnutrition and infection (which will be discussed in more detail later), but the episodes of disease differ in frequency, duration, and severity, and in catch-up during convalescence; these factors largely determine the outcome. We know now that growth failure, correlated with immune competence, relates particularly to the duration and severity of disease; if the children are in the same environment, disease frequency is less affected. Child C, illustrated as in a better environment than children A and B, has less frequent infections.

The difference between children A and B is that child B is better fed and better cared for. Child B regains lost weight faster during convalescence, and has less severe and shorter periods of ill health. At six months both are near the reference weight–for–age, with the immune system developing and the child becoming increasingly independent from immunity inherited at birth, but still deriving protection from breastfeeding. However, child A has less care, being sick longer and more severely; during convalescence, the weight lost is not fully recovered on a bulky, monotonous diet. In contrast, child B is fed more frequently with diverse and energy-dense foods. And so the cycle continues. Each episode not followed by full recovery reduces both growth and immune competence. Thus a vicious spiral develops. In the illustration, child A is shown dying around 18 months of age.

Child C is included to illustrate that in a better health environment, with good access to services and better care, the frequency, duration, and severity of disease are all improved. Catchup growth during convalescence is easier, and less catchup is needed. Both good nutrition and better health, which are linked, work in favor of survival. These two factors very often are correlated and interact, so that we might expect quite a fine balance between serious growth failure and good growth and health. Within a given environment, nutrition substantially controls this balance.

Malnutrition and Infection

Cyclic interactions between malnutrition and infection are diagrammed in Figure 2 (from ACC/SCN, 1989a), which essentially elaborates on the "immediate causes" box in Figure 6, to be discussed later. Inadequate dietary intake causes weight loss or growth failure in children, and leads to low nutrient reserves. This is associated with lowered immunity – probably with almost all nutrient deficiencies (Chandra, 1991). Particularly in protein-energy and vitamin A deficiencies there may be progressive damage to mucosae, lowering resistance to invasion and colonization by pathogens. Lowered immunity and mucosal damage are thought to be the major mechanisms by which defenses are compromised. The disease processes themselves increase nutrient loss, both from the intestine and through the host's metabolic response. These factors exacerbate the malnutrition, leading to further possible damage to defense mechanisms. In addition, many diseases are associated

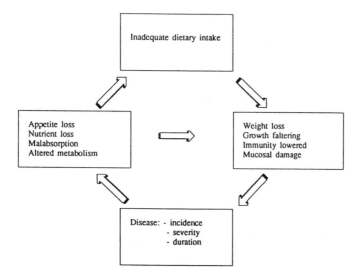

Figure 10.2. The Malnutrition-Infection Cycles
Source: ACC/SCN, 1989a.

with a loss of appetite and other possible disabilities, thus further lowering dietary intake. The synergistic effects of malnutrition and infection in relation to mortality risk have recently been demonstrated quantitatively (Pelletier *et al.*, 1994).

This cycle can lead to a downward spiral of increasing malnutrition (e.g., child A in Figure 1). Alternatively, if there is full recovery and if growth is adequate during healthy periods – in other words, if normal physiological responses are enabled – then the child survives and thrives. Factors within the cycle that can be improved are precisely those shown as underlying causes in the conceptual framework (Figure 6): a better diet related to household food security; less exposure to infection and better access to services when sickness occurs; and improved care of the individual. These factors especially affect dietary intake, treatment of the disease (e.g., ORT, antibiotics), and the careful feeding of a child with poor appetite. The immune response is compromised even with mild degrees of malnutrition, and requires adequate nutrition in terms of many essential nutrients. In effect, there is competition between the immune-response cycle – exposure to a pathogen, eliciting an immune response that kills the pathogen and returns the individual to health – and the malnutrition/infection cycle. In well-nourished individuals the immune-response cycle normally wins.

Malnutrition and Growth Failure

So far, most of this paper has dealt more with "growth" than with "malnutrition." Growth failure is widely used to provide indicators of "malnutrition": individual children's weights are converted to a weight-for-age index, and the prevalence below a cut-off gives the indicator of the prevalence of underweight children. This indicator is widely used, and is centrally incorporated in international goals. Moreover, policy choices are made depending on how directly one wishes to affect the indicator. Thus, understanding the meaning of indicators such as underweight prevalence in young children is of considerable importance.

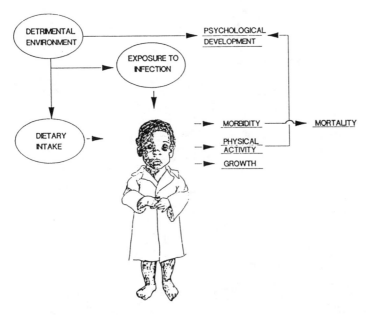

Fig 10.3. Environmental effects on the child
Source: SCN News No. 5, 1990: 9.

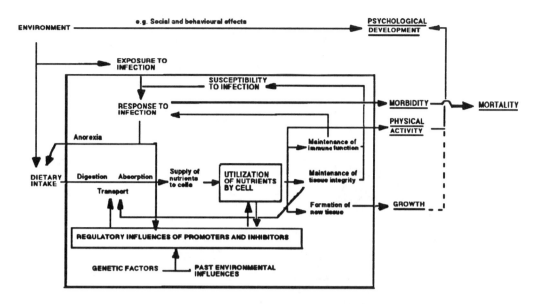

Figure 10.4. Influence of diet and other environmental factors (outside box) **on physiological processes in children** (inside box) **and outcomes** (on right, outside box, underlined)
Source: Beaton et al., 1990: 4.

Growth failure in young children is probably more important in terms of the disabilities *associated* with it (but not directly caused by it) and the deprivations that lead to it than in terms of the growth failure *itself*. In the illustration in Figure 1, the main problem is not so much the weight deficit in children A and B as their suffering during early childhood, the mortality risk, and the lingering long-term effects. In other words, it is the *process* of becoming small that is significant (ACC/SCN, 1989b; Beaton, 1989) rather than just *being* small. In Figure 3, these environmental risks and their effects on the child are summarized. Figure 4 elaborates this – the physiological processes affected by low individual dietary intake and exposure to infection (arrows on the left-hand side) are shown within the box: these processes are related to the physiology of nutrition. On the right-hand side, the four associated outcomes are shown: effects on immunity and, hence, mortality risk; on physical activity; on growth; and, related to the above, on psycho-social development. In individuals or populations with growth failure, these factors are usually all negatively affected.

Many of the disadvantages associated with growth failure are experienced at the time. It used to be considered that if a child survived to (say) age five, even if stunted, there was little continuing disability. However, recent work has begun to demonstrate that better nutrition in early childhood improves outcomes (such as educational attainment) in adults, even if other conditions from early childhood do not improve (Martorell *et al.*, 1992; Pollitt *et al.*, 1993).

Using Underweight for Goals and Indicators

An important implication of setting goals in terms of the prevalence of severe and moderate malnutrition, as measured by indicators of growth failure of children, is to provide indicators of the health, development, and well-being of children themselves. The appeal of these indicators is intuitive: it is easy to understand and

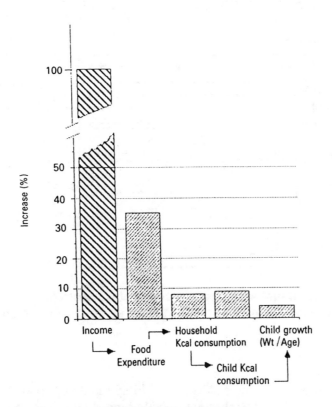

Figure 10.5. Effects of doubling income on nutrition
Illustration of data from project in the Philippines: dilution of income effects, through food consumption, on child growth.
Source: SCN News No. 3, 1989: 6, from Kennedy et al. 1988.

communicate that when children are healthy and growing well, things cannot be too bad; and that when children are failing to grow, something needs to be done. But there is a second implication of "malnutrition," measured thus, which is that indicators of child malnutrition also become a measure of (or proxy for) broader nutritional problems in the community – access to food (or household food security), health environment, and care – as shown in the conceptual framework discussed below.

How far are underweight prevalences in young children, and trends in these, in fact related to broader nutritional problems in society? The short answer is, in general terms and at the population level, reasonably closely; at the individual level, much more loosely. Numerous studies have shown that the children of better-off groups in poor countries grow better than those of worse-off groups. Associations with long-term factors such as employment, housing, income/expenditure, and so on, show the expected relationships, although often not as strongly as once thought. An example is shown in Figure 5. Here, a doubling of income leads to a 35% increase in food expenditure, but less than a 10% increase in calorie consumption. Between countries, associations of underweight prevalences are readily demonstrated with measures of national income (e.g., GNP in ACC/SCN, 1992a, p.9), and moreover *changes* in prevalence are associated with *changes* in purchasing power at national average level (see ACC/SCN, 1994). Shorter-term changes have also been observed between underweight prevalences and such factors as seasonality (ACC/SCN, 1989c) and relative price of food, as well as, more obviously, with acute food shortages. Anthropometry has not often been studied in relation to household, still less individual, food consumption, but tends to show the expected relationships; between countries, the association with estimates of calorie availability, GNP, and other such highly averaged variables (from food-balance sheets) is reasonably close (ACC/SCN, 1993).

At the individual level, more careful studies focusing on children at the most vulnerable age of less than three years have recently modified earlier pessimism about the effects of supplementary feeding (Beaton and Ghassemi, 1982), demonstrating in controlled intervention trials in deficient children that increased food intake does indeed lead to increased growth (ACC/SCN, 1992b). Important but more subtle effects, such as food intake offsetting the effects of diarrhea on growth, have been clearly demonstrated (Lutter et al., 1989).

Thus the chain between conditions at the level of society through the household to the individual, finally affecting child growth, is clear, but certainly does not show a strict proportionality. One reason for this is that the care available to the child radically modifies the effect of household food security, health environment, and services on the individual. Not only does this partly explain fuzzy relationships, and observations such as there being healthy, well-grown children in some poor households (and the opposite), but it has important policy implications because improving care (or, at the extreme, reducing neglect) has a direct effect on child growth and welfare. This is discussed further in the next section. The point here is that prevalences of underweight children are a meaningful measure of a range of nutritional problems from the individual to the population level.

Underweight: A Non-specific Nutritional Indicator

The dietary aspect of growth failure is not confined to protein and energy. First, an inadequate intake of a number of micronutrients that could well be deficient in diets of poor children is almost certainly a direct cause of growth failure (Golden, 1991). Second, specific nutrient deficiencies have an indirect effect through their effects on the immune system (e.g., vitamin A), intrauterine growth (e.g., iron and anemia in pregnant women), appetite, intestinal absorption, and the like. The designation "protein-energy malnutrition" stems from the incorrect view that protein supply is often the limiting factor in the diet, and the conjunction was coined in part to emphasize (correctly) that protein and energy trade off against each other (protein being used for energy when the latter is deficient). However, growth failure is non-specific with respect to nutritional causes, and certainly is not a specific indicator of – although it is probably sensitive to – protein-energy malnutrition. The term "general malnutrition" has been adopted (e.g., ACC/SCN, 1992a, p.2) to deal with this.

The issue goes beyond strict scientific correctness, because direct prevention of the problem may not involve protein and energy at all. For example, an infant may be underweight because of its low birth weight caused by iron-deficiency anemia in the mother; it may be underweight because of ill health or poor appetite associated with a specific nutrient deficiency; and indeed, other deficiencies, as yet ill-defined, could be playing an important role. The unexplained high prevalences of underweight in South Asia should be considered in this context. These prevalences are higher, in comparison with other regions, than might be expected

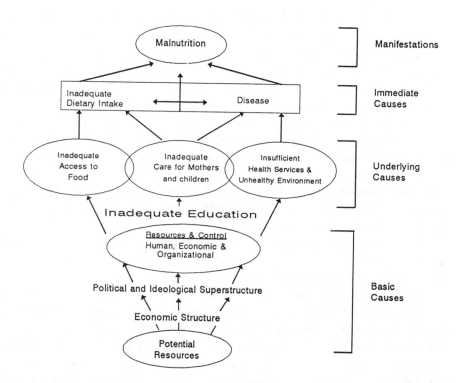

Figure 10.6. Causes of malnutrition: the UNICEF Conceptual Framework
Source: developed from UNICEF, 1990.

from environmental and socioeconomic conditions, indicating that some of the causes are not well enough understood to know all the interventions required.

A Conceptual Framework for Causes of Malnutrition

For some time, there has been a tendency to reduce child malnutrition to a technical problem amenable to ready, unisectoral solutions. For many years, policy-makers and academic experts associated malnutrition most directly with food production or food availability, and a common approach to malnutrition was food-distribution or feeding programs. Now it is somewhat better understood that multisectoral approaches are needed, although emphasis on food often still dominates policy making and program planning for nutrition.

A conceptual framework developed by UNICEF (1990) depicting the multidimensional and multisectoral causation of child malnutrition has proven useful (Figure 6). This framework shows malnutrition to be the outcome of three levels of causes: 1) immediate causes – inadequate dietary intake and illness at the individual level, which represent a synergy discussed earlier; 2) underlying causes – access of households to food, access to health services and a healthy environment, and care of children and women; and 3) basic causes – technical/ecological, social, economic, political, and ideological (including cultural) factors, especially those that are disempowering to people and which impede their capacity to control resources. Access to information through training, education, and other communication channels is a key to enabling communities and households to assess and analyze the constraints and determine appropriate actions.

This framework has been used in many countries to accelerate consensus building at government and community levels on causes of malnutrition and appropriate responses to the problem. Focusing not just on food, but on food, health, and care, it represents the best scientific understanding of the nature of the malnutrition problem and reflects the experience of many communities where access to food is not a widespread problem but child malnutrition is. It is a central idea in this framework that food, health, and care are necessary conditions for adequate dietary intake and control of diseases, and so for good individual nutritional status. None of these conditions is sufficient by itself, but when all *three* are fulfilled, the likelihood of good nutrition is high. Although this framework does not dictate particular actions to be taken in response to child malnutrition, it suggests clearly that simple injections of food aid or supplementary feeding programs are unlikely to be sufficient in many situations.

The conceptual framework implies relationships between the ICN/WSC nutritional goals and several other goals. Control of diarrhea and measles, for example, is very important in reducing malnutrition. This means that improved water and sanitation also contribute substantially to the achievement of nutritional goals. Exclusive breastfeeding is the only single human action that fulfills the conditions of "food," "health," and "care" simultaneously. Sustained breastfeeding during weaning is equally important for nutrition, because this makes it easier to ensure adequate dietary intake using foods available in the household. In the conceptual analysis, education was identified as crucial in increasing a household's capacity to use available human, economic, and organizational resources to satisfy the essential "food," "health," and "care" conditions.

The Convention on the Rights of the Child (CRC) identifies correlative rights for all these goals. While the WSC and the ICN transformed children's nutritional needs into claims, the CRC transformed the claims into rights. Claims are recognized needs, worthy of sympathy and attention, but without any obligations. Rights, on the other hand, are correlative obligations of the states that have ratified the Convention, and therefore a base for international law.

The ICN/WSC nutritional goals can be seen as "cross-cultural moral minima" (Sen, 1984), and their achievement can be seen as a necessary condition for the realization of children's nutritional rights. However, achievement of the goals is not a sufficient condition. The challenge, therefore, is to reach them through such means that the achievement becomes a realized right, including ownership, sustainability, and empowerment.

Recent Trends: Will the Goals be Met?

The Current Situation

Estimates of trends in prevalences of underweight children in the early 1990s are shown in Figure 7. For Sub-Saharan Africa, seven of the eight trends show recent deterioration, the exception being Tanzania. This may indicate a general worsening of the trends in this region. In the Near East and North Africa, and in South America, it seems likely that the generally improving trends of the 1980s are continuing, and that at the present rate both these regions are likely to reach prevalences now typical of developed countries by about the year 2000. The situation is perhaps similar for many countries in Middle America and the

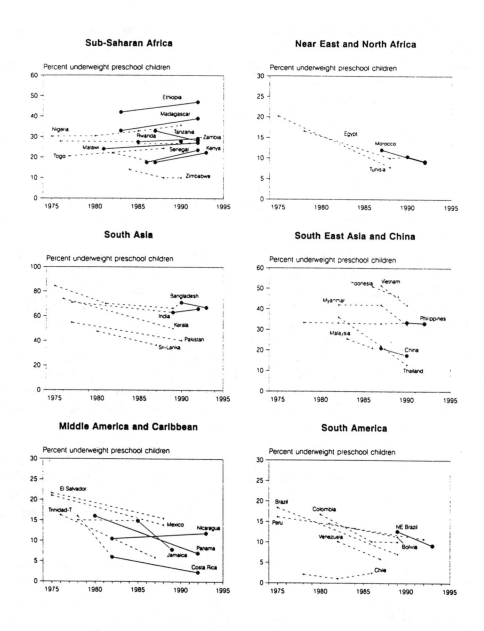

Figure 10.7. Trends in prevalence of underweight children. Results available after 1992 are solid lines, earlier ones are dotted.
Source: ACC/SCN, 1994: 2.

Caribbean; however, deterioration was noted in Nicaragua, and trends are unclear in Mexico and Cuba. In South East Asia, in which China is included (Figure 7), the rapid rates of improvement of the late 1980s probably continued. New data from China indicate rapid improvement in underweight prevalences from 1987 to 1990. The Philippines remains an exception, not yet having reached economic growth rates similar to the rest of the region.

Over half the underweight children in the world are in South Asia; thus estimates of trends in this region have enormous importance. New data are scarce. A surveillance system established in Bangladesh does appear to show improvement from 1990 to 1993 (mainly in 1992), and this is included in Figure 7. Recent changes in the situation in India are harder to assess, as data gathered in 1991/92 are from a rather small sample. Of the seven states surveyed, three showed a deterioration, and four had no significant change; this contrasts with the general improvement previously estimated between 1975-79 and 1988-90. India suffered an economic slowdown in the early 1990s, and there is reason to hope that the reversal of the improving trend may be temporary. Efforts to estimate the prevalences more precisely have been renewed, and results reported here should only be taken as an interim assessment.

More details of these estimated trends, including rates of change in percentage points per year, are shown in Table 1. Newer trend estimates (up to 1990 or later) are highlighted in gray. The results in this table in terms of rising or falling trends reflect those seen in Figure 7. Thus it is evident that most of the estimates for Sub-Saharan Africa indicate a deteriorating situation, whereas in other countries (except India) the fall in prevalence observed earlier has generally continued.

Rates of change in the prevalences observed can be compared with rates necessary to reach the nutrition improvement goals for the year 2000, endorsed by the World Summit for Children (1990) and the International Conference on Nutrition (1992) (ACC/SCN, 1992a, p.67; ACC/SCN, 1993, p.5). In Table 1, the rates of prevalence change (in percentage points per year) are shown in the right-hand column. The new data show the trends into the early 1990s (i.e., when the latest survey is after 1990) for 18 countries. Also shown in the right-hand column are regional rates of change in prevalence, in percentage points per year, required to meet the year-2000 goals. Thus, for example, in Sub-Saharan Africa a average change of -1.5 percentage points per year would be required to meet the goal of halving the prevalence by the year 2000; but most of the observed trends are positive, indicating deterioration.

A different picture emerges in other regions. In the Near East and North Africa, the signs are that the rate of improvement is about that necessary to meet the goals – although starting from a low prevalence the required improvement rate is lower than elsewhere. As noted earlier, similar relatively encouraging conclusions can be seen in South East Asia, China, Middle America/Caribbean, and South America, with rates of improvement usually similar to those necessary to reach the year-2000 goal.

Again South Asia has a larger task, starting with the highest prevalences; although the rate of improvement is estimated to be fairly similar to that in other improving regions – with the notable recent exception of India – these rates are not enough to meet the halving-the-prevalence goals. The rate required (because the starting prevalence is so much higher) is almost twice that of other regions: at nearly 3% per year, compared with 1.5% for Sub-Saharan Africa or South East Asia.

These figures are summarized in Table 2, which also includes for comparison the average rate of change in prevalence from 1985 to 1990 at the regional level. The required rate to meet the goals is also shown in this table, and the observed ranges are given in the right-hand column. This again focuses attention on Sub-Saharan Africa and South Asia. In Sub-Saharan Africa a trend reversal is needed. In South Asia, particularly if the possible deterioration in nutrition in India is

Table 10.1. Estimated trends in prevalence of underweight children
Results available since 1992 are highlighted in grey.

Country	Earlier Year	Earlier Prevalence	Later Year	Later Prevalence	Trend	Rate (pp/yr) (rate for goals)
Sub-Saharan Africa						(-1.5)
Ethiopia	1983	37.3	1992	46.9	Rising	1.07
Kenya	1982	22	1987	17.5	Falling	-0.8
Kenya	1987	18	1999	22.3	Rising	0.34
Lesotho[1]	1976	17.3	1981	13.3	Falling	-0.8
Madagascar	1984	33	1992	39	Rising	0.75
Malawi	1981	24	1992	27	Rising	0.27
Rwanda	1976	27.8	1985	27.5	Static	-0.03
Rwanda	1985	27.5	1992	29.4	Rising	0.34
Senegal	1986	17.5	1992	20.1	Rising	0.43
Tanzania	1987	33	1991	28	Falling	-1
Togo	1977	20.5	1988	24.4	Rising	0.35
Zambia	1985	26.5	1991	26.8	Static	0.05
Zambia[2]	1991	27.4	1992	29	Rising	0.3
Zimbabwe	1984	14	1988	10	Falling	-1
Near East and North Africa						(-0.6)
Egypt	1978	16.6	1988	10	Falling	-0.66
Egypt	1990	10.4	1992	9.4	Falling	-0.5
Morocco	1987	12	1992	9	Falling	-0.6
Tunisia	1975	20.2	1988	7.8	Falling	-0.95
South Asia						(-2.9)
Bangladesh	1981	70.1	1989	66.5	Falling	-0.45
Bangladesh[3]	1990	71	1993	67	Falling	-1.33
India	1977	71	1988/90	63	Falling	-0.67
India[4]	1987/90	69	1991/92	66	Rising	1
Pakistan	1977	54.7	1990	40.4	Falling	-1.1
Sri Lanka	1980	47.5	1987	36.6	Falling	-1.56
South East Asia						(-1.6)
Indonesia	1986	51	1989	46	Falling	-1.7
Malaysia	1983	25.6	1986	21.1	Falling	-1.5
Myanmar	1982	42	1990	32.4	Falling	-1.2
Philippines	1982	33.2	1990	33.5	Static	0.04
Philippines	1990	33.5	1992	34	Falling	0.23
Thailand	1982	36	1990	13	Falling	-2.88
Vietnam	1987	51.5	1990	41.9	Falling	-3.2
China[6]	1987	21.7	1990	17.5	Falling	-1.4
Middle America/Caribbean						(-0.8)
Costa Rica	1978	16	1982	6	Falling	-2.5
Costa Rica	1982	6	1992	2.3	Falling	-0.37
El Salvador	1975	21.6	1988	15.5	Falling	-0.47
Jamaica	1978	15	1985	14.9	Static	-0.01
Jamaica	1985	14.9	1989	7.2	Falling	-1.93
Nicaragua	1982	10.5	1993	11.9	Rising	0.13
Panama	1980	16	1992	7	Falling	-0.75
Trinidad/Tobago	1976	16.3	1987	5.9	Falling	-0.95
South America						(-0.4)
Bolivia	1981	14.5	1989	11.4	Falling	-0.39
Brazil	1975	18.4	1989	7.1	Falling	-0.81
Brazil (NE)	1989	12.7	1991	8.2	Falling	-1.17
Chile[6]	1978	2.1	1986	2.5	Static	0.01
Colombia	1980	16.7	1989	10.1	Falling	-0.73
Peru	1984	13.4	1992	10.8	Falling	-0.33
Venezuela	1982	10.2	1987	5.9	Falling	-0.85

Note: The purpose of this table is more to give prevalence trends than levels comparable across countries. Most prevalences given are of children 0-59 months, <-2 SDs by NCHSA standards. In some of the recent cases, however, this indicator was not available and could not be estimated (e.g. 0-36 month age range, <80% w/a cut-off), in which case priority was given to deriving identically-defined prevalences comparable within country across time. This has minor effects on the estimated rates, in percentage-points per year (pp/yr), which are considered generally comparable across countries.

1 These data not included in figure 2 as too old
2 Zambia 1990-1992, rural. In figure 2, period taken as 1985-1992 and rate calculated as 0.2 pp/yr
3 Bangladesh data for 1981/1989 from surveys, 1990/1993 from surveillance, thus levels not comparable but trends should be reliable

4 Data from Karnataka, Maharashtra, Gujarat, Kerala, Tamil Nadu, Andhra Pradesh, and Orissa
5 1987, five provinces, 1990, seven provinces. Five provinces have data for both years in these, the prevalence trend (weighted average by sample size) was -1.1 pp/yr
6 Not included in figure 2 as both prevalences approximately equivalent to NCHS prevalences

Source: ACC/SCN, 1992: 3.

temporary, the issue is to accelerate the improving trend, particularly since the underlying prevalence is nearly double that of the rest of the world.

An important determinant of nutrition trends is the economic growth rate. Comparing rates of change of GDP with rates of change in prevalence shows a moderately close fit. In Figure 8 the rates of change in prevalence are plotted against the rates of change in GDP as percent per year (discussed further in the next section). The association between the two variables is significant and the slopes of the associations were shown not to be significantly different for two periods (1980s, early 1990s). Linear and non-linear (quadratic) regressions are both significant, the latter being drawn in Figure 8.

Table 10.2. Regional rates in underweight prevalence change (pp/yr)

Region	Regional average 1985-90[1]	Required in 1990-2000 for goals[2]	Observed range in late 1980s and early 1990s (see Table 1)
Sub-Saharan Africa	0.00	-1.5	+1.1 (Ethiopia) to -1.0 (Tanzania), typically +0.4
Near East/N. Africa	-0.34	-0.6	-0.6 (Egypt, Morocco)
South Asia	-0.52	-2.9	+1.0 (India), -1.3 (Bangladesh)
South East Asia	-0.68	-1.6	-0.3 (Philippines) to -3 (Thailand, Vietnam); typically -1.5
China	+0.10	-1.1	-1.4
Middle America/ Caribbean	+0.04	-0.8	+0.1 (Nicaragua) to -1.9 (Jamaica)
S. America	-0.10	-0.4	-0.3 (Peru) to -1.2 (Brazil, NE)

[1] From Table 1.2, Second Report on the World Nutrition Situation, Volume I, p.10. (ACC/SCN, 1992a)

[2] From Table 6.1, Second Report on the World Nutrition Situation, Volume I, p.67 (ACC/SCN, 1992a): Goals of World Summit for Children (1990) and International Conference on Nutrition (1992).

Is the trend in the early 1990s (1990-92) worse than that in the late 1980s? Nutritional trends in Sub-Saharan Africa were estimated to be static in 1985–90 (ACC/SCN, 1992a, p.10), and (as discussed above) prevalences on average are likely to have increased in 1990-1992. Thus the trend probably worsened in Sub-Saharan Africa in the early 1990s. This is in line with the reduction in real GDP growth in the region, from -0.4% in 1985-1990 to -1.9% in 1990-1992 (ACC/SCN, 1994, Table 2, p.6). On average, the situation in South Asia depends largely on India. On the other hand (except for India) in other areas of the world the underweight trends available in the early 1990s were similar to those in the late 1980s. Average GDP growth rates in other regions were generally similar or better in 1990-92 than in 1985-90, again predicting a continuation of improving nutritional trends into the early 1990s.

Thus, except for India and Sub-Saharan Africa, it seems likely that the early 1990s would have seen a nutrition improvement rate similar to that of the late 1980s.

Categories of Countries

Any attempt to reduce malnutrition involves a wide range of actors at all levels of society. Although the process differs from place to place, some of its key components can be identified and are described in more detail in the next section. It may be useful to classify countries with respect to their current progress in nutrition, and in particular to note whether a consensus has been reached on the causes of malnutrition and has led to the formulation of appropriate actions and the assignment of a high political priority to the problem. By these two criteria, countries may be divided into the five groups, as shown in Table 3. The countries listed here are those for which data are available and where elements of country programs and strategies are well known.

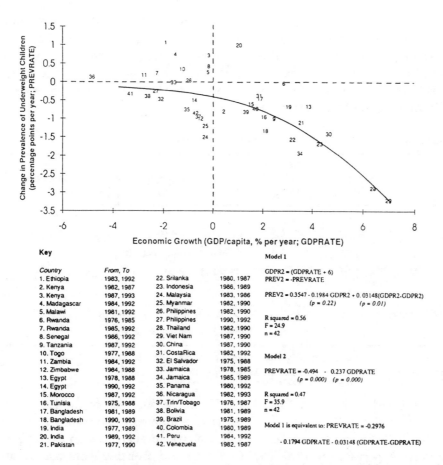

Key

Country	From, To			
1. Ethiopia	1983, 1992	22. Srilanka	1980, 1987	
2. Kenya	1982, 1987	23. Indonesia	1986, 1989	
3. Kenya	1987, 1993	24. Malaysia	1983, 1986	
4. Madagascar	1984, 1992	25. Myanmar	1982, 1990	
5. Malawi	1981, 1992	26. Philippines	1982, 1990	
6. Rwanda	1976, 1985	27. Philippines	1990, 1992	
7. Rwanda	1985, 1992	28. Thailand	1982, 1990	
8. Senegal	1986, 1992	29. Viet Nam	1987, 1990	
9. Tanzania	1987, 1992	30. China	1987, 1990	
10. Togo	1977, 1988	31. CostaRica	1982, 1992	
11. Zambia	1984, 1992	32. El Salvador	1975, 1988	
12. Zimbabwe	1984, 1988	33. Jamaica	1978, 1985	
13. Egypt	1978, 1988	34. Jamaica	1985, 1989	
14. Egypt	1990, 1992	35. Panama	1980, 1992	
15. Morocco	1987, 1992	36. Nicaragua	1982, 1993	
16. Tunisia	1975, 1988	37. Trin/Tobago	1976, 1987	
17. Bangladesh	1981, 1989	38. Bolivia	1981, 1989	
18. Bangladesh	1990, 1993	39. Brazil	1975, 1989	
19. India	1977, 1989	40. Colombia	1980, 1989	
20. India	1989, 1992	41. Peru	1984, 1992	
21. Pakistan	1977, 1990	42. Venezuela	1982, 1987	

Model 1

GDPR2 = (GDPRATE + 6)
PREV2 = -PREVRATE

$PREV2 = 0.3547 - 0.1984\ GDPR2 + 0.03148(GDPR2 \cdot GDPR2)$
$\qquad\qquad (p = 0.22) \qquad\qquad (p = 0.01)$

R squared = 0.56
F = 24.9
n = 42

Model 2

$PREVRATE = -0.494 - 0.237\ GDPRATE$
$\qquad\qquad (p = 0.000)\ (p = 0.000)$

R squared = 0.47
F = 35.9
n = 42

Model 1 is equivalent to: $PREVRATE = -0.2976$

$- 0.1794\ GDPRATE - 0.03148\ (GDPRATE \cdot GDPRATE)$

Figure 10.8. Relation of change in underweight prevalence with economic growth, by country
Source: ACC/SCN, 1994: 5.

In Table 3, progress in nutrition is shown, first, as the change in the prevalence of childhood malnutrition in percentage points per year (pp/yr); for example, a change from 40% in 1985 to 35% in 1990 would be -1.0 pp/yr. Second, it is shown as the percentage change in prevalence: for example, 40% to 35% in five years is 2.5% per year (not compounded: [5/40*100]/5). The pp/yr indicator is not affected by the prevalence itself, and allows direct comparisons of the *absolute* rate of prevalence change (e.g., of slopes in Figure 7). For guidance, the global rate from 1975 to 1990 was -0.5 pp/yr, with regional rates, for example, of: -0.1 for Sub-Saharan Africa; -0.6 for South Asia; and -0.8 for South East Asia (from ACC/SCN, 1992a, Table 1.2). A rate of -1.0 pp/yr represents substantial progress. The %/yr indicator, that is, change *relative* to the prevalence itself, is the one used for direct assessment of progress towards ICN and WSC goals. UNICEF's mid-decade goal of a 20% reduction of 1990 prevalences by 1995 implies a decrease of about 4% per year. These two indicators have been used, with an assessment of the policy position, in classifying countries in Table 3.

Countries in Groups 2 and 3 are thought to have appropriate strategies for improving nutrition. Those in Group 2 were improving, in the late 1980s and early 1990s, at a rate sufficient to meet the mid-decade goals – more than 4% per year. Countries such as those in Group 3 have been progressing more slowly. But given appropriate policies, it is reasonable to suggest that greater resources could

Table 10.3. Classification of selected countries by (a) whether policies are generally agreed for nutrition improvement and (b) progress towards nutritional goals

Group 1: Developing countries in which malnutrition prevalence is 10% or below (of those in which the prevalence was significantly higher a generation ago). Recent prevalences of underweight children are given as calculated for 1990 from SCN model (ACC/SCN, 1993, Table 2.6), or recent survey where data shown (ibid, Table 2.1)

	Prev		**Prev**		**Prev**
Algeria	9%, '87	Cuba	8%	Paraguay	4%
Argentina	1%	Jamaica	7%	Trinidad & Tobago	9%
Brazil	7%, '89	Jordan	6%	Tunisia	9%
Chile	2%	Kuwait	5%	Uruguay	7%
Costa Rica	8%	Libya	4%	Venezuela	6%

Group 2: Examples of countries for which recent trend data suggest that the 1995 goal will be met or nearly met. In most of these countries, consensus has been built on causes of malnutrition and appropriate strategies, and reducing malnutrition is given some degree of political priority. Recent prevalences of underweight children are given as for Group 1, then prevalence changes in percentage points/yr (pp/yr, negative is improving), then % prevalence improvement per year (4%/yr needed for 1995 goal).

	Prev.	**pp/yr**	**%/yr**		**Prev.**	**pp/yr**	**%/yr**
China	18%	-1.4	8%	Malaysia	18%	-1.5	5%
Colombia	10%	-0.7	7%	Thailand	13%	-2.9	12%
Egypt	10%	-0.5	5%	Vietnam	42%	-3.2	8%
Indonesia	38%	-1.7	5%	Zimbabwe	14%	-1.0	10%

Group 3: Examples of countries in which appropriate strategies to reduce malnutrition are in place or are planned but a significant allocation of resources will be needed to establish an adequate trend to meet the goal. Data from most of these countries indicate that malnutrition is declining, though not rapidly enough by current trends to meet the goal.

	Prev	**pp/yr**	**%/yr**		**Prev.**	**pp/yr**	**%/yr**
Bangladesh	66%	-0.5	1%	Nicaragua	19%	+0.1	-1%
Bolivia	11%	-0.4	3%	Peru	13%	-0.3	3%
El Salvador	19%	-0.5	3%	Philippines	34%	-0.3	1%
Myanmar	33%	-1.2	4%	Tanzania	24%	-1.0	4%

Group 4: Examples of countries in which appropriate strategies to reduce malnutrition are not in place and consensus on causes of malnutrition has not been reached. Meeting the goal is unlikely in these countries, even with additional resources. Data from such countries indicate that malnutrition is increasing or not declining significantly.

	Prev	**pp/yr**	**%/yr**		**Prev.**	**pp/yr**	**%/yr**
Ethiopia	47%	+1.1	-2%	Malawi	24%	+0.3	-1%
India	63%	+1.0	-2%	Pakistan	42%	-1.0	3%
Kenya	17%	+0.7	-3%	Zambia	26%	+0.6	-2%

Group 5: Countries currently or recently affected by war or internal strife. Although it is possible with effective planning for countries to make progress in reducing malnutrition even during emergencies, these countries are unlikely to reach the goal.

	Prev.		**Prev.**		**Prev.**
Afghanistan	40%	Liberia	20%	Somalia	39%
Angola	35%	Mozambique	47%	Sudan	34%
Burundi	29%	Rwanda	32%	Zaire	33%
Haiti	24%	Sierra Leone	26%		

Source: From data available to ACC/SCN and UNICEF.

accelerate the improvement to meet the goals – if not now the mid-decade goals, then those for the year 2000.

Countries classified in Group 4 have a more serious problem: not only slow progress, but a prior need for policy development and consensus. Indeed, some of these – in fact, most countries in Sub-Saharan Africa – are actually deteriorating nutritionally. India is clearly of particular importance, and, as we have already indicated, the trend estimate here may be unduly pessimistic; nonetheless, there is no doubt that accelerated improvement is needed.

Group 1 is included to stress that already a substantial number of countries have reached relatively low levels of malnutrition. In fact, other projections

(ACC/SCN, 1992a, pp. 66–67) envisage much of South America, and Near East/North Africa, reaching this situation by 2000. On the other hand, countries affected by internal conflict (Group 5) can hardly benefit from improved policies and resources, and their nutrition is likely to deteriorate until the situation changes.

Policy Implications

Reduction of childhood malnutrition, like all social action, can be accomplished in many ways. Poor households and communities are engaged in constant action to cope with factors that may engender nutritional problems and to use resources as effectively as possible to improve their lives. At the household and community level as well as at more aggregated levels, it is important to strengthen the capacity of poor people to assess and analyze their problems and to realize appropriate actions to reduce or prevent malnutrition. Actions must then be reassessed, reanalyzed, and so on, leading to the "triple-A cycle" depicted in Figure 9. Useful information can accelerate triple-A cycles and improve people's abilities to use resources well and mobilize support for positive actions. Structural changes – political, social, economic, etc. – can enhance or constrict the environment in which this cycle of assessment, analysis, and action takes place. Triple-A cycles imposed on communities or households from outside are not likely to help reduce malnutrition. Problems must be assessed, analyzed, and acted upon by the poor and not just on their behalf by others.

Achieving international goals is especially difficult in Sub-Saharan Africa and South Asia. In the former, the situation is generally static, with some deterioration resulting from economic recession, drought, and the like in a number of countries. Nonetheless, there are examples of important progress that could perhaps provide lessons for other regions. South Asia has the highest number of underweight children, because its population numbers are huge and prevalences are much higher. This region is showing only rather slow improvement, and several generations would pass at the present rate before the problem is fully controlled.

ASSESSMENT - ANALYSIS - ACTION

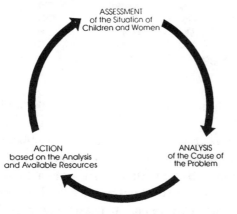

Figure 10.9. The "Triple-A cycle"
   Source: UNICEF.

Under these circumstances, it is necessary to understand where there has been success and what brought it about, and then (next section) to explore whether there are reasons for supposing that a rapid acceleration in improvement could be achieved, and how.

From many perspectives – poverty alleviation and human development in particular – the combined effects of economic growth that involves the poor, plus investments in human capital and improved social services (including safety nets) are regarded as the way ahead (UNDP, 1990; World Bank, 1990; Gillespie and Mason, 1991, pp.12-13). In specific relation to hunger and malnutrition Dreze and Sen (1989) referred to "growth-led," and "support-mediated" approaches to national success. In the present context, we need to add the role of specific nutrition programs. In analyzing a number of national case studies, the impact on malnutrition of public policies and programs was looked at under the headings of: economic growth; health and education; nutrition programs; and institutions (Gillespie *et al.*, 1995). These headings are used to comment on success factors in the next section. The case studies themselves were undertaken by national institutions, supported by UNICEF and coordinated by the ACC/SCN, in nine countries. Results have been published, in the countries concerned, from six of these: Brazil (Iunes and Monteiro, 1993); India (Reddy *et al.*, 1992); Indonesia (Soekirman *et al.*, 1992); Tanzania (Kavishe, 1993); Thailand (Kachondham *et al.*, 1992); and Zimbabwe (Tagwireyi *et al.*, 1992).

Success Factors

The relation of economic growth to improved nutrition can now be better understood using the newly available data on nutrition trends described above together with national income trends. The results have limitations; for example, the estimates of prevalence changes are for varying periods, depending on when nutrition surveys were done, and the rate of change is estimated as an average over these periods. Figure 8 shows the general relationship between economic growth rates and declining underweight prevalence. Using the UNICEF framework (Figure 6), the effect is likely to be both through basic causes (e.g., improved income, hence access to food), and through underlying causes (e.g., improved health environment and access to health services). Improved education and other social factors that go along with economic growth no doubt lead to improved nutrition. It should be reemphasized that the effect of economic growth is broader than simply that of improved income.

One way of examining influences other than income is to look more carefully at countries that have shown an improvement substantially greater or less than the average, performing significantly better or worse in terms of nutrition than might have been expected from the economic picture. These can be identified from Figure 8, where the deviation from the average (i.e., the "residual") can be examined in relation to likely influences on nutrition improvement, such as expenditure in the social sector, which may be estimated, for example, by the percentage of government expenditure on health and education. This relation is illustrated in Figure 10, which demonstrates broadly that countries with higher expenditures on health and education do indeed show more nutrition improvement (negative prevalence pp/yr) than accounted for by economic growth. The positive association of education and literacy, especially of women, and of access to health services with improved nutrition has been quite widely demonstrated at the intercountry level (e.g., Berg,1981; ACC/SCN, 1993, p.111), and in many

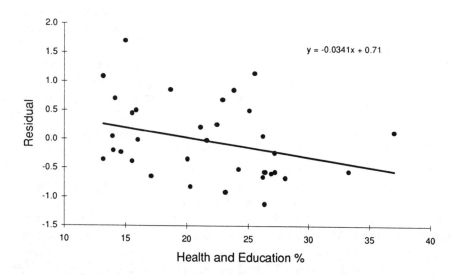

$y = -0.0341x + 0.71$

Regression statistics: n = 34. R²= 0.11, coefficient, p = 0.09

Note: Residual from linear model shown in Figure 8.

Figure 10.10. Relation of underweight prevalence change, removing effect of economic growth (residual) with government budget percent for health and education.
Source: ACC/SCN, 1994: 5,86.

individual-level studies. It can also be seen that countries with rather low commitments to health and education (e.g., less than 20% of the government budget) also tend to be those with a worse performance in terms of nutritional improvement (i.e., more data points above zero residual). Yet again we should emphasize that *how* government budgets are spent greatly affects their impact on nutrition – for example, a high health expenditure on capital-city hospitals is clearly less effective than primary health care in rural areas. Similar considerations apply to education expenditures.

To strengthen the financing of nutrition and related human development spending by governments and donors, the so-called "20/20" initiative has recently been promoted by UNDP, UNICEF, and other organizations. The initiative calls for a minimum of 20% of the total government budget to be allocated to basic social needs, arrived at on the basis of a recommended 40% of national budgets going to the social sectors, with 50% of this amount going for basic services. This national allocation would be supported by a commensurate level of foreign aid for social priorities. The 20/20 proposal was debated at the World Summit for Social Development held in Copenhagen in March 1995, and it received significant attention. Donors as well as recipient countries considered that a 20% target might be too restrictive, but there was agreement on the need to allocate additional spending for social development. In the Summit's Programme of Action, developed and developing countries were encouraged to make mutual commitments to allocate 20% of aid and national budgets for basic social services. Analyses are now being carried out in a number of countries to identify opportunities to restructure budgets to increase allocations for basic services directly or indirectly related to nutrition.

The effects of nutrition-oriented programs cannot readily be assessed from intercountry data (e.g., as in Figure 8) by this method, and here we need to look more carefully at specific countries, such as those included in the case studies mentioned earlier. It seems plausible that those with effective community-based nutrition programs had more rapid improvements in nutrition. Four of the countries with a known high awareness of nutrition and related programs – Tanzania, Indonesia, Thailand, and Zimbabwe – showed improvements greater than would be expected from economic growth; this is perhaps in contrast to the two other countries – India and Brazil – whose nutrition improvement was the same as or less than would have been expected on this basis.

What are the characteristics of more specifically "nutritional" activities? They include the requirements that such programs be community–based, that their planning and implementation empower people to identify and solve their own problems, and that they do this in a way that controls and maximizes the use of their own resources, through local decision making (i.e., the Triple-A process shown in Figure 9). The actual content of the activities is relatively familiar: improved local health services; improved awareness of nutrition and related practices; growth monitoring; micronutrient programs; local food production, etc. *How* these activities are carried out seems to be what makes them successful and sustainable. Having said that, there are a number of other straightforward but crucial differences between programs that appear to have a significant impact and those that do not.

One important difference concerns the *coverage* of programs and their *targeting*. For example, the nutrition programs in Indonesia and Thailand cover the majority of the population, in contrast to ICDS in India, which perhaps reaches 15%. Even if these latter programs were equally effective where they operate, clearly the overall effects on the entire population would be very different. This is related also to the targeting of programs – the clearest means of focusing resources to get better coverage of the needy. In practice, programs are targeted by three methods (Jennings *et al.*, 1991 p.11): geographically; selection of participants, especially by age; and screening methods such as growth monitoring. It remains common that programs tend not to optimize their potential by focusing on the most vulnerable age group: children under three. This simple targeting change could have significant effects, increasing program coverage and impact. A number of other factors are of similar importance in ensuring effective programs, such as adequate levels of resource availability, management, and so forth – these are covered in more detail in a publication in preparation which synthesizes the experience of the case studies (Gillespie *et al.*, 1995). Experience from the countries considered in the case studies referred to above seems fairly consistent in suggesting that two different types of institutions are usually involved in generating effective nutrition-relevant actions. On the one hand, a focal-point institution usually provides for research, advocacy, planning, and monitoring. Examples are TFNC in Tanzania; government planning departments like BAPPENAS in Indonesia; universities such as Mahidol in Thailand; and government-supported research institutes such as NIN in India. These, however, do not usually have responsibility for operating large-scale programs; this comes within the realm of governmental and political structures. In Tanzania, the structure was that of the party (CCM) *and* the Government; in Zimbabwe it was the district administrations; in Indonesia and Thailand it was within government departments, including the Ministry of Health; in India, it was under a special department of Social Welfare. The line ministry itself is not usually the starting point of nutrition activities, and the institutional focal points for nutrition have not usually been able to run programs effectively. In seeking to enhance programs it may be important to consider the capabilities of both types of institutions.

Fulfillment of the three necessary conditions for nutritional well-being – food, health, and care – requires scarce human, economic, and organizational resources. To fulfill one condition often means competing for the same resources needed to fulfill any of the others, for example, the time available to the mother or household income. It is important to recognize that even in situations when all three conditions have been fulfilled, there might be a problem if this requires a very large proportion of available resources. For example, households that must use 80% of their income to achieve food security have a food security problem.

Is Accelerated Improvement Possible and Likely?

Current trends, at least in Sub-Saharan Africa and South Asia, make it tempting to conclude that any conceivable acceleration is very unlikely to be adequate to meet the goals. In fact, one would be entering what would historically be seen as the rapid downward path of an S-shaped curve. Have we any reason to believe that improvement in nutrition does follow a non-linear, S-shaped path? Is it in reality the case of a relatively steady state, which then in a fairly short period takes a quantum step to a much-improved situation? If so, do we have any idea of the factors that cause this step? And indeed could we influence them?

Existing data on trends in nutrition are very recent, covering at the most the last 15-20 years. Nonetheless, it is obvious that at least those countries showing a rapid improvement – for example in South East Asia – must be on the fast track of an S-shaped curve. For a start, they presumably were never at 100% prevalence, so that sometime in the recent past they must have been in a fairly steady state of, for example, 50% prevalence of underweight; they are heading towards zero prevalence, which should then persist, so inevitably the shape will historically turn out to be S-shaped. In fact, if we look at Costa Rica and Jamaica in Figure 7, it seems probable that these are indeed portions of such a curve. Trends in regions of Tanzania with effective community-based programs – earlier Iringa, more recently the Child Survival and Development (CSD) regions – show patterns that may be similarly interpreted.

Infant mortality varies in rate of improvement, and rapid steps have been observed in history. Studies in Sweden (Corsini and Viazzo, 1993) have shown these effects. Fogel (1994) has postulated that improvements in overall (crude) death rates in France and England took place in various waves. In England this apparently happened from the second quarter of the 18th century through the first quarter of the 19th, then resumed again in the late 19th century. In France, Fogel sees a first wave of decline moving more quickly than in England, and about half a century earlier. Infant mortality rates (IMR) tend to fall more rapidly (once they start falling) – from, say, 150 deaths per 1000 live births to around 50 – then to slow down; this is usually explained as the first improvements (e.g., immunization and better neonatal care) being somewhat easier to achieve. After the IMR has initially been reduced lives are more difficult to save because the next improvements are more difficult to make. Again, these occurrences must logically be parts of S-shaped curves, since they clearly could not be extrapolated backward to 100% IMR.

We also know that economic growth rates can show periods of rapid change, and indeed seem to be related to nutrition improvement, as currently seen in South

East Asia and China. There is also some evidence that the relation itself of income with nutrition (measured by underweight prevalence) is non-linear. In the rather few cases where this has been observed, it seems that a rapid fall in underweight prevalence begins when a certain level of income is reached – an example is in Costa Rica (Mason *et al.* 1984, p.110). Therefore, based on income alone, if there is steady improvement, one might expect the point to be reached at which accelerated improvement in nutrition is observed.

The mechanisms involved in generating malnutrition are complex, and again this would argue that non-linear changes are likely. The malnutrition-infection cycle has been described, as was the synergism (multiplicative interaction) between malnutrition and infection in causing mortality (Pelletier *et al.*, 1994). We also referred earlier to competition between the malnutrition-and-infection cycle and the immune-response cycle. There are longer-term cycles also, such as the intergenerational perpetuation of growth failure, whereby low-birth-weight girls become small mothers having low-birth-weight babies. One could imagine that preventing this for a generational cohort could abolish underweight for all time. It is precisely when there are competing non-linear cycles in biological systems that major shifts can occur. As we said much earlier, quite a fine balance between thriving and malnutrition could be expected. Thus there are further reasons to argue that in principle we could look for the possibility of a major acceleration in improvement.

Since the determinants are multi-factorial, as shown in the UNICEF conceptual framework (Figure 6), it is likely that a number of pieces need to be in place to bring about the acceleration. Looking at the community and individual level, where this all has to happen, one could use the concept of the need for resources – organizational, human, and economic – for guidance.

The conclusion is probably that the slow rate of improvement in Africa and South Asia should be an alarm, but should not be interpreted as proving that the type of improvement called for to achieve the goals is impossible. On the contrary, it should lead to better analyses of where best to invest resources to bring about a self-perpetuating and increasingly rapid improvement. The good news is that some of the necessary resources are indeed coming into place: education improves human resources, information in the hands of better-educated people can help bring about better organization. As economic growth continues, the economic resources required may also become available. Looking more closely at this part of the framework should be one step in trying to accelerate improvement.

Elements of the Strategy to Improve Nutrition
During preparation of the UNICEF Nutrition Strategy a large number of nutrition-oriented programs and projects were reviewed. A number of factors associated with success were identified:

a)   Use of an explicitly formulated conceptual framework that reflects the biological and social causes of the nutrition problem, as well as the importance of causes at both macro- and micro-levels. Such a framework should reflect the multisectoral nature of the problem, accommodating a number of potential causes, but also allowing for a reduction to the most important causes in a particular context.

b)   Early establishment of a community-based monitoring system. The generation and analysis of data are of great importance for program modifications and mobilization. Data that are useful for resource management (from the household to the national level) should have priority. Analysis of information on the nutrition problem will act as a stimulus and a mobilizing force. It will also ensure that interventions are more relevant because they consider local conditions and are understood by the people concerned.

c)   Involvement of communities, particularly the women, in planning, implementation, and monitoring. The people concerned are the most capable of understanding the context.

d)   Strengthening of formal and non-formal organizations. This also requires local knowledge and often involves leadership training.

e)   Mobilization of resources at all levels. This involves both creation and reallocation of resources and planning for their use.

f)   Early provision of essential services such as immunization and the control of diarrheal diseases contributes to visibility and enthusiasm, both of which are important for social mobilization.

g)   Training at all levels plays a crucial role in increasing the capability to assess and analyze the problem of malnutrition and to design appropriate action.

h)   Recognition that, although the nutrition problem is most often multisectoral and multilevel, which should be reflected in any assessment and analysis, intervention need not always be multisectoral. A sequencing of actions, based on identification of priority actions and their feasibility, is often more efficient than multisectoral interventions.

i)   Recognition that the context in which a nutrition–oriented program is planned and implemented usually changes during the course of the program, making it difficult to plan many years in advance. Planning, implementation, and monitoring should have built-in flexibility to accommodate and facilitate modifications. Government commitment regarding personnel, resources, and advocacy should be long-term.

j)   Improved management at all levels, particularly the district level. Flexibility means continuous replanning, which requires efficient use of information. This does not necessarily mean more information, but rather more appropriate and timely information.

In sum, during the last decade improved information about nutritional trends in developing countries has made it possible to identify countries that have managed to reduce malnutrition over and above what would be expected from their level of *per capita* income and economic growth rates. Approaches to solving the nutrition problem in these successful countries reflect an emerging new development paradigm in which poor people are recognized as key actors in poverty reduction, rather than passive beneficiaries of transfers of commodities and services. Poor people are put first; development is achieved through a learning process rather than a blueprint, leading to capacity-building and empowerment; and participation, decentralization, and effective communication are encouraged. Priority is given to human-resource development, with special emphasis on reducing gender disparities. Successful approaches are also most often a combination of "top–down" promotion of sound policies and political commitment to achieving human-development goals, and "bottom-up" planning and demand for higher-level support. In most successful countries the approach has been integrated, multi-sectoral, and has used multi-level information systems, including growth-monitoring and promotion, and surveillance.

As we have seen, some countries have already established trends that are adequate for achieving the mid-decade targets for nutrition and the year-2000 goals; others will need to accelerate their implementation of existing sound strategies; another group of countries will need to develop new strategies to reduce malnutrition. The following four strategies seem particularly important:

a)   Support for consensus building on the causes of malnutrition at all levels, including the international level. At the international level the ACC Sub-Committee on Nutrition plays an important role in harmonizing policies and strategies among UN agencies and concerned bilaterals. At the national level, nutrition-relevant policies are required, including legislation for universal salt iodisation, implementation of the Code on Marketing of Breastmilk Substitutes, and universal access to health, education, and other social services. An increased awareness of the problem of malnutrition is essential, together with changed perception of the nature of the problem, and making the solutions of the nutrition problem "good politics" for leaders.

b)   People do not live at the "national level"; they live in communities. Actions are therefore required at community level. The strategy must aim at strengthening the capacity of communities and their leaders to assess and analyze their nutrition problems and to design and implement resource-relevant actions (Triple-A strategy). "Top-down" promotion of a "first call for children" to achieve human development goals, including the nutritional goals, should be done in such a way that capacities are built and communities are empowered to create a "bottom-up" response and articulated demand for support from higher levels. Among the three necessary conditions for nutritional well-being – food, health, and care – the last has been most neglected. Emphasis must therefore be given to improving care practices, including breastfeeding, complementary feeding, hygiene, and young-child stimulation. Women should be recognized as key actors and special attention should be given to reducing gender disparities. A third emphasis should be given to the promotion of environmentally sustainable actions.

c)   Improved nutrition information will be required in all the above-mentioned strategies. Current systems need to be revised so that decisions are based on more valid information. Nutrition-information systems must become more demand driven. This will require more emphasis on changing perceptions and knowledge through advocacy, training, and education. It is not until mothers demand and understand nutrition information that growth monitoring and promotion works; it is not until national decision-makers demand nutrition-relevant information that it is worthwhile to establish a nutritional surveillance system.

d)   A combination of support for service delivery and capacity building for empowerment must be promoted. Service delivery – for example, distribution of vitamin A supplements through the health care system – should be done in such a way that it encourages and enhances capacity building, i.e., knowledge about how to grow and use vitamin A-rich foods. This in turn should be done in such a way, in combination with other activities, that people are empowered, for example to ensure availability of land to cultivate these vegetables and fruits. The final goal of empowering women to breastfeed will require more basic changes in the position of women in society, often changes in perception and attitudes, and legislation to support women.

Conclusion

Consideration of past success and failure leads to several important conclusions: instead of adopting and trying to implement "pre-packaged" technical interventions, more appropriate actions should emerge from assessment and analysis of the particular context. Regular monitoring at all levels makes the nutrition problem more visible and serves as a mechanism to assess the impact of actions taken. The shortcoming of most nutrition–oriented programs today is not the lack of well–documented, scientifically proven technical interventions, but rather the failure of most programs to explore fully how existing local skills and resources should be mobilized and supported in concert with technical interventions to create an environment and a support structure more conducive to improved nutrition.

1. This paper was prepared for the World Hunger Program meeting on "Overcoming Hunger in the 1990s", Institute of Nutrition, Mahidol University, Thailand, 7–11 November 1994. The material used draws on the work of many colleagues. Recent nutritional data come from the ACC/SCN's "Update on the Nutrition Situation" (1994), assembled by M. Garcia and A. Qureshi, with further analysis by H. Bouis, B. Rodriguez, V. Elliott and J. Wallace. The views expressed are largely drawn from those elaborated from ACC/SCN and UNICEF publications as referenced, but additional speculations are the authors' own views and not those of their institutions.

2. Technical Secretary, ACC/SCN, c/o World Health Organization, 20 Avenue Appia, CH–1211 Geneva 27, Switzerland.

3. Regional Director, UNICEF Regional Office for South Asia, P.O. Box 5185, Lekhnath Marg, Kathmandu, Nepal.

4. Nutrition Advisor, Nutrition Section, UNICEF, 3 U.N. Plaza, New York NY 10017, U.S.A.

References

ACC/SCN (1989a) Introduction and Operational Implications in *Malnutrition and Infection: A Review*. ACC/SCN State-of-the-Art Series, Nutrition Policy Discussion Paper No. 5 by A. Tomkins and F. Watson. ACC/SCN, Geneva.

ACC/SCN (1989b) The Significance of Small Body Size in Populations. In: *Report on the Fifteenth Session of the Sub-Committee on Nutrition and its Advisory Group on Nutrition*, New York, 27 February – 3 March 1989. ACC/1989/PG/2 also in SCN News No.5, 1990, p19.

ACC/SCN (1989c) *Update on the World Nutrition Situation: Recent Trends in Nutrition in 33 Countries*. ACC/SCN, Geneva.

ACC/SCN (1992a) *Second Report on the World Nutrition Situation*. Volume I. Global and Regional Results. ACC/SCN, Geneva.

ACC/SCN (1992b). ACC/SCN Statement on the Benefits of Preventing Growth Failure in Early Childhood. *Report of the Subcommittee on Nutrition on its Nineteenth Session*, WFP, Rome, 24-29 February 1992; also in ACC/SCN (1993). *Nutritional Issues in Food Aid*. ACC/SCN Symposium Report. Nutrition Policy Discussion Paper No.12. ACC/SCN, Geneva; also in *SCN News No.10* (1993), p.4, ACC/SCN, Geneva.

ACC/SCN (1993) *Second Report on the World Nutrition Situation. Volume II. Country Trends*. ACC/SCN, Geneva.

ACC/SCN (1994) *Update on the Nutrition Situation, 1994*. ACC/SCN, Geneva.

Beaton, G. (1989) Small but Healthy? Are We Asking the Right Question? *Human Organization*, **48**(1), 30-39.

Beaton, G.H. and Ghassemi, H. (1982) Supplementary Feeding Programs for Young Children in Developing Countries. *Am. J. Clin. Nutr.* **35** (4), 864-916.

Berg, A. (1981) *Malnourished People: a policy view*. Poverty and Basic Needs Series, World Bank, Washington D.C.

Chandra, R.K. (1991). 1990 McCollum Award Lecture. Nutrition and Immunity: Lessons from the Past and New Insights for the Future. *American Journal of Clinical Nutrition*, **53**, 1087-1101.

Corsini, C.A. and Viazzon, P.O. (eds) (1993) *The Decline of Infant Mortality in Europe, 1800-1950*. National Case Studies, ICDC/UNICEF, Florence.

Dreze, J. and Sen, A. (1989) *Hunger and Public Action*. Clarendon Press: Oxford.

FAO/WHO (1992) *International Conference on Nutrition Goals. World Declaration and Plan of Action*. FAO, Rome & WHO, Geneva.

Fogel, R. (1994). Economic Growth, Population Theory, and Physiology: The Bearing of Long-Term Processes on the Making of Economic Policy. *American Economic Review*, **84**(3), 369-395.

Gillespie, S., Mason, J., Martorell, R. & Sanders, D. (1995). *How Nutrition Improves*. ACC/SCN. Forthcoming. See draft by Gillespie, S. & Mason, J. (1993) *How Nutrition Improves*. Background Paper for the ACC/SCN Workshops on "Nutrition-Relevant Actions in Developing Countries – Recent Lessons" at the XV IUNS Congress, 25-27 September 1993, Adelaide, Australia.

Gillespie, S. and Mason J. (1991) *Nutrition-Relevant Actions*. ACC/SCN State-of-the-Art Series, Nutrition Policy Discussion Paper No 10. ACC/SCN, Geneva.

Golden, M. (1991) The Nature of Nutritional Deficiency in Relation to Growth Failure and Poverty. *Acta Paediatr Scnd Suppl*, **374**: 95-110.

Iunes, R., & Monteiro, C. (1993). *The Improvement in Child Nutritional Status in Brazil: How did it occur?* UN ACC/SCN Country Case Study supported by UNICEF. Center for Epidemiological Studies in Health and Nutrition, University of Sao Paulo, Brazil.

Jennings, J., Gillespie, S., Mason, J., Lotfi, M. & Scialfa, T. (1991). *Managing Successful Nutrition Programmes*. ACC/SCN, Geneva.

Kachondham, Y., Winichagoon, P., Tontisirin, K. (1992). *Nutrition and Health in Thailand: Trends and Actions*. UN ACC/SCN Country Case Study supported by UNICEF. Institute of Nutrition, Mahidol University, Thailand.

Kavishe, F. (1993). *Nutrition-Relevant Actions in Tanzania*. UN ACC/SCN Country Case Study supported by UNICEF. Tanzania Food and Nutrition Centre.

Kramer, M.S. (1987). Determinants of Low Birth Weight: Methodological Assessment and Meta-Analysis. *Bulletin of the World Health Organization*, **65**(5), 663-737.

Lutter, C.K. , Mora, J.O., Habicht, J.-P., Rasmussen, K.M., Robson, D.S., Sellers, S.G., Super, C.M. & Guillermo Herrera, M. (1989) Nutritional Supplementation: Effects on Child Stunting because of Diarrhoea, *Am. J. Clin. Nutr.* **50**, 1-8.

Martorell, R., Rivera, J., Kaplowitz, H. & Pollit, E. (1992) Long-term consequences of growth retardation during early childhood. In: *Human growth: Basic and clinical aspects* (Hernandez, M & Argente, J. eds). Elsevier.

Mason, J.B., Habicht, J-P, Tabatabai, H. and Valverde, V. (1984) *Nutritional Surveillance*, World Health Organization, Geneva.

Pelletier, D. *et al.* (1994) The Relationship Between Child Anthropometry and Mortality in Developing Countries . Supplement to *Journal of Nutrition*, October 1994, **124** 10S. Contains: Pelletier, D. The Relationship Between Child Anthropometry and Mortality in Developing Countries: Implications for Policy, Programs and Future Research (2047S); Pelletier, D., Low, J.W., Johnson, C. and Msukwa, L.A.H. Child Anthropometry and Mortality in Malawi: Testing for Effect Modification by Age and Length of Follow-up and Confounding by Socioeconomic Factors (2082S); and Pelletier, D., Frongillo, E. Shroeder, D. and Habicht, J.P. A Methodology for Estimating the Contribution of Malnutrition to Child Mortality in Developing Countries (2106S).

Pollitt, E., Gorman, K.S., Engle, P.L., Martorell, R. and Rivera, J. (1993) Early Supplementary Feeding and Cognition. *Monographs of the Society for Research in Child Development*, **58** (7, Serial No. 235). The University of Chicago Press, Chicago, USA.

Reddy, V., Shekar, M., Rao, P. & Gillespie, S. (1992) *Nutrition in India*. A UN ACC/SCN Country Case Study supported by UNICEF. National Institute of Nutrition, Hyderabad, India.

Sen, A. (1984). *Resources, Values and Development*. Harvard Unv. Press, Cambridge, Mass. 1984.

Soekirman, Tarwotjo, I., Jus'at, I., Sumodiningrat, G. & Jalal, F. (1992). *Economic Growth, Equity and Nutritional Improvement in Indonesia*. UN ACC/SCN Country Case Study supported by UNICEF.

Tagwireyi, J., Jayne, T. & Lenneiye, N. (1992). Nutrition-Relevant Actions in Zimbabwe. UN ACC/SCN Country Case Study supported by UNICEF. National Nutrition Unit, Zimbabwe.

UNDP (1990) *Human Development Report*, Oxford University Press for UNDP.

UN (1990) *World Summit for Children. World Declaration and Plan of Action for Implementing the World Declaration on the Survival, Protection and Development of Children in the 1990's*. United Nations, New York.

UNICEF (1990) *Strategy for Improved Nutrition of Children and Women in Developing Countries*. UNICEF Policy Review, 1990-1.

UNICEF (1993a) *Operationalization of Mid-Decade Goals*. Executive Directive, CF/EXD/1993-008, 24 June 1993.

UNICEF, ICDC (1993b) *Nutrition and the United Nations Convention on the Rights of the Child.* Innocenti Occasional Papers, Child Rights Series, No. 5, November 1993.

UNICEF (1994) *Medium-Term Plan for the Period 1994-1997*, UN Economic and Social Council, UNICEF Executive Board, Annual Session 1994, E//CEF/1994/3 p.30.

World Bank (1990) *World Development Report*, World Bank, Washington D.C.

WHO (1986) *The Growth Chart: A tool for use in infant and child health care.* WHO, Geneva.

CHAPTER 11

Trends in Household Poverty and Hunger

Pierre Landell-Mills[1]

In recent years the world has not been short of food. Nonetheless, as the *Hunger Report: 1993* (Messer, 1994: ix) states bluntly, "over three-quarters of a billion people still do not have sufficient access to food to meet their basic human needs". This contradiction is evidence of a massive failure of public policy. But there are also grounds for optimism.

The second report on the *World Nutritional Situation* (ACC/SCN, 1992) gives the latest data on the nature and extent of global nutritional deficiencies. Statisticians may argue about the exact numbers of children who are stunted or the precise figure for adults who are unable to lead productive lives for lack of food, but the basic fact remains: hunger and malnutrition still stalk the land. Few analysts of global hunger would disagree that the reason for this shameful deprivation lies not in capacity of the world's farmers to produce food, but in the simple fact that those who go hungry lack the means either to buy or produce food. Peter Uvin's chapter in the *Hunger Report: 1993* (Uvin, 1994) summarizes the global food supply and consumption situation well .

The purpose of this paper is to examine briefly the other side of the equation – trends in incomes, which determine the ability of households to meet their food needs – and to discuss some key conceptual and analytical issues that must be addressed to improve our understanding of data on poverty and hunger trends.

Poverty Trends

In the past year or so there has been no attempt – in the World Bank at least – to re-estimate global poverty trends. The main focus has been on improving country data. Thus, the latest data remain those set out in *The World Bank's Strategy for Reducing Poverty and Hunger* which was an update of the number given in the 1990 *World Development Report* on poverty and from which this section is drawn (World Bank, 1995; World Bank 1990).

The data on poverty are notoriously weak, and while considerable efforts are being made to expand the number of household budget surveys and improve their quality, we are far from achieving comprehensive coverage. The World Bank's most recent estimates suggest that in 1990, 1.1 billion people were living in developing countries on less than $1 a day (at 1985 prices).

Table 1 summarizes the latest available estimates of the number of poor people and of the poor as a percentage of the population (the *headcount* index) in 1985 and 1990. The table shows that there was little progress in reducing poverty during the second half of the 1980s. The proportion of the developing world's population living in poverty has fallen slightly since 1985, but the absolute number is estimated to have risen.

These aggregates hide marked differences across regions. In South Asia, and in East Asia and the Pacific the proportion of the population living on less than $1 a day has declined. By contrast, this proportion has increased in the Middle East and North Africa, and in Latin America and the Caribbean. Although there has been only a negligible change in the percentage of the population of Sub-Saharan Africa living on less than $1 a day, the number of poor in the region has grown at roughly the same rate as the population: about 3% per year. This was the largest estimated increase in the number of poor in any region.

Table 11.1. Estimates of the Magnitude and Depth of Poverty in the Developing World, 1985-90

Region	Number of poor (millions)		Headcount index (percent)		Poverty gap index (percent)	
	1985	1990	1985	1990	1985	1990
Aggregate	1051	1133	30.5	29.7	9.9	9.5
East Asia and the Pacific	182	169	13.2	11.3	3.3	2.8
Eastern Europe	5	5	7.1	7.1	2.4	1.9
Latin America & the Caribbean	87	108	22.4	25.2	8.7	10.3
Middle East & North Africa	60	73	30.6	33.1	13.2	14.3
South Asia	532	562	51.8	49.0	16.2	13.7
Sub-Saharan Africa	184	216	47.6	47.8	18.1	19.1

Source: World Bank, 1993.

The proportion of the population considered poor in Sub-Saharan Africa is now estimated to be almost equal to that in South Asia, which still has the highest poverty incidence among all the regions and where about half of the world's poor live. Although the percentage of the South Asian population estimated to be living in poverty fell, this was not enough to prevent the estimated number of poor people from rising. During the same period, the number of poor people in the Middle East and North Africa was estimated to have increased by more than the rate of population growth, as was also the case in Latin America and the Caribbean. East Asia and the Pacific is the only region where the number of people living in poverty and the proportion of the population in poverty are estimated to have decreased.

Table 1 also provides estimates of the *poverty gap index*. This index reflects the depth of poverty by taking into account how far the average poor person's income is from the poverty line. The table shows that in some regions (Latin America and the Caribbean, the Middle East and North Africa, and Sub-Saharan Africa) the poor have become poorer. The poverty gap estimate is highest for Sub-Saharan Africa. Thus, while a slightly higher percentage of the population is living on less than $1 a day in South Asia, the depth of their poverty is estimated to be less than in Sub-Saharan Africa.

Differences in the rate of growth of average household living standards have been an important percentage increase in per capita consumption, which is on average associated with a 20% fall in the percentage of the population who are poor. This relationship varies from country to country. Figure 1 compares the percentage change in the proportion of the population living on less than $1 per day with the percentage change in real consumption per capita across those countries (in all regions) for which reasonably comparable observations for two dates during the 1980s are possible.

Other factors affecting changes in poverty are the initial income distribution and how that distribution changes. Poverty reduction is swifter when a higher proportion of the gains from growth reach the poor. In Brazil, average per capita income grew by 220% from 1960 to 1980 to achieve a 34% decline in the headcount index of poverty, whereas in Indonesia per capita income grew by 108% from 1971 to 1987 to bring about a 42% decline in poverty incidence. This difference in performance is because of the less equal initial distribution of income in Brazil and the broad-based growth achieved in Indonesia.

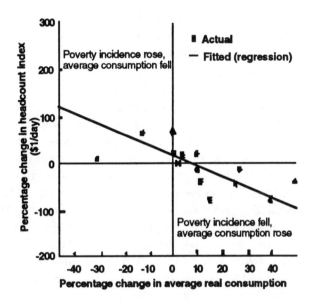

Figure 11.1. Change in poverty against change in household mean consumption between survey dates in the 1980s.

Table 2 presents estimates of the minimum rate of growth in aggregate consumption necessary to achieve a reduction in the number of the poor. It reflects the estimated relationship between increases in per capita consumption and declines in the percentage of the population who are poor (see Figure 1) with the observed rates of population growth by region in the 1980s. The comparison between this critical minimum rate with actual rates of growth during the decade (the first two columns of Table 2) shows that both East Asia and the Pacific and South Asia achieved rates of growth in consumption in the 1980s that were enough to bring down the number of the poor (although the slowing of progress in South Asia during the latter half of the decade resulted in an increase in the number, as indicated in Table 1). In East Asia and the Pacific, the rate of growth in aggregate consumption is considerably more than the estimated minimum that would be needed to reduce the number of the poor. The reverse is true for Sub-Saharan Africa and Latin America and the Caribbean; in both cases the rate of growth is well below the critical value - markedly so in the case of Sub-Saharan Africa.

**Table 11.2. Minimum Rates of Growth to Reduce the Number of the Poor
(percent per year)**

Region	Minimum rate of growth in aggregate consumption needed to achieve reduction in number of poor	Actual rate of growth in aggregate consumption 1980-90	Projected rate of growth in aggregate consumption 1993-2000
East Asia & Pacific	2.4	6.1	7.7
Latin America & Caribbean	3.2	1.2	4.7
South Asia	3.3	5.1	4.9
Sub-Saharan Africa	4.7	0.8	3.3

Source: World Bank, 1993

It is instructive to examine trends in two regions for which more detailed data exist. One is Latin America and the Caribbean, in which the living standards of the poor have declined over the decade. The other is East Asia and the Pacific, in which the poor have fared better in the 1980s than before.

Recent estimates of the size of the poor population in Latin America and the Caribbean, using a regional poverty line of $2 per day (higher than is typical of some other regions), show that the number of the poor in this region increased by more than 40 million between 1980 and 1989. Across the region during the 1980s, per capita income fell by 11%, real wages declined, and unemployment increased sharply. In many countries in the region during the recession of the 1980s, the income of the poor declined more than average income. In almost every country in the region the rise in urban poverty was greater than that in rural poverty; the number of poor people was estimated to have increased by more than 30 million in the urban centers compared to around 10 million in the rural areas. Of the overall increase in poverty, about 44% was accounted for by the increase in poverty in the cities of Brazil alone. Another 17% took place in Peru.

For East Asia and the Pacific, nutrition-based poverty estimates show a dramatic decrease in the incidence of absolute poverty – from one-third of the population in 1970 to one-fifth in 1980 and down to one-tenth in 1990. Although much of the reduction in the number of the poor in East Asia and the Pacific took place in rural areas, poverty in the region still remains mostly a rural problem.

There are, however, some differences in performance, as progress in reducing poverty has been slower in some countries in the region than in others. Of the estimated 180 million absolute poor in 1990 in East Asia and the Pacific, China accounted for 100 million. China achieved an average annual economic growth rate of 8.5% over the 1980s – the highest rate recorded by any developing country during the decade. This contributed to spectacular declines in the incidence of poverty, from about one-third in 1980 to barely one-tenth in 1990, which was largely because of broad participation in strong rural economic growth. This progress now appears to be slowing down, however, and there were signs of a modest increase in rural income disparities in China during the late 1980s. In two rapidly industrializing countries (the Republic of Korea and Malaysia) with GNP growth rates that averaged 6-8% during the 1980s, the incidence of absolute poverty was more than halved, to less than 5%. In contrast, in Thailand the high economic growth rate during the 1980s had little impact on the incidence of poverty, since this growth was not sufficiently broad-based. Indonesia started the 1970s with more than half its people in poverty (some 70 million), but by 1990 the incidence had fallen to 15% and the number of poor to 27 million. Steady gains have been made by Indonesia over a sustained period as economic growth has coincided with increasing overall equality.

Measures to Improve Poverty Data

The profile of global poverty set out above gives a false sense of accuracy. In practice, measuring global poverty trends is technically difficult and the estimates are inevitably imprecise. Household surveys are still available for only a limited number of countries, with particularly poor coverage in Africa and the former socialist economies. A census of household surveys conducted by the World Bank in 1993 revealed that usable household survey data are available for only about 40 developing countries (Chen, Datt and Ravallion, 1993). To help overcome this problem, five years ago the World Bank (with the support of UNDP and a number of bilateral donors) launched a program of priority household surveys and of integrated household surveys in Sub-Saharan Africa as part of a Social Dimensions of Adjustment project.

The priority surveys aim to collect basic information as rapidly as possible to achieve a first "fix" on household welfare. The integrated surveys are more ambitious multi-topic surveys akin to the Living Standards Measurements Studies (LSMS) initiated in the early 1980s. Even these modest surveys place a heavy burden on limited statistical resources in the countries concerned. Consequently, the coverage is still incomplete. In all, data now exist for some 20 countries in Africa, but resources were available to initiate new surveys in only five African countries in fiscal 1994. In addition, LSMS surveys were completed in 1994 in Nicaragua and Guyana, and were started in Nepal and Kyrgysztan.

Household surveys provide the raw data for country poverty assessments and for the design of targeted interventions to reduce poverty, hunger, and malnutrition. To date, 39 such assessments have been completed by World Bank staff, and 66 more are scheduled over the next three years.

Increasingly, household surveys have been defined to identify the poorest and most vulnerable families and to try to understand better the nature of their poverty, and the extent and causes of hunger and malnutrition. In Pakistan, for example, the recent integrated household survey provided information on access to and consumption of food, as well as basic social services. In Jamaica a comparative analysis of food subsidies and food stamps, using household data, demonstrated that the food stamp program was much more successful in reaching the poorest groups. Given this evidence, the Government decided to withdraw food subsidies and double the size of the food stamp program.

The objective of a poverty assessment is, in the first instance, to construct a country poverty profile. But that is only a first step. To detect the impact of poverty programs, time-series data are needed. Therefore, governments are being helped to create the capacity to monitor poverty trends through a series of priority and integrated surveys. For example, in Africa nine countries have either completed or started follow-up surveys.

To improve our understanding of the complex factors that affect the living conditions of the poor, increasing reliance is being put on a participatory approach to poverty assessments. This includes seeking the views of intended beneficiaries in the design of programs to reduce hunger and malnutrition, in the belief that this will greatly improve these programs' relevance and effectiveness, as well as strengthen all stakeholders' ownership and commitment to the successful completion of the programs. There is already strong evidence that this approach increases the uptake of services and decreases their delivery costs.

Income Distribution and its Impact on Poverty and Growth

While higher incomes are generally associated with improved well-being and better nutrition, as Dreze and Sen (1989) have shown, income distribution is also a crucial factor. Indeed, if economic growth is associated with sharply increased inequality, its impact in reducing poverty is not assured. However, there are few documented cases of "immiserizing" growth.

Studies by Kuznets (1955), Ahluwalia, Carter, Chenery (1979), and others in the 1950s to 1970s appeared to substantiate the so-called Kuznets inverted-U hypothesis, which argued that economic growth in its early stages was generally accompanied by a movement of population from low-inequality, low-mean-income rural areas to higher-mean-income, high-inequality urban areas. Consequently, according to Kuznets, inequality first increased and only later decreased as the process of economic growth proceeded. Recent work by Anand and Kanbur (1993) has shown with improved data sets that the Kuznets hypothesis does not hold. There is now good evidence that economic growth is usually associated with greater, not less, equality even for countries with low incomes. This is because the simple assumptions about rural and urban-sector inequalities do not hold.

Cross-section evidence from four regions in the world also puts the Kuznets hypothesis into question, as can be seen from the following aggregate data estimated by Milanovic (1994) (Table 3).

Table 11.3. Relationship between income and income inequality

	Gini ratio %	Per capita income (purchasing power in 1988 $$)
OECD Countries	31.2	12501
Asia	41.0	4851
Latin America	49.2	4156
Africa	52.3	1778

Source: Milanovic, 1994

The analysis of time-series data for income levels and inequality since 1960 for 11 countries revealed that only two countries (Brazil and Costa Rica) experienced growing inequality with economic growth. For the remainder the opposite was true. Indeed, study of a wider panel of less complete data for the 1980s indicates that in only three countries (China, Mexico, and Thailand) is it possible that growth has been accompanied by an increase in the proportion of the population in absolute poverty. Nonetheless, the fact that economic growth is not infrequently associated with greater inequality and greater inequality is per se associated with an increase in the number in poverty (and hence malnourished) means that careful attention must be given to the distributional impact of economic policies.

While much attention has been given to the distributional effects of growth, the reverse effects have been relatively ignored in recent years. In the 1960s Kaldor argued that income inequality tended to be associated with more rapid economic growth because the rich saved more than the poor and hence countries with greater income inequality would have higher levels of investment. This simplistic view of the growth process took no account of investment in human resource development. It is well established that the most significant factor determining income inequality is the extent to which education is made available to the population. A growing body of work substantiates that the more widespread is education, the greater is not only income equality but also economic growth (Demery et al., 1995). It has also been clearly demonstrated that family nutrition improves as the level of education rises, particularly with increased *female* education.

Conclusion

Although data from household surveys is still very patchy, there is a steady accumulation of evidence that while the absolute numbers in poverty – and hence suffering from food insecurity and malnutrition – is still on the rise, those countries that have achieved rapid growth have been most successful in reducing the proportion of their populations in poverty. Also, on the positive side there is strong evidence that economic growth is not favored by a highly-skewed income distribution – quite the contrary. And there is a happy link between investment in human resource development, accelerated growth, and reduced income inequality which reinforces the welfare argument that developing countries should invest heavily in education, health, family planning, and sanitation.

1 .   Pierre Landell-Mills has recently become Chief of Mission of the World Bank's Resident Mission in Bangladesh. Prior to August 1994 he was Senior Policy Adviser in the World Bank's Vice Presidency for Environmentally Sustainable Development.

192   Pierre Landell-Mills

References

ACC/SCN (1992). *Second Report on the World Nutrition Situation; Volume 1 Global and Regional Results*. Geneva: Administrative Committee on Coordination/ Sub-Committee on Nutrition.

Ahluwalia, M.S., Carter, N.G., Chenery, H.B. (1979). Growth and Poverty in Developing Countries. *Journal of Development Economics*, 6: 299-341.

Anand, S. & Kanbur, S.M.R. (1993). Inequality and Development. A Critique. *Journal of Development Economics*, 41: 19-43.

Birdsall, N. (1994) Macroeconomic Reform: Its Impact on Poverty and Hunger, in Serageldin, I. and Landell-Mills, P. (eds.) *Overcoming Global Hunger*. Washington DC: Environmentally Sound Development Proceedings Series No. 3.

Chen, S., Datt, G. and Ravallion, M. (1993). *Is Poverty Increasing in the Developing World?* Washington DC: World Bank Policy Research Working Papers, WPS 1146.

Demery, L., Sen, B. and Vishwanath, T. (1995). *Poverty, Inequality and Growth*. Washington DC: World Bank Education and Social Policy Department Discussion Paper Series No. 70.

Dreze, J. and Sen, A. (1989). *Hunger and Public Action*. Oxford: Clarendon Press.

Kuznets, S. (1955). Economic Growth and Income Inequality. *American Economic Review*, 45, 1 (March): 1-28.

Milanovic, Branko (1994). *Determinants of Cross-Country Income Inequality: An "Augmented" Kuznets Hypothesis*, Policy Research Working Paper, Washington DC: World Bank.

Messer, E. (1994). Overview, in Uvin, P. (ed.) *The Hunger Report 1993*. Yverdon: Gordon and Breach.

Uvin, P. (1994). The State of World Hunger, in Uvin, P. (ed.) *The Hunger Report 1993*. Yverdon: Gordon and Breach.

World Bank (1990). *World Dvelopment Report 1990*. New York: Oxford University Press.

World Bank (1992). *World Development Report 1992*. New York: Oxford University Press.

World Bank (1995). The World Bank's Strategy for Reducing Poverty and Hunger: A Report to the Development Community. Washington DC: World Bank, Environmentally Sound Development Series No. 4.

DISCUSSION

Is Economic Growth Really the Remedy for Overcoming Hunger and Poverty?

Shlomo Reutlinger

Landell-Mills article "Trends in Household Poverty and Hunger" offers a succinct prognosis for the food/poverty problem. It notes the paradox of an ample food supply in a world with over two-quarters of a billion people hungry because they lack access to food, and attributes it to "a massive failure of public policy." Landell-Mills' article provides a succinct summary of a position taken by a large number of ecomonists. Below I first summarize and question the central proposition of this position, that the public policy failure is a failure of growth, and then present some alternatives.

What Policies Have Failed?

According to Landell-Mills and many others, countries with rapid growth rates have been the most successful in reducing poverty: "...while the absolute numbers in poverty are still on the rise, those countries that have achieved rapid growth have been most successful in reducing the proportion of their populations in poverty...". In addition, a "less than highly skewed income distribution" is desirable for achieving better growth, and "there is also a happy link between investing heavily in human resource development (in education, health, family planning, and sanitation) and rapid growth." By this reasoning, doing what is best for growth is the solution for poverty, and even over the short run there is no conflict between growth and poverty alleviation: poverty and hunger persist because of the policy failure to achieve more rapid rates of growth.

"Trickle-down" theories (do what is best for economic growth and the wealth generated by a nation's new industries and successful entrepreneurs will "trickle down" to take care of the rest of the population) have been around since the 1950s. The new idea suggested in this chapter is that there is no conflict between having a "less than highly skewed income distribution" and more investment in human resource development and growth. This is an important addendum, but Landell-Mills is not clear about the solution when what is best for growth conflicts with effective efforts to alleviate poverty.

Other authors have also papered over the possible conflict between growth and poverty alleviation. Lipton and Ravallion wrote in *Poverty and Policy* (1993):

> ... *some observers have read the recent evidence that economic growth is rarely associated with sufficiently adverse changes in relative inequalities to prevent a decline in absolute poverty as suggesting that the role of government in reducing poverty can safely be confined to promoting growth. That does not follow...*

Having correctly made this observation, the authors go on to "soften" their appeal against relying on growth:

> ... *even though past growth has often helped reduce poverty, some growth processes may do so more effectively than others...*

Lipton and Ravallion emphasize the importance of choosing the right "pattern of growth," and insinuate that concern about poverty should lead to investment in sectors that allocate a larger share of growth to the poor; by definition, the more incomes of the poor grow, the less poverty. But the authors admit in passing: "growth in favor of the poor may come at a cost", and they are unclear whether they think governments should trade off some growth by choosing growth patterns that lead to greater reductions in poverty. Unfortunately, the apparently minor adjustments that may need to be made in the growth process lead to the persistent belief "that the role of government in reducing poverty can safely be confined to promoting growth."

Questions Regarding the Growth Thesis.

Landell-Mills, and quite a few others, indicate that doing what is good for growth is not only necessary but also sufficient; that growth per se can alleviate poverty and hunger. However, if slow growth is the cause of poverty, then the chapter should also deal with the many factors other than initial income distribution and insufficient investment in the development of human capital that may contribute to slow growth – factors such as faulty price and exchange-rate policies, excessive government regulation, public-investment policies, and excessive military expenditures. But perhaps the importance of a more equitable income distribution and investment in human resource development is highlighted because these contribute directly to poverty alleviation, as well as indirectly via growth. It is correct that investment in human resources and a more equitable income distribution, which are good for the alleviation of poverty, are good for growth, but many other things are also good for growth. At the margin hard choices must be made. In the 1970s and 1980s, during "the McNamara Era," the World Bank began to recognize the need to implement policies based on explicit recognition of multiple objectives, not just of growth alone. Does Landell-Mills' perception reflect a reversal in the Bank's position? Does the Bank now advocate growth primarily, and income distribution and human capital development only when there is no conflict, i.e., when they also contribute to growth?

Many specialists nowadays seem to be quite comfortable with the notion that doing what is good for growth is necessary *and* sufficient for poverty alleviation. A review of recent literature (Annand and Kanbur, 1984) refutes earlier work by Kuznets (1955) on the relationship between growth and income distribution. Kuznets had concluded, on the basis of statistical analysis of data across countries, that in the early stages of development, growth and income equality are negatively correlated, while in later stages growth and income equality move together. Recent investigations, based on new data and different analytical techniques, have concluded that no negative - perhaps even a positive - relationship exists between growth and income equality even in the early stages of development.

At least on average, growth is associated with poverty reduction. But rather than take comfort from these results, one might be impressed with another finding of these statistical investigations: the instability of this relationship between growth and poverty. Landell-Mills suggests several reasons why growth may be effective in some countries and not in others, *e.g.*, the initial distribution of wealth and how the fruits of growth are distributed. And there are many other explanations.

The same authors who see growth as the primary source of poverty alleviation attach much importance to the exercise of calculating the rate of growth required to reduce poverty. But how valid are calculations based on the average response rate of poverty reduction to growth? Countries with little growth and little reduction of poverty are unlikely to have as high a response rate as the average country. The poorest countries, particularly those in Africa, have a highly skewed initial distribution of wealth and lack many of the factors that contribute to high resource mobility. The positive correlation between growth and poverty reduction observed in Latin America does not bode well for a strategy aimed at reducing poverty merely by raising the growth rate.

Growth per se may contribute very little to poverty alleviation in countries with a very unequal initial distribution of wealth and vice versa. It remains to draw implications for policy. The new optimism about poverty being swept away by growth is primarily based on the recent experience in East Asia. However, similarly high growth rates in South Asia have hardly made a dent in the poverty levels there. And in many other countries, particularly in Sub-Saharan Africa, growth rates have been too low to expect any noticeable impact. The "Asian Miracle" is not understood well enough to be used as the sole source of universal prescriptions for action.

As Landell-Mills documents, the fundamental human problem with pursuing a single-minded strategy to combat poverty and hunger through growth alone is that very little can be done for hundreds of millions of impoverished people in this generation. In South Asia, ten years of growth (1980-1990) at the respectable annual rate of 5.1% have not managed to reduce the number of poor during the five year period from 1985 to 1990. In East Asia, the region in which growth and poverty alleviation might be expected to be most closely correlated, the same ten years of growth have been accompanied by a five-year poverty decline (1985-1990) of only 13 million people (182 to 169 million).

Another View of Failed Policies

An alternative strategy based on non-acquiescence with poverty in both the long and the short term has been enunciated in two separate World Bank Publications, *Poverty and Hunger* (World Bank, 1986) and the *World Development Report 1990: Poverty* (World Bank, 1990). Both offer the central thesis that growth is essential, but not sufficient for the alleviation of poverty. Both recognize that trading growth for poverty alleviation is sometimes necessary but should be accomplished with as little cost for growth as possible:

> ...*Any policies that raise the incomes of the poor and increase economic growth should obviously be given high priority, since they can reduce poverty at no additional cost to the economy. Such policies may involve shifting resources from large to small farms, from industry to agriculture, or from capital-intensive activities to labor-intensive activities. They may involve also removing price and trade interventions that reduce incentives to farmers...* (Poverty and Hunger).

> ... *Some measures in some circumstances [to reduce poverty] are fully compatible with efficient economic growth. Others involve some tradeoff. Cost-effective measures can minimize this tradeoff...* (Poverty and Hunger).

> ... *In the 1950s and 1960s many saw growth as the primary means of reducing poverty...in the 1970s attention shifted to the direct provision of*

health, nutritional and educational services... (World Development Report 1990: Poverty).

...The evidence in this Report suggests that rapid and politically sustainable progress on poverty has been achieved by pursuing a strategy that has two important elements. The first is to promote the productive use of the poor's most abundant asset - labor. The second is to provide basic social services to the poor... Even if this basic two-part strategy is adopted many of the world's poor - the sick, the old, those who live in resource poor regions, and others will experience severe deprivation ... A comprehensive approach to poverty reduction, therefore, calls for a program of well-targeted transfers and safety nets as an essential complement to the basic strategies... (World Development Report 1990: Poverty).

In *Poverty and Hunger*, the World Bank took strong issue with those who would pursue growth without making concessions to poverty alleviation. The Bank was equally critical of those who for the sake of "helping the poor" were ready to justify a wide range of growth-inhibiting protectionist policies and implement costly and ineffective special programs. Instead of emphasizing the importance of growth, *inter alia*, for the alleviation of poverty, the publication recommended that countries pursue efficient policies for growth while implementing cost-effective measures specifically directed at hunger and poverty.

The central proposition in *Poverty and Hunger* is that, in terms of results, public interventions are usually more cost-effective in the short and intermediate run if they are well targeted to the poor. For example, many attempts to stabilize food prices for the entire population have been very costly and rarely adequate to meet the needs of those in poverty. A price reduction of 10 or 20 percent – through whatever government intervention – is a very costly undertaking, yet provides little relief to people whose source of livelihood has been seriously damaged by a drought or flood or who are chronically unemployed.

Similarly, the *World Development Report 1990: Poverty* targeted growth, based on promoting "the productive use of the poor's most abundant asset - their labor." Another important strategy advocated in the same report is to focus investments in human resource development on the poor. Suggestions for enhancing their access to public services, such as education and health, and adopting employment-promoting policies and investments, clearly indicate the World Bank view that undifferentiated growth is not a sufficient and timely remedy for poverty.

The World Bank's policy pronouncements and actions in regard to the relationship between growth and poverty alleviation show that even an organization primarily in the business of promoting growth has long given up on claims that growth is a sufficient remedy. They contradict those authors whose central theme is the sufficiency of growth to eradicate hunger.

Summing It All Up

The central conclusion in Landell-Mills' "Trends in Household Poverty and Hunger" is that "...those countries that have achieved rapid growth have been most successful in reducing the proportion of their populations in poverty...". This, and other substantive points presented in the text, might lead readers to conclude that policies which lead to rapid growth are the primary (and sufficient) method for alleviating poverty within any reasonable time. But the evidence points to other equally plausible remedies:

- The statistical evidence linking growth to the alleviation of poverty is very weak. The results are primarily driven by the recent excellent performance of East Asia on both growth and poverty alleviation. But the "Asian Miracle" is still not well enough understood. Factors other than those that usually "explain" growth have contributed to the observed high growth rates; factors other than growth have contributed to the observed high rates of poverty reduction and, particularly, to the decrease in malnutrition and ill health.

- Reliance on growth ignores time frames. As Landell-Mills observes, countries with more equal distribution of wealth and investment in human resources have a better chance of realizing rapid growth and of distributing that growth widely. Countries with great numbers of poor people will take many years to realize these conditions. To achieve rapid growth, such countries need to invest in income-augmenting programs of many kinds (e.g., land reform, selective subsidization of employment, and outright distribution of income or food) and in human resource development (e.g., education, health).

- An alternative approach to combat abject poverty has been advocated for quite some time in policy papers by the World Bank and other development institutions, such as the International Fund for Agricultural Development (IFAD), and by many bilateral aid agencies. The policies are being implemented in many countries, often with the assistance of international aid programs. The approach is based on the recognition that growth is essential and central to the alleviation of poverty, but that many other actions need to be taken as well. Poor countries cannot eliminate poverty without growth. But there must be no illusion: some growth needs to be traded off if poverty is to be alleviated.

To achieve both high rates of growth and poverty alleviation, policy instruments and programs need to be conceived and implemented in as cost-effective a way as possible. Anything less sacrifices growth essential to reduce poverty. And anything less makes special poverty-alleviating programs unaffordable.

There are many recent instances where heightened attention to efficient growth and special programs to enhance human capital and provide some relief from the worst aspects of poverty have borne fruit, but much remains to be done, as the grim statistics on poverty show. Some of the failures are due to politics, a subject I will not discuss here. But much more could be accomplished even with the limited resources governments are able and willing to devote to the objective, if they consider and have at their disposal answers to some of the following questions:

- What precisely is the role of central vs. local government? What is best left to the private sector and NGOs? Is it politically thinkable to institute some form of radical redistribution schemes, such as land reform?

198   Shlomo Reutlinger

- Under what circumstances are policies that provide incentives to all producers or consumers more or less cost effective than programs directed to the poor exclusively? Examples are a policy that subsidizes the price of basic foods vs. a food- or income-distribution scheme for particular segments of the population, or a public investment in irrigation vs. a subsidized credit scheme strictly targeted to poor farmers.

- What is the cost-effectiveness of schemes to augment household income vs. investing more in providing greater access for the poor to public services, such as schools or health facilities?

For a program to be cost effective, the answer usually is not to do one thing rather than another, but to devote some resources to each. This is an alien approach for those accustomed to dealing with policy questions in the attention-seeking framework of academic, national, and international debates. However, each alleged panacea by itself – for example, growth, income distribution, or access to public services – exhibits diminishing returns. Thus, it is wasteful to commit all available resources to any single program, and especially unfortunate in view of the immense magnitude of the poverty problem and the very limited resources available for or allocated to its eradication.

References

Annand, S. and Kanbur, R. (1984). Inequality and Development: A Reconsideration, in H.P. Nissen (ed.) *Toward Income Distribution Policies*, Tilbury: EADI Book Series 3.

Kuznets, S. (1955). Economic Growth and Income Inequality, *American Economic Review* 45:1-28.

Landell-Mills, P. (1995). Trends in Household Poverty and Hunger, E. Messer and P. Uvin (eds.) *The Hunger Report 1995*, Yverdon: Gordon & Breach.

Lipton, M. and Ravallion, M., (1993). Poverty and Policy, Chapter 42 in Jere Berman and T.N. Shrinivasan (eds) *Handbook of Development Economics, Vol. 3*, Amsterdam: North-Holland.

World Bank (1986). *Poverty and Hunger*. Washington D.C.: World Bank.

World Bank (1990). *World Development Report 1990: Poverty*, Washington D.C.: World Bank.

CHAPTER 12

The Future of Food Trade and Food Aid in a Liberalizing Global Economy

H. W. Singer

After offering some overall thoughts on the recent Uruguay Round, I propose to discuss, first, some conceptual problems that arise when distinguishing between food trade and food aid. I hope to show that these conceptual problems are by no means only matters of statistical significance but have important policy implications. Secondly, I will discuss some of the problems arising from the Uruguay Round which will now have to be faced by the new World Trade Organization (WTO).

The title of this paper may suggest that food trade and food aid can be neatly separated by drawing some kind of boundary line between the two. My contention will be that this is not the case, and that any boundary line – including the present boundary line – fails to do justice to the facts of life and obscures some important policy matters. Economic life does not lend itself to a separation of the two into neat statistical boxes.

The Impact of the Uruguay Round

The liberalization of agricultural policies and agricultural trade will mainly affect the food exporting countries, the US and the EU in particular. For this reason it would be likely, rather than increasing the volume of trade, to affect prices and market shares. To the extent that food-importing countries such as Japan are also expected to liberalize policies and trade under the Uruguay Agreement, this in itself would tend to increase trade. However, the developing food-importing countries are partially or wholly exempt from the duty to liberalize. In particular, in developing countries subsidies for agricultural inputs and for purposes of diversification – out of narcotics, for example – are explicitly exempt. Together with the higher international prices it may be hoped that this will increase domestic food production in developing countries. This, however, is on the assumption that the increase in prices will be passed on to local farmers and that the infrastructure facilities exist to cope with additional food output – two big "ifs" in many developing countries!

The reduction in domestic subsidies by the EU, US, Japan, etc., will only be partial. The Aggregate Measure of Support (AMS) will be reduced by 20% only, although the Agreement has built-in provisions for further reductions on a continuing basis at the end of the initial period. Even this partial reduction, however, would reduce domestic subsidies in these three major areas from $198 billion to $162 billion. The budgetary saving of $36 billion, if added to aid budgets, would go a long way to bring aid up to the UN target of 0.7% GNP. If the saving of $36 billion is added to food aid, it would bring food aid up from some 11-12 million tons to something more like 80-90 million tons – far above the wildest estimates of need or absorptive capacity.

The 20% AMS reduction is, however, an exaggerated measure of the degree of liberalization. Since it is an aggregate measure, it is open to the subsidizing countries to concentrate the reduction on unimportant products, while leaving subsidization and protection for the more important products intact. Moreover, subsidies not directly linked to production are exempt; this would include both the EU "compensation payments" and the US "deficiency payments." While such payments are not directly linked to production, and may in fact be linked specifically to keep land out of production, the effect may well be to induce farmers to concentrate productive inputs on the rest of their land and to stay in production, thus also serving to maintain or increase production (although probably to a lesser extent than direct production subsidies).

Export subsidies are to be reduced in the developed countries by 36% in value and 21% in volume of subsidized exports over a period of six years. For the developing countries the required reduction is less: 24% in value and 14% in volume over 10 years, and there are also various exemptions. However, developing countries cannot usually afford to subsidize their exports, and any such subsidies are largely defensive in character. The reduction of export subsidies by developed countries under the Uruguay Round would reduce budgetary expenditure from $21.3 billion to $13.8 billion. The resulting saving of $7.5 billion, if applied to food aid, would almost treble it to something like 30 million tons – close to the current FAO/USDA estimates of present requirements.

It has by now become conventional wisdom (a) that there will be losers as well as winners in the Uruguay Round both within countries and between countries; and (b) that the poorer net food-importing countries, especially in Africa, will be among the losers as a result of higher food import prices (as well as possible reductions in food aid). The higher international food prices are only one of the factors. Others include the erosion of preferences inherent in general liberalization and possible higher costs of imported technology under the new agreement affecting TRIPS (Trade-Related Intellectual Property Rights) and TRIMS (Trade-Related Investment Measures). The higher cost of imported technology may also extend to items needed for food production, including seeds.

It is also relevant in this context to note that restrictive business practices that were included in the Havana Charter for an International Trade Organization (ITO) are not included in the World Trade Organization (WTO). Thus there is no bar in the WTO on the multinational corporations exercising market power in international food trade to use the reduction of pressures of surplus production in the US and EU to increase international prices even more than the reduction in supply would cause in itself. Restrictive business practices are to be dealt with separately in the UN, mainly by UNCTAD, but given the lack of financial and political support for the UN it is not very likely that this will have effective results. All this suggests a definite need for a safety net for the food-importing developing countries. Such a safety net could be financial, which would involve the Bretton Woods institutions and perhaps the WFP, or trade-related, which would involve future discussions within the WTO, or generally related to global governance, which would involve the UN. Most likely it would be a mixture of all three.

The reduction in surplus stocks and in the general willingness to hold stocks involved in higher food prices (which increase the cost of holding stocks) may have the incidental effect of increasing price instability or volatility as well as raising the overall price level. However, this prospective risk of increased volatility is based on the assumption that the surplus stocks and commercial stocks were previously used in a counter-cyclical manner, that is, reduced when world prices were rising and vice versa. More seriously, perhaps, it would also make the holding of domestic reserve stocks in disaster-vulnerable countries as well as the advance positioning of international food aid in such countries more expensive.

To keep this discussion in perspective, it should be emphasized that the impact of the Uruguay Round will be only one of many factors affecting future food prices, and not necessarily the most important. However, it may well be that the Uruguay Round will provide the swing factor, with the other forces more or less canceling each other out. For reasons already explained, this is much more likely to be true for international prices than for volume of trade.

Food Aid – A Conceptual and Statistical Quagmire

The present statistical convention is that food aid is distinguished from food trade or commercial transactions by an element of concessionality. This has been arbitrarily defined as a grant element of at least 25% below the commercial price.

Some immediate problems arise. The commercial price of food in international trade is itself a policy-determined quantity. It is not a textbook free market price with a significant reference function.[1] The policies of subsidizing national agricultures in the main industrial countries result in surpluses and surplus capacities. It is these surpluses which both enable and induce the countries producing them to tie their aid to food. But these same surpluses and surplus capacities also depress the commercial price of food in international trade. Hence the 25% concessionality limit which defines food aid is not 25% off a truly free market price, but 25% off a world price which is already itself at a discount from what commercial prices would be in a free, fully liberalized market. In other words, if the 25% concessionality were measured from a truly free market price in international food trade many more transactions would come to be defined as food aid.

Furthermore, over half of total food "trade" (so-called) is covered by various forms of bilateral agreements, providing discounts from the "commercial" international price (itself reduced by overhanging surpluses and domestic production subsidies) in many direct and indirect ways difficult or impossible to quantify, such as export credits, linkage with other trade concessions, linkage with financial aid, and the like. With "commercial" imports of Third World countries running at seven times "food aid," it would only need an overall subsidy factor of 14% to double real (as distinct from statistical) food aid. The 14% figure, while no more than a guess, seems well within the realm of the possible – probably even an understatement. The effective international price of wheat has been estimated to be 30-40% below the official Chicago price, with similar discrepancies for coarse grains and rice.

Under the Uruguay Agreement, such export subsidies are to be reduced by 36% over six years, and subsidized exports to be reduced by 21% in volume, but it is doubtful whether these reductions will really catch all the hidden and indirect subsidies involved in this game. For example, subsidies tied to acreage (rather than production tonnage), or set-aside subsidies, are exempted from the reduction, although their ultimate effect may not be all that different.

We have thus a "double whammy." Real food aid may have to be doubled to allow for international prices being lower than truly free market prices, and then doubled again to allow for direct and indirect discounts from this already-lowered international price. While difficult to quantify statistically, this does illustrate the precariousness and conservatism of the traditional 11-12 million tons statistical figure for food aid.

This point has acquired current realistic importance by the "stylized fact" of agreement on the partial reduction of agricultural policies recently reached in the GATT/Uruguay Round. On the basis of various economic models with more-or-less plausible assumptions, different authors have made quantitative estimates of the rise in prices in international food trade consequent upon agricultural protection reductions in the US and Europe. The best known of these models is the Rural/Urban – North/South (RUNS) model developed by the OECD Development Center and the World Bank. This model suggests that even the relatively mild degree of partial reduction under the Uruguay Round agreement (20% reduction in subsidies to national food producers and 36% reduction in subsidized exports spread over six years) would result in a rise in world wheat prices of 5.9%, with rises of 3.6% in coarse grains, 7.2% in dairy products, and 4.1% in vegetable oils. If we take an average of 5.5% for these four main items of food aid (giving them appropriate weights according to their importance in food aid) we would find that the present 5.5% discount from the higher commercial price without the partial GATT is roughly equal in value, as to an income transfer to food importers, to what is now statistically defined as food aid (which also comes to 5-7% of world food trade).

In other words, if we include the present 5.5% discount from the higher genuine commercial price in our definition of food aid, food aid would be approximately doubled compared with the present figure. This would raise the current tonnage of food aid from around 12 million tons per annum to around 24 million tons. This higher figure makes talk of "the decline of food aid" (Clay, 1994) somewhat questionable. It also brings food aid within the range of the status quo assessments of needs by the USDA and the FAO. It also raises the share of food aid in total development aid from around 8% to about 15%, giving it a distinctly more important profile.

With more radical assumptions, moving from the partial GATT to full liberalization, and defining any discount from a fully liberalized commercial international free market price for food as food aid, we might well find the true volume of current food aid thus broadly measured further increased – quadrupled rather than doubled – to something in the nature of 40 to 50 million tons equivalent.[2] This would bring food aid to the level of the USDA estimate of food aid needs, including nutritional requirements. The important qualification to such comparisons must be that the food aid implicit in the artificial lowering of international food prices and trade discounts – the food aid that dare not speak its name – is not in any way targeted on food needs, food security, or nutritional requirements. It is broadly and blindly given across the board to all commercial importers, regardless of need. In fact, the really needy, almost by definition, are not commercial importers. If this hidden food aid could be brought into the open and properly targeted on needs, the world would have taken an important step in dealing with the hunger problem.

Another implication of including this "grey area" in food aid is that much food aid is in fact, although involuntarily, given not by the countries that appear statistically as "donors," but by food exporters among developing countries – such as Argentina, Thailand, or Zimbabwe – which do not appear as "donors" at all (except insofar as they figure as sources of procurement in triangular transactions). If these countries can step up their food exports to take the place, in a more level playing field, of the present subsidized exports of the EU and US and the liberalized markets in Japan, the rise in world prices projected by the models may not in fact materialize.

In fact, such developing country food exporters are doubly hit by the present situation. In the first place, they suffer from the downward pressure on international food prices due to overhanging surpluses and surplus capacities of countries protecting and subsidizing their agriculture. In the second place, they see their normal markets preempted by food aid (including "grey area" food aid, subsidized exports, export credits, etc.) which they cannot afford to give. Theoretically this second burden should not exist: their sales should be protected by the provision for "Usual Marketing Requirements" (UMRs) monitored by the FAO Committee for Surplus Disposal. However, it is generally accepted that in fact at least a part of program food aid replaces commercial imports – that indeed is one of the strong arguments in favor of program food aid. Since it replaces commercial imports, it amounts in fact to the provision of balance of payments support and foreign exchange, and thus has all the advantages of the greater flexibility of financial aid and built-in monetization. Moreover, insofar as commercial imports are displaced, the program food aid does not add to total food supplies and hence, unless sold at subsidized prices, cannot have disincentive effects on local food production. On the other hand, by the same token, it does not in itself deal with hunger and nutrition problems. There is, however, a secondary exception to this: if the foreign exchange set free by the food aid is at least partially used to import additional food, then we might have not only the risk of disincentive effects but also the potential nutritional benefits.

The prospective rise in international food prices as a result of agricultural liberalization will also affect the UMRs. The commercial market requirements – or rather commercial market possibilities – of the poorer food-importing countries will be less at the higher prospective post-liberalization prices, given their limitation of foreign exchange earnings and the drain of debt service. It can be hoped that the higher international prices will stimulate domestic food production in these countries, but this will require major investments in infrastructure, R&D, etc.; the elasticity of supply to price alone, without such complementary investment, may not be high enough.

So far we have identified two types of "grey" food aid that are not included in the statistical definition. These are the "light grey" area of subsidized exports, export credits, and other forms of concessionality that remain below the 25% concessionality limit but apply to a very high proportion of total food exports by food aid donors. In addition, we have identified a "dark grey" food aid consisting of the concealed subsidy to food importers as a result of the lower prices in international food trade due to the pressure of overhanging surpluses and surplus capacities. But beyond these two "grey" categories there looms yet another statistically unrecorded set of transactions which in economic effect amount to food aid. Once we cross the Rubicon into the "grey area" there are no obvious landmarks telling us where to stop. At least some of the financial aid, especially financial program aid including structural adjustment lending, finances balance of payments deficits, thus enabling countries to acquire additional imports. Insofar as some of these additional imports are food, we could say that this segment of financial aid is in fact aid for food finance or food aid. As a first approximation, we may assume that financial aid which in effect finances additional imports should be classified as food aid in the same proportion as food imports to overall imports of recipient countries. Even project aid, as a result of fungibility, has the ultimate effect of freeing foreign exchange (Singer, 1965). Since for the low-income and lower-middle-income countries (other than China and India) food represents 14% of total imports, we may roughly assume that of the $50 billion of annual financial ODA (Overseas Development Assistance) some $7 billion represents finance for food imports or, in the broader sense, food aid. The inclusion of this latter sum would almost treble food aid by comparison with its present highly limited definition.

This would also apply to the IMF Food Financing Facility, which was added to the Compensatory Financing Facility in 1981. Although it has not been much used and under the stringent IMF rules may not be much used in future (and also only doubtfully treated as "aid"), yet it was specifically intended to enable food-insecure low-income countries to maintain cereal imports in the face of supply failures or unexpected drops in export earnings. With this mandate, it is difficult to avoid the conclusion that, at least conceptually, transactions under the FFF should be treated as food aid – presumably part of emergency food aid. This is particularly the case since the IMF has recently developed sources of funds on highly concessional terms with interest – as low as 0.5% in the case of the Expanded Structural Adjustment Facility (ESAF).

All these are areas in which the present statistical definition of food aid appears too limited; broader definitions may well be suggested. There is also, however, a countervailing element where the present definition of food aid could be said to be excessively wide. Some food aid represents in fact financial aid in that it sets free foreign exchange. This relates to that part of program food aid that in fact replaces commercial imports. This type of food aid is equivalent to financial aid in the form of free foreign exchange. In any functional definition of food aid, distinguishing it from financial aid, it may well be that the border line should be drawn to bring the import-replacing element in program food aid into the category of financial aid. This is easy to suggest as a conceptional procedure, but statistically it will be very difficult to determine which part of program food aid replaces commercial imports and which part is additional. Under the UMR rule in principle all food aid should be additional, as already pointed out. This is a principle rather than a fact. There is no doubt that there is some substitution, but its magnitude is a matter of counterfactual evidence which is notoriously difficult. Saran and Konandreas put substitution as high as 60-70%, but this may be on the high side (Saran and Konandreas, 1991). How much would a country have imported commercially if no program food aid had been available to it? The same question could also be asked in respect of emergency food aid, although in this case it would be much less likely that commercial imports could have been afforded. In the circumstances, the size of this sector of statistical food aid which in fact amounts to financial aid must remain more a matter of speculation than of practical adjustment – more in the nature of a statistical footnote.

A second dimension in which the present food aid statistics may in fact be overstated relates to value figures rather than tonnage. Food aid is usually valued by donors at the budget cost to themselves, but this is inflated by the subsidies and high domestic prices involved in their own agricultural policies. According to Saran and Konandreas, the actual value of the food donated at international prices is only about one-half of the budgeted value (Saran and Konandreas, 1991). (On the other hand, it must be remembered that international prices are themselves artificially lowered by the same agricultural policies, so the true value would be somewhere between the international price and the budget-cost price. Nothing could better illustrate the quagmire of concepts and statistics.)

A third cause of possible overvaluation of food aid in present statistics relates to triangular transactions and local procurement. Some of the food aid donors without any surplus food (yet committed under the Food Aid Convention to participate in "food aid") give cash instead to buy food in other countries or locally in the recipient country. These triangular transactions are an increasing element in total food aid and by many criteria a particularly desirable element. However, it is by no means clear how they should appear in food aid statistics. If the UK buys surplus white maize from Zimbabwe to transport as food aid to Zambia, it seems pretty clear that Zambia is a recipient of food aid. But the case could well be presented as a combination of UK-financed expansion of South-South trade between Zimbabwe and Zambia. From the UK point of view this is a case of double benefits, of killing two birds with one stone: the transaction represents financial aid to Zimbabwe by providing foreign exchange for their maize surplus, and it also provides food aid to Zambia. Yet it would clearly be double-counting for the same transaction to be counted both as financial aid to Zimbabwe and food aid to Zambia. Which is it to be? To count it as food aid only would in effect understate financial aid, and to count it as aid to Zambia only would understate the aid figures for Zimbabwe. To count it as financial aid would run the opposite risk. The road of the food aid statistician is clearly full of dangerous land mines.

This last example illustrates clearly that the real quagmire is conceptual rather than statistical. When we deal with subsidized and financially promoted trade what part of it is trade and what part of it is aid? What is the grant element that distinguishes trade from aid – is it 10%, 25%, 50%? Why should 25% (the DAC-agreed benchmark) act as a "magic number"? Where is the borderline between financial aid and food aid? On which side of the borderline do the following fall: monetized food aid; triangular transactions; balance of payments support either through financial or program food aid? How should the hidden subsidies to food importers arising from the agricultural policies pursued by the US and EU be treated? Where is the bench mark for full commercial prices as against actual prices in international food trade? The more we broaden our definition of food aid and ask some of the foregoing questions, the more it becomes clear that food aid must be understood as an element in world food policy and world food security.

Such a shift towards a broader conception of food aid will be all the more necessary since the historical link with surplus disposal and the resulting popularity of food aid, especially in the farming communities of the industrial countries, are now likely to be weakened as a result of agricultural policy. Partly as a result of this link, and partly because of the direct association of food aid with poverty alleviation and humanitarian relief, food aid has consistently enjoyed greater political support than financial aid. While financial aid is stagnating at below 0.35% of donor GNPs – less than half the accepted UN target – food aid, even on the narrow definition, has amounted to around 2% of total food production in the major donor countries (US, EC, and Canada)[3] and has consistently exceeded the minimum target under the Food Aid Convention. Moreover, the Food Aid Convention represents a multi-annual commitment of a kind never achieved in the case of financial aid. But, on the supply side, food aid is now threatened both by a reduction of surpluses and by higher food prices, which will mean less volume of food aid for given budgetary appropriations. Yet at the same time, on the demand side, the need for food aid will increase as a result of higher costs of commercial food imports. According to the Final Act of the GATT Uruguay Round Agreement, a balance between reduced willingness to supply and increased need should be found in the maintenance of food aid in the post-liberalization era – presumably in volume terms.

Cutting the historical link between surpluses and food aid may be a blessing in disguise. Surplus disposal and the resulting popularity of food aid for this reason was always a flawed motivation for food aid. We have heard a lot about possible disincentive effects of food aid on policy makers as well as producers in recipient countries. We have heard less about the disincentive for policy makers in the industrial countries: an incentive to continue with harmful agricultural policies on the grounds that some of the resulting surpluses could be disposed of by food aid. Similarly, if the hidden food aid which dared not speak its name is now forced to come out into the open, it could then be more purposefully targeted on developmental and humanitarian objectives. This will not only help to clear up the present conceptual and statistical quagmire, but, more important, it will also promote the fight for development and against poverty.

Problems of Implementation

It was explicitly recognized in the decisions of the Uruguay Round that liberalization of agricultural trade held dangers for the food security of developing countries. Such worries came on top of other worries, such as erosion of preferences and the like. Worries were clearly concentrated on the low-income food deficit countries (LIFDCs), particularly in sub-Saharan Africa. It was recognized that special measures would be needed to avoid such potentially harmful effects. To this end, a series of counter-measures were proposed.

The first such measure relates to the Food Aid Convention. The basic decision was that genuine or bona fide food aid would be exempted from the provision to abolish or reduce export subsidies. Presumably the definition of bona fide or genuine food aid is to be based on the current definition of 25% or more concessionality. This principle of the maintenance – or possible strengthening – of genuine food aid leads automatically to the Food Aid Convention, which was established for precisely this purpose and strengthened after the experiences of the 1974 food crisis. The Uruguay Round suggests "a periodic review" of the minimum food aid supply laid down by the Food Aid Convention. The present minimum commitment is for 7.5 million tons, well below the actual level, which in recent years has not been less than 10-11 million tons. This suggests that, in the spirit of the Uruguay Round decision, the minimum target should be raised closer to the actual level to provide a more effective safety net. Whether the domestic policies of major contributors will permit such an improved safety net remains to be seen. The omens are not good, but there is certainly a moral commitment in the spirit of the Uruguay Round.

The fact that actual food aid has been consistently above the minimum commitment under the Food Aid Convention can be interpreted in one of two ways. Either it can be held to indicate that food aid, particularly in emergencies, is a relatively popular form of aid, as distinct from financial aid, where the accepted UN target of 0.7% of donors' GDP has never been reached and the movement is away from the target rather than towards it. An alternative interpretation would be that the 7.5 million ton target has been excessively modest, and that the time has come to bring it more in line with the facts of life. This second interpretation would strengthen the implications of the Uruguay Round decision to maintain genuine food aid. One possible suggestion arising from the proposal to bring the minimum target into line with the facts of life would be to base it on some kind of average food aid during the preceding three or five years or so and subsequently adjust it automatically on a sliding basis. That would be an effective safety net, but may be beyond what food aid donors are presently willing to approve.

The reference to emergency food aid suggests still another possibility: while total food aid has been maintained or increased in recent years, this is not true of developmental food aid. Developmental food aid has been increasingly squeezed by the needs of emergency food aid. While we are all groping to create links between emergency relief and development, there still remains a worrying squeeze on developmental food aid. Hence a possible suggestion would be that under the Food Aid Convention there should be a new and separate commitment for the maintenance of non-emergency or developmental food aid. This would be in line with the Uruguay Round decision, which was not directly concerned with emergencies. The proposal would be based on an assumption that there is no need for any specific formal commitment in connection with emergency food aid, on the grounds that emergencies will always call forth a non-controversial response. If such a proposal is considered, it would be possible perhaps to maintain the present level of 7.5 million tons but to define the commitment more narrowly, to exclude emergency food aid.

The Uruguay Round specifically asked donors to give more food aid to LIFDCs on a grant or concessional basis. This suggests the possibility that under the Food Aid Convention separate minima should be guaranteed for LIFDCs and/or there should be a commitment to supply food aid to LIFDCs on a full grant basis. This should be in addition to the more general overall present commitment, but if political necessity so requires, could also be substituted for it.

The Uruguay Round also decided that the rise in food prices should be considered as a factor in determining access to existing and new facilities from international financial institutions. This is a clear reference to the IMF Food Financing Facility. But it was also meant to be a hint to the IMF and World Bank to take the rise in food prices into account in their stabilization and structural adjustment programs, as well as a hint to the World Bank and regional development banks to consider additional lending, including lending on concessional terms, to countries affected by the rise in food prices, especially the LIFDCs. It was also specified that there should be additional lending to agricultural development projects in LIFDCs to enable them to respond to the higher prices for imported food by increasing domestic food production. It is to be hoped that these decisions, although not in very concrete and binding terms, will be remembered if and when the expected rise in international food prices and reduction of export subsidies materialize.

This last proviso is necessary. Although the models developed by economists agree that food prices will rise – and this was accepted as a basis for the decisions of the Uruguay Round – economists have been known to be wrong in their forecasts. In any case, the models only predict that food prices will be higher than they would otherwise be, other things being equal. In the past, international food prices have been on a long-term declining trend, quite a sharp one in recent years. (The last year has seen a rise, but this may just be normal volatility rather than a reversal of the trend.) So it may be that in fact there will be no actual rise in food prices but only a reduction of the trend decline. There are many unknown factors that could reduce the actual rise below the predicted figure: agricultural production in Russia and eastern Europe; increased food exports from Argentina, Thailand, and other exporters outside the EU and US; new breakthroughs in agricultural R&D; beginnings of a Green Revolution in Africa, etc. – all are presently unknown "black boxes" which could affect international food prices in a downward direction. There are also "black boxes" which might affect future food prices in an upward direction: signs that the rapid yield increases in the US and EU may be petering out; restrictions on the use of fertilizer, pesticides, etc., for environmental reasons; general effects of environmental degradation; the impact of global warming and climatic change; a shift of food production into increasingly fragile areas and soils; possible major food import needs of China; a reduction in the supply of food crops in favor of fodder and cash crops, etc. Compared with such major other factors, the impact of the Uruguay Round may be small, but it may be the straw that breaks the camel's back.

Thus there is no justification to dismiss the rise in food prices predicted by the models in a spirit of complacency. Malthus is not by any means dead yet. Amartya Sen may have told us that Malthus should have talked less of diminishing returns in food production and increases in population and more about increasing difficulties faced by increasing numbers of people in obtaining access or entitlement to food. The declining trend of international food prices may be as much due to lack of effective demand – need backed by purchasing power – as abundance of supply. In fact, it is due to the ratio or interaction between the two. But that does not offer an escape from Malthusian gloom – only a shift in analysis, from Malthusian supply-side Malthusianism to Keynesian-Senian effective demand-side Malthusianism. This shift does serve to draw our attention to the real underlying problems of food insecurity – poverty, unequal income distribution, unemployment, etc. – rather than merely to food production, food trade, or food aid. It is quite possible that the initial rise in food prices predicted by the models will provide incentives to step up food production in the deficit countries and counteract incentives to reduce production in the surplus countries. But this will involve long-run adjustments, and these may take longer than we can afford to wait. Since we are dealing with food, Keynes's statement, "in the long run we are all dead" may be literally true. It is as well to be prepared and to take the warning signals of the Uruguay Round seriously.

1. Peter Uvin, 1994, describes it as 'residual' and 'largely devoid of significance.'

2. For example, under the RUNS model the price of wheat would increase by 30.2 per cent instead of 5.9 per cent; coarse grains by 19.0 per cent instead of 3.6; dairy products by 52.6 per cent instead of 7.2; and vegetable oils by 17.7 per cent instead of 4.1 – see Goldin et al. (1993).

3. See Peter Uvin (1994) who points to the remarkable similarity of this percentage in the US, EC, and Canada as evidence of wider and more general forces determining the willingness of major donors to give food aid.

References

Clay, E. (1994) The Decline of Food Aid: Issues of Aid Policy, Trade and Food Security, in Prendergast, R. and F. Stewart (eds). *Market Forces and World Development*. New York and London: Macmillan.

Goldin, I., O. Knudsen and D. van der Mensbrugghe (1993) *Trade Liberalization: Global Economic Implications*. Paris and Washington DC: OECD and World Bank, 91, Table 3.1.

Saran, R. and P. Konandreas (1991) An Additional Resource? A Global Perspective on Food Aid Flows in Relation to Development Assistance in Clay and Stokke (eds). *Food Aid Reconsidered: Assessing the Impact on Third World Countries*. London: Frank Cass.

Singer, H.W. (1965) External Aid: for plans or projects?. *Economic Journal*, 75, (September).

Uvin, P. (1994) *The International Organization of Hunger*. London: Kegan Paul International.

CHAPTER 13

Visions of the Future: Food, Hunger and Nutrition

Ellen Messer

In 1993, two reports about the world food outlook reached opposite conclusions. The first, a product of the International Economics Department of the World Bank, concluded that the supply situation has been steadily improving, and that prospects for sustaining this positive trend are encouraging. Although rates of growth for cereals appear to be plateauing, so are rates of growth of demand because of changes in economies and diets across the world (Mitchell and Ingco, 1993). The second, a product of Lester Brown's World Watch Institute, continued to announce a world food crisis. This doomsday perspective insists that current levels of food production cannot be sustained, and that a crisis of non-renewable resources in agriculture (soils, water, biodiversity, energy) exacerbated by population growth is underway (Brown, 1994).

These reports are two among many examples of future projections into the next century, spanning the year (decades) 2000 through 2060 (Table 1). As a group, they examine the technological, institutional, policy, and socioeconomic dimensions of food supplies. They also address the nutritional, economic, technological, and sociocultural dimensions of food demand. They differ in whether the focus is principally on supply or on demand, and on whether they project more food might become available through greater production or through increased efficiency, and also on the relative weight placed on agricultural prices and trade. All agree, nevertheless, that biotechnology or other forms of agricultural intensification have great potential, as yet unproven, to provide additional food and efficiency for the world food system. They also agree that meeting the food needs of the poor, especially the increasing numbers of urban poor, will continue to be difficult.

The reports are also similar in what they leave out. They provide background information only; if they offer recommendations, they do so without suggesting

Table 13.1. World Food, Agriculture, and Hunger Projections from Year 2000

2000	(FAO, 1981, 1987)
2000	(SADCC, 1984)
2010	(FAO, 1993)
2010	(World Bank [Mitchell and Ingco, 1993])
2020	(IFPRI, 1994)
2050	(World Resources Institute [Bender, 1993])
2060	(World Hunger Program [Chen and Kates, 1994])

priorities. They pay scant attention to the institutional mix that will be necessary to achieve sustainable yields and a sustainable end to hunger. Instead, they tend to focus on what governments or international agencies might be doing and funding, and less on the activities of NGOs and the private sector. They give little thought to how global or national efforts can connect with local ones. Moreover, their scenarios, however conventional or "surprise"-oriented, miss at least four conditions that might significantly brighten otherwise dismal spots in the world food and hunger outlook, namely, (1) what peace might contribute to future food supply and demand – particularly in sub-Saharan Africa, where food supply per capita is dismal and projected in most scenarios to become even more so, and (2) what effective grassroots participation might mean for rural development and transformations of the food economy, including incorporation of indigenous ideas and materials and appropriate advances in agrobiotechnology. Although all are interested in how income affects food choices and possible improvements in dietary quality, most of the discussion focuses on livestock and meat consumption, not vegetable consumption which can also improve diets and lower the demand for cereal grains. As a corollary, they fail to consider (3) what diversified dietary-nutritional strategies, especially those incorporating micronutrient goals, might offer to future scenarios of adequate food and nutrition. Finally, they do not seriously look at (4) what difference a woman-centered approach to food and nutrition planning, from agricultural research and extension to efficient processing and consumption, might yield.

These four points relate the four Bellagio goals for overcoming hunger to a longer term vision for adequate food and nutrition and freedom from hunger. They are followed up here in passing as we review very briefly certain assumptions and findings of the most recent efforts to address food and hunger beyond the year 2000, especially the International Food Policy Research Institute's (IFPRI) 2020 Vision and World Resources Institute-Santa Fe Institute-Brookings Institute 2050 Project. This presentation is meant to generate discussion and does not claim to completely represent the views of all participants.[1] In addition, the analysis largely leaves open for discussion the distinction between "visions" and "projections" of future food supply and demand.[2]

2010

Analysis begins with the very explicit anti-Malthusian predictions of The World Bank economics department's food outlook for 2010 (Mitchell and Ingco, 1993), whose authors envision technology, trade, and the market basically adjusting to increasing population numbers with increasing food demands. Current production techniques, with increments from biotechnology, adjustments of price and income, will make Malthus wait, they insist. There is minimal attention to possible changes in diet or possible sources of downturns in certain regions, such as the "conflict" factor (1) mentioned above. The scenarios, while acknowledging increasing hunger in sub-Saharan Africa, are uniformly optimistic.

Agcaoili and Rosegrant of IFPRI (1994a:2) provide a somewhat more nuanced analysis. Disaggregating their data analysis according to major food crops and regions of the world, they suggest why growth in average per capita cereal production seems to be diminishing in Asia (e.g., market prices or government price policies make it less attractive to grow rice versus other cash crops on the best lands, while intensified production on more marginal lands also lowers the averages). Their simulation models use three major factors to estimate global and regional food markets in the next twenty years: population growth and urbanization; improvement of general economic conditions; and increases in food production through yield increases. Varying these factors, their findings predict substantial differences in regional commodity demands, according to population and income. In view of more optimistic scenarios (low population growth, high income and agricultural investment) they emphasize that "the biggest challenge in the next two or three decades is the development of more efficient production technologies," which are already resulting in some reduction in production costs in middle income economies (p.25). (Their outlook might be even more attractive if the simulation model included important staple crops such as roots, tubers, and pulses.) They conclude that if the international community maintains investments in agriculture for LDCs, as well as for human capital and rural infrastructure, the food supply picture, even with rising populations, should be secure. But they caution that efforts to reduce population and retain agricultural production growth may be daunting.

2020

The aforementioned 2010 paper in part provides background for a larger IFPRI effort: "A 2020 Vision for Food, Agriculture, and the Environment," subtitled, "The Unfinished Agenda – Famine and Poverty in the 21st Century." The project, initiated in 1994, ambitiously aims to bring together opposing views on the future of world food security (optimistic, pessimistic) and set priorities and actions to avoid a future world food crisis. Concept papers examine opposing views on soil and water resources, biological resources, and agricultural chemicals and fertilizers. Additional papers explore trends in population, trade, income, and poverty. Related research on agricultural intensification argues that new technology is necessary to prevent environmental degradation and overcome poverty. Conceptually more than an agricultural outlook, the 2020 Vision constitutes a defense of international agricultural research at a time of imperiled funding, but also a response to the lack of follow-up of the unfulfilled promises of the UNCED and the ICN. The 2020 Vision tries also to provide a locus for discussion of the impact of AIDS, political change (governance), trade patterns, urbanization, and technical change in food, agriculture, and environment. The 2020 vision therefore offers a review and synthesis of current knowledge on food production, population, and economic development.

The 2020 Vision also promises to provide some priorities for a global plan of action in agriculture for the next century. The plan is supposed to suggest strategies to meet the burgeoning food demands of growing populations that will also demand higher quality diets. Relatively the same quantity of land must simultaneously provide increasing numbers of rural poor in LDCs with jobs and income. Agricultural production must somehow keep up with continuing if not accelerating population growth (relative to food supply), avoid environmental degradation, and alleviate rural poverty. The underlying theme of all background papers is that a better life for all can be achieved only through investment in rural people via agricultural research.

Information and debates are presented through a series of short briefs. "World Production of Cereals, 1966-90," also by M.C. Agcaoili and M.W. Rosegrant (1994b) concludes that the world needs certain "innovations" in policies: more investment in research and extension with better interactions with farmers; more efficient fertilizer use; integrated pest management; improved efficiency of irrigation water use; appropriate price incentives; reformed trade and macroeconomic policy regimes to improve long-term performance of the agricultural sector. "World Supply and Demand Projections for Cereals, 2020" offers a global food model that can be used to estimate future world food prices, supply, demand, and trade of cereals, which they have divided into "baseline," reduced production, and reduced production and income scenarios. The current rate-of-growth scenario predicts that global food supply will be adequate and that prices will fall. But increases will continue to accrue in the developed countries, and South Asia and sub-Saharan Africa will suffer deficits more than triple those of today. However, these scenarios do not account for some changes in crop mixes as a result of changing price ratios and production abilities. Nor do they assume that somehow African communities might recover and grow more than they do now. They conclude that investment in cereal production for LDCs must be maintained and expand to prevent LDCs from suffering a bleak future.

Rajul Pandya-Lorch finds in "Economic Growth and Development" (Pandya-Lorch, 1994) that both are uneven across regions. Africa does most poorly; parts of Asia surge at an average of 5.3% per year. This report also looks at where the billion or more impoverished are located. Poverty is increasing in Sub-Saharan Africa, Latin America, and the Middle East. Although decreasing in East Asia and the Pacific, the numbers in South Asia are still enormous – roughly a half billion. Although this report stresses the strong correlation between poor performance in agriculture and poor overall economic performance, it does not consider conflict as a contributing factor – especially in Africa.

The environmental context is presented in "Conservation and Enhancement of Natural Resources" (Stephen Vosti and Sara Scherr, 1994), in which the 2020 project seeks to identify trends and sources of trends in soil degradation or enhancement, forest conversion, and land use. The authors trace various policy scenarios and their impacts. They emphasize that there is much more speculation on patterns of deterioration (desertification, salinization) than of improvement, such as treeplanting, soil remediation, or intercropping. Investigators know almost nothing about what leads farmers to improve rather than degrade land, or what happens to land, including former forest, once degraded. Much better use might be made of environmental data collected by non-governmental organizations and international agencies to learn what types of behaviors favor sustainable agriculture.

Sustainable agriculture is addressed more directly by Robert Paarlberg in a brief on "Sustainable Farming: A Political Geography" (Paarlberg, 1994). He summarizes the controversy surrounding high input farming, with its load of chemicals and fertilizers. The high monetary and environmental costs of these technologies are blamed at least in part for the cutbacks in funding for international agricultural research centers. Using India as an example, Paarlberg argues that high input farming is crucial to raise food output. But he does not analyze in depth the argument that more efficient use might lower inputs. He compares farming practices and yields associated with traditional versus modern varieties and farming techniques but does not consider the possible range of alternative farming practices. Paarlberg argues that environmental pollution can arise out of power (as in East Asia, where Chinese farmers pollute the waterways) or powerlessness (as in Africa) but in either case the powerless suffer the damaging impacts of environmental degradation. These are vast generalizations, as is the "solution" of reform in the countryside, not just more technology.

"Malnutrition and Food Insecurity" (Garcia, 1994) projects that the number of malnourished (underweight) children will increase to about 200 million by 2020 and then remain stable, given reductions in fertility. Three possible alternative scenarios are the goals of the World Summit for Children and the International Conference on Nutrition (ICN): to reduce childhood malnutrition by half to around 90 million; an "optimistic" scenario that would reduce numbers to about 110 million; and a pessimistic scenario that would leave numbers around 200 million. None of these scenarios envisions the impacts of breakthroughs in food supply or devastation from AIDS. Garcia notes that most of the malnourished (underweight) children will continue to reside in Asia, although reductions might come about through wider application of effective health policies, as has been shown in Tamil Nadu, Indonesia, and Thailand as well as on other continents, Chile and Zimbabwe.

Population scenarios are reviewed by David Nygaard in "World Population Projections, 2020" (Nygaard, 1994). Estimates for population in 2020 vary from 7.5 to 8.5 billion people, and nothing can be done about these very large numbers over the next twenty years, given the numbers of children already born. But he probably is wrong to state that "virtually nothing can be done in a short period of 20 years" in the sense that this generation can experience substantial changes in fertility behavior if the social, cultural, economic, and health conditions are favorable.

With this background, an opening advisory committee meeting was convened in Uganda in June, 1994. Discussion was organized around five issues: population; food supply and demand; economic growth and development; food insecurity, malnutrition, and poverty; and natural resource degradation. Usual buzzwords, such as "participation," "grassroots," and other mechanisms for "involving" the producer and consumer were missing. Additional topics proposed by participants, but not reported, included how to generate more employment and income, and by what "social technologies" to foster greater involvement of community members with the process of food, agricultural, and environmental improvement. The discussion on "food insecurity, malnutrition, and poverty" did, however, include the suggestion that "the conference agenda should consider an explicit role for NGOs in delivering nutritional improvement knowledge." Also discussed were decisionmaking capacities of women and biotechnology's potential to feed the world. Some of these topics have been followed up in subsequent 2020 issues papers and briefs. The advisory group also asked IFPRI to consider public-private linkages with respect to agricultural research and related issues such as intellectual property rights, and urged studies to critique aid and all the recent UN conferences. People seemed not to agree on where aid was most needed and where it might be most effective.

All these themes are brought together by Per Pinstrup-Andersen and Rajul Pandya-Lorch in the discussion paper, "Alleviating Poverty, Intensifying Agriculture, and Effectively Managing Natural Resources" (Pinstrup-Andersen and Pandya-Lorch, 1994). They conclude that only agricultural intensification, via new technologies yet to be identified and disseminated, can prevent food insecurity, poverty, and environmental degradation.[3] Their research promises "a comprehensive set of policies to encourage and facilitate long-term sustainable agricultural development while alleviating poverty and conserving natural resources."

Their recommendations for sustainable agriculture run the full spectrum of policies. These involve improvements to both the most favored and the marginal lands, off-farm income for the poor to acquire and hold on to land, and sustain investments in water management, seeds, and chemicals that working the land entails. Their principal remedy for increasing agricultural production in the future is more research to further yield improvements on all types of land. But recommendations are non-specific. To benefit from the research, farmers need income for access to technology. They also need credit, reasonable prices, and technical assistance.

Pinstrup-Andersen and Pandya-Lorch point out also that "indigenous practices for resource conservation could benefit from research" but not the converse (agricultural research and applications might benefit from research on what farmers are already doing right, whether or not such "right" actions might be further improved by research). Rural people also need to participate productively in mixed economies, with off-farm income targeted for farm investments. Additionally, production inputs must be priced to encourage sensible use.

Overall, the 2020 Vision offers not a strategy, but an extensive menu of actions that might (or must) be taken to promote agricultural yields, food security, and environmental protection. In its effort to be inclusive, to represent all possible interests and points of view, it sets no priorities. Potential actors, be they governments, IGOs, or NGOs, are therefore left without guidance as to what needs and actions are most urgent and who should take responsibility. Some recommendations in August 1994, for example, listed:

1. Diversify the income base so that families do not have to rely solely on rainfed agriculture.

2. Invest in agricultural research and transferring technology (e.g., drought-resistant and high-yielding crops) to farmers;

3. Allow markets to function freely so that buying and selling food is not affected by artificial restrictions and political turmoil;

4. Provide some of the poor with food subsidies such as food stamps;

5. Make credit available to the poor for building up assets and purchasing needed farm supplies;

6. Invest in road building and other infrastructure because markets cannot work if there are no roads on which food can be delivered;

7. Promote sustainable use of the natural resources base;

8. Focus on social issues that contribute to poverty, including inadequate health care and sanitation, lack of literacy, and discrimination against segments of the population based on race or ethnicity.

9. Avert severe impacts of crop failures by effective early warning and timely response.

10. Prevent hunger due to political conflict: "the international donor community should step in and reward peace and political stability with long-term development aid wherever and whenever it occurs" (IFPRI *News & Views*, August 1994, p.2).

Apart from these recommendations, project papers conclude that the food picture will depend on effective demand and investment in technology. They envision a dual challenge: to produce food sustainably and to increase employment, especially in urban areas, to protect food security.

The Vision background papers tend to be government-centered, especially when one examines in detail the analyses and recommendations for specialized topics, such as eliminating famine.[4]

Unlike the "Overcoming hunger..." initiative, the 2020 Vision, at least up to the time of its major conference, June 1995, displays little interest in making choices or setting priorities. The writers lamely reiterate the poverty and hunger statistics and thereby the enormity of the problem. They report and accept some disagreements over the hunger numbers, and based on alternative formulations of minimally adequate diets, child survival, and government investment and trade, trace out different scenarios for the future of hunger (e.g., Garcia, 1994). But they do not suggest how different understandings or selections of the numbers might guide priority-setting. Publications announce that the 2020 Vision initiative "seeks to bring together divergent schools of thought in order to identify more productively those solutions that seem the most promising" but have not identified any particular plan. Although the 2020 Vision is presented as an initiative on hunger, hunger here seems to mean "agriculture".[5] The effort straightforwardly is to offer evidence and results that will help reverse the decline in long-term international investment in agriculture.

Sustained investment in agriculture, without argument, is necessary to ensure steadily upward trends in food production and sustainable livelihoods for the rural poor, since agriculture still provides their major source of income. But whether and in what particular directions this IFPRI 2020 Vision process can move international investment through a series of issues papers, briefs, and one central three-day meeting in Washington (the "focal point" of the activities) is doubtful. As their economic growth discussion noted, "solutions to poverty, food insecurity, and environmental degradation were likely to be country-specific and local in nature, rather than global." Priorities need to be set in many de-centralized places by the people involved most closely with the problems. But it is not clear that the Vision has planned in advance for follow-up.

What is absent in this Vision, in addition, is clear non-governmental presence. The key words identified for the mid-1990's are "shared vision," "consensus," "how to meet future world food needs" while "reducing poverty," and "protecting the environment." The Vision says little about diet (discussion of diet is subsumed under discussions of urbanization). It says little about decentralized decisionmaking. And it says little about the role of grassroots or non-governmental organizations, which were brought into the discussions by IFPRI well after the first phase of the process.[6]

Finally, the earlier phase of the 2020 Vision was silent on the issue of human rights, although as the vision evolved – and by the June conference – achieving adequate food and nutrition as human rights constituted the starting point for this very ambitious IFPRI agenda.

2050

The 2050 Project, by contrast, is a large-scale, multi-year non-governmental "think-tank" consortium effort that examines the transition to "sustainability." Overall, the project has tried to arrive at new visions of what might be desirable and doable in the next 50 years: to describe a decent global future and then figure out how to get there. Its ultimate goal is to link environment, food, and population visions through modelling. The participants hope that innovative models will offer fresh insights about how to create a better, more sustainable world.

The 2050 food and agriculture sector, in contrast to the agricultural visions already discussed, begins from the premise that "the purpose of the food system is not agricultural production, but is the satisfaction of nutritional requirements of the world's population, along with providing an enjoyable, healthy, and palatable diet." William Bender, who led the food and agricultural sector studies, utilized "end use analysis" rather than production, price and trade, nutrient intake, or other functions to estimate how the world might continue to meet food and nutritional needs through 2050 (Bender, 1994). Background on additional issues was provided in the 2050 food and agriculture papers on: "Agriculture and Global Entitlements to Food" (Bender, 1993); "Soil Erosion and Effects on Crop Productivity" (Jarnagin and Smith, 1993); "Crop Plant Productivity" (Smith, 1993); and "Nutrient Flows in Agriculture" (Smil, 1993). Vaclav Smil, who participated in 2050 discussions of energy sustainability, drew on many ideas of the group for his essay, "How Many People Can the Earth Feed?" (Smil, 1994). His figures on energy needs for agriculture through 2050 are used as estimates by Bender (1994), as well as by Kates (see his 2060 vision, this volume).

The 2050 Project in general addressed such questions as how a sustainable global society might be defined; the time frame and indicators of sustainability; and what strategies and actions might be necessary to bring it about. For the food and agriculture sector, such questions led to an analysis that focused more on demand than supply, and on how to achieve sustainable food availability by eliminating waste rather than by greater production. The analysis challenges the assumption that links remain static between levels of income and food demand, and instead seeks to clarify what might be changing and the potential impacts of change on food demand. In his end-use analysis, Bender (1994) identified four sources of potential change in global per capita food requirements:

- changes in global calorie requirements stemming from improved nutritional status and (lower) activity levels;

- efficiency changes in the storage, handling, transportation, and consumption losses of food;

- changes that result from shifts in diet, particularly the increasing demand for meat; and

- changes in dietary structures resulting from increasing knowledge and concerns about diet and health.

Calculations of a future potential sustainable food supply are offered in terms of the percent of 1990 calorie consumption that might be "saved" by shifts to alternative nutritional and activity patterns; greater food system efficiency; healthier diets (fewer animal products which are costlier in calories to produce); and (to a lesser extent) global transfers (remittances) that might allow resources to be produced, distributed, and consumed more efficiently at a global level. Precision is limited, in that the model rests on shaky estimates of wastes and savings at each step in the food chain (see Tables 2 and 3 in Kates, this volume). The model rests also on the unstated assumption that somehow calories saved by avoiding waste or not eating meat might be channeled into the general food supply for the poor. It offers no suggestions or indications of how behaviors and choices might be moved in the direction of greater efficiency, such as recycling in multiple contexts. Nevertheless, the paper provides a fresh and much-needed focus on efficiency that considers how consumer behavior and technological choices might affect the future of food, hunger, and nutrition.

The numbers economists use to make food and agriculture projections are also questioned by Smil, who notes that estimates of carrying capacity vary widely as do estimates of how much food the world community has and consumes. Both production and consumption surveys are highly inaccurate and out of synchronization. Concluding that the world already has almost enough food to feed everyone an adequate diet, Smil (1994) suggests that the world community already has the know-how to be more efficient, but there remains the question of providing consumers with incentives to change toward more efficient and healthful eating patterns and of providing international actors with incentives for cooperation in further efficiencies. Both Bender and Smil accept the 2050 findings that the major problem in food sufficiency will remain distribution, especially (over) allocations of basic food products to animals that utilize both food energy and water relatively inefficiently. Another major determinant of future efficiencies will be crop choices and management methods – who controls land, water, and technological research and development decisions. Drought-tolerant crops such as sorghum might produce more food than maize in the dry lands of Africa, for example. But returning to more appropriate crops depends on who owns the land and can access suitable technologies. People must also be willing to eat coarser grains, such as sorghums, in a shift away from maize or rice, the grains that increasingly dominate urban diets. Urbanization (both migration and population growth), one large social transformation already well underway, will have tremendous implications for food and nutrition. By 2050, in contrast with today, worldwide the greatest numbers of people and most severe poverty will be located in urban, not rural, areas. The factors that affect population movements and poverty trends will also shape the future of food. These include rules of ownership, entitlements to land and water resources, decision-making power over technological research and development for agriculture and food processing. Whoever decides what crops and crop characteristics will receive priority in plant breeding and biotechnological development, or what foods or processing characteristics will be the focus of food technology research and development, will largely determine who goes hungry.

Like the 2020 researchers, the 2050 investigators find many of the ecological data problematic: things could get worse or better, depending on who decides food and agriculture priorities and plans of action. They recognize the many areas where savings could assure adequate food for the foreseeable future, but still acknowledge the need to discover, in Bender's (1994) terms, why there appears to be so much inefficiency in the food system, and how it can be eliminated.

2060

Robert Chen and Robert Kates, researchers at the Brown University World Hunger Program, summarizing perspectives developed over seven years and drawing on the 2050 data on food availability, present an even more comprehensive vision for world hunger in the year 2060. Accepting predictions of global change, they note that the world might be warmed by 1.5 to 4.5 degrees, and that it might be more crowded – at least 10 billion people, 85% of whom will live in LDCs. Given trends in electronics and trade on the one hand, and late 20th century political culture on the other, they suggest that this world will be more interconnected but also more diverse. People who will have access to more information and more of the same standardized things will also be searching for additional ways to differentiate themselves from one another. The arguments are summarized in Kates (in this volume). Here are listed only their five criteria or scenarios by which he and Chen examined the potential for all people to feed themselves adequately in this warmer, more crowded, more diverse and interconnected world: (1) food as a human right; (2) sustainable food availability; (3) adequate household income; (4) social security safety nets; and (5) flexibility – the capacity to deal with surprise. None of the measures is developed in detail. An additional weakness of the presentation is their heavy reliance on "safety nets" to overcome hunger, where all else fails. Safety nets, almost by definition, cover only a small fraction of the global population at risk for hunger. Examples of successful interventions to prevent hunger are derived from a scattering of case studies from all over the globe whose effectiveness in both their original and proposed additional locations remains problematic.

Visions New and Old

The visions presented above share a basic faith in technology and an essential skepticism that there will be available the necessary political will and cultural behavioral changes necessary to give the world's growing population food security. They acknowledge, furthermore, that future food resources and hunger will be shaped enormously by dietary preferences that tend to move toward consumption of more meat and higher-quality grains and vegetables as incomes improve and urbanization proceeds. Distribution, not food per se, will remain the crux of the hunger problem in these visions of the future. But just how many people will be hungry and where they will be located depends on whose numbers the analysts accept, and all of our visionaries are rightly skeptical of the accuracy of the numbers.

In these assessments, the scientists both continue and depart from past efforts to monitor and manipulate the future of food.

Ecological Concerns: How Many People can the Earth Feed?

These visions of the future food-population equation address most of the same natural environmental issues that were raised by Lester Brown (1974) and his then-critics (e.g., Joy, 1973; Taylor, 1975): whether energy, fertilizer, water, soils, and seeds can be combined to feed the world, and whether such combinations are sustainable. Answering this question depends on how agricultural intensification will improve food supplies and income while protecting the environment. This applies to both the most favored irrigated lands as well as more marginal zones that are being brought into cultivation. Agroforestry and diversified cropping and livestock schemes are the wave of the future to be adapted on a case-by-case basis to suit local conditions. But most scientists and policymakers "agree[d] that low-input agricultural technologies cannot generate the yield growth required to match population growth over the long run." (MSU, 1994:5). They wonder how to give farmers incentives to use new input and management practices to improve performance (ibid). Case studies show that the entire economic environment and infrastructure, including local organizations and NGOs, must be geared to such positive change if achievements are to be realized. These systems need adequate channels to the marketplace, from which vantage point local farmers generate their own demands for input supply (Scherr and Hazell, 1994). But they also need capital, natural, human, and financial, to bring about transformations in agricultural production and livelihoods.

An increasing worry is who will provide extension services, seeds, and innovative ideas to respond to the needs of the resource-poor farmers, especially as the private sector takes over plant breeding and sales of inputs. The worry increases as the public sector cuts back funding for LDC agricultural research and plant breeding generally. Will agricultural research and extension systems be sufficiently well organized to keep us with crop pests and other physical environmental threats? Who will set priorities in research and then see results through to applications? A host of studies have noted that existing technology packages do not always reach the poor, and, in particular, female farmers who dominate food production in Africa. Although technologists tend to worry about the presence or absence of future breakthroughs to expand agricultural production and the investment conditions under which small holders will invest in new technologies, field practitioners are equally concerned about whether advances in technology can be tailored to local conditions so that even marginal lands will be able to supply food and income sustainably. These are some of the additional questions being addressed under the rubric of "intensification" (e.g., Scherr and Hazell, 1994), accumulating local case studies and examples. Off-farm and on-farm income growth historically have gone hand-in-hand. But most of the investigations tracking such trends in livelihood fail to establish what happens to subsistence food production and consumption within rural localities, as farmers shift away from food self-reliance. Specialization and market integration remain extremely risky in an era of persistent political instability and market volatility – let the cash crop seller beware.

Curiously, again, very few of these case studies pay much attention to the social organization of production, as they focus on land, water, seeds, chemicals, and technology. Some exceptions are studies of successful small-holder investments in agricultural improvement (e.g., diversified agroforestry in Kenya; elevated maize production in Zimbabwe) that show small holders do take stock of their resource base and advantage of production and market opportunities to improve land and livelihood. Common features appear to be strong farmers' organizations that are able to communicate effectively with those who offer goods and services; supportive community government or NGO organizations that can mobilize support for supra-household improvements; a supportive national market environment that offers inputs as well as outlets for goods produced; a strong research arm that offers improved crops suited to the local land and economy; and a general economic environment that may allow credit for capital improvements and a political environment and that, if not directly supportive, at least does not interfere with such endogenous intensification efforts (Scherr and Hazell, 1994). The economic advantages of "diversified" agriculture and income are clear; beneficiaries are less subject to the vagaries of the risk for failure of production or market for any single crop. But the ecological implications or benefits of diversified cropping, especially agroforestry, alley-cropping, or other designated "regenerative agriculture," still need further research to establish them on a scientfic and more beneficial basis (Silberstein, 1992).[7]

To answer these questions, researchers need better information on total production, as aggregated from all localities. As it stands, much of the food that may be produced at home to ensure self-sufficiency as a hedge against local food shortages may not be accounted for in national food balance sheets. An additional issue in food and nutrition projections is how much food production is *not* in the food balance sheets, e.g., roots and tubers, mixed crops from farming systems?

Disagreements persist also over the basic soil-water requirements of different cropping regimens and whether it will be possible to grow sufficient crops (including livestock and fish) if current climatic, pollution, and land-water utilization trends continue.

Dietary Issues: whether there is enough food depends on what people will be eating

Current visions of the future of food and nutrition differ from earlier (1960s-1970s) approaches in that they seem to have abandoned many of the food science and technology sidelines which characterized visions of twenty years ago. There is no mention here of unusual protein sources from single cells, fish, or leaves (e.g., Taylor 1975). But neither is there mention of the more unusual or indigenous food plants and animals as contributors to human nutrition, diet, and income, although study of these potential sources of food, fodder, income, and fuel are more recent and ongoing (e.g., FAO, 1989-90).

Meat consumption is still an issue, although it is as hard as ever to argue that grain saved in livestock feed will be redirected to the poor; the economics, values, politics, and infrastructure still must be right. But the new health concerns about overconsumption of fat may result in some downturn in animal product consumption in middle-income countries and so adds a new dimension to future projections.

Outside of meat consumption, most scenarios still remain reluctant to consider carefully dietary issues in the food supply, although both economic and cultural data are slowly accumulating. Economists at IFPRI, for example, have been examining how individual food commodity pricing affects demand for staple cereal grains (e.g., Kennedy and Reardon, 1994) or micronutrient-rich vegetables (Bouis, 1994). Another dimension is lifestyle, be it urbanization that affects how much of what grains African consumers may consume already prepared outside the household (Kennedy and Reardon, 1994), or modernization that limits the amounts of rice the Japanese consumer now buys and eats (Bouis, 1991). IFPRI also has a series of investigations on intrahousehold resource allocation rules that might affect food preferences. All of the above may be lumped into cultural changes in perceived needs: i.e., combined changes in life style, body size and composition, health and nutritional wisdom, prestige values of foods (advertising).

Factors affecting household food security need to be investigated on a country-by-country basis. Curiously, few of the global analyses are asking the obvious question: how might national policies protect the supply of affordable staple foods to provide an adequate diet for all? Most Asian nations, for example, have official rice policies and rice research that include certain scientific, technical, market and trade priorities to meet national goals. Does the existence of grain marketing boards increase production and supply of basic grains at local levels where they have been employed in African nations, such as Tanzania or Kenya? More systematic analyses of such data are needed.

Finally, diversified cropping goes hand in hand with diversified diets. Initiatives on food-based strategies for meeting vitamin A and iron needs involve more attention to vegetables and fruits as sources of these nutrients. Alternatively, plant breeders are suggesting that it might be possible for individuals to consume (at least) more iron via their staple grain or legume since nutrient-dense cereal varieties promise to deliver better nutrition through hardier plants.[8] If such varieties are identified *and adapted to local conditions*, including high yield conditions, they might prove both acceptable to farmers and more cost-effective in reaching the iron-deficient population than supplementation or fortification programs that incur recurrent costs. The latter benefit depends also on their being good sources of available micronutrients, a nutritional dietary study which has not yet been done.

Alternatively, economists have been examining the characteristics of mixed occupational systems, including various forms of agricultural technology, for the ways work and income patterns influence consumption behavior, including food choices and intra-household allocation of resources that affect the micronutrient intakes and status of women and children. Systematic studies of what combinations of nutrients people consume as they move away from self-sufficiency are few, except insofar as they address questions of grain and animal product substitutions. Yet such dietary choices would seem to hold the key to whether there will be savings and greater efficiencies all along the food chain.

Finally, instead of asking whether the earth can produce enough food, it might also be appropriate to ask: "do people live in the right places?" (to produce food) or "do people want the right foods?". That is, are food production and consumption choices appropriate for where people live, if they have to produce food themselves? From a water perspective, for example, more and more people may be living in the "wrong" places (plagued by drought) and growing the "wrong" crops (maize rather than drought-tolerant sorghum) and demanding the "wrong" foods (water-thirsty rice or wheat rather than more water-sparing staples, such as millet). Some scientists have argued that if people live in the "wrong" places – and demand the "wrong" diets – they will never have food security, and furthermore, attempts to support the preferred dietary life style may be mining agricultural production resources – especially water – and undermining future food security. But such judgmental analysis raises the important issue of individual human rights to an adequate diet, including culturally desirable food patterns, and returns the discussion to social and technological pessimism, which our visionaries have consciously rejected.

Conclusions

This analysis began with certain optimistic and doomsday scenarios of the future food supply, which have been further refined in the future food projections offered for the years 2020, 2050, and 2060. In their conclusions, the 2020, 2050, and 2060 visions share a basic faith that human technology can allow nutrient production to keep up with population growth but also some essential skepticism that political or cultural decisionmaking will result in the best possible, most optimistic outcomes. They expect that incremental improvements in conventional technologies can lead to more food at lower prices and provide better nutrition for the poor and that new biotechnologies, among other innovations, hold additional promise. But they are not sure the financial or strategic social resources will be available to press progress in that direction. They are knowledgeably skeptical of all the numbers on which predictions are offered but nevertheless continue to project numbers into the future.

All these scenarios are realistic and possible but are compilations of aggregate data that devote insufficient attention to intervening factors, which tend to be national or smaller in scale and in measurement. Four of these factors which will shape outcomes are the ecological parameters of agricultural biotechnology and other forms of agricultural intensification; the dimensions by which food and nutrition goals are established and implemented in national economic plans; the ways in which the international and national food (and agri-) business and culture interact with local food systems; and the impacts of all of these factors on local to global ideas and practice of good, healthy diets and nutrition.

Additional factors will be the modes by which grassroots interests participate in the agricultural development process and the ways in which participatory farmer research leading to action can turn locality-specific production upward in a sustainable fashion. In particular, women's contributions to transforming food systems have been underutilized and underestimated at every point from agricultural research priority setting to extension and food processing (see Ferguson, 1994). Also underdeveloped is the possibility of utilizing indigenous knowledge and resources to provide income and food from a more diverse set of food species and processing methods where conventional crops and food technologies fare poorly (see US National Research Council, FAO, 1989 to 1990). All might contribute to adjustments in food systems to use productive resources more efficiently and to eliminate additional sources of waste all the way through the food system, as suggested by Bender (1994).

On balance, the visions just presented have made a start, but remain more projections than visions and certainly are not prophecies. They work from questionable numbers to identify trends. They suggest, but do not preach change or even set priorities or plans of action toward improvements. They are researchers, not advocates, except so far as their findings lead them to recommend certain changes in the ways the world pursues agriculture, so that there will be greater production, more efficiencies, and less waste. They do not suggest in sociocultural terms what a future food-secure global society might look like or by what ethical agenda(s) it might come about.

Although the analysis has focused on the technical issues and questions of collecting the right numbers and asking the right technical questions to arrive at alternative visions for the future of food, additional and equally significant dimensions are cultural and moral, i.e., if or how the world will create a society which cares that everyone achieves a right to adequate nutrition and no one goes hungry. This is less a technical, and more a cultural concern, and is treated elsewhere in this volume.

1. The analysis here is based on the 2020 and 2050 written materials available through October, 1994 and was presented at Mahidol University, October, 1994.

2. Since this essay was prepared in October, 1994, the 2020 Vision project has incorporated some of its suggestions for further research; the 2050 project has closed for lack of funding; and additional scientists have offered their assessments of agriculture and food needs well into the 21st century (e.g., McCalla, 1994). These efforts are acknowledged here and are the topic of a separate essay.

3. Unfortunately, their evidence that lack of technology is more destructive than modern technologies is questionable. It is never quite clear what degraded lands they are measuring or comparing. They argue that agricultural chemicals, such as pesticides, should continue to be used even where they have proved destructive until scientists come up with safer integrated pest management. In addition, their analysis runs into the problem that sustainable agriculture counts on decreasing chemical use, more sparing water use, and improved cultivation (tillage) and mixed cropping methods.

4. i.e., "Famine is ultimately the responsibility of governments both in its cause and in its resolution...Famine is the final manifestation of government's failure to serve and protect its citizens." (Patrick Webb cited in The Unfinished Agenda – Famine and Poverty in the 21st Century, IFRPI *News &Views*, August 1994, p.1). "The bottom line is that it is up to the government to take action to prevent hunger and future famine." (p.8) Although community breakdowns and households are also involved ("Famine also represents a breakdown in the community's ability to protect itself and its weaker members." [p.2]), no research or analysis has been expended on investigating how communities continue to function in the face of government intervention, or how governments might pay more attention to avoiding actions which interfere with community functioning. Under what circumstances should government stay out of the way, or play an assisting but not fundamental transformative role? Although the same article cites Food Aid Management Consultant Tom Zopf, that "the people" need to tell the development consultants which solutions are the "right ones" (p.7), there is no specified process by which this happens. The article also carefully notes, again citing Zopf, that so-called "coping mechanisms" which allow people to survive in desperate periods, lead to destitution and famine. But which coping mechanisms are not so destituting? And are there ways in which governments can assist or not interfere with their functioning, if they might continue to work without permanently disabling the population? (In fact, to call sale of material assets that permanently impoverish a household a "coping mechanism" is a misnomer.)

5. Later papers and presentations dealt with additional issues of micronutrient malnutrition, but still without offering any priorities or plan that would join these observations to earlier ones.

6. IFPRI invited a group of Washington-based NGOs, and a few non-local NGOs (including the author, Director of Brown's World Hunger Program and part of the steering committee for the NGO, Overcoming Hunger in the 1990s, to Washington, 12 October 1994 for a half-day meeting to react to (brainstorm) about the Vision's conceptualization.

7. Silberstein (1992) investigated claims about the ability of agroforestry systems to increase nitrogen, control erosion, and promote nutrient pumping from deep soil layers. For example, mixed cropping systems with leguminous trees are claimed to contribute to the nitrogen available for companion crops through natural litter fall, green manuring, and transfer of nitrogenous compounds from root nodules. But the scientific literature bears out only the claimed nitrogen contributions of green manuring and even in this case, management practices must synchronize decomposition of prunings with the nitrogen demands of the growing companion crop. Moreover, people may be reluctant to leave prunings on the ground if they function alternatively as fodder or fuel.

8. Plant breeders now are making the argument that breeding for higher iron and zinc content holds great promise for alleviating these deficiencies in human diet and also for plant nutrition and the sustainability of agricultural production (Graham and Welch, 1994; Bouis, 1994). Not only humans, but plants do better (e.g., have more resistance to disease) when they are well nourished minerally. Seeds that have a superior ability to uptake minerals from "deficient" soils produce seeds with high nutrient loads that outperform their unloaded counterpart varieties. They are more vigorous and disease resistant. They also may need fewer inputs, since their performance is based on tailoring the seed to the soil rather than the soil to the seed. Both features make them attractive candidates for farmer adoption. They meet the breeders' priority to breed for higher and more stable crop yields and the growers' focus on performance. CGIAR funding is now investigating whether superior Australian varieties of wheat can be adapted to Turkish growing conditions, where the problem of soil depletion (of zinc) is great. Plant breeders are searching for superior mineral-efficient varieties of the other major cereal grains.

References

Agcaoili, M. and M.W. Rosegrant (1994a). Global and Regional Food Demand, Supply, and Trade Prospects to 2010. Paper presented at the roundtable meeting: Population and Food in the Early 21st Century: Meeting Future Food Needs of an Increasing World Population, Washington DC.

Agcaoili, M. and M.W. Rosegrant (1994b). World Production of Cereals, 1966-90. 2020 Vision for Food, Agriculture, and the Environment brief. Washington DC: IFPRI.

Bender, W.H. (1993). Agriculture and Global Entitlements to Food. Background paper. Washington DC: World Resources Institute, 2050 Project.

Bender, W.H. (1994). An End Use Analysis of Global Food Requirements. *Food Policy* 19:381-95.

Bender, W.H., M. Smith, and S. Jarnagin (1993). Project 2050: Food and Agriculture Sector Summary. Mimeo. Washington DC: World Resources Institute, 2050 Project.

Bouis, H. (1991). Rice in Asia: Is It Becoming a Commercial Good? Comment. *American Journal of Agricultural Economics*, 522-27.

Bouis, H. (1994). *Agricultural Technology and Food Policy to Combat Iron Deficiency in Developing Countries*. IFPRI Food Consumption and Nutrition Division Discussion Paper No. 1. Washington DC: IFPRI.

Brown, L. (with E.P. Eckholm) (1974). *By Bread Alone*. New York: Praeger.

Brown, L. (1994). Facing Food Insecurity. In *State of the World: A Worldwatch Institute Report on Progress Toward a Sustainable Society.*, pp.177-97. New York: W.W. Norton & Company.

Chen, R.S. and R.W. Kates (1994). World Food Security: Prospects and Trends. *Food Policy* 19 (2):192-208.

Ferguson A. (1994). Gendered Science: A Critique of Agricultural Development. *American Anthropologist*, 96,3:540-52.

FAO (1981). *Agriculture: Toward 2000.* Rome: FAO.

FAO (1987). *Agriculture: Toward 2000.* (Revised Version). Rome: FAO.

FAO (1989-90). *Utilization of Tropical Foods* (series). FAO Technical Food and Nutrition Papers 47/1-8. Rome: FAO.

FAO (1993). *Agriculture: Towards 2010.* C93/24. Rome: FAO.

Garcia, M. (1994). Malnutrition and Food Insecurity. 2020 Vision for Food, Agriculture, and the Environment brief. Washington DC: IFPRI.

Graham, R.D. and R.M. Welch (1994). Breeding for Staple-food Crop with High Micronutrient Density: Long-term Sustainable Agricultural Solutions to Hidden Hunger in Developing Countries. Paper prepared for presentation at an organizational workshop on Food Policy and Agricultural Technology to Improve Diet Quality and Nutrition, Annapolis, Maryland, January 10-12.

IFPRI (1994). A 2020 Vision for Food, Agriculture, and the Environment. Mimeo.

IFPRI *News & Views* (August 1994). The Unfinished Agenda – Famine and Poverty in the 21st Century, 1,2,7,8.

Jarnagin, S.K. and M.A. Smith (1993). Soil Erosion and Effects on Crop Productivity. Background paper. Washington DC: World Resources Institute, 2050 Project.

Joy, L. (1973). Food and Nutrition Planning. *Journal of Agricultural Economics* 24: 1-22.

Kennedy, E. and T. Reardon (1994). Shift to Non-Traditional Grains in the Diets of East and West Africa: Role of Women's Opportunity Cost of Time. *Food Policy* 19:45-56.

McCalla A. (1994). Agriculture and Food Needs to 2025: Why We Should Be Concerned. Sir John Crawford Memorial Lecture. Washington DC: Consultative Group on International Agricultural Research.

Mitchell, D.O. and M.D. Ingco (1993). *The World Food Outlook.* Washington DC: International Economics Department of the World Bank.

MSU (Michigan State University) (1994). Confronting the Silent Challenge of Hunger: A conference synthesis. Mimeo. Conference held at IFPRI, sponsored by USAID, with support from Michigan State University Department of Agricultural Economics, and the US Department of Agriculture, June 29-29, 1994, Washington DC.

Nygaard, D. (1994). World Population Projections, 2020. 2020 Vision for Food, Agriculture, and the Environment brief. Washington DC: IFPRI.

Paarlberg, R. (1994). Sustainable Farming: A Political Geography. 2020 Vision for Food, Agriculture, and the Environment brief. Washington DC: IFPRI.

Pandya-Lorch, R. (1994). Economic Growth and Development. 2020 Vision for Food, Agriculture, and the Environment brief. Washington DC: IFPRI.

Pinstrup-Andersen, P. and R. Pandya-Lorch (1994). *Alleviating Poverty, Intensifying Agriculture, and Effectively Managing Natural Resources*. 2020 Vision for Food, Agriculture, and the Environment discussion paper no. 1. Washington DC: IFPRI.

SADCC (1984). *Agriculture: Toward 2000*. Rome: FAO.

Scherr, S.J. and P.B.R. Hazell (1994). *Sustainable Agricultural Development Strategies in Fragile Lands*. IFPRI Environment and Production Technology Division Discussion Paper No. 1. Washington DC: IFPRI.

Silberstein, K. (1992). Agroforestry: Does It Nourish the Land as Experts Claim It Does? B.A. Thesis, Environmental Studies, Brown University.

Smil, V. (1993). Nutrient Flows in Agriculture. Background paper. Washington DC: World Resources Institute, 2050 Project.

Smil, V. (1994). How Many People Can the Earth Feed? *Population and Development Review* 20:255-92.

Smith, M.A. (1993). Crop Plant Productivity. Background paper. Washington DC: World Resources Institute, 2050 Project.

Taylor, L. (1975). The Misconstrued Crisis: Lester Brown and World Food. *World Development* 3 (11-12): 827-37.

Vosti, S. and S. Scherr (1994). Conservation and Enhancement of Natural Resources. 2020 Vision for Food, Agriculture, and the Environment brief. Washington DC: IFPRI.

CHAPTER 14

Ending Hunger: 1999 and Beyond

Robert W. Kates[1]

According to the most-detailed computer simulation of the long-term future of food availability, a projection of current demographic, economic, and agricultural trends will find as many or more hungry people in the year 2060 as there are today (Fisher and others, 1994). For those of us who would halve hunger in this decade and end hunger in the decades to come, this is a sobering conclusion. But it should not and need not happen. It is possible to visualize a world without famine, with little seasonal or chronic undernutrition, and with virtually no micronutrient deficiencies and nutrient-depleting illness. But to end hunger will require a broad recognition of food as a basic human right, an increased food availability far in excess of increased population, an extensive growth in household income, a pervasive safety net of emergency assistance, entitlements, and special needs programs, and a capability to cope with the surprises of the future. And all of this will need to happen in a warmer, more crowded, more connected but diverse world with its economy, environment and institutions under considerable strain.

The Hunger Agenda for the 90s

The onset of a new century or millennium such as will be marked by the year 2000 has always been a time of hope and fear, with apocalyptic fears dominating for much of human history until the idea of progress began to take hold in the 18th century. Over the next five years, we will be bombarded with taking stock of the past, future visions and warnings, and agenda of tasks to be accomplished. As we assess the effort to date and contemplate the hunger agenda beyond the turn of the century, it may be helpful to recall the context of the effort to overcome hunger by half.

By one estimate, the proportion of the world population that was hungry was cut in half between 1950 and 1980, although the numbers that were hungry stayed about the same as population increased during that 30 year period (Grigg, 1985). But this progress against hunger slowed during what many have called the lost '80s. The conventional wisdom attributed this lack of progress to the worldwide slowdown of economic growth and development and to the failure of growth, where it had occurred, to benefit the poorest segments of society. The enormous increase in third world debt brought about a reversal of resource flows – a net flow of money from the south to the north. The euphemistically called structural adjustment of economies in Africa and Latin America has almost invariably been accompanied by reductions in health, nutrition, and welfare programs. In Africa, this was exacerbated by agricultural decline, population growth, armed conflict, and environmental degradation. And in the United States the decade of the 1980s has been characterized as the "me" decade, the self seeking obverse of the "lost '80s" in hunger reduction and poverty elimination.

But as the decade closed, groups and agencies concerned with hunger came together to propose a renewal in the long struggle against hunger. In retrospect, 1989 can mark not only the end of the cold war but also the beginning of a great renewal in overcoming hunger. If words can do it justice, it was surely an auspicious year. In 1989, good words came from the intergovernmental World Food Council, The Interagency Task Force on Child Survival, and in September 1990 from the World Summit for Children. And they came from the 23 planners, practitioners, opinion leaders, and scientists meeting at the Rockefeller Foundation Center in Bellagio, Italy who produced the major nongovernmental initiative: *The Bellagio Declaration: Overcoming Hunger in the 1990s.*

The message of the Bellagio Declaration was a simple one. It was possible to end half the world's hunger before the year 2000 through four achievable goals: (1) to eliminate deaths from famine; (2) to end hunger in half of the poorest households; (3) to cut malnutrition in half for mothers and small children; and (4) to eradicate iodine and vitamin A deficiencies. Together, these comprised a comprehensive yet practical program to end half of world hunger in the 1990s by building on the better and best of programs and policies for overcoming hunger. The most promising programs, the Declaration found, were those that empowered people to assess their own condition and to act in their own behalf, that provided short-term hunger relief while addressing deeply rooted causes, and that could be sustained over the long term.

In the 60 months since its production, the Declaration has been broadly disseminated, even emulated; the individual goals have been widely adopted, and

Table 14.1. Recent Estimates of Hunger

Dimension of Hunger/Food Security	Population Affected (millions)	Population Affected (percent)	Year	Source
Famine (population at risk)	272	5	1994	Uvin
Undernutrition (chronic and seasonal)				
FAO food poverty (1.54 BMR)	786	20	1990	FAO
Child malnutrition (weight below -2 s.d.)	184	34	1990	ACC/SCN
Micronutrient deficiencies				
Iron deficiency (women 15-49)	370	42	1980s	ACC/SCN
Iodine deficiency	211	5.6	1980s	ACC/SCN
Vitamin A deficiency (children <5)	14	2.8	1980s	ACC/SCN
Nutrient-depleting illness				
Diarrhea, measles, malaria (deaths of children <5)	6.5	0.8	~1990	UNICEF
Parasites (infected population)[a]				
Giant roundworm	785-1,300	15-25	1980s	World Bank
Hookworm	700-900	13-17	1980s	World Bank
Whipworm	500-750	10-14	1980s	World Bank

Sources: Uvin, this volume. FAO (Food and Agriculture Organization of the United Nations): FAO Statistical Analysis Service, 1992. ACC/SCN (Advisory Committee on Coordination – Subcommittee on Nutrition): ACC/SCN, 1992. UNICEF (United Nations Children's Fund): Grant, 1991. World Bank: Warren and others, 1993. See too Chen & Kates, 1994: 195.

[a] Includes those people expected to have multiple infections.

major efforts at implementation are underway. That the task of halving hunger was enormous is shown by the numbers in Table 1. And renewed conflict, slowed economies, and population growth have increased some of the numbers at risk of hunger and make the halving of hunger more difficult to achieve. But the need to end hunger is, as Ismail Serageldin has said, the modern equivalent of abolishing slavery. A vision of ending hunger needs to be formulated if it is ever to end. To begin, consider some of what we know of the world beyond the 1990s.

Beyond 1999: A Warmer, Crowded, Connected, Diverse World

A child born today has an average life expectancy of 65 years, in the course of which he or she will experience a warmer and more crowded, more connected but more diverse world. Environmental change, population growth, and increasing connectedness and diversity are powerful trends as deep-running as the great ocean currents, trends that will impact the task of ending hunger in different ways.

The world is already deeply committed to a warmer world unless there is some basic failure in present-day scientific understanding. In the lifetime of a child born today, there may well be a doubling of atmospheric carbon dioxide concentrations and other increases in trace gases that will lead to an average temperature rise of 1.5-4.5°C with much spatial and temporal variation from this mean. (Houghton and others, 1992) The resulting changes in precipitation, cloudiness, humidity, sea level, weather extremes, and other aspects of the environment will only add to the other human-induced changes in local and regional environments including the large scale introduction of pollutants: acid rain in the atmosphere, heavy metals accumulating in the soils, chemicals in the ground water and the massive assault on the biota – specifically deforestation in the tropical and mountain lands – desertification in the dry lands, and species extinction, particularly in the tropics.

There is much that we do not know about such a warmer, environmentally stressed world. What we do know suggests that the impacts might be very different in different parts of the world and even for any given place there may be offsetting phenomena. A warmer climate may also grow more and bigger plants. The sulfates that create acid rain may also reflect the sun's heat and thus offset the warming trends. Indeed, several major studies of the effects of climate change on world agriculture find that on balance the changes are small for a doubling of carbon dioxide (Fischer and others, 1994; Reilly, Hohmann, and Kane, 1994). But those same studies find important differences in impacts on developed vs. developing countries. The poor will grow poorer in a warmer world, while the rich may actually be richer or at least no worse off.

Also within the lifetime of the child are many more children. For almost two decades now the United Nations, the World Bank, and individual demographers that make 50-150 year forward population forecasts have projected a world population of between 8-12 billion that stabilizes sometime within the next century compared to today's 5.6 billion (United Nations, 1992). Such agreement needs to be taken with many proverbial grains of salt since all the forecasters seem to use similar methods and assumptions and upward creep is more likely than downward error. In recent years, expectations of future population growth have steadily increased as present trends toward lower fertility rates have slowed. In that more crowded world, the proportion of population living in what is now considered the developing world will have grown from 77% in 1990 to more than 85%. More than half of the world's population will be living in urban areas, and the populations of the largest cities will likely grow into the tens of millions. These trends will weigh most heavily on the children yet to be born. For in an extraordinarily short period enormous numbers of clinic, creches, schools, and jobs will need to be produced.

The children of the future will also be much more closely connected by ties of communication, economic production and consumption, interlinked technologies, and migration. By the end of this decade, at least three major common-market, free-trade blocs are likely to emerge, each with associated blocs in the south. Such flow of goods, capital, and technology will most certainly be accompanied by flows of people. New information technologies and mass communication techniques will continue to penetrate many different geographic, temporal, linguistic, cultural, and political barriers. However, such connectedness will not necessarily make us all alike but may well increase the diversity of people as well as the availability of things. Places of wealth or opportunity towards which people and products are drawn actually become more diverse. In response, there are strong counter currents which emphasize ethnic, national, and religious distinctiveness.

Superimposed on these great underlying currents will be many other changes, some in the form of alternating tides of cyclical phenomena or fashion. These might range from short term recessions of the business cycle and multiple year fluctuations of climate to decades-long swings toward the left or right of the political spectrum or the growth and decline of the economy from the introduction of new technologies. These in turn will be punctuated by the many surprises, the undertows, riptides, and storm surges that batter our conventional expectations. Indeed, since our initial meeting in Bellagio, some surprise has been the order of the day (Hyden, this volume).

A tale of two scenarios

The implications of these long-term currents can be examined through scenarios and models. Consider the contrasting implications of two sets of scenarios generated by the International Institute of Applied Systems Analysis in Laxenburg Austria.

The 2-4-6-8 Scenario

In 1989, an Institute study (Anderberg, 1989) explored the implications of a doubling of population under the assumption that the doubled world population (at that time 10 billion people) should have modest access to varied and nutritious diets, industrial products, and regular jobs. The study found that in this somewhat more humane and equitable world, a doubling of population would require a quadrupling of agriculture, a sextupling of energy, and an octupling of the economy, given the then current trends in economy and technology.

Since then, many have found this 2-4-6-8 scenario unbelievable and certainly unsustainable because of the extraordinary increases in production and consumption required by "just" the doubling of population. Can the world economy grow rapidly enough, can the required technology be clever enough, and can the social institutions be both stable and innovative enough to provide what would be needed by a doubling of population? And if successful, could such increases be sustained in a human environment that already has seen substantial transformation of its atmosphere, soils, groundwater and biota? Indeed, for some, a world of over 5 billion people is already overpopulated because they find that virtually every nation is depleting its resources or degrading its environment (Ehrlich & Ehrlich, 1990; Meadows, Meadows, and Randers, 1992).

The 2-2.25-X-4.4 Scenario

A more likely scenario is the one employed recently to study issues of climate change and food security. It brings together the work of economists, agriculturists, geographers and others concerned with the supply and demand for food with the work of those involved in assessing climate change and its implications for agricultural systems (Fischer and others, 1994). It utilizes a set of 35 different country and country-group agricultural policy models designed to simulate the national or regional agricultural sectors linked together through trade, world market prices, and financial flows.

These linked models were used to generate a "reference" scenario for the year 2060 by integrating in the model annual changes in expected population growth, labor force participation, and technological change. Overall, this scenario projects that Gross Domestic Production (GDP) will increase by a factor of 4.4 over 1980 levels by 2060. Total cereal production will increase by a factor of 2.25 over this period, barely keeping up with population growth and assuming no change in income distribution, the number of undernourished (computed according to the older FAO methodology) will rise from 501 million in 1980 to 641 million in 2060.

These models were also used to test global sensitivity to a changing climate by linking models of global climate under conditions of doubled atmospheric concentrations of carbon dioxide (CO_2) with crop models for wheat, maize, rice, and soybeans and for different agricultural practices with the economic models described above. In the 12 different simulated cases, climate change leads to net declines in cereal production and in agricultural GDP in the developing world. There are modest increases in production in the developed world, but in most instances these do not fully counterbalance the developing world declines. Thus world market prices would increase at the same time that developing countries are forced to import more cereals. As a result, the estimated number of undernourished people is projected to increase in 11 of the 12 climate change scenarios examined. Under the most adverse climate changes considered, the number of undernourished could increase drastically to more than 2 billion, or 20% of the 2060 population.

Scenarios As Cautionary Tales

Scenarios of course are not forecasts of the future, but are systematically created "what if" statements. The two scenarios serve as contrasting cautionary tales as to the inadequacy of current trends to end hunger, even if we are willing to wait a lifetime in order to achieve it. The 2-4-6-8 scenario posits a world without hunger, with a modicum of economic justice and opportunity for all. But even if we could achieve such a daunting goal, we have reason to fear for the ability of the earth to sustain the enormous increases in production and consumption required under current institutions and technology. And in the more likely 2-2.25-X-4.4 scenario, there is reason to reject a prospect that, after a lifetime of change, there will be even more, and possibly many more, hungry people than today.

The scenarios, while cautionary, do not bound the possibilities for ending hunger in the future. It is possible to imagine a world without hunger that does not necessarily require, for example, the ending of poverty, only the raising of the poverty line above the level required to provide sustainable dietary sufficiency for most people. A goal that has already been partly achieved in a number of poor countries as well as in all rich ones. Equally, it is possible to imagine significant increases in production and consumption achieved in ways compatible with sustaining the ability of the earth to support human life. Indeed it is possible to go beyond imagination, to define a set of requirements for a world without hunger that go beyond "business as usual" or "current trends" and yet are consonant with some of these trends.

Requirements for a World Without Hunger

A world without hunger, a food-secure world, would be a world in which:

> ... *famine will be an historic occurrence of the past, less than 1% of the world's population would experience extremes of seasonal or chronic undernutrition, endemic micronutrient deficiencies would virtually disappear, and nutrient-depleting illness would be prevented or controlled. To move towards such a food-secure world requires a global implementation of food as a basic human right. Food supply would have to grow at rates as great as in the previous half century. International and regional welfare systems will need to be institutionalized to provide for famine prevention, emergency assistance, maintenance and supplementation of entitlements, and special programs addressed to the distinctive needs of women, children, and other groups vulnerable to hunger. And in a highly connected world of 2060, there should be much interest in learning how to cope with surprise, to achieve resilience by maintaining flexibility.* (Chen and Kates, 1994:199)

The Right to Food

A world without hunger is a world in which the right to food is a human right that has become a norm of social behavior, an expectation upheld and enforced by all for all. There is a continuing trend in this direction with the elements for the international recognition of a human right to food coexisting in the form of the Universal Declaration of Human Rights, the International Covenant on Economic, Social, and Cultural Rights, and for armed conflict, in the 1977 protocols to the Geneva Conventions of 1949. Yet as one legal expert wrote in 1984:

> *Few human rights have been endorsed with such frequency, unanimity, or urgency as the right to food, yet probably no other human right has been as comprehensively and systematically violated on such a wide scale in recent decades.* (Alston, 1984:162)

The most widespread recognition of a right to food is in the provision of humanitarian assistance in cases of widespread disaster caused by natural or technological hazards or war. Indeed, preventing or mitigating famine is the oldest form of collective human assistance and may have been one of the bases for the early organization of urban society. The latest development in this long evolution has been the establishment of a human right to food by civilians in zones of armed conflict even when such conflicts are within national borders or are condoned or encouraged by national governments. Simply stated, there is growing agreement that no nation, governmental authority, or faction has the right to starve its own or neighboring people.

In the years since 1989, major precedents for the enforcement of such a right are found in Bosnia, Northern Iraq, and Somalia. But humanitarian assistance becomes increasingly complex as the cold war definitions of self-interest wither away and new agreements as to common interest have yet to emerge. With waves of human tragedy in Bosnia, Rwanda and Somalia overwhelming us, it is easy to lose sight of the continuing success in coping with famine as evidenced by the continuing decrease in the numbers affected by famine or the recent successful prevention of famine in southern Africa in the face of extraordinary drought.

The transition to a world where all nations and peoples live up to their responsibilities to ensure that everyone is adequately fed will be a long and difficult one, but with uneven steps forward and occasional retreats a global ethic is emerging to serve as the ideological requirement for a world without hunger.

Sustainable Food Availability

A world without hunger has food enough for all. As we come to the close of the century and consider a future of doubled or perhaps tripled population, the classic Malthusian concern rises again. In the last two years there has been a sudden spate of books and papers asking the question, "Will there be enough food to feed the population of tomorrow?" (Bongarts, 1994; Brown and Kane, 1994; Crosson and Anderson, 1994; Ehrlich, Ehrlich, and Daily 1993; Mitchell and Ingco, 1993; Pinstrup-Andersen, 1994; Smil, 1994).

While there is widespread interest in the overall adequacy of a future food supply, there is much less current interest. It is generally accepted that there is plenty of food in the world. Hunger, it is argued, results mainly from lack of access to the available food supply. This seems to be the case for a nutritionally adequate, primarily vegetarian diet. In a recent paper Smil (1994) has estimated that current consumption (drawing on work by Bender, 1994), if distributed according to need, comes close to meeting most nutritional needs requiring perhaps a 10% increase (200 calories) in current calorie availability (Table 2). This could easily be met from the 1300 calories of grain that go into the feeding of animals.

In a somewhat different calculation, Chen (1990) has shown that if we could distribute food to all according to each person's nutritional need, then the vegetarian food supply plus meat and dairy production from naturally grazed animals could feed as much as 120% of the world's current population. However, there is only enough food produced at present to meet the nutritional needs of about three-quarters of the world's population if they were given access to a diet that contains a modest amount of products from animals fed with cereal grains. And there would be only enough food for a little more than half of the world's population if they were fed with a healthy but animal-rich industrialized nation diet.

This does not mean that there is or will be a global food shortage. Economists and others rightly point out that the world has much unused capacity for producing food. If poor countries and poor people had greater purchasing power then more food would be produced and made available. Nor does it mean that a vegetarian solution, eliminating in particular animal products fed with cereal grains is a practical solution. Direct consumption of grain would still require increased purchasing power or food aid. And there is a clear preference in most parts of the world for diets with some animal products. With increased income, most poor people want to spend some of that income for a diverse diet that includes animal products except where restricted by religious preference.

Table 14.2. Estimated Global Per Capita Averages (kcal/day) of Food Harvests, Availabilities, Losses, Consumption, and Requirements in 1990

	Global average	Subtotals
Edible crop harvests	4,600	
Cereals		3,500
Tubers		300
Pulses		100
Vegetables, fruits, nuts		150
Oils		350
Sugar		200
Less Animal feed	1700	
Grain		1,300
Grain milling residues		300
Other crops and processing residues		100
Less apparent postharvest losses	600	
Available Plant Food	2,300	
Available animal Food	400	
Available food (FAO)	2,700	
Less apparent restaurant, institution, and household losses	700	
Food Consumption	2,000	
Food Requirements		
Healthy, active smaller children (2.6% over consumption)	2,050	
Healthy, active, taller children; active adults universal development (10% over consumption)	2,200	
Healthy, active, taller children; active adults but current development (19.3% over consumption)	2,360	

Source: (Smil, 1994:266)

It is this recognition of unmet nutritional need and the desire for more varied diets that led to the 2-4-6-8 scenario, in which a doubling of world population might require as much as a quadrupling of agricultural production to provide both for food and evolving alternative uses for biomass. Such a quadrupling of food production could be attained in 70 years at a rate of 2% per annum which is a little below the historic (1934-1989) rate of food production growth of 2.1%.

How likely are we to achieve such increases in the next century? Some recent trends have raised questions as to maintaining the historic rate of growth in food production. For example, Ehrlich, Ehrlich, and Daily (1993) offer eleven "biophysical" constraints to maintaining the growth in food production: 1) losses of farmland, 2) limits to freshwater supplies, 3) erosion and degradation of soils, 4) biological limits to yields, 5) diminishing returns from fertilizers, 6) problems associated with chemical control of pests, 7) declining genetic diversity, 8) increased ultraviolet radiation, 9) air pollutants, 10) climate change and sea-level rise, and 11) a general decline in the free services of natural ecosystems.

These biophysical constraints are in addition to the many socioeconomic constraints. For example, in the short term, Pinstrup-Andersen (1994), reflecting mainstream agricultural economic thinking, cites the dependence of increases in food production on economic policies that would: 1) complete structural adjustment and economic reforms, 2) remove subsidies, trade and market distortions in developed and developing countries, 3) enhance access by the poor to land, capital, and technology, 4) expand investment in rural infrastructure, health, education, and agricultural research and technology, 5) facilitate sustainability in agricultural production, and 6) reverse the decline in international assistance to agriculture.

As alternatives to these specific biophysical and socioeconomic constraints, agricultural scientists are quick to point out at least four major opportunities for increased production: 1) the unrealized potential to increase yields from the application of current techniques and technologies, 2) the possibilities provided by the biotechnological revolution just underway, 3) the development of organic and sustainable agriculture techniques, and 4) the opportunity to increase efficiency in the end use of food.

While the increases in yield potential from improved seeds, fertilizer, pesticides, and water have slowed in both industrialized and the developing countries of Asia, considerable opportunities exist for yield increases by the application of readily available technology. Yields of cereals in Asia and Latin America are twice those of most African countries. It is argued that even modest increases in seed quality, fertilizer, pesticide and water use, encouraged by appropriate policies, prices and markets, could lead to a rapid increase in yields. For example, Smil (1994) argues that it would be possible by 2050 to increase by 35% current food availability with no additional inputs just by improving the efficiency of production through the use of better agronomic practices, increased uptake of available nitrogen, and more efficient use of the available water (Table 3, line 1). All told, an additional equivalent of three quarters of current production could be had, he claims, from very conservative assumptions as to agricultural progress between now and 2050 (Table 3).

Table 14.3. Conservative estimates of additional harvest achievable by the year 2050 in harvest equivalents (MT unmilled grain/per year).

Agronomic Measures	Million metric tons
Intensification of existing cropping practices (raise yields 35%)	700
Extension of cultivated land (20% increase compared to 1990)	500
Cultivation of idle land	75
High-efficiency irrigation	100
No beef production with intensively grown feed	50
Irrigation with saline waters	25
Agrisilviculture, aquaculture, and new crops	50
Total	1,500

Source: Smil, 1994:280.

Beyond the intensive utilization of what is already available, are the new possibilities provided by the promise of the biotechnological revolution just getting underway. A new set of molecular, cellular, and whole-plant biology techniques are tailoring plants used in agriculture to respond more efficiently to nutrients and moisture, to tolerate heat and drought, and to resist pests. For example, pest-resistant seeds for legumes widely used in developing countries have just been genetically engineered to provide post-harvest protection against weevils (Schmidt, 1994). While the first biotechnology products in the marketplace will primarily benefit farmers in rich nations, progress into the next century will depend greatly on improved capabilities on the part of developing country scientists and farmers (Messer & Heywood, 1990).

Whether we take comfort from the technological optimists or concern from the biological pessimists, there is widespread agreement that trebled or quadrupled food production could not be sustained under current practices with the additional burdens of soil and water loss, pesticide and fertilizer use, and the potential for changing climates. Thus there is much interest in developing a "sustainable" agriculture of the future. But there is also much division in the directions such a sustainable agriculture might take, roughly divided between those who would encourage "natural" or organic methods, often built on indigenous knowledge, and those who would apply technology, including biotechnology, to developing farming techniques that minimize negative environmental impacts while still maintaining high productivity.

Finally, the global food system is not very efficient in transforming raw agricultural products into usable food (Chen 1990). Bender (1994) has shown that over 50% of the available food is wasted, most of it in richer countries and most of it in waste at "end uses" – food sold retail and used in restaurants, institutions, and households. The least wasteful systems found in developing countries can keep such waste to 30%. An estimated 62% of the world's population lives in countries where waste is over the 30% best-practice threshold. Diets rich in fat from animal sources are harmful and are wasteful as well because of the grain required to feed the animals. Thus Bender estimates that an amount almost equal to a quarter of the world's food consumption could be created by using the current best practice in limiting waste and adopting the minimal healthy diet of 30% or less fats from animal sources.

It is clear that trebling or quadrupling food production is within the range of the possible. But to do so, much that is different will need to happen in farmer's fields, in research institutions, in agricultural markets, and in consuming households.

Adequate Household Income

For most of the world's hungry people, the major determinant of their hunger is poverty or inadequate income. The largest source of entitlements for the food required by the household is from income obtained by the sale of household labor or the sale or trade of household products which are made, grown, fished, or hunted (Sen, 1982). As of 1990, such income is currently inadequate in households with a total population of more than 786 million (Table 1). Inadequate household income also indirectly affects the size of the available food supply by failing to provide the market required to encourage greater production.

Poor countries are also among the most inequitable. While the gap between the amount of wealth commanded by the upper and lower fifths of society diminishes with rising national income from 15-20:1 in poor countries to the 5-7:1 found in wealthy countries, the process is slow, inequitable and uncertain. For the poor, trickle down is not very efficient. So for example, in the 2-2.25-X-4.4 scenario, after 70 years of GNP growth to 4.4 times that of 1980, there would still be more hungry people in the world in 2060 than in 1980. This suggests that in a world of somewhat more than doubled population, national income will have to increase four to six fold (depending on the pattern of income distribution) in order to meet the food requirements and modest expectations of improved diets in the poorest households.

Increasing income as a prime mode of ending hunger is also not enough. Some of the additional income is spent on more diverse but costly foods and some on non-food related expenditures. From a number of studies, it appears that in general a 10% increase in income increases dietary calories only by 4-6%, even though the poorest households spend up to 85% of household income on food (Marek, 1992). And within the household there may be an inadequate distribution of food to household members, favoring some and not others. Even after most household income is raised on average above the poverty level, there is still need for a pervasive safety net.

Safety Net

A world without hunger will still continue to have natural and technological disasters that will require emergency assistance. Poor people, even those whose average income is above the food poverty level, will nonetheless require occasional income maintenance and supplementation as the cycles of crop production, income, illness, and family creation and loss will continue to generate a need for additional entitlement. Within the individual life course, the special needs of women and children will have to be met by responsive maternal and child care systems just as such systems are required in the wealthiest of countries today. Ending hunger will require a pervasive safety net.

It is difficult to know how such a safety net will evolve and be supported decades in the future, or whether the nation-state would still constitute the basic unit of social organization required for its implementation. However, the elements of a pervasive safety net can be foreseen, both in the prototypes now operating within many developing countries and the advanced systems in place in the wealthiest countries. They include famine prevention, emergency assistance, entitlement maintenance, and special needs programs.

Famine Prevention. In 1992-93, a major drought affected southern Africa, reducing crops in some countries by as much as 50%. Yet there was no famine. Indeed, the remarkable achievement in preventing famine in Botswana, Malawi, Mozambique, South Africa, Zambia, and Zimbabwe was further evidence for the maturity of national and international efforts to end famine deaths. These efforts, beginning in the 1980s and designed to cope with drought, flood, war, and famine had led to great improvement in the global system for providing emergency food aid. International early-warning systems coordinated by the United Nations Food and Agriculture Organization were established in 1975, and national early warning systems are in operation in many countries. Efforts to improve understanding of the underlying vulnerability of particular groups to famine and to coordinate development, response, and relief efforts based on this understanding hold promise of more timely and effective interventions before famine conditions spread. The importance of providing income and not just food to prevent famine is increasingly recognized and the use of emergency work programs has increased in both Asia and Africa.

Thus it is now possible to anticipate widespread food shortages and to bring food quickly almost anywhere in the world. It is increasingly possible to identify vulnerable groups and famine potential even where national food stocks may be sufficient (Downing, 1991; Bohle, Downing, and Watts, 1994; Babu and Quinn, 1994). It is also increasingly possible to rally international concern when justified even in the face of national denial. It is only in zones of armed conflict that the major obstacles to eliminating deaths due to famine remain.

The rudiments for international protection of civilian rights to food are provided by the 1977 protocols to the Geneva Conventions of 1949 that prohibit the starvation of civilians as a means of combat. Recent interventions in conflicts in Angola, Bosnia, the Kurdish regions of Turkey, Iraq, Iran, Liberia, Mozambique, Rwanda, Somalia and the Sudan have had mixed success in alleviating mass starvation but do provide a series of precedents in which humanitarian concerns can overcome the barriers posed by national sovereignty if necessary to prevent famine. But they also provide a series of cautions as to how difficult it is to intervene in these renewals of political, ethnic, religious, and even clan-based rivalries and civil wars, how narrow the line is between humanitarian assistance, peacekeeping, and enforced peacemaking; and how easily the commitment of even the greatest of powers can be diverted by armed resistance. Nonetheless, it is clear that in this painful search for a new post-cold war standard of international responsibility, there is also the opportunity for a major breakthrough in the standards of international conduct. Indeed, hunger cannot be ended without it.

Emergency Food Assistance. Along with effective early warning and response mechanisms, famine prevention requires emergency food assistance from national and international sources. In recent years, the international community has distributed some 2-4 million metric tons (MMT) of food aid annually for emergency situations in developing countries, and an additional 1-2 MMT to feed a growing number of refugees and other displaced peoples. It has also been possible to place emergency stocks nearer to where they may be most useful and to deliver them when and where needed. Food aid availability in the future will depend on a range of factors, including national agricultural and trade policies, world food markets, and international use of food aid as a tool for humanitarian assistance, socioeconomic development, and foreign policy, but emergency aid seems to have a high priority.

As noted above, progress in emergency assistance efforts are still spotty, however, only in those situations related to armed conflict or political repression. In developing countries, local capacity to assist those in need in times of disaster is often limited not by concern but by resources. International responses to such disasters are frequently haphazard, delayed, and at times counterproductive, as evidenced by the latest tragedy in Rwanda. Nevertheless, there appears to be a slow but steady improvement in the logistical, institutional, and legal capabilities to deal with complex humanitarian situations. Whether this trend will be reversed by the burgeoning number of refugees and other displaced persons around the world and the unwillingness of developed nations to accommodate them remains to be seen.

Entitlement Maintenance. The need to subsidize or distribute food or their income equivalents is at least as old as the Roman empire. Maintaining a general entitlement to food can be quite costly, whether done as a direct subsidy or gift or whether by mandating an artificially low consumer price, which if not directly costly to governments, can discourage needed food production. But food or income maintenance can be quite effective when targeted to the truly needy.

The most effective distributions utilize existing markets to distribute food through food stamps, ration shops, or specially subsidized foods. This is more difficult in rural settings where it may be harder to reach households on a sustained basis with food-welfare programs. Notwithstanding, even in rural areas, there has been considerable success in providing work opportunities during drought and flood crises that provide some income in return for labor to construct needed agricultural infrastructure and to restore environmental resources. This has been harder to do in Africa where low densities of population and smaller numbers of technicians make the organization of such projects more difficult. Nonetheless they have succeeded in Botswana and elsewhere.

All told some 11-15 million metric tons of food aid have been distributed annually in recent years to both developing and transitional countries, only a quarter of which has been used for emergency assistance. Aid if maintained at that level can serve as a core for entitlement maintenance programs, whether monetized (sold commercially) to provide general assistance or distributed directly or through employment schemes. But the total amount is still much below the 20-60 MMT that might be needed in this decade both to provide emergency assistance and to stabilize food prices in developing countries. (BOSTID, 1989; Bender, 1990)

Creating diverse sources of income can also help maintain the entitlements of the poor by making them less vulnerable to post-harvest seasonal hunger or the threat of natural disaster imposed by the sole reliance on agriculture. In encouraging such diversity, community and women's banking programs which provide self-sustaining sources of credit to start small businesses or to produce handicrafts and services have proven very effective.

Many of the world's food-poor households still raise much of their own food. For them, maintaining access to the natural resource base and the inputs needed for agriculture, herding, or fishing is becoming increasingly difficult in the face of growing population and increased competition for land. In some places, there are still opportunities for redistribution to smallholders of land that are little used. Everywhere, there are low-cost techniques that can be used to sustain productivity, provide fuelwood, limit soil erosion, and increase food and income. Nonetheless, agricultural smallholders are still at the mercy of "too perfect" markets as well as the imperfect ones economists frequently complain about. In such markets, what smallholders have to sell is at low prices in highly competitive markets and .what they have to buy is at high prices from relatively restricted ones. Thus, it seems likely that the developing countries will have to follow the path of the developed countries in providing subsidies and basic entitlements to their rural populations in order to stem the flow of population into urban areas and retain a viable agricultural economies.

Special Needs Programs. The special needs of women, children, and the sick for additional food will always have to be met if hunger is to be ended. Such systems need to be maintained even in wealthy countries. For children, immunization and low-cost treatment of diarrhea, malaria, and measles promise to reduce the impact of disease on nutrition even as early as the end of this century. In many developing countries, the use of breastfeeding remains stable or is even increasing, possibly as a result of continuing efforts to encourage and maintain the practice. Sustained breastfeeding, in combination with limiting the effects of childhood illness, expanded supplemental feeding, and growth monitoring, could eliminate much childhood wasting and stunting. Most of these needs – breaking the disease-nutrition nexus and meeting the special dietary needs of women and children – can be handled well within the context of effective low-cost systems of maternal and child health care supported by adequate nutrition education.

More troublesome for the health of women is anemia, especially among pregnant women, as it requires regular iron supplementation. Universally troublesome are the burdens imposed by intestinal parasites on two billion or more people which prevent them from absorbing the full nutritional value of the food which they ingest. For those most severely affected, deworming drugs hold much promise. But to end hunger, basic improvements in sanitation and safe drinking water will be necessary. To date, while there has been much progress, the pace of improvements has not kept up with the growth of population in rapidly growing cities, densely populated watersheds, and environmentally threatened rural areas.

Coping with surprise

Ending hunger will be easier and harder, and certainly different because of unexpected surprises. The surprises themselves are by definition unpredictable, but the mechanisms are easily imaginable. New breakthroughs in biotechnology can provide substantial improvements in yields and nutrition while new disease outbreaks can seriously disrupt plant or animal production. Social and religious movements can enhance the development of global responsibility while unexpected sources of conflict may well interfere with the flow of food, people, and caring. Some of today's so-called "basket cases" will confound the conventional wisdom while some favored regions will prove more troublesome in outlook. Thus, ending hunger will require a capacity to deal with surprise – to take advantage of surprising opportunities and to maintain social and technical flexibility to cope with surprising adversity.

Hunger and the Great Global Concerns:

A world without hunger must not only have plenty of food, but have food produced in ways that are sustainable to the environment and supportive of the income needs of poor people. A world without famine requires not only a surplus of food and a willingness to distribute it in times of emergency but also a widespread recognition of the human right to food and effective mechanisms to prevent armed conflict. A world with relatively low levels of undernutrition must not only be more wealthy, but also willing and able to provide food entitlements to poor and vulnerable groups as needed. A world without the wasting and stunting of children and the exhaustion of their mothers requires a rate of population growth that provides adequate spacing between children sufficient to allow for their and their mothers' nutrition and for society's ability to provide the needed services, education, and jobs to support them. A world with virtually no micronutrient deficiencies and nutrient-depleting illness must not only have more diverse diets, but also the income to support widespread access to adequate sanitation, safe water, public health and primary care services, and nutritional and health education.

Thus to end hunger, the other great global concerns over population, economy, environment, and world order need to be addressed. In turn, addressing the great concerns can also provide great opportunities to end hunger. The focus on women that has emerged from the Cairo Conference on Population and

Development will hasten the end of maternal anemia and child wasting and stunting. The painful but inexorable restructuring of the global economy will provide new sources of income to many parts of the world. The vision of sustainable development arising from the Rio Conference on Environment and Development can only assist the effort to create a sustainable, but much enlarged food production system. The struggle to strengthen the United Nations and collective action for human rights and international order can make the elimination of famine more feasible. To end hunger none of the problems from which these concerns arise needs to be fully solved, but all need to be engaged, now, in 1999, and beyond.

1 .   In preparing this paper, I draw heavily on both the ideas and language from a recent paper jointly-authored with Bob Chen (Chen and Kates, 1994).

References

ACC/SCN (Advisory Committee on Coordination – Subcommittee on Nutrition) (1992). *Second Report on the World Nutrition Situation, Vol I, Global and Regional Results*. Geneva: ACC/SCN.

Alston, P. (1984). International law and the right to food, in *Food as a Human Right*, A. Eide *et al.* eds. Tokyo: United Nations University.

Anderberg, S. (1989). A conventional wisdom scenario for global population, energy, and agriculture 1975-2075, in *Scenarios of Socioeconomic Development for Studies of Global Environmental Change: A Critical Review*, RR-89-4, F.L. Toth, E. Hizsnyik, and W. C. Clark eds. Laxenburg: International Institute for Applied Systems Analysis, 201-229.

Babu, S.C. and V. Quinn (1994). *Household Food Security and Nutrition Monitoring: The African Experience*. Special Issue. *Food Policy* 19(3):211-343.

Bender, W. H. (1990). Food aid and hunger, *The Hunger Report: 1990*, R. S. Chen, gen. ed, HR-90-1. Providence RI: Alan Shawn Feinstein World Hunger Program, Brown University, 49-70.

Bender, W. H. (1994). An end use analysis of global food requirements. *Food Policy*.

Board on Science and Technology for International Development (1989). *Food Aid Projections for the Decade of the 1990s*. Washington DC: National Academy Press.

Bohle, H.G., T.E. Downing, and M.J. Watts (1994). Climate change and social vulnerability. *Global Environmental Change* 4(1): 37-48.

Bongarts, J. (1994). Can the growing human population feed itself? *Scientific American,*. (March 1994) 36-42.

Brown, L. and H. Kane (1994). *Full House: Reassessing the Earth's Population Carrying Capacity*. New York: W. W. Norton.

Chen, R. S. (1990). Global agriculture, environment, and hunger: past present, and future links. *Environmental Impact Assessment Review*, 10 (4):335-358.

Chen, R. S. and R. W. Kates (1994). World food security: prospects and trends. *Food Policy* 19 (2):192-208.

Crosson, P. and J. R. Anderson (1994). Demand and supply: trends in global agriculture. *Food Policy* 19 (2):105-119.

Downing, T. E. (1991). *Assessing Socio-economic Vulnerability to Famine*. Providence: Brown University, Alan Shawn Feinstein World Hunger Program.

Ehrlich, P. R. and A. H. Ehrlich (1990). *The Population Explosion*. New York: Simon and Schuster.

Ehrlich, P.R., A. Ehrlich, and G.C. Daily (1993). Food security, population, and environment. *Population and Development Review* 19(1): 1-32.

FAO Statistical Analysis Service (1992). *World Food Supplies and Prevalence of Chronic Undernutrition in Developing Regions As Assessed in 1992*, ESS/MISC/1/92. Rome: FAO Statistical Analysis Service, Statistics Division, Economic and Social Policy Department.

Fischer, G. K. Frohberg, M. L. Parry, and C. Rosenzweig (1994). Climate change and world food supply, demand and trade: who benefits, who loses? *Global Environmental Change*, 4(1):7-23.

Grant, J. P. (1991). *The State of the World's Children 1991*. New York: UNICEF.

Grigg, D. (1985). *The World Food Problem 1950-1980*. Oxford: Basil Blackwell.

Houghton, J. T., B. A. Callander, and S. K. Varney, eds. (1992). *Climate Change 1992: The Supplementary Report to the IPCC Scientific Assessment*. Cambridge UK: Cambridge University Press.

Meadows, D. H., D. L. Meadows, and J. Randers (1992). *Beyond the Limits: Confronting Global Collapse, Envisioning a Sustainable Future*. Post Mills VT: Chelsea Green.

Marek, T. (1992). *Ending Malnutrition: Why Increasing Income Is Not Enough*, Population, Health, and Nutrition Division, Technical Working Paper No 5, Africa Technical Department. Washington DC: The World Bank.

Messer, E. and P. Heywood (1990). Trying technology: neither sure nor soon. *Food Policy*, 15(4): 336-345.

Millman, S. R. with R. S. Chen, J. Emlen, V. Haarmann, J. X. Kasperson, and E. Messer (1991). *The Hunger Report: Update 1991*. Providence RI: World Hunger Program, Brown University.

Mitchell, D.O. and M.D. Ingco (1993). *The World Food Outlook*. Washington: World Bank, International Economics Department.

Pinstrup-Andersen, P. (1994). *World Food Trends and Future Food Security*. Washington: IFPRI.

Reilly, J., N. Hohmann, and S. Kane (1994). Climate change and agricultural trade: who benefits, who loses? *Global Environmental Change*, 4 (1): 24-36.

Schmidt, K. (1994). Genetic engineering yields first pest-resistant seeds. *Science* 265 (5 Aug): 739.

Sen. A. (1982). *Poverty and Famines: An Essay on Entitlement and Deprivation*. Oxford: Clarendon.

Smil, V. (1994). How many people can the earth feed? *Population and Development Review* 20(2): 255-292.

United Nations, Department of International Economic and Social Affairs (1992). *Long-Range World Population Projections: Two Centuries of Population Growth 1950-2150*. New York: United Nations.

Warren, K.S. D.A.P. Bundy, R. M. Anderson, A.R. Davis, D. A. Henderson, D. T. Jamison, N. Rescott, and A. Senft (1993). Helminth infections, in *Disease Control Priorities in Developing Countries*, Dean T. Jamison and W. Henry Mosley eds. Washington DC: The World Bank.

The Salaya Statement on Ending Hunger*

THE MORAL IMPERATIVE • The persistence of hunger in a world of plenty is immoral. In a world of 5 billion people, more than 1 billion are desperately poor and face food insecurity. 800 million are chronically malnourished. Every day, 35,000 children under age five (14 million a year) die of malnutrition and related preventable diseases. Millions more become blind, retarded or suffer other disabilities that impair functioning for lack of vitamins and minerals (micro-nutrients), robbing the human community of valuable gifts and talents. Hunger increases pressures that lead to a growing tide of refugees and migrants. Hunger and poverty are at the base of much political turmoil and armed conflict.

PROGRESS BEING MADE • Food security is a fundamental human right. Although still far from being generally accepted, significant progress is being made. Community and nongovernmental organizations are implementing successful programs against hunger. A number of governments have adopted national policies addressing hunger, in some cases, especially in East Asia, cutting malnutrition in half in a single decade. Diseases caused by the hidden hunger of micro-nutrient deficiency are being dramatically reduced and could largely be eliminated by the year 2000. Early warning systems and humanitarian responses have virtually eliminated deaths by famine due to natural disasters such as drought, floods and earthquakes. Today's famine is likely to be triggered by armed conflict and civil war. National and inter-governmental conferences on women, children, nutrition, population, social development and the environment indicate by their plans of action a growing moral consensus that preventable suffering will no longer be tolerated. Popular movements for democracy and equity testify to the grassroots character of the changes required.

STRATEGIES FOR CHANGE • Ending hunger is a credible and achievable goal. Increased funding needs to be re-directed to programs addressing the needs of poor people, especially rural and urban households at risk of food insecurity. Beginning with the Bellagio Declaration of 1989, major public statements to overcome hunger have focused on (1) eradicating vitamin and mineral deficiencies, (2) reducing malnutrition among women and young children, (3) diminishing hunger in the poorest households, and (4) eliminating deaths from famine. Continued progress especially toward the first two goals can be achieved by improved communication, community organization and collaboration with local governments. In particular, this includes empowering poor communities, education for women and providing safety nets for vulnerable populations.

Diminishing hunger in the poorest households requires first of all strong commitment by national governments to develop adequate infrastructure, increase agricultural productivity, minimize rural indebtedness, and implement land reform. Governments and the private sector should insure that poor people are active participants in the economic life of their communities. Balance must be sought between economic growth and government regulation on behalf of poor people. To secure timely and effective intervention in famines requires an unwavering commitment to civilian rights to food in armed conflicts and better coordination of international humanitarian responses.

WIDER HUNGER LINKAGES • Consumerism, unsustainable population increases, wastage, trade imbalances and other misguided private and public actions could worsen an already tragic situation. Since hunger is the worst manifestation of a complex set of political, economic and social problems, durable solutions require linkages with peoples' movements for peace, justice, equity and sustainable development. To overcome hunger, we must all join together to create a world in which children and adults can thrive as well as survive.

*Formulated by 31 local organizers, opinion leaders, technical and policy experts from 18 countries at the Institute of Nutrition, Mahidol University, Salaya, Thailand, November 6-11, 1994 as part of a mid-course review of the Bellagio Declaration: Overcoming Hunger in the 1990s.

Contributors

CHEN CHUNMING is Professor at the Chinese Academy of Preventive Medicine, Beijing, China. She is a researcher in population nutrition and nutrition policy since the 1960s.

JOANNE CSETE is Nutrition Advisor at UNICEF. She holds a Ph.D. in Nutrition from Cornell University and an M.P.H. from the Columbia University School of Public Health.

GORAN HYDEN is Professor of Political Science and Interim Director, Center for African Studies at the University of Florida. He holds a Ph.D. from the University of Lund, Sweden.

URBAN JONSSON is Regional Director for South Asia at UNICEF. He holds a Ph.D. from Chalmers University of Technology, Sweden.

ROBERT W. KATES is Co-Chair of Overcoming Hunger in the 1990s and Director Emeritus of the World Hunger Program, Brown University. He holds a Ph.D. in Geography from the University of Chicago.

PIERRE LANDELL-MILLS is Chief of Mission at The World Bank Resident Mission in Bangladesh. He holds an M.A. from Cambridge University, UK.

JOHN B. MASON is Technical Secretary at UN ACC/SCN. He holds a Ph.D. in Nutrition from the University of Cambridge, UK.

ELLEN MESSER is Associate Professor (Research) and Director of the World Hunger, Brown University. She holds a Ph.D. in Anthropology from the University of Michigan.

ANNE LALSAWMLIANI RALTE is Deputy Project Director, Opportunities for Micronutrient Interventions (OMNI) at Helen Keller International. She holds an M.P.H. in Public Health Administration from the Institute of Public Health, University of the Philippines.

SHLOMO REUTLINGER is an economist at Food Economics International. He holds a Ph.D. from the University of North Carolina.

HANS SINGER is Professor Emeritus, University of Sussex and Fellow at the Institute of Development Studies. He holds degrees from Bonn University and Cambridge University.

SOEKIRMAN is Deputy Chairman for Human Resource Development at the National Development Planning Agency and Professor of Nutrition at the University of Agriculture, Indonesia. He holds a Ph.D. in International Nutrition from Cornell University.

KRAISID TONTISIRIN is Professor and Director of the Institute of Nutrition, Mahidol University. He holds an M.D. from Sririraj Hospital Medical School and a Ph.D. in Nutrition from Massachusetts Institute of Technology.

PETER UVIN is Joukowsky Family Assistant Professor and Assistant Professor (Research) at the World Hunger Program, Brown University. He holds a Ph.D. in International Relations from the Graduate School of International Studies, University of Geneva.

PATTANEE WINICHAGOON is Assistant Professor and Head of the Community Nutrition Division, Institute of Nutrition, Mahidol University. Winichagoon holds a Ph.D. in International Nutrition from Cornell University.